THE FIRST GHETTO

Alexander Lee is a fellow in the Centre for the Study of the Renaissance at the University of Warwick. Educated at the universities of Cambridge and Edinburgh, he has previously held positions at the universities of Oxford, Bergamo, Luxembourg, Lyon 2 and Lyon 3, amongst others. He is the author of five acclaimed books, including *Machiavelli: His Life and Times* (a *Financial Times* and *New Statesman* 'Book of the Year') and *Humanism and Empire: The Imperial Ideal in Fourteenth-Century Italy*. He writes a regular column for *History Today* and frequently appears on television, radio, and podcasts. He is a fellow of the Royal Historical Society.

THE FIRST GHETTO

Venice and the Jews

Alexander Lee

PICADOR

First published 2026 by Picador
an imprint of Pan Macmillan
The Smithson, 6 Briset Street, London ECIM 5NR
EU representative: Macmillan Publishers Ireland Ltd, 1st Floor,
The Liffey Trust Centre, 117–126 Sheriff Street Upper,
Dublin 1 DOI YC43
Associated companies throughout the world

ISBN 978-1-5290-6650-0

Copyright © Alexander Lee 2026

The right of Alexander Lee to be identified as the
author of this work has been asserted in accordance with
the Copyright, Designs and Patents Act 1988.

All rights reserved. No part of this publication may be reproduced,
stored in a retrieval system, or transmitted, in any form, or by any means
(including, without limitation, electronic, mechanical, photocopying, recording
or otherwise) without the prior written permission of the publisher.

Pan Macmillan does not have any control over, or any responsibility for,
any author or third-party websites (including, without limitation, URLs,
emails and QR codes) referred to in or on this book.

1 3 5 7 9 8 6 4 2

A CIP catalogue record for this book is available from the British Library.

Map artwork copyright © ML Design.

Typeset by in Adobe Caslon Pro by Six Red Marbles UK, Thetford, Norfolk
Printed and bound in the UK using 100% Renewable Electricity by CPI Group (UK) Ltd

This book is sold subject to the condition that it shall not, by way of
trade or otherwise, be lent, hired out, or otherwise circulated without
the publisher's prior consent in any form of binding or cover other than
that in which it is published and without a similar condition including this
condition being imposed on the subsequent purchaser. The publisher does not
authorize the use or reproduction of any part of this book in any manner
for the purpose of training artificial intelligence technologies or systems.
The publisher expressly reserves this book from the Text and Data Mining
exception in accordance with Article 4(3) of the European Union
Digital Single Market Directive 2019/790.

Visit **www.picador.com** to read more about all our books
and to buy them.

*Pour mes chers beaux-parents
Henri et Catherine Sebban*

Contents

List of Illustrations ix
Maps xi

Introduction 1

Part I Origins

1 An Uncertain Refuge (to c.1440) 9
2 Borrowed Time (c.1440–1492) 28
3 Confinement (1492–1516) 41
4 'Under the Protection of the Lord' (1516–1541) 69

Part II The Golden Age

5 Expansion (1541–1553) 93
6 The Great Fiction (1553–1589) 105
7 The Golden Age (1589–1630) 121

Part III Decline

8 Bodily Sickness (1630–1663) 147
9 A Spiritual Crisis (1663–1688) 163
10 Orphans of the Storm (1688–1714) 176
11 The Age of Unreason (1714–1789) 186

Part IV Death and Afterlife

12 The Burning of the Gates (1789–1797) 199
13 The Price of Freedom (1797–1835) 209

14 Risorgimento (1835–1866) 224
15 The Emptying of the Ghetto (1866–1945) 242
16 Epilogue (1945–present) 266

Acknowledgements 275
Notes 277
Index 371

List of Illustrations

1. Jacopo de' Barbari's *Veduta di Venezia* (1500), a depiction of Venice as it would have appeared shortly before the Ghetto's foundation. (Archivart / Alamy)
2. The martyrdom of Simon of Trent as shown on a broadsheet printed in 1475. (Bayerische Staatsbibliothek)
3. A portrait of Doge Leonardo Loredan by Giovanni Bellini, 1500. (FineArt / Alamy)
4. The Senate decree establishing the Ghetto Nuovo in March 1516. (Archivio di Stato di Venezia)
5. The Campo del Ghetto Nuovo. (FredP / Alamy)
6. Bricked-up windows and quays along the Rio di Ghetto Nuovo. (Courtesy of the author)
7. Facade of the Scuola Italiana. (imagoDens / Alamy)
8. View of the Scuola Canton from the Campo del Ghetto Nuovo. (Oleg Znamenskiy / Alamy)
9. Interior of the Scuola Spagnola (or Ponentina). (James Talalay / Alamy)
10. Portrait of Ludovico Beccadelli by Titian, painted in 1552, the year before Beccadelli oversaw the burning of Jewish books in the Piazza San Marco. (Heritage Image Partnership Ltd / Alamy)
11. Portrait of Leon Modena, shown here in a detail from the title page of the 1638 edition of his *Historia de' riti Hebraici*. (Fine Art Images / Heritage Images / Getty)
12. Portrait of a young woman thought to be Sara Copia Sullam, attributed to the artist Antonio Lagorio. (Wikimedia Commons)
13. Title page of Sara Copia Sullam's 1621 *Manifesto*, a masterpiece of wry condescension in which she rebutted accusations that she had denied the immortality of the soul. (Wikimedia Commons)
14. Santa Maria della Salute, commissioned by the Venetian government at the height of the plague of 1630–1. (Wolfgang Moroder / Wikimedia Commons)

15. The Banco Rosso – one of the three Jewish loan banks in existence by the end of the sixteenth century – as it appears today. (Lois GoBe / Alamy)
16. Eighteenth-century drawing of a Jewish body being carried by gondola to the cemetery on the Lido. (Archivio di Stato di Venezia)
17. A drawing of the Canale degli Ebrei from July 1688. (Archivio di Stato di Venezia)
18. The Jewish Cemetery on the Lido. (Maspez / Wikimedia Commons)
19. Images from Giovanni Grevembroch's richly illustrated volume of Venetian dress. (MS Gradenigo Dolfin 49. Biblioteca del Museo Correr, Venice)

    a. A Levantine Jew.
    b. A banker.
    c. 'Jewish refinement'.
    d. A Jew wearing the yellow circle.

20. Cross-section of buildings in the Ghetto Nuovo, by Giorgio Fossati and Pietro Checcia, February 1778. (Archivio di Stato di Venezia)
21. The 'tree of liberty' erected in the Piazza San Marco after Napoleon's troops entered the city, as depicted by Giuseppe Borsato in 1797. (Alamy)
22. An 1865 engraving of Samuel David Luzzatto, one of the leading Jewish scholars of his generation. (The Picture Art Collection / Alamy)
23. Portrait bust of Margherita Grassini Sarfatti, while she was Mussolini's mistress, by Adolfo Wildt, 1929. (DeAgostini / Getty)
24. Portrait of Letizia Pesaro Maurogonato, daughter of minister of finance Isacco Pesaro Maurogonato, by the painter Giacomo Balla, 1901. (Ca' Pesaro International Gallery of Modern Art, Venice)
25. Antisemitic cartoons from *Il Travaso delle idee*, a satirical magazine, in August 1938. (Biblioteca Nazionale Centrale di Roma)

    a. 'Business is business'.
    b. 'At the beauty salon'.

26. Arbit Blatas's *Monument to the Victims of the Holocaust* in the Campo del Ghetto Nuovo, installed in 1980. (Andrea sabbadini / Alamy)
27. Arbit Blatas's *The Last Train*, erected in 1993 to commemorate the fiftieth anniversary of the deportation of Venetian Jews from the Ghetto. (lowefoto / Alamy)
28. The Calle di Ghetto Nuovissimo. (Courtesy of the author)
29. Aerial view of the Ghetto Nuovo. (San Marco Venice / Wikimedia Commons)

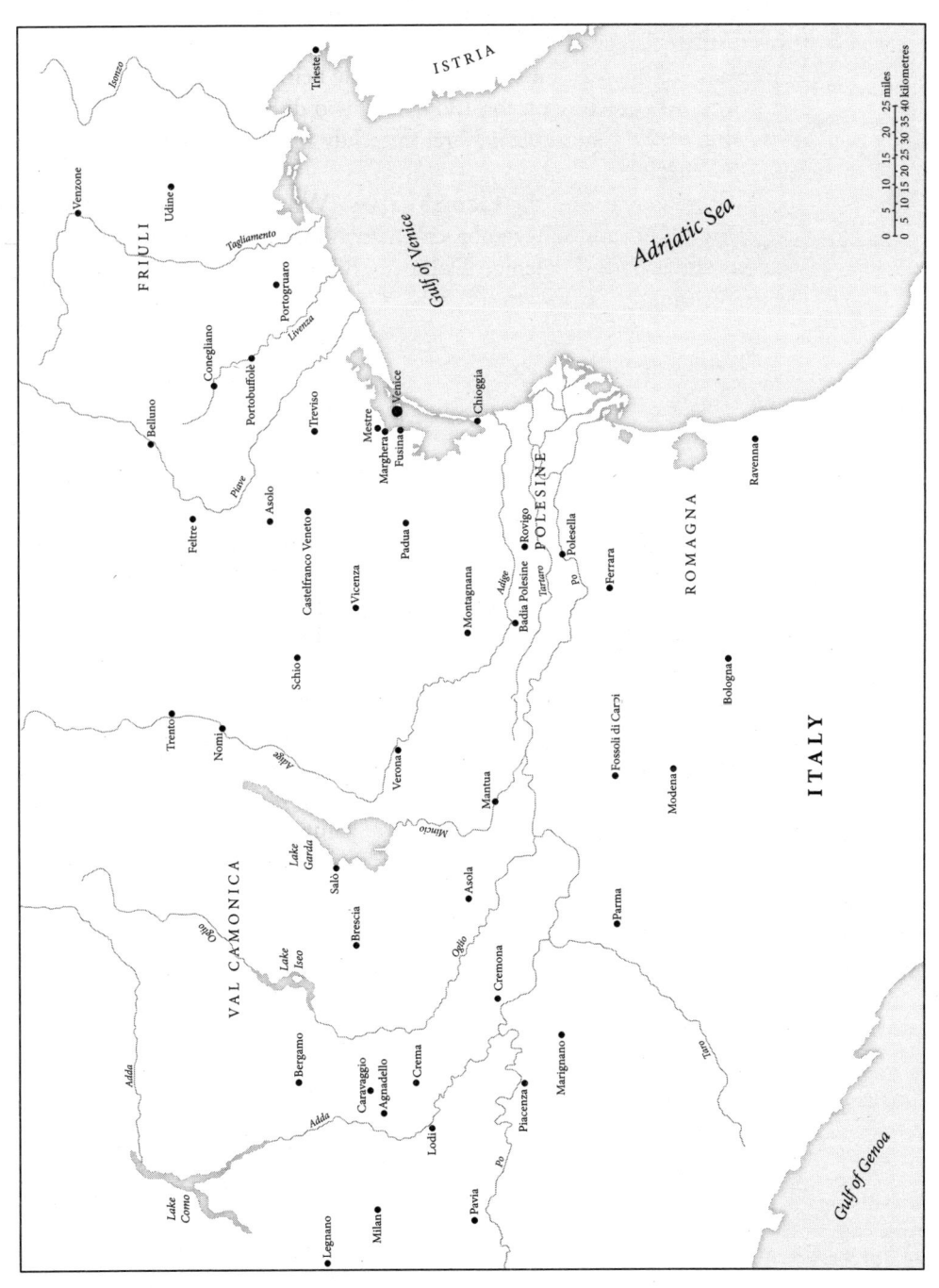

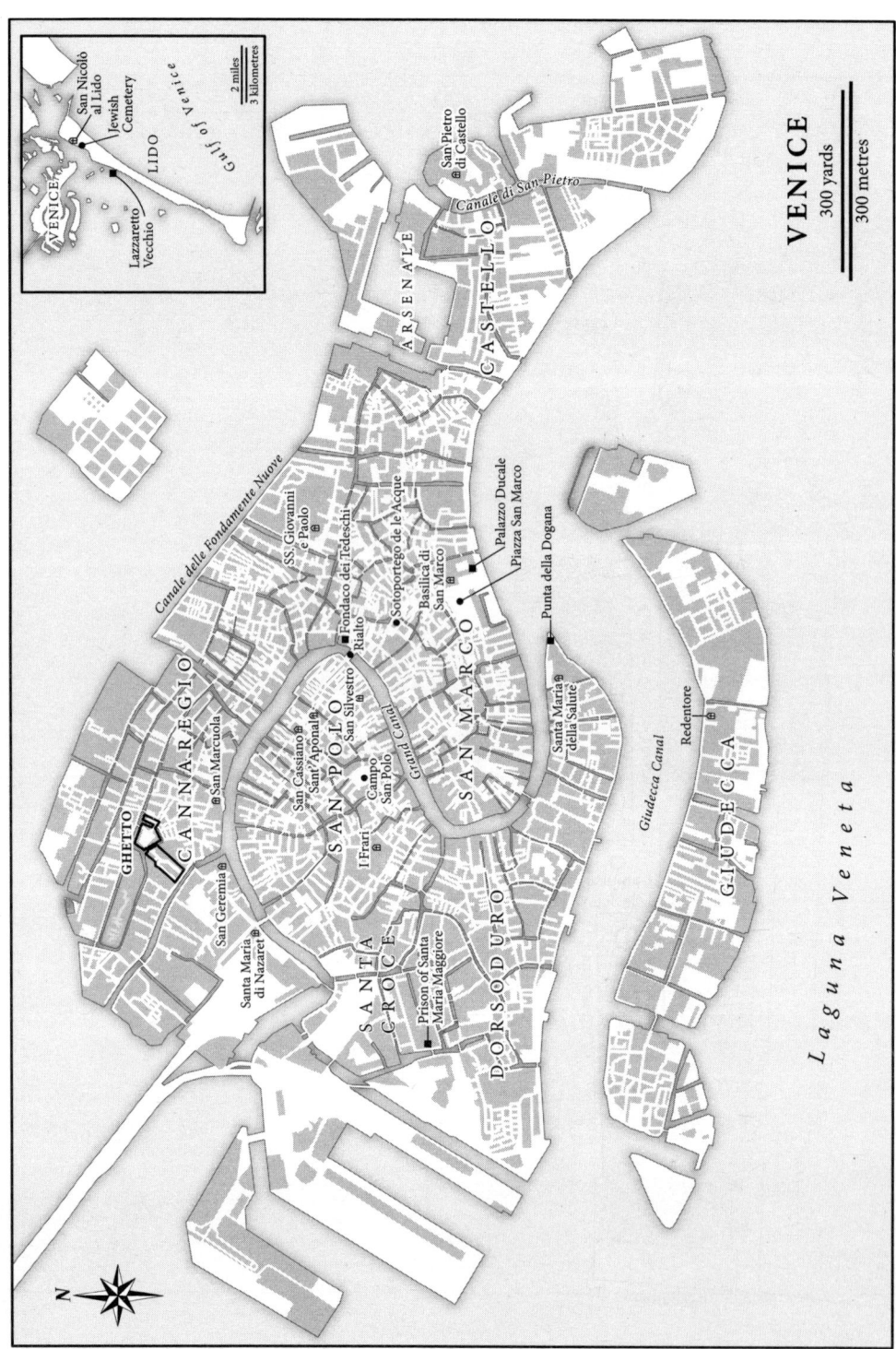

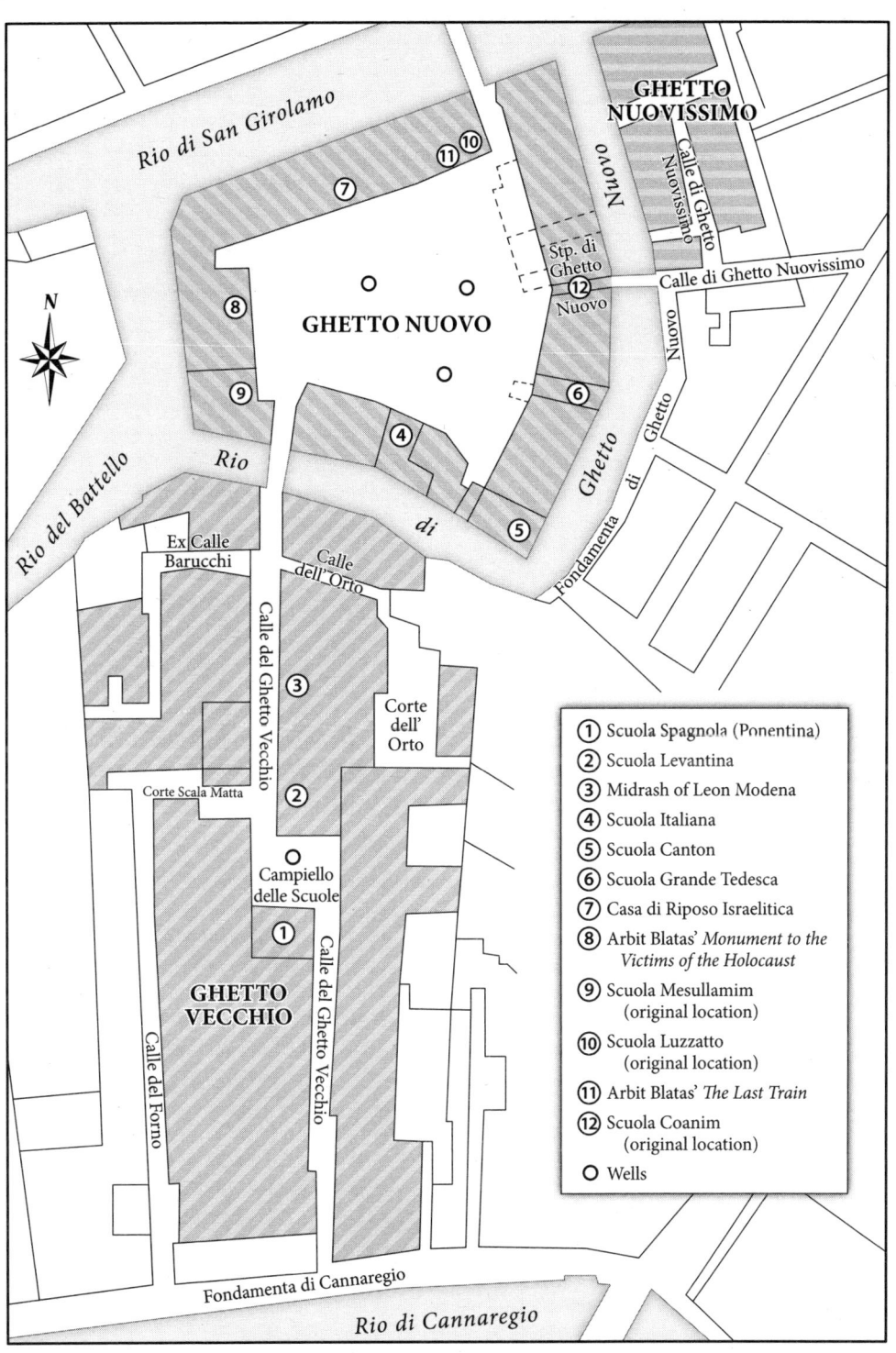

Introduction

'But how I caught it, found it, or came by it,
What stuff 'tis made of, whereof it is born,
I am to learn . . .'
William Shakespeare, *The Merchant of Venice*, 1.1.3–5

It was a cold January afternoon when I first came to the Ghetto. I got there much later than I had hoped. I had spent much of the day elsewhere and had lost track of time. It was already beginning to get dark. The *campo* seemed deserted. Shutters were closed and, apart from the tinkling of water in the wells, there was hardly a sound. There were no streetlights; barely even the glimmer of a lamp. But in the branches of the trees, thousands of tiny lights were shining.

Having nothing else to do, I wandered idly across the square. On a wall opposite, I spotted an imposing bronze plaque. It was hard to make out in the gloom. Squinting, I could just see the image of a train pulling what looked like trucks. Hundreds of people – and around them, soldiers with guns. I caught my breath – a sharp intake of icy air. Behind the plaque, in a large, irregular recess set with a metal grille, there was an inscription with names. Not far off, there was another with a date. I picked out the numbers slowly. 5 December 1943. I stopped. 5 December. My birthday.

Just then, I heard a sound coming from my right. A gentle song, joyful and defiant. Turning, I saw a light in a ground-floor window and a small group of men dressed in black, shawls pulled up, nodding their heads in prayer. Then it struck me. It was Friday. The Sabbath was beginning. Something stabbed at my heart. Without knowing why, I burst into tears.

It was in that moment that my fascination for the Venetian

Ghetto began. Although I did not realize it at the time, I had glimpsed – *felt* – the essence of its past. To most of us, the word 'ghetto' will be familiar. We know the tragic stories of the Warsaw Ghetto, the Łódź Ghetto, and the horrors which followed. We have heard it used of the 'imprisoned cities' of Black Americans, in parts of Harlem and Chicago, Brownsville and Detroit. We have seen it reimagined in poems and songs. But it was there, in an out-of-the-way corner of Cannaregio, that the word – and its benighted history – was born.[1]

*

In many ways, there was nothing particularly new about the Venetian Ghetto. It was certainly not the first time Jews had been confined to a quarter which was 'obligatory, separate, and enclosed'.[2] Far from it: by the time it was established on 29 March 1516, the practice of enforced segregation was already a painfully familiar feature of European life.[3] From at least the thirteenth century, Jews in Prague, Frankfurt-am-Main, Marseilles, and more than a dozen other cities had been required to live in specified neighbourhoods, cut off from the surrounding area by barriers and iron gates.

But the Ghetto was not 'just' the culmination of earlier trends. There was no conscious effort to model it after Jewish quarters elsewhere, no clear awareness of its past, and no vision of how it might evolve more than a handful of years in the future. Rather, it was an ad hoc creation, occasioned by the tumult of the Italian Wars, and framed by Venice's – perhaps myopic – determination to reconcile religious prejudice with its most pressing economic needs.

Like many other European states, Venice had long regarded Jews as a threat to its Christian identity. Preachers and patricians constantly warned that, if allowed to live unchecked in the city, Jews would 'infect' the Christian faithful, poisoning the minds of the pious and stealing souls away from salvation. Yet the Venetian government knew that it could not manage *without* a Jewish presence, either. By the early sixteenth century, the Republic's economy was already showing signs of decline. The 'working poor' were especially vulnerable; but since the Venetians were unable – or unwilling – to offer any form of credit on their own account, they had no choice but to rely on Jewish moneylenders instead. The Ghetto was simply the easiest way of allowing Jewish loans to keep flowing while keeping the spiritual 'risks' to a minimum.

At first, it was intended to be a temporary measure; yet the collapse of Venice's maritime trade – once the guarantor of its prosperity – demanded that the Ghetto not only be retained but expanded. Jewish merchants, originally from Spain and Portugal, were invited to make the Ghetto their home and, in doing so, help revive Venice's flagging commerce with the Levant. One Ghetto swiftly became three; and as long as Venice's fortunes continued to worsen, their existence was all but guaranteed – so much so that, by the mid-seventeenth century, their status could well be regarded as a barometer of Venice's decline.

Though each of the Ghetto's three areas (the Ghetto Nuovo, the Ghetto Vecchio, and the Ghetto Nuovissimo) retained its own, distinct character until remarkably late, it was always cramped, unsanitary, and marred by privation. Its residents were subject not just to innumerable petty restrictions, but to an ineradicable, if often variable, hostility. Comparisons with Shakespeare's *The Merchant of Venice* are invidious, but perhaps unavoidable. Although most scholars now agree that Shylock's 'pound of flesh' owes more to antisemitic hysteria in London than to daily life in the lagoon, the abuse he suffers at Antonio's hand in the Rialto market would not have been all that unrecognizable, at least in a slightly earlier period.[4] Insults were common, threats familiar. Accusations of blood libel periodically recurred. Physical attacks were not unknown. There are cases of Jewish corpses being abused on their way to the cemetery; and even one instance of a father watching as his son was stabbed to death in the street.

Over the 300 years of its existence, the Ghetto became a byword for the forcible segregation of Jewish communities. And after its gates were finally pulled down, it lived on – as much in mind as in space. To borrow James Baldwin's phrase, its limits were 'set forever'.[5] Jews, though relieved of their financial burdens and recognized as citizens, often struggled to escape the Ghetto's shadow, and Venetian antisemitism, shorn of its religious mantle, took on the more vicious garb of race.

The Ghetto's tale is anything but simple, however. Though its high walls were intended to protect the Christian population, they sometimes did more to defend the Jewish people within. Particularly after Venice's break with the papacy in the early seventeenth century, the government went to great lengths to shield judaizers from the Inquisition's glare and recast the Ghetto as a refuge. On other occasions, its walls could be remarkably porous. The Ghetto was, after all, founded in the expectation of regular exchange between Jews and Christians and was enlarged in the hope that it would be a window of sorts onto the East. Jews often lived outside the Ghetto; and, at times, Christians made their homes inside its walls. Conversions were common; apostasy not unknown; and the presence of so-called Marranos (Jews from Spain or Portugal who had converted to Christianity) made it virtually impossible to draw a clear distinction between religious communities. Even at the height of Jewish segregation, Jews might work in partnership with Christians, call on Christians to arbitrate in disputes, or be welcomed into Christian homes as friends. And once segregation was ended, we find Jewish councillors at the heart of civic politics, Jewish restaurants being haunted by Venetian gourmands, and Jewish soldiers taking their place in the struggle first for Italian unity, then for Italian freedom.

Most of all, the Ghetto's story is a testament of hope. Despite all they endured, its inhabitants not merely survived but thrived. They were, in a sense, a microcosm of the Jewish world. Having all fled persecution abroad, the early residents belonged to three 'national' groupings, worshipped according to two separate rites (Ashkenazi and Sephardic), and spoke any number of different languages. At various times, they practised a dizzying range of professions: from doctors and rag-traders to merchants and copy-editors. More than once, they helped keep the Venetian economy from collapse. They founded no fewer than eight glittering synagogues, each a masterpiece of its kind; they founded innumerable charities; and they administered their own affairs with democratic probity. They were poets and scientists, musicians and philosophers; they put on plays and held festivals; and they transformed Venice into the greatest centre for Hebrew printing in the world. And almost five centuries after the Ghetto's foundation – long after the horrors of the Holocaust – I found them still there, on that cold winter evening, proud, defiant, and full of hope.

*

In looking back at the Ghetto's past, I have used three lenses. The first is context. As will perhaps already be apparent, the Ghetto is a product of much wider Jewish diasporas. Those who lived there came as refugees or migrants from Germany, Spain, Portugal, the Ottoman Empire, modern Ukraine – and perhaps even beyond; and the Ghetto's story cannot be told except through their own. At the same time, it is equally impossible to understand the Ghetto except in relation to Venice's own fortunes. Just as the Ghetto's foundation was precipitated (if not necessarily caused) by the catastrophic defeats Venice suffered during the Italian Wars, so its subsequent history was shaped by the decline of Venetian shipping, its fractious relationship with the Ottoman Empire and the papacy, its shift towards the land, and its subjugation – to France, to Austria, and finally to Italy. I have therefore tried to link the daily happenings in Cannaregio with the bigger picture as clearly as I can. As will become clear, this has often necessitated giving a good deal of attention to Venice's economic situation, the state of its public finances, and – most of all – the workings of credit markets. These are, understandably, often rather tricky topics; but I have done my best to avoid unnecessary technicalities whenever possible.

The second lens is environment. Although the Ghetto's story often unfolds across a large canvas, as a tale of negotiations and charters, wars and finances, the Ghetto itself was never anything less than a lived environment. Whatever the squalls raging about, those few small blocks structured and shaped the daily lives of Venice's Jewish population. It was there, in those squares and streets, that people had their homes, ate their meals, celebrated, worshipped, and mourned. The fabric of the Ghetto is the warp and weft of its social existence. At each stage of the narrative, I have therefore tried to give as clear an impression as I can of the built environment and its evolution: the state of the tenements, the shops and synagogues, the wells, drains, and bridges. In this, I have been helped immeasurably by the abundance of primary materials still available and by the many wonderful studies which have been produced in recent decades, most notably by Donatella Calabi, Ennio Concina, and Ugo Camerino – not to mention the outstanding conservation work which has preserved so many of the Ghetto's buildings for posterity.

The third is personalities. Although this book traces the Ghetto's history from the arrival of the first Jews in Venice down to the present day – a period of some 700 years – it is above all a story of individuals. The Ghetto itself was a place to live; and though its fate was often shaped by factors beyond the control of any one person, it was always a living community, of families, friends, acquaintances, and rivals. As such, I have tried to tell the Ghetto's tale through the experiences, and (where possible) the voices, of its inhabitants. Particularly for earlier periods, this has, admittedly, not always been easy. Far fewer first-hand accounts have come down to us than we might like. As a result, non-Jewish sources have necessarily had to be privileged, a fact which has the unfortunate effect of reinforcing Jewish exclusion. From the mid-sixteenth century onwards, however, the situation is quite different. Thanks to the wealth of materials which have survived, we are fortunate to be able to reconstruct many lives in exceptional detail. Some of these are 'significant' figures, who made some noteworthy contribution to cultural, political, or religious life, or who are otherwise well represented in the documentary record, such as the poet Sara Copia Sullam, the learned rabbi Leon Modena, the revolutionary Daniele Manin, and the doctor Giuseppe Jona. But I have tried to balance these with the lives of more ordinary people, too, like Simcà Todesca, the housewife who found a baby on her doorstep, and the children who were separated from their parents during the Second World War.

This book cannot pretend to completeness, however. It is the historian's curse to see the past through a glass darkly; and even the most strenuous efforts afford nothing more than a brief and incomplete glimpse into the Ghetto's history. Yet the longer I have studied this most remarkable place, the more deeply I have dug into its records and remains, the more clearly have I come to see its essential truth: that its greatest monument is its endurance; its greatest blessing, its memory; and its greatest hope, its people.

PART I

Origins

1

An Uncertain Refuge

(to c.1440)

At some point in the early 1380s, a small boat made its way across the lagoon to Venice. It was not a long journey – perhaps an hour or two at most – but it was treacherous nonetheless. As any boatman could have told you, the waters are seldom more than a metre deep, even at high tide. Only skilled pilots knew where the deep channels lay; and even then, there were no guarantees. Hidden dangers lurked just beneath the surface; and when the wind was up, the waves could sweep lightly loaded vessels onto the sandbanks in the blink of an eye. It is unlikely Anselmo, the son of Samuel, paid much heed, though. Like many other Jews who made the crossing in the late fourteenth century, he had left the German lands some years earlier, fleeing either the pogroms which had broken out after the Black Death, or the waves of economic persecution which had followed.[1] Together with his two brothers, Giacobbe and Abramo, he had trekked from his native Nuremberg across the Alps and over the Lombard plain.[2] Now, at long last, his journey's end seemed to be in sight.

Even approached from the north – its least favourable side – Venice would have been an impressive sight. Writing a few decades later, the Milanese pilgrim Pietro Casola doubted whether any city on earth could compare with it.[3] Though still reeling from a recent war, it radiated the brash, unvarnished confidence of a Republic in the first flush of its 'imperial' glory.[4] As a sketch by the traveller Niccolò da Poggibonsi shows, it already bristled with fine buildings.[5] By then, the bronze *quadriga* had already stood atop the Basilica di San Marco for more than a century; the Palazzo Ducale was being rebuilt in a grand new style; and the canals were lined with palaces worthy of kings. Its wealth was palpable. From atop the Adriatic, it had come to dominate European trade. State-owned galleys plied the routes to Flanders, Romania, Alexandria, and Beirut; commercial outposts had been established throughout the Mediterranean; and a fledgling overseas empire (the so-called Stato da Màr) was growing apace. Already, Crete, Istria, Ragusa, Negroponte (Euboea), the ports of Coron and Modon, and a host of smaller towns answered to Venetian rule; and in the years that followed, more territories would be added. The fruits of these connections could be seen everywhere. In the market at the Rialto, there were goods of every kind, from Saxon timber and English wool to Indian spices and Chinese silks. Along the quays thronged people from far and wide. According to one visitor, there was such a 'babel of strange tongues' that the 'rough accents of the Venetians' could hardly be heard.[6] German merchants sold their wares at a dedicated *fondaco* (warehouse) in San Bartolomeo; Armenians prayed at their own church in Castello; Moorish servants, wearing long scarves and elaborate turbans, were immortalized in the stones of Cannaregio; and here and there, in streets and squares throughout the city, Jews, too, plied their trades.[7]

Jews had long been familiar to Venetians. Since at least the tenth century, Jewish traders from Dalmatia and the Levant had been travelling aboard Venetian ships;[8] and, as Venice's overseas possessions had grown, so too had its acquaintance with Jews from around the Mediterranean. By c.1300, Jews were even living under Venetian rule in the Republic's Levantine colonies. Like many other 'foreigners' (Greeks and Syrians among them), they were not eligible for citizenship, for which residence in the capital was a precondition; but they were recognized as Venetian nationals (*fideles*) from the first.[9] This allowed them to benefit from legal and diplomatic protection, lower tariffs on goods, and immunity from local taxation. It also gave them the right to use Venetian warehouses and, in some cases, even access to state-owned ships. This did not mean that they were always treated equally or even fairly: in the colonies, the Venetian government generally subjected Jews to harsher restrictions than any other minority. A separate Jewish quarter existed in Candia, the capital of Venetian Crete,[10] and in 1242, Venetian Jews living in Tyre were required to pay a special tax.[11] In 1325, the Republic even attempted to impose segregation throughout the Stato da Màr.[12] But such measures were usually respected more in the breach than in the observance and did nothing to stop Jews from playing a prominent part in Venice's maritime trade.[13] By the early fourteenth century, Venetian Jews in Crete were selling cloth as far afield as Cyprus, Armenia, and Egypt; and a few decades later, Jews living in the Venetian settlement in Constantinople were dealing in furs from Crimea.[14]

Some Jews travelled to Venice itself, though exactly when they first did so is something of a mystery. A fleeting – if ambiguous – reference in the binding of the Damascus *Keter*, now in the National Library of Israel, hints that Jews may have been present in the city as early as the twelfth century.[15] Similarly, an oft-repeated but probably apocryphal story suggests that the celebrated Talmudist Isaiah di Trani (c.1180–c.1250) sparked controversy by crossing the canals in a gondola on the Sabbath during a stay in the city in c.1244.[16] But the earliest securely documented Jewish visitor only appears in 1314. An inhabitant of Venetian Crete, he had been deputed to petition the doge – Venice's head of state – on behalf of the island's Jewish community and had most likely been chosen for the role because he was already going to Venice on other business.[17] Others soon followed. Though their numbers were never great, they came regularly enough that they would have been a common sight.

A few even settled in the city. In the late 1310s, Messer Nicola Bongi, a Friulian doctor who had converted to Christianity, but whom official documents still referred to as a Jew (*judeus*), had a house in San Cassiano; and in 1321, a Jewish merchant from Ancona is known to have imported wine for his Venetian friends.[18] But these were exceptions rather than the rule. Only a handful have ever been identified, and the grounds for believing that there was fully fledged Jewish community are dubious at best. A census purportedly conducted in 1152, indicating that 1,300 Jews were then living in the city, actually dates to 1552 or 1555; a law of 1290 supposedly requiring Venetian Jews to pay a 5 per cent tax on all imports and exports applied only to Jews in Euboea, rather than in Venice itself; and the island of Giudecca – often said to have been named for a group of Jewish inhabitants – seems to have owed its name to some other, unknown etymology.[19]

Most Jews who came to Venice from the Stato da Màr and elsewhere in the Mediterranean were hence a transient presence, staying only as long as it took to transact their business or unload a cargo, and then setting off for harbours new. Anselmo and the German Jews (*ebrei Tedeschi*) were different. They had come not as visitors, but as refugees. Back in 1348, Europe had been struck by the Black Death. Estimates of how many died from the pestilence vary, but recent data suggests that in most regions the mortality rate may have been at least 30 per cent. What caused the plague, no one knew. Some attributed it to the corruption of the air, or even the alignment of the planets. Many more pointed the finger at Jews. The Franconian friar Herman Gigas recorded that they were accused of planning 'to wipe out all the Christians' by poisoning 'wells and springs'.[20] A torrent of popular outrage followed – and Jews everywhere became the target of brutal attacks. The worst atrocities occurred in the German lands. According to the chronicler Heinrich von Herford, Jews 'throughout Germany . . . were cruelly and inhumanly killed . . . either by the sword or with fire'.[21] Entire communities were massacred, often at the instigation of local elites. In Frankfurt, the Jewish quarter was razed to the ground;[22] in Basel, 600 Jews were burnt to death on the banks of the Rhine;[23] while in Strasbourg, the slaughter is said to have gone on for six days.[24] Those who could, fled. Taking only what essentials they could carry, they sought refuge wherever they were able: some in nearby forests, others further afield.

When the violence eventually abated, some Jews were persuaded to return by local rulers, often encouraged by assurances of protection and offers of special privileges. But many preferred to seek new homes elsewhere. Their destinations varied, with Italy proving particularly popular. With rare exceptions, it had not experienced anything like the same violence, and its commercial prowess was too tempting to resist – no more so than in the case of cities like Venice.

After making their way across the Alps and through Friuli,[25] those attracted by the Republic's wealth first settled in Mestre, on the opposite side of the lagoon. A Venetian subject city, looking out at the domes and towers from across the water, it was a thriving port, and the Jews quickly prospered. Much of their early activity is unclear; but later records suggest that they followed a variety of trades. Some settled into manual labour, while others became merchants or rag dealers (*strazzaruoli*) or took up skilled professions like jewel-cutting, medicine, and tailoring. But it was as moneylenders – or more properly, as pawnbrokers – that they found their niche.

As a business, moneylending was relatively straightforward. Working from rented premises or makeshift tables in the marketplace, lenders would offer loans for a fixed length of time at an agreed rate of interest on the security of a pledge (usually an item of roughly equivalent value) or a promissory note. If a borrower was unable to repay what he owed, the lender would be entitled to sell any unredeemed pledges or notes to recover the loss.

There were risks to this, of course.[26] It was not always easy to raise enough capital to make loans; pledges could be inaccurately valued or suffer damage through inadequate storage; occasional downturns might mean that pledges were rarely redeemed, but difficult to sell; and disgruntled employees might be tempted to put their hands in the till. But such hazards were no different from those facing any business – and certainly did not stop the Jewish moneylenders of Mestre from prospering.

Their success was hardly surprising. Since the mid-twelfth century, the Church had forbidden Christians from lending money at interest. At the Second and Third Lateran Councils, it was decreed that any usurer who refused to mend his ways was to be cut from the body of the Church, denied the sacrament of communion, and refused burial in consecrated ground.[27] As the canons pointed out, this had a clear basis in scripture: both the Old and the New Testaments had emphasized that, while it was legitimate – even laudable – to help those in need, it was wrong to charge interest on food or money.[28] According to the prophet Ezekiel, it was one of the basest crimes, comparable in gravity to theft and murder.[29] There were other reasons for banning usury, too.[30] As Dante later noted, one was that it 'went against ... nature' (*natura ... dispregia*).[31] Whereas other 'arts' created things in imitation of God, usury produced nothing – and actually made other activities *less* productive. If a farmer took out a loan, for example, the interest he would have to pay 'devoured' money that he might otherwise have used to buy more seeds for next year's crop – meaning that his harvest would be smaller and his belly emptier. What was more, usury was based on a legal absurdity. If I lend you money, and you spend it – the argument went – there is no sense in which the money still belongs to me; so how can I charge you interest for something I no longer own?[32]

Of course, some enterprising souls had found a way around this – at least insofar as large sums were concerned. All you had to do was disguise interest as something else. Canon lawyers like Hostiensis (c.1200–71) argued that if, in lending someone money, a creditor could claim that he had lost an opportunity to make a profit, he could reasonably expect to receive some compensation for the loss, in addition to the principal. How much 'compensation' was charged varied; but in twelfth-century Venice, rates of 20 per cent were not unknown.[33] Alternatively, if no fixed rate of interest was set, a loan could be dressed up as an 'investment' and the relationship between lender and borrower treated as a partnership like any other. In Venice, such an arrangement was known as a *colleganza* and was much favoured by merchants planning risky voyages by sea.[34]

Small loans were another matter. As the sums involved were too minor either to be considered an 'investment' or to turn a conventional profit, such loans were plainly usurious. Yet it was precisely this sort of loan for which there was greatest need, especially among the urban poor – with the result that there were plenty of Christian moneylenders who were ready to defy the Church's prohibition. Unlike some other Italian cities, Venice – which prided itself on its piety – was troubled by this at first. From the mid-thirteenth century onwards, the government made repeated attempts to stamp out small-scale lending. In 1254, it forbade Venetians to lend at interest, either in Venice or anywhere else; in 1281, the Great Council (*Maggior Consiglio*) – Venice's principal legislative body – tried to drive Tuscan moneylenders out of Mestre; and in 1333, loans of less than 100 *lire di piccolo* were banned.[35] But it was clear that small loans could not be eradicated altogether. On the contrary, given how heavily the poor relied on them, many Venetians recognized that it would be positively dangerous to do so.

The Jews of Mestre provided a convenient alternative. Technically, they were also forbidden to lend each other money at interest, but there was nothing, in principle, to stop them from lending money to Christians. As the Fourth Lateran Council pointed out in the canon *Quanto amplius* – and as many halakhic authorities agreed – the divine law only prohibited interest-bearing loans between people of the *same* faith.[36] Provided interest rates were not 'excessive', the Council argued, Jews could therefore practise usury without incurring any sin. As such, Christian rulers were free to welcome Jews into their territories – and even grant them licences to lend.[37] Many Italian states leapt at the opportunity. Orvieto and Perugia, for example, had 'extended charters of privileges . . . to Jewish moneylenders as early as 1287'.[38] And in Mestre, German Jews were well placed to make a similar arrangement work, to both Venice's advantage and their own. Although they were neither licensed nor in Venice itself, they were close enough to serve the city's population with relative ease – and to grow prosperous in the process.

As fate had it, they arrived at just the right moment. After the Black Death, Venice's economy was in a fragile condition. A costly war with Genoa had drained the treasury; taxes had been raised; and the debasement of silver coins had weakened confidence.[39] Trade had suffered. Though Venice's dominance of the Adriatic remained unchallenged, galleys to the Levant had been interrupted, while the outbreak of the Hundred Years War between England and France had closed the route to Bruges. As a result, prices began to rise – not dramatically, but certainly enough to hurt. Everyone from the humblest plebeian to the most powerful patrician began clamouring for loans; and the more who came flocking, the higher interest rates climbed.

For the Jewish moneylenders of Mestre, it was an excellent opportunity to make money. The surge in demand held out the possibility of other advantages, too. As interest rates had risen, the Venetian government had grown increasingly alarmed. With images of impoverished families and bankrupt businesses dancing before their eyes, some patricians came to believe that loans would have to be made more affordable – and that, to do so, a deal should be struck with moneylenders. A range of proposals were put forward, all of which were rejected.[40] In June 1366, with interest rates on small loans now touching 25 per cent, and abuses becoming common, it became clear there was no other choice. The Great Council instructed the *podestà* of Mestre to negotiate a contract (*condotta*) with any moneylenders willing to lend at more reasonable rates, for the benefit of the poor.[41] Lasting for five years, this granted the signatories a protected status and a host of additional rights.

The *condotta* was open to any moneylenders, regardless of their religion or background. While it is possible – even likely – that some Jews were among the signatories, no conclusive evidence has yet been found. It was, however, an encouraging development. The German Jews in Mestre could have been forgiven for hoping that, before long, Venice might offer them a *condotta* of their own – and maybe even allow them to live in the city itself. There were huge benefits to the latter: not only would it have been safer, both legally and practically, but the commercial opportunities were greater, too. With more clients closer to hand, and the shipping routes to the east open before them, there was no telling what they might achieve.

Even at this time of need, however, the obstacles were considerable. Though the Venetians were happy to accept loans when it suited them, many still harboured a horror of moneylending in Venice itself – and almost all regarded the Jews with unconcealed hostility. Granted, there was little sign of the violent abuses seen in Germany and France, but the vehemence of antisemitic feeling was no less keenly felt than anywhere else in Italy. Though there was obviously a great deal of regional variation in both legal provisions and social attitudes, the belief in Jewish 'wickedness' was pervasive.[42] From every pulpit, in every town, priests and friars denounced the Jews as enemies of the Christian religion. As the Dominican Giordano da Rivalto (c.1260–1311) told the Florentines in 1304, the Jews were 'evil at heart and hate[d] Christ with evil hatred'. If they could, he claimed, 'they would crucify him anew every day'.[43] Their mere presence in society threatened the well-being of Christian believers. Whenever they could, the inquisitor Bernardo Gui (1261/2–1331) warned, they tried 'secretly to pervert Christians' and to convert them to their 'Jewish perfidy'.[44] Their supposed methods varied, but moneylending was thought to be among the most favoured. Inherently greedy for profit, it was believed that they would drag unsuspecting Christians into debt and then coerce them into abandoning their faith. However willing Venice might have been to avail itself of the German Jews' services, this prejudice still far outweighed its financial need. There was hence no question of Jewish moneylenders being granted a special status – let alone permission to reside in Venice permanently.

A few years later, all that changed. Not long after the *condotta* had been agreed, tensions between Venice and Genoa began to rise once again. In October 1372, a quarrel at the coronation of King Peter II of Cyprus sparked a riot in which Genoese merchants suffered enormous losses. Outraged, Genoa retaliated by attacking the island and seizing the port of Famagusta. At a stroke, this transformed the balance of power in the eastern Mediterranean. From Famagusta, Genoa could challenge Venice's trade with Beirut and Antioch, potentially reducing the river of silk and spices flowing into the Rialto to a mere trickle. This was bad enough; but when Genoa also acquired the island of Tenedos – guarding the entrance to the

Dardanelles – Venice realized the time had come to act. On 22 April 1378, war was declared.[45]

After an initial victory at sea, near Anzio, Venice soon found itself on the back foot. On 6 August 1379, a huge Genoese fleet landed at San Nicolò al Lido, just opposite Venice itself. A week later, it attacked Chioggia, 25 kilometres to the south, while Genoa's ally Francesco da Carrara of Padua besieged the town from the landward side. Within a matter of days, Chioggia fell. An attack on Venice seemed imminent. Food and supplies were already running low. Uncertain how long the city could hold out, the Great Council offered to negotiate terms. The Genoese commander refused. Still giddy from victory, he swore that there would be no peace until he had bridled the horses of San Marco.

Venice had never been in greater peril. To meet the threat, forced loans were imposed, mercenaries hired, new ships built, and sailors wooed with promises of sweeping political reforms. Even women and children stood ready to fight. But Genoa had gravely miscalculated. While its forces were tied down in Chioggia, a Venetian fleet blockaded their ships back home, and an allied army from Milan crossed into Genoese territory. On the night of 22/23 December 1379, Venice launched a furious attack on Chioggia. Though its troops failed to take the town straight away, they nevertheless succeeded in cutting it off completely. The Genoese, once the besiegers, now became the besieged. For six months, they held out; but eventually, the hunger and disease became too much. On 22 June 1380, they surrendered. By then, both sides were exhausted. Unable to go on, Genoa agreed to a peace.

For Venice, survival was victory enough – but it had come at a price.[46] Already fragile, Venice's economy was virtually ruined. Despite the forced loans, the public debt had grown to previously unimaginable levels, while the value of government bonds had collapsed. Stringent measures were hastily introduced to reduce the deficit. But the effect was to limit both the number of galleys and the volume of trade even further. Many of the old nobility saw their fortunes evaporate. For those lower down the social scale, the situation was even worse. Inevitably, the demand for loans shot up – and the cost of borrowing, already exorbitant, climbed to an all-time high.

More so than ever before, Venice needed cheap credit – and fast. Even before the Treaty of Turin had been signed, Marco Corner had put forward a proposal to invite moneylenders to live in Venice for at least four years, on the condition that they lend at more reasonable rates.[47] This had been defeated in the Great Council, but the vote had been close – and as the crisis worsened, the remaining opposition crumbled. When, in February 1382, the heads of the Quarantia, the committee responsible for finance – Giovanni Corner and Giovanni da Canal – presented a similar bill again, prejudice took a back seat to pragmatism.[48] Passing the Great Council on the first ballot, the legislation offered anyone willing to lend at a maximum of 10 per cent on pledges and 12 per cent on notes the chance to live in the city itself for up to five years. Their activities would be carefully regulated, and oversight given to the Magistrato del Piovego – a magistracy primarily responsible for administering public land.[49] All unredeemed pledges were to be auctioned publicly at the Rialto or San Marco. And anyone who charged too much, or who engaged in illicit practices, was to be severely punished. Other than that, those who took up the government's offer would be free to do as they pleased.

Designed to 'avoid the highest interest rates' (*pro evitandis maximis usuris*), this *condotta* was, in theory, open to anyone: Venetian or foreigner. No mention was made of Jews – but with only one exception, all those who took up the chance to live in Venice were Jewish.[50] The first in line were the Tedeschi of Mestre. Before long, however, they were joined by another wave of migrants from the north. Following another outbreak of plague in the Holy Roman Empire just a year later, persecution resumed – albeit of a more economic nature. In 1384, Jews in Anselmo's native Nuremberg were taken prisoner and released only when they agreed to pay a large sum of money.[51] The next year, all debts owing to Jews in Nuremberg and thirty-seven other cities were cancelled. Facing financial ruin, and fearing there was worse to come, many left and made their way to Venice, where they eagerly took advantage of the *condotta*.

Settling in the northern *sestieri* of Cannaregio and Santa Croce, Anselmo and his colleagues were soon doing good business. Like most other types of enterprise, loan banks came in all shapes and sizes.[52] Some were loosely knit affairs, while others took the form of a 'family company' (*fraterna societas*), or partnerships reaching well beyond the immediate kinship group. In addition to their Venetian activities, many had branches elsewhere. Either the branches were run as separate enterprises, with occasional ad hoc co-operation, or they were managed in a more coherent fashion, with shared profits and common procedures. Some even retained links with associates in Germany or further afield.[53] Take the Jew Salomon:[54] together with his partner, Auser, Salomon ran a loan bank in Venice, and another in Zara (today Zadar in Croatia) with his brother Caser. Though each was notionally separate, there was a constant exchange of letters, bills of exchange, and credit between the two. Anselmo of Nuremberg was more unusual.[55] He and his two brothers, Giacobbe and Abramo, financed a loan bank in Venice run by their Christian partner, Giacomo Panigo (or Panichi). While Anselmo lived in Venice itself – presumably so that he could oversee operations with Giacomo – Abramo looked after a branch in Verona, and Giacobbe seems to have taken care of another in Vicenza. Here too, cooperation appears to have been the norm.

Anselmo and his colleagues lent to people from all walks of life. Little is known about pledges; but notarial documents suggest that the primary recipients of loans on promissory notes were not the poor, but patricians – including some from extremely eminent families. Of nineteen such loans examined by Richard Mueller, fourteen (74 per cent), including one renewal, were for sums of 100 ducats or more; and six (32 per cent) were for 400 ducats – over four times the annual salary of a foreman shipwright.[56] All those for which a duration was specified were to be repaid within four or five months, and all but three were charged at the maximum permissible rate. On 30 August 1385, for example, Crisano de Spier (Speyer) lent 400 ducats to Ludovico di Bernardo Bragadin at a rate of 12 per cent, to be repaid by the end of the following January; while on 1 August 1386, Salamon and Caser lent the more modest sum of 30 ducats to Catarino Zane, who was active in managing the family's property on Torcello.[57]

Old prejudices continued to bubble away beneath the surface, though. On at least one occasion the Jewish community found itself the victim of malcontents. In 1384, five Jews were robbed, tied to an anchor, and thrown into the sea by three sailors who had brought them by ship from nearby Portogruaro.[58] But such abuses were rare – and for a time, Venice's arrangement with the Tedeschi seemed to be working to everyone's advantage.

The city's economic recovery was slow, however. Three and a half years after the *condotta* came into force, money was still scarce, and business had not yet returned to its pre-war levels. On 4 August 1385, a ducal councillor, Pietro Morosini, therefore proposed that a special committee should be appointed to explore whether the Jews might be willing to offer better rates in return for a longer *condotta*.[59] After some initial difficulties, this was approved about a month later, and on 24 November 1385 a new agreement with the German Jewish community was concluded.[60] When the existing *condotta* expired, in 1387, it would be revoked and replaced by another, lasting for ten years.[61] In a break with the past, this would be open to Jews alone. They would be given a choice between paying a tax of 4,000 ducats per year and continuing to charge the same interest rates as before (up to 10 per cent on pledges and 12 per cent on notes) or paying *no* tax and lending at lower rates (up to 8 per cent on pledges and 10 per cent on notes). The thinking was that, if they chose the higher rates – as the Venetians evidently hoped – the tax would push them to lend more than 200,000 ducats a year, since anything less would represent a loss on the other option; whereas if they chose the lower rates, they would make credit more affordable for the poor. Either way, Venice would benefit – in theory, at least.

At the same time, steps were taken to make the city more attractive to Jews – both as a continued place of residence and as a refuge from persecution elsewhere. If the Jews chose to charge higher rates, the legislation stipulated that they would be allowed to elect their own leaders to collect the taxes owed. This was a major concession: fiscal self-regulation was not something the Venetians allowed lightly. But while it established a formal structure for collective action, it also laid the foundations for a more stable community life.[62] More importantly, the Jews were to be provided with a quarter of their own. Where this would be situated was not specified, but the intention was clearly to give them a comfortable, coherent base in the city. This was not all. The following year, the Piovego also granted the Jewish community a vineyard next to the Benedictine monastery of San Nicolò al Lido for use as a cemetery.[63] Measuring 70 by 30 Venetian *passi*, this was a sizeable plot; and, with views of the lagoon, it would have been a fitting resting place for even the most discerning. Anselmo and his friends would have had good reason to hope that a new era of fruitful co-existence was about to begin.

No sooner did the new *condotta* come into force, however, than all its promise was shattered. Despite what the Venetian government had hoped, the German Jews chose to charge the lower rates and avoid the tax. Either they did not think that there was enough demand to lend more than 200,000 ducats, or more likely, they preferred not to take the risk. On its own, this need not have been a problem. What alarmed the Venetian government was that they were also being highly selective in their lending. While they were happy to lend large sums to rich individuals – such as Antonio della Scala, the former *signore* of Verona, who borrowed 40,000 ducats against his family jewels – they were reluctant to lend smaller amounts to the poor.[64] From the moneylenders' perspective, this made good business sense: when storage and administrative costs were taken into account, it was hardly worth lending people a few ducats here and there when all they could offer as collateral was a few pewter bowls or a bolt of linen. But that was hardly the point.

The Venetian government reacted quickly and harshly. On 24 September 1388, following a complaint from the ducal councillor Michele Contarini and the head of the Quarantia, Rosso Marino, the Senate passed a bill clamping down on moneylending operations.[65] Claiming that the whole point of the *condotta* had been to help the poor, this obliged Jewish banks to lend sums of up to 30 ducats to anyone who asked, on pain of a fine. Later that day, the Senate, outraged that loans were being made to priests, and that unredeemed religious treasures were being sold at the Rialto, banned Jewish lenders from accepting any items used in Christian worship as pledges.[66] In both cases, oversight was transferred from the Piovego to the more powerful Sopraconsoli dei Mercanti, who were responsible for regulating all other areas of Venetian business.

The following month, the Senate ratcheted up the pressure still further. Recalling that, in 1385, provision had been made for a separate Jewish quarter, it decreed that a suitable location should now be found as a matter of urgency – ostensibly because the housing in which they were then living was unsuitable.[67] But whereas in the past, this measure had been intended to attract more Jews to the city, its purpose was now to segregate them from the rest of the population.

The German Jews were appalled. In protest, they refused to lend the government the money needed to support the Flanders galleys that year.[68] It was a petulant and short-sighted gesture, which only served to make things worse. A proposal to force them to make the loan was only narrowly defeated in the Senate; and among the common people, violent resentment began to break forth. So severe did this become that, the next year, the Jewish community was forced to petition the Piovego for permission to erect a fence around the cemetery at San Nicolò al Lido to protect their graves from desecration.[69]

In early June 1389, the Sienese merchant Biago di Ruberto reported that the German Jews were at breaking point.[70] Disgusted by how the Venetians were treating them, many were already leaving the lagoon for the nearby cities of Padua, Treviso, Verona, and Vicenza. The Sienese government – eager to attract extra moneylenders – offered them a home in Tuscany; and no doubt other states did the same.

Facing a potential exodus – and the imminent collapse of two major Christian banks[71] – the Venetian government finally realized it would have to compromise.[72] On 22 June 1389, Michele Giustinian put forward a plan for a small-loans fund, which would have allowed Jewish lenders to serve the most vulnerable while protecting them from undue losses. This failed to pass, but it paved the way for further negotiations – and the following month, an agreement was reached. The Jewish community would maintain a reserve of 50,000 ducats, with each resident contributing a share. This would be lent to the poor in sums of between 1 and 30 ducats at moderate rates of interest. To safeguard the lenders' interests, they were allowed to refuse pledges of low value; and the manner of redeeming pawns was more tightly regulated. This arrangement was far from perfect, but in theory it settled the major difference between Venice and the Tedeschi.

Breathing a sigh of relief, the German Jews picked up the threads of daily life and went about their business as before. The first signs of cultural activity began to emerge. Manuscripts were copied, including a magnificent collection of kabbalistic writings transcribed by Abramo ben Isacco ha-Yerushalmi;[73] and when Barcelona was rocked by pogroms, the community sent one of their number, Salamone Sansone di Vinegia, to rescue any Hebrew books in danger of destruction.[74] Works of poetry, theology, and liturgy were written, and a lively trade in books even sprang up. Early in the fifteenth century, Mosè ben Joseph bought a manuscript copy of Jeremiah and Ezekiel from a certain Issachar ben Mosè, also known as Ber of Zurich.[75] Meanwhile, German Jews made loans, albeit still more on notes than on pledges. They welcomed a further wave of refugees from Spain and Germany,[76] and availed themselves of the courts – sometimes recklessly so. Anselmo was particularly rash. In 1393, he and his brothers became embroiled in a quarrel with their Christian partner, Giacomo Panigo.[77] Alleging that Panigo had failed to hand over the notebooks in which he recorded all the pledges he had received, they had him arrested by the authorities in Vicenza and thrown in jail. If the charge was true, they were well within their rights; but Anselmo would soon realize that a more moderate course of action might have been wiser.

From 1390 onwards, Venice's economy at last began to regain its former strength. The city's old rival, Genoa, was exhausted, leaving Venice's navies in sole command of the eastern Mediterranean. Maritime trade rebounded.[78] As prosperity returned, so the need for Jewish moneylenders diminished – and prejudice resurfaced. Shopkeepers who had been only too glad to accept loans grew restive; the poor no doubt grumbled that they had not been lent enough; and doughty patricians – cursing their previous willingness to compromise – began looking for ways to get rid of the Jews altogether. For a time, Venice's involvement in a war with Milan prevented any definite action being taken;[79] but in August 1394, during a brief lull in hostilities, the Senate decreed that when the current *condotta* expired in three years' time, Jewish moneylenders would have to leave the city.[80] After that, they would not be allowed to visit for more than fifteen days at a time. To ease identification – and to prevent them from 'deceiving' the rest of the Christian population – they were also required to wear 'a yellow circle the size of a loaf of bread worth four denarii' on their outer clothing.[81]

Seeing the writing on the wall, many Jews left for Mestre straight away. Some of the more far-sighted had already made preparations. Two men named 'Magister Moyse' and 'Ber' had registered themselves with the authorities in Mestre several months before. As soon as the decree of expulsion had been approved, they had signed an agreement with the *podestà* and the *capitano* allowing them to continue lending money at interest.[82] Those who remained in Venice were worryingly vulnerable – none more so than Anselmo. In September 1395, just over a year after the decree, his former partner Giacomo Panigo brought their dispute back to court.[83] This time, Anselmo and his brothers were charged with burning the notebooks they had accused Panigo of withholding, and of procuring his arrest on false pretences. All three were found guilty, thrown in jail, and fined. Whether there was any truth to the charges is difficult to tell – but the timing of the case suggests Panigo may simply have been taking advantage of the change in the government's attitude to exact his revenge. Others likely followed suit.

For many Jews – Anselmo included – the day of expulsion must have been a bitter release. But it quickly dawned on the Venetian government that it had made a mistake. While it had seemed easy enough to get rid of the Jews, it proved almost impossible to do without them. Even at a time of economic recovery, the city relied on Jewish moneylenders – and despite everything, they were anxious for its business. Soon, Jews from Mestre were flocking back, with every intention of bending the rules. After spending their allotted fifteen days in the city, they would go back to Mestre for a short time and then return, restarting the clock as they did so. By doing this regularly enough, they were effectively able to become permanent residents once again, much to the chagrin of the Venetian authorities.

At first, the Senate had tried to clamp down on rule-breakers. In late 1402, it decreed that, after staying in the city for fifteen days, no Jew could return for four months.[84] But the effect was limited – and even the Senate had to recognize that there would have to be exceptions. Clearly, Jews who had legal business in the city would need to stay longer – especially if they had come from the Stato da Màr. The Venetian courts were not as quick as many would have liked, and cases, even those involving Jews, could not be impeded without eroding confidence in the legal system. Doctors, too, were a case apart: though they were not mentioned explicitly, legislation passed in 1395 had clarified that the restrictions did not apply to them, either.[85]

By 1408, it was evident that merchants also required special treatment.[86] Since the expulsion, Jewish merchants from elsewhere in Italy who had previously brought silks, tanned skins, and foodstuffs to Venice had started taking their goods to Ancona instead, causing Venice an annual loss of more than 60,000 ducats – a staggering sum. Such a loss was manifestly unacceptable. In the wake of the Milanese war, Venice had greatly expanded its territories on the mainland (known collectively as the *dominio di terraferma*) – gaining Belluno, Feltre, and Vicenza in 1404, and Padua and Verona in 1405 – but the effects of such a prolonged economic depression were still keenly felt. As such, Jewish merchants, too, would be allowed to come to Venice, to buy, to sell, and to live, just as they pleased.

Before long, there were as many Jews in Venice as there had ever been. Some areas, such as the parishes of Sant'Aponal and San Silvestro (both in San Polo), were reputedly full of them;[87] and, in addition to the German Jews, appreciable numbers also came from the Venetian *terraferma*, Spain, and southern Italy.

Even the Venetian government could see how absurd the situation was. Though determined not to revoke the expulsion of moneylenders, it had to accept that a Jewish presence of some sort was inevitable – even desirable. Its attitude therefore shifted from rejection to containment. Rather than fight economic and social realities, it tried instead to cut the interest rates on loans outside Venice (albeit unsuccessfully)[88] – and to limit the 'harm' Jews could do to Christians in the city itself.

Efforts were made to enforce the wearing of distinguishing signs. On 5 March 1408, the government stipulated that, in light of repeated violations, the yellow circle, in addition to being the same diameter as a 4*d.* loaf of bread, should also be made of a braided rope the width of a man's finger.[89] The following year, after receiving reports of Jews falsely claiming exemptions, or dressing up as Christians so that they could commit 'evil deeds with women', the Senate ruled that, from then on, all Jewish men would have to wear the circle all the time. Exemptions would only be made in rare cases, and even then, only with the approval of the ducal councillors, the Quarantia, and 600 members of the Great Council.[90] In 1430, a further raft of legislation extended the requirement to Jews both in the Venetian *terraferma* and in the Stato da Màr.[91]

Worship was also tightly regulated. At the time, there were no true synagogues in Venice – or at least no buildings set aside specifically for acts of communal devotion. However, reports had reached the authorities that Jews were regularly gathering for prayers in houses rented from Christian landlords. Outraged by the temerity of this and alarmed by the possibility of spiritual 'infection', the government decreed that, if any Jews were caught doing this again, the leaseholder would be locked in jail for a year and fined 1,000 lire, while anyone else found there would be sentenced to six months in prison and obliged to pay 300 lire.[92] In 1426, the penalties were increased. New legislation passed by the Great Council categorically forbade Jews from gathering for prayers, and threatened anyone who disobeyed – whether tenant, participant, or Christian landlord – with a 1,000 lire fine and a year's 'hard' imprisonment.[93]

Even greater care was taken to prevent 'sexual pollution'.[94] Following a visit by the fiery Franciscan preacher Bernardino da Siena in 1422,[95] the Quarantia banned all sexual contact between Christian women and Jewish men.[96] Harsh penalties were imposed for the women, with the severity of the punishment being determined by their status. A Christian prostitute plying her trade at the Rialto, for example, could expect to spend six months behind bars and pay a fine of 500 lire, whereas any other would be sentenced to a full year in prison and face a similar fine. Male partners were punished too, although their sentences were often somewhat lighter. Just days after the law was promulgated, for example, Samuel Astruc was fined – but not imprisoned – for pretending to be a German Christian and having sex with a Christian woman.[97] Though less common, Christian men who slept with Jewish women were of equal, if not greater, concern. Indeed, the Avogadori di Comun (state attorneys) were instructed to proceed even more harshly against them than against Christian women.[98] More troubling to the state was male homosexuality. Long a preoccupation of the Venetian authorities, this had been treated with increasing severity since at least 1406;[99] and, thanks in part to the preaching of friars like Bernardino da Siena, a discreet but potent connection was now being drawn between sodomy and Judaism.[100] Accusations were admittedly difficult to substantiate. In 1422, for example, the Christian Johannes Caliva accused a Jew named Ioste (or Joste) Astru of committing a homosexual act with a boy; but when repeated attempts to locate the boy failed, the judges had no choice but to imprison both accuser and accused until further enquiries could be made.[101] Yet this did nothing to lessen the seriousness of the perceived offence – or the determination of the Venetian authorities.

Such a conflicted legal attitude inevitably resonated in other aspects of Venetian culture. Venice's humanists were equally tortured. Like other adherents of the new learning elsewhere in Italy – such as the Florentine Giannozzo Manetti – they could not suppress a fascination for Hebrew texts and took advantage of the Jews' presence both in the city and further afield to pursue their new-found enthusiasm.[102] Eagerly learning the Hebrew language, they sought out Hebrew manuscripts, studied Jewish history, and corresponded with leading Jews. The patrician Marco Lippomano, for example, exchanged letters with the Jew Crescas Meir during his time as *podestà* of Belluno, and asked for books on a wide range of subjects, including philosophy and magic.[103] This interest in Hebrew learning was driven less by a yearning to understand Jewish thought per se than by the pious antisemitism familiar to men of their social background. Their principal goal was to recover 'Christian' truths from Jewish texts, refute Jewish beliefs, and – if possible – induce Jews to convert.[104] When Crescas refused Lippomano's request for magical books, the Venetian launched a brutal attack on the Talmud, affirmed that the Jews had long been deprived of wisdom, and urged his correspondent to become a Christian.[105]

It was a paradoxical situation. Despite intense Venetian prejudice, the Republic seemed unable to part with a people it loathed. Its laws, though stern in language and sterner still in the penalties prescribed, were irregularly enforced; the ban on residence was quietly ignored; and its outbursts of hostility masked the reluctant acceptance of a Jewish presence. So much was typical of the Venetian character. For all their vaunted piety, all their proud cries of *fiat iustitia*, its citizens were pragmatists at heart. '[N]aturally timid and averse to any doubtful . . . measure' – as Machiavelli later put it – they were slow to decide, and avoided taking any precipitous action.[106] They preferred compromise to consistency, and would rarely, if ever, do anything which might endanger their commercial interests. This was only natural. The sea on which their prosperity was founded was proverbially unpredictable, and the ferment of Italian affairs, into which they were increasingly drawn, was turbid, even in times of peace. Given how quickly things could change, it paid to be flexible – most of all with creditors. And while Venice's 'arrangement' with Jews might have been strained, all that mattered to the Venetians was that it worked. Whether it would last was another matter.

2

Borrowed Time

(c.1440–1492)

By the middle of the fifteenth century, a fresh wave of hostility had begun to sweep across Italy. For some time, the Observant Franciscans had been calling for a crackdown on Jewish activities;[1] but a letter from King Juan II of Castile, complaining about the 'scandalous' offences Jews were supposedly committing against the Christian religion, persuaded Pope Eugenius IV to take action. In a sharp break with his predecessors' policy of toleration, Eugenius' bull *Dudum ad nostram audientiam* (1442) set out to protect Christians from the Jewish 'threat' by separating the two faiths as completely as possible.[2] All the privileges Jews had previously been granted were revoked, and severe limits were placed on social interaction. Henceforth, Castilian Jews were banned from practising medicine, renting property from Christian landlords, or belonging to the same guilds as Christian merchants. They could no longer enter the same bathhouses, share the same houses, or even break the same bread. Harsh new legal restrictions were also imposed. Though Christians could still testify against Jews in court, Jews were barred from giving evidence against Christians. Most important were the curbs on usury. Despite the fact that many jurists were still convinced that Jewish moneylenders, if properly regulated, had a valuable and even necessary part to play in Christian society, Jewish bankers were now forbidden to lend money at interest – and were required to reimburse those who had borrowed from them in the past.[3]

Eugenius' bull was only intended to apply to Castile, but in Italy, the mendicant orders were quick to seize on its implications. Trudging from town to town in worn-out sandals, friars like Domenico da Leonessa preached violently against the Jewish 'disease'. From pulpits and in squares, they thundered against usury with renewed vigour and demanded that municipal authorities expel local Jews once and for all. They knew this wouldn't be easy. As Venice had already discovered, once a population had come to rely on Jewish loans, it was difficult to do without them. But the friars now proposed a solution. With the papacy's approval, they encouraged communes to establish *monti di pietà* (literally 'banks of compassion'). Funded by public donations, these would make small loans on a charitable basis. They would cater not to the destitute, for whose benefit a number of other charitable institutions already existed, but to *pauperes pinguiores* (the 'fatter poor') – that is to say, working people with some possessions, who occasionally struggled to put food on the table or keep a roof over their heads, and who were most likely to resort to Jewish lenders when times were tight. Depending on how the *monti di pietà* were set up, they would either ask for no interest at all or charge rates no higher than needed to cover their running costs.[4]

Although some scholars have suggested that a *monte di pietà* may have existed at Ascoli Piceno as early as 1458, the first securely attested institution was founded in Perugia in 1462.[5] Over the next ten years, around forty were established throughout Umbria, Tuscany, Le Marche, Lazio, and the Abruzzo.[6] Almost all followed the same pattern. After a friar delivered a series of violent sermons calling for the annulment of any existing *condotte*, the town council would sanction the creation of a *monte* and invite the friar to oversee its statutes. Once the *monte* was up and running, the Jews would be ordered to wind up their businesses and leave the town for good. In some cases, they were even required to stump up capital for the *monte* before they left.[7]

Admittedly, the break wasn't always as clean as some friars would have liked. No matter how carefully their statutes were crafted, *monti di pietà* couldn't replace Jewish moneylenders entirely. While they were admirably suited to alleviating the suffering of *pauperes pinguiores*, it quickly became clear that they were not designed to cater to the needs of other – less hard-up – borrowers who had also come to rely on the Jews' services, such as merchants, lawyers, and patricians. To prevent a shortage of credit holding up the local economy, many towns therefore decided to allow Jews to continue lending money 'unofficially' alongside the *monti di pietà*; and in many places, Christian businessmen who publicly opposed Jewish lending actually invested in these 'clandestine' Jewish banks.[8] Now and then, the popes intervened on the Jews' behalf, too. Though they firmly supported the foundation of *monti di pietà*, they recognized that the financial needs of communities often took precedence, and were not above providing Jewish moneylenders with the means to circumvent, or even ignore, their own decrees. On 29 April 1463, for example, Pope Pius II (r. 1458–64) approved the prohibition on Jewish moneylending in Perugia – but only after he had granted a group of Perugian Jews permission to open loan banks in nearby Deruta.[9] Similarly, in 1474, Pope Sixtus IV attempted to save the commune of Terni from bankruptcy by inviting expelled Jewish moneylenders to return and reopen their businesses – provided, of course, that they did not interfere with the work of the *monte di pietà*.[10]

Yet for many local people who had heard the friars' message, the goal was always to rid their towns of Jewish 'perfidy'. Even before the first *monte di pietà* was established, petty-minded attacks had become a familiar occurrence in Tuscany and the Papal States. So severe did this become that, on 27 July 1459, Pope Pius II stepped in to restrain the violence.[11] In response to complaints from several Jewish communities, he issued a bull prohibiting anyone from forcing Jews to attend sermons, baptizing Jewish children, or obliging Jewish employees to work on Saturdays. He also confirmed that Jews should be allowed to have their own synagogues and schools and gave them permission to keep Christian servants. This was to little avail – and in the years that followed, the foundation of *monti di pietà* was rarely unaccompanied by agitation of one sort or another.

*

Venice could not help being swept along. After almost thirty years of near-constant warfare, another bitter conflict with Milan was drawing to a close. Though it would never entirely trust its neighbours again, the Peace of Lodi (1454) brought much-needed stability to its Italian affairs. Its territories on the *terraferma* now stretched from Istria in the east to the banks of the river Adda in the west.[12] Now that its borders were secure, it could at last turn its attention to the growing threat of the Ottoman Empire, which had captured Constantinople less than a year before the Peace of Lodi, and which was already beginning to cast greedy eyes on the Balkans. Venice's economic prospects were, admittedly, still fragile. During the final stages of the Milanese wars, prices were high, trade was struggling, and many of the city's greatest trading houses were staring bankruptcy in the face. But by the late 1440s, there were already signs of recovery – and a new sense of civic optimism was in the air. Under Doge Francesco Foscari (r. 1423–57), 'a forceful and self-willed man' whose boldness was matched only by his ambition, the city burst into a flurry of architectural and artistic creativity, reinforcing its self-image as a providential power predestined to greatness.[13]

All this made Venice receptive to the friars' message. Since the mid-1420s, subject towns on the *terraferma* – which enjoyed a measure of self-government – had been growing steadily more resentful of the Jewish presence. Following the promulgation of *Dudum ad nostram audientiam*, many felt emboldened to act. On 5 November 1442, Treviso, home to one of the Veneto's longest-established Jewish communities, banned Jews from lending at interest. Although this decision was rescinded a few years later, Jewish banking never regained its former vigour, and criminal accusations against Jews became more frequent.[14] In 1445, Vicenza followed suit. Jewish moneylending was forbidden, and while some Jews were allowed to remain in the city, most were obliged to leave for villages in the surrounding countryside.[15] The following year, Verona did the same,[16] and in 1453, Padua was given permission to expel its Jews, too.[17]

Meanwhile, the Venetian government passed a raft of legislation designed to prevent Jews from 'contaminating' Christian life. On 11 April 1443, the Senate reaffirmed that Jewish men were required to wear the yellow circle at all times and imposed new restrictions on some Jewish activities. Although Jews were still allowed to practise medicine, they were forbidden to operate 'a school of games, *arte*, *dottrine*, dancing, singing, playing instruments or anything else' on pain of a 500-ducat fine and six months in prison.[18] This was ostensibly just another attempt to limit the opportunities for social interaction. But as Guido Ruggiero has argued, it was also likely underpinned by growing fears of sexual 'pollution' – and intended to prevent any inappropriate contact between teachers and students.[19] The following month, the Senate took this a step further. It had dawned on Venice's patricians that, since previous statutes had required only Jewish men to wear the yellow circle, there was a danger that (married) Jewish women might still be concealing their identities and seducing unwitting Christian men. If this was indeed taking place, as many feared, any children arising from such liaisons would be raised as Jews. To prevent this, the Senate ordered Jewish women to wear the same yellow circle as men – or be subject to the same fine, to be paid by their husbands.[20]

*

Venice was nevertheless divided over how far this should be taken.[21] While some patricians fully supported the mendicants' hard-line approach, others were unsettled by the anti-Jewish agitation in Tuscany and the Papal States – and had grave concerns about the financial damage it was causing. Given rising tensions in the eastern Mediterranean and uncertainties about Levantine trade, they were reluctant either to expel Jews from the Veneto as a whole, or to interfere with Jewish business any more than they already had. With no agreement in sight, the Council of Ten – a 'proverbially powerful' magistrature, responsible for state security[22] – therefore asked Doge Cristoforo Moro (r. 1462–71) to write to the papal legate, Cardinal Bessarion (1403–72), for advice.

Why the Council chose Bessarion is not recorded, but if moderates were hoping to find an ally, they were not disappointed. A Greek-speaking Neoplatonic philosopher with a long, aquiline nose, receding hairline, and flowing beard, Bessarion was among the most cosmopolitan members of the Sacred College.[23] Unlike many of his fellow cardinals, he was largely untroubled by prejudice and shared none of their hostility towards Jews.[24] More importantly, he was keenly aware of how pivotal Jews were to the Church's plans. Since the fall of Constantinople, successive popes had called for a crusade against the Ottoman Empire; but while the Christian states of Europe had been quick to promise their support against the Muslim 'infidels', no one had wanted to be the first to commit troops.[25] Either they were too mistrustful of their neighbours to risk exposing their defences, or – like Venice – they simply believed that the profits to be made from Ottoman trade still outweighed the dangers of growing Turkish power. When the Ottomans captured the kingdom of Bosnia and pushed into southern Greece in mid-1463, however, Pope Pius II spied a way of overcoming their reluctance. Seeing that Venice had lost Argos to the sultan's advance, he suspected that the Venetians' attachment to Ottoman trade might be wavering and, in July, sent Bessarion to persuade them to declare war. After much debate, the Senate eventually agreed. Pius used this as a pretext to call a new crusade in support of the Venetians. Announcing that he would lead the campaign himself, he summoned Christian princes to take the cross and was gratified when European princes began rallying to the cause. The challenges were as much economic as political. Mounting an expedition of this scale would be expensive, far beyond anything the pope and his allies could afford. Some of the costs could be covered by a tithe on the Italian laity, but it was on Jews that Pius pinned his hopes. In October 1463, he imposed a new tax, requiring all Jews to hand over a twentieth of their property and income, regardless of how it had been earned – even if by usury.[26] This tied Bessarion's hands. Even if he wanted to, it was clear he could not condone any action against Venetian Jews without putting the tax – and the crusade – in direst jeopardy.

Bessarion replied to the doge's request on 18 December 1463.[27] As Moro's advisers had perhaps been hoping, his letter was a masterpiece of diplomatic firmness. In the past, Bessarion argued, everyone had benefitted from the agreements which Venice and its subject towns had signed with Jewish bankers. Ready loans had kept the economy afloat in times of trouble, while low interest rates had kept debts to a minimum. As such, there was no reason why Jews should not be allowed to go on living in Venetian territory. Naturally, Bessarion was too canny to risk appearing to justify usury per se, much less mention the money it would bring the crusade, but to assuage those worried about spiritual 'contamination', he ventured that being in close proximity to Christians might actually persuade Jews to convert. Though the friars might argue that previous popes had forbidden Christians to contract with Jews, Bessarion reassured the doge that there was no need to worry on that account. No one was going to get excommunicated for signing a simple *condotta* – especially not in these circumstances.

Enough patricians were swayed by Bessarion's letter that the Venetian government agreed to let Jews live in its territories, much as they had done before. Efforts were even made to make their lives slightly more agreeable. In February 1464, as Venetian colonists were beginning to push back against Turkish troops in the Peloponnese, the Council of Ten decreed that, in principle, subject towns would be free to sign their own *condotte* with Jewish bankers.[28] And the more that did, the more taxes could be raised.

Preparations for the crusade were soon underway.[29] On 18 July, Pius II set off for Ancona, where the armies had agreed to embark for Greece. While he was waiting for the Venetian fleet to arrive, a chill he had caught in Rome developed into a 'phlegmatic fever'. His condition rapidly deteriorated. A few days later, he died – and with him, the crusade. Within days, the remaining troops had melted away, leaving Venice and its Hungarian allies to fight the Ottomans alone.

Facing a lengthy struggle, and reeling from an outbreak of the plague, the Venetians needed the Jews even more than before.[30] In response to a request from 'Jews living in or travelling to' the city, it therefore agreed to relax restrictions on religious worship. Henceforth, Jews throughout Venetian territories would be allowed to gather for prayer provided that no more than ten people took part, and that they refrained from reciting *officii* or performing *sacrificii*. Since Jewish law stipulates that at least ten people must be present for a *minyan* (quorum), this allowed a number of important rites to be observed legally for the first time in almost forty years.[31]

*

While a majority of the Council of Ten had voted in favour of allowing the Jews to remain in Venetian territories, the decision had been far from unanimous.[32] And as the war against the Ottoman Empire deteriorated, opposition began to grow.[33] In subject towns, governors found themselves struggling to balance the Republic's official policies with mounting popular animosity; while at the University of Padua, jurists engaged in a furious debate about the legitimacy of Jewish usury. Although some believed that commerce between Jews and Christians was permissible under certain conditions, others, like Alessandro Nievo, insisted that the continued presence of Jewish lenders represented a clear danger to Christian believers.[34] Taking aim at the compromises struck by recent pontiffs in his *Consilia contra iudeos foenerantes* (1469), Nievo argued that Jews were committing a grave sin in lending at interest, and that the pope could therefore neither dispense with earlier prohibitions on usury nor consent to the *condotte* that some towns granted to Jewish bankers.[35]

At the same time, the first attempts were made to establish a *monte di pietà* in the Veneto – in spite of the Venetian government's policy of commercial tolerance. In 1469, a Franciscan friar, Michele Carcano da Milano, who has recently helped establish the *monte di pietà* in Perugia, arrived in Padua and urged the citizens to found their own – albeit without success.[36]

Over the next few years, Venice's position in the eastern Mediterranean became perilous. On 5 August 1470, Negroponte, the most prized of its Greek possessions, was captured; and despite a brief recovery under Moro's successor, Nicolò Tron (r. 1471–3), further losses seemed inevitable.[37] With disaster looming, and Levantine trade at a standstill, a wave of fear and resentment swept the Veneto. As it did so, the Venetian government came under mounting pressure to take a firmer stance towards the Jews. An incident in nearby Trent provided the impetus. On 26 March 1475, a toddler named Simon was found dead after going missing three days earlier. Suspicion immediately fell on local Jews: accused of having murdered the child for ritual purposes, the entire community was arrested. The ensuing investigation was a sham. Despite the lack of evidence connecting the Jews with Simon's death, there was no doubt they would be found guilty. Even before the official investigation was concluded, news of the 'outrage' had already spread to neighbouring Venetian towns.[38] On 4 April, the physician Giovanni Mattia Tiberino, who had helped examine the boy's body, sent an account of the Jews' supposed 'crime' to the Senate of Brescia.[39] Based more on antisemitic fantasy than on proven facts, this painted the Jews of Trent as cold-hearted killers driven by an uncontrollable hatred of Christianity, who deserved the harshest punishment. Within a few weeks, an Italian translation of Tiberino's text had been printed at Verona; and by the beginning of the summer, a rhymed account of Simon's 'martyrdom' (*Li horribili tormenti del beato Simone di Trento*) had been published in Treviso.[40] A pictorial version followed soon after.[41] Coupled with the lurid rumours already circulating, these texts helped foster a burgeoning cult of the murdered child and provided the Jews' enemies with grist for their mill. In Venetian subject towns, popular resentments began to bubble over. Within a month of Simon's death, accusations of ritual murder were levelled against the Jews of Padua, and there were calls for expulsions – or worse.[42] Many Venetian patricians sympathized.[43]

Others were more doubtful, however. Recognizing the accusations for the nonsense they were, more level-headed patricians feared that if the public mood was not calmed, the resulting violence might quickly spiral out of control. The doge, Pietro Mocenigo (r. 1474–6), agreed, and on 5 November 1475 issued a decree denouncing the attacks on Jewish communities and clamping down on the veneration of the murdered child. Quoting a letter sent by Pope Sixtus IV to the 'rulers and officials of Italy' less than a month earlier,[44] Mocenigo ordered that

> no person of any condition may dare or presume in any place to depict or have depicted, or buy or sell [images] of that little boy called Simon of Trent who was killed, as they say, by the Jews, or to preach about him in either public or private places, or to make *any* reference to his sanctity . . .[45]

It was to little avail. Although the *podestà* of Brescia had copies of the doge's decree posted throughout the city,[46] the first of many miracles associated with images of the 'martyred' child was reported on 13 April 1476.[47] Soon, frescoes of the boy's murder appeared on the walls of churches throughout the val Camonica,[48] and over the next few years, broadsheets with pictures of his agony circulated freely – all of which fanned the flames of popular antisemitism.

Anti-Jewish feeling was further intensified by Bernardino da Feltre.[49] A short, wiry man in his thirties, he had recently emerged as one of the Franciscan Order's most formidable preachers. He was deeply committed to the defence of the Christian life, the renewal of public morals, and the relief of the poor. With his booming voice and simple, earthy language, he railed against vanity, greed, and corruption. He condemned the failings of secular governments and poured scorn on venial officials. But he reserved particular hatred for the Jews. Since embarking on his mission almost a decade before, he had preached against Jewish usury in towns throughout Lombardy, Aquila, and the Veneto, whipping up storms of hatred as he went. In 1475, he had delivered the Lenten sermons in Trent just before Simon's 'martyrdom', and his fiery rhetoric had undoubtedly contributed to the arrest of the town's Jews. Now, in 1477, he was back in Venetian territory. Exploiting the popular fervour provoked by the trial of Simon's alleged 'murderers', he urged Venice's subject towns to expel their Jews (if they had not already done so) and called for the establishment of *monti di pietà* throughout the *terraferma*.

The Venetian government's attitude began to harden. Exhausted by sixteen years of fighting, the Republic had tired of the Ottoman war.[50] Too much had already been lost, and with no prospect of help from either the papacy or its Italian allies, Doge Giovanni Mocenigo (r. 1478–85) – the brother of Pietro – glumly sued for peace. Though the sultan's terms were harsh, Venice had no choice but to agree, and in the calm which followed the signing of the treaty, a growing consensus supported tougher measures against the Jews. To limit Jewish movements – and, by extension, trade – the rules governing the yellow circle were tightened. Whereas, in the past, exemptions had been granted to ensure Jews' safety while travelling, or for a host of other understandable reasons, the Council of Ten decreed that Jews would henceforth be obliged to wear the mark at all times – with exceptions being made only for 'reasons of state'.[51] Accusations against Jews were also treated more indulgently, no matter how spurious the charges, or how grave the penalty. When in 1480 three Jews in Portobuffolè, near Treviso, were condemned to death for the ritual murder of an Albanian beggar boy on Holy Thursday, the government was sufficiently alarmed to send a public prosecutor to investigate. By all accounts, the Jews should have been acquitted, but after a somewhat one-sided trial, the sentence was confirmed, and the Jews were burnt at the stake.

*

Worse was soon to come. Although Sultan Mehmed II had promised to respect Venice's sovereignty and guaranteed its trading rights in the eastern Mediterranean, tensions with the Sublime Porte remained high. There was no doubt about the Ottomans' territorial ambitions and, while the Venetians were anxious to avoid another war, few had any illusions about the chances of lasting peace. The Ottoman capture of Otranto on 11 August 1480 caused understandable alarm – as much for the brutality of the attack as for the threat to Venice's strategic interests. During the sack, 800 inhabitants who refused to convert to Islam were beheaded; children were sold into slavery; and churches were turned into stables.[52] Fearing this might be the prelude to a wider campaign in the Adriatic, the Venetian government immediately ordered a new fleet to be armed, and there was even talk of drumming up support for a new crusade. The sultan's unexpected death on 3 May 1481 forestalled any immediate danger, but fears of an Ottoman attack were still acute when, less than a year later, war broke out with nearby Ferrara over control of the salt trade.[53] Though there was never any serious risk of an attack on Venice itself, the effects were grave. Pope Sixtus IV promptly took Ferrara's side, and Venice was placed under interdict. Food supplies ran short, and by early 1484, famine had set in.[54]

Even before hunger had started to bite, Venice had been struggling to meet its obligations. Although attempts had been made to trim the Republic's bloated budget some years before, the cost of war had far outstripped the treasury's resources. In a bid to stave off the looming crisis, the government hastily established a new loan fund, known as the *Monte nuovo*.[55] More ominously, it also tried to wring money out of the Jews. At first, it merely asked for 'contributions'. In March 1481, the Senate ordered an unspecified group of Jews to hand over 1,000 ducats for arming the war fleet in September, and a further 1,200 ducats three months after that.[56] Then, on 26 April 1483, special taxes were levied on the Jews of the *terraferma*,[57] and by December that year, Jews throughout Venetian territories were required to provide a forced loan of 10,000 ducats.[58] At the same time, restrictions were placed on Jewish trade. Some years before, at the height of the war with the Ottoman Empire, the Republic had tried to safeguard the interests of Venetian merchants – and the state's tax revenues – by banning Jews from importing or exporting goods from Greece and the Levant. Rightly or wrongly, the government believed that some Jews were getting around this by persuading Venetians to act as 'front men' for their operations, 'to the . . . total ruin of all the other Venetian merchants'. To prevent this, the Senate reaffirmed the existing laws, decreeing that any Venetian ship-masters (*patroni*) who carried Jewish goods on board their vessels would be deprived of their positions for ten years.[59]

Meanwhile, on the *terraferma*, Venice's subject towns were taking things even further. Although Bernardino da Feltre was obliged to leave Venetian territory in 1483, the vicissitudes of the war with Ferrara rendered the people of the Veneto more receptive to the idea of establishing *monti di pietà*. Instrumental in this was another Franciscan friar called Marco da Montegallo.[60] Arriving in Venetian territory, he went first to Vicenza, where anti-Jewish feelings were already running high. Just a few weeks earlier, amidst accusations of another ritual murder, it had voted to expel its Jewish inhabitants, and it greeted his proposals with enthusiasm. On 3 August 1486, the statutes of the new *monte* were approved.[61] A second was founded in Brescia, at the urging of Marco's colleague Michele da Acqui.[62] Unlike in Vicenza, expulsion was never seriously considered, but the *monte* was founded along similar lines, with small loans being offered free of charge. In 1490, a third *monte* was established in Verona.[63]

The return of Bernardino da Feltre only accelerated this trend. By then, his preaching had grown so fiery that even the Venetian government was uneasy. Afraid that he might incite subject towns to further violence, it reaffirmed that, in the absence of contrary legislation, Jews still had the right to lend money at interest, and that they should not be molested in any way. It warned preachers – by which it really meant Bernardino – to refrain from inflaming tensions, on pain of the harshest punishment.[64]

Bernardino had no intention of moderating his tone, though. Under his influence, another *monte* was founded in Padua in 1491.[65] In contrast to the *monti* established in Vicenza and Brescia, this one charged interest. Towards the end of the same year, Ravenna asked for permission to set up another.[66] Realizing that the genie was now out of the bottle, the Venetian government reluctantly agreed. Although it stressed that the local Jews were not to be expelled, it acknowledged that, once the *monte* was operational, Jewish moneylending would have to be banned, and that the Jews would be forbidden to 'defile' Ravenna's squares with a synagogue. Over the next few years, a stream of other *monti* followed.[67]

Such measures were, however, sporadic and disorganized. Subject towns acted on their own initiative, and there was no sign of a co-ordinated, let alone consistent, policy. Even with the Jews' opponents in the majority, the Venetian government fought shy of taking any irrevocable decision about their status. Wary as it may have been of their trading activities, and distasteful though many patricians found their lending, the Republic could not deny the contribution they made to its prosperity. When necessary, it was even prepared to protect those whose skills marked them out as particularly valuable. In June 1490, for example, the Collegio approved a petition from the arms manufacturer Sigismondo Alberghetti to allow certain Jews who were specialists in the founding of bombards to work with him on projects for the Venetian war fleet.[68]

Amidst all this uncertainty, Jewish communities proved remarkably resilient. In those parts of the Veneto where no expulsions had occurred, they even flourished. In 1483, the Venetian diarist Marin Sanudo reported that while the Venetians still refused to have Jews in the capital, there was nevertheless a 'beautiful synagogue' in Mestre.[69] In Brescia, the Jewish population grew so rapidly that within a few years of the *monte*'s approval, voices were being raised in the town council about the sheer number of Jewish people thronging the streets.[70] The Jewish population of the Veneto was even beginning to develop its own form of corporate self-organization. Just over a decade after the *monte* in Vicenza opened its doors, the Jewish *università* (community) sent representatives to the capital to negotiate on behalf of co-religionists throughout Venetian territories.[71]

Yet however uncoordinated the subject towns' actions, however numerous the exceptions, it seemed clear that *monti di pietà* would continue to proliferate – and that further expulsions would follow. How far and how fast this would go was anyone's guess. As the events of recent years had shown, the fate of communities throughout the Veneto would be shaped by Venice's wider interests. But to many Jews, it must have seemed as if they were living on borrowed time.

3

Confinement

(1492–1516)

For the Jews of Venice, the year 1492 was pregnant with ill omen. Even before Columbus had landed in the New World, strange and terrible changes had begun to sweep the Old. In Spain, the Catholic monarchs Ferdinand of Aragon and Isabella of Castile captured the Muslim emirate of Granada, and celebrated their 'reconquest' of Spain by expelling all Jews from their territories. In Rome, amidst unprecedented bribery, the College of Cardinals elected Rodrigo Borgia as Pope Alexander VI, and near the Alsatian town of Ensisheim, a meteorite crashed to earth, a portent – claimed the chronicler Sebastian Brandt – of war and bloodshed.[1] Yet no event proved more portentous, or consequential, than the coming of age of the young King Charles VIII of France.

Charles was far from an imposing figure. The Venetian ambassador reported that, at just twenty-two years old, he was 'small in size and malformed in body, with an ugly face . . . large white eyes . . . an aquiline nose . . . and fat lips, which he always keeps open'. Although he was reputedly a keen sportsman, he had a severe twitch and was unusually 'slow in speech'.[2] He did not seem to have any of his father's cunning; and, but for a distant claim to the kingdom of Naples – which he had inherited from his great-grandfather – there was little reason to suppose he would ever cast his rheumy gaze beyond the Île-de-France, let alone across the Alps. No member of Charles' family had sat on the Neapolitan throne in over fifty years, and to his predecessors, the prospects of recovering the crown had seemed slight indeed. Yet so unstable had the Italian peninsula grown in the intervening years that previously hostile states now saw in that tenuous claim hopes for much-needed alliances – and what had once seemed an impossibility now took on a different colour.

The Serenissima – as Venice was often known – had been among the first to recognize the significance of Charles' Neapolitan inheritance. In 1483, at the height of the Ferrarese War, it had appealed to him for help.[3] Extolling the justice of his claim to the *Regno*, the Venetians had urged him to cross into Italy to take what was rightfully his and put their enemies to flight in the process. Nothing had come of this at the time. Then just thirteen years old, Charles had still been a minor; and, in the eyes of his ministers, the subjugation of Brittany took precedence.[4] Now that Charles was of age, however, all that changed. Proud and impetuous, he found the temptations of an Italian crown almost irresistible. Following the death of Ferrante of Naples on 25 January 1494, the balance of power in Italy suddenly swung in Charles' favour. Fearing that the new king, Alfonso II, might have designs on Lombardy, the duke of Milan hastened to solicit French support;[5] and when Alfonso started to meddle in the delicate politics of the Papal States, Pope Alexander VI invited Charles to invade. Confident of success, Charles wasted no time, and by mid-October was encamped on the Lombard plain.

Charles had every reason to expect Venice's support. They were natural allies. Not only had the Republic encouraged him in the past, but it had also come to see Alfonso as a threat to its position in the Adriatic. Despite the obvious benefits, however, Venice remained neutral. The Senate's official explanation was that it needed to devote all its energies to guarding against the possibility of an Ottoman attack. The real reason, however, was that the Venetians were wary of what Charles might do and wanted to see how his expedition would turn out before committing themselves.[6]

The Venetians' caution was vindicated when Charles captured Naples, almost without a fight, on 22 February 1495.[7] After putting his new kingdom in order, Charles announced his intention of returning to France within a few months. But so easily had he defeated his enemies that the states of Italy began to wonder if he might be tempted to try his luck elsewhere before leaving. On his march south, he had already driven the Medici out of Florence, and his cousin, Louis d'Orléans, was openly talking about pressing his own claim to the duchy of Milan. Like many other states, Venice was alarmed. On 31 March, it therefore formed an anti-French league with Pope Alexander VI, Emperor Maximilian I, King Ferdinand of Aragon, and the duke of Milan.[8] Charles immediately saw the danger. Hoping to make it back to France before the league could block his path, he hastily set out from Naples. But he was too late. A day after he was forced to give battle, Alfonso's son, Ferrandino, re-entered Naples in triumph. Surrounded by enemies, and exhausted by the struggle, Charles had no choice but to limp back over the Alps, his grand schemes in ruins.

Venice was exultant. With the French retreat, it had secured its borders against a potentially devastating threat, while from a grateful Ferrandino, it received three ports on the Apulian coast which it had long coveted. Its commercial prospects were bright – brighter, indeed, than many could remember. Around the corner, the Republic espied the promise of increased trade with southern Italy and a much-needed boost to the state coffers. A renewed self-confidence was in the air. Completed a little over a year after the Battle of Fornovo, Gentile Bellini's *Procession in Saint Mark's Square* shows the city resplendent in its order and unity; while in Vittore Carpaccio's *Miracle of the Cross at the Ponte di Rialto* (c.1496), we glimpse a growing sense that God had marked Venice out for special favour.[9]

Yet war had cost the city dear. The army it had fielded, while not excessive, had badly strained its finances; and the Republic still had to reckon with heavy military obligations on the mainland. In the months after the battle, the government was so short of money that it had to resort to forced loans; but even these did little to stem the outflow. Things were not made easier by a severe famine the following year, which caused prices to drop and borrowing to become more expensive.[10] Barely a year after Charles VIII had left Italy, government bonds had slumped to 62 per cent of their former value.[11] If Venice was to reap any benefits at all from its gains in Apulia, it would first have to put its finances in order. In practice, this meant maximizing tax revenues accruing from trade and controlling the supply of credit more closely.

Attention focused on the Jews of Venice. Just ten days after Ferrandino's return to Naples, and with a trading boom on the horizon, the Council of Ten attempted to clamp down on illicit business transactions by cancelling all badge exemptions, except for those granted for reasons of state.[12] Evasion was, however, so widespread that the following spring, the Senate felt obliged to legislate further.

As the preamble to the new law explained, some Jews were allegedly hiding the yellow sign under their outer clothing, so that they could remain in the city unrecognized for as long as they wanted, all the while 'committing many evils to the offence of God and the . . . city of Venice'.[13] To stop this, Jews throughout Venetian territories would now be required to wear a yellow *baretta* or a similar type of hat – instead of the yellow circle – at all times, on pain of a 50-ducat fine and a month in prison.[14] It was also decreed that, after spending their allotted fifteen days in Venice, they would not be allowed to return for a full year. The only exceptions would be the Jewish bankers of Mestre. Whenever the Venetian authorities held a sale of pledges, each bank could send one representative to the city to handle its business; but they were warned not to stay any longer than absolutely necessary. In the event, this quickly proved impracticable. As the Jewish bankers in Mestre pointed out, earlier legislation had required them to register every transaction with the Sopraconsoli in Venice. If they were now prohibited from coming to the city except on rare occasions, their businesses would simply cease to function. Realizing its mistake, the government hastily granted them leave to stay; but the desire to reduce the Jewish presence in the capital nevertheless remained.

A little under two years later, in February 1498, the Great Council took aim at Jewish dealers in *strazzaria* (second-hand goods).[15] Rather shamelessly, it claimed that, in the past, no Jews had ever resided in the city, nor had any been allowed to visit, except for public fairs. But just recently, a Jew had been caught selling *strazzaria* outside of the permitted times. This risked setting a precedent. It would be all too easy, the Council reasoned, for Jews to use this as an excuse to come to the city whenever they wanted – and for as long as they wanted. Appalled, the Council declared that henceforth, Jews would be forbidden to come to Venice to sell second-hand goods, or transact any other sort of business, except during fairs. Just to be sure, it also stipulated that they were forbidden to reside in the city for any length of time outside the allotted periods – and that any Christian who rented them somewhere to stay or store their goods on unauthorized days would be heavily fined.[16]

*

Had French ambitions been curtailed forever by the ill-fated Neapolitan expedition, it is possible that Venice's relations with its Jews may simply have reverted to the uneasy equilibrium which had existed at the beginning of the fifteenth century; but the unexpected death of Charles VIII on 7 April 1498 – and the terrible wars it unleashed – propelled them along the path that led to the Ghetto.

Having no children of his own, Charles was succeeded by his cousin, Louis d'Orléans, who, as Louis XII, made no secret of his desire to return to Italy as soon as possible. It was, however, not Naples which drew him – or at least, not so much. Though he fully intended to recapture it at some point, his priority was to conquer the duchy of Milan, which he had already begun eyeing some years before. As soon as he had secured France against its enemies, he began negotiating with potential allies.[17] Pope Alexander VI, whose son, Cesare Borgia, was intent on carving out a kingdom for himself in the Romagna, readily agreed. But of all the cities and states in Italy, none was more central to the king's plans than Venice. Since its lands on the *terraferma* bordered on the duchy of Milan, Louis would not be able to do anything without its support (or at least its neutrality); but, given its previous hostility to Charles VIII, most doubted that it would even listen to the French proposals. The Venetians, however, had been impressed by the strength of the French army. Weighing this against the feebleness of Naples and Florence – on whose support the duke of Milan was pinning his hopes – they realized that there was more to be gained from an alliance than from opposition. On 9 February 1499, Venice and Louis therefore signed the Treaty of Blois, and agreed to divide the duchy between them.

Victory came swiftly.[18] Crossing the Alps in August, Louis' forces swept all before them. Within a few weeks, French troops had captured Milan; and on 6 October, the king made his ceremonial entry into the city. Meanwhile, the Venetians raced across the Po, occupying Cremona and the Gera d'Adda. It had almost been too easy. There was some lingering resistance; but a brief rally by the deposed duke was soon brushed aside – and the victors were left to enjoy their spoils.

With Milan now firmly in his grasp, Louis was able to turn his attention to Naples. It was obvious this would be a much trickier prospect. He was no longer the only interested party. Barely a year after retaking the kingdom, Ferrandino had fallen ill and died, leaving the throne to his uncle, Federico. But Ferdinand of Aragon now claimed that *he* was the rightful heir – and there were plenty of Neapolitan nobles who were ready to back him. Rather than having Ferdinand as a rival, Louis therefore made him an ally. On 11 November 1500, the two kings agreed to mount a joint invasion and divide the kingdom between them.[19] As many contemporaries noted, it was naive to suppose that such an arrangement would last long; but for the moment, it served both of their needs. The following June, advancing rapidly in a pincer movement, the two armies encountered little resistance. On 2 August, Naples fell.

The Venetians were justifiably pleased. As the diarist Girolamo Priuli recorded, the Senate was quick to congratulate Louis on his success, and no doubt hoped that its gains in the north would soon be followed by further privileges in the south. But unlike in Florence and Rome, there were no public celebrations.[20] For while Venice's standing on the *terraferma* was improving, its position overseas had suddenly deteriorated. In April 1499, just two months after the Treaty of Blois had been signed, the Republic had once again found itself at war with the Ottoman Empire over trade in the eastern Mediterranean.[21] From the outset, it was on the back foot. In August 1499, its fleet was defeated; in September, Friuli was raided; and in the following year, the ports of Coron and Modon were lost. The shock was terrible; but before it had a chance to recover its strength, the Ottomans were already advancing on Dalmatia.

To make matters even worse, Venice's wider trading interests were also under threat. On 9 September 1499, a week before the fortress of Milan surrendered, the Portuguese explorer Vasco da Gama landed at Lisbon after rounding the Cape of Good Hope and opening the sea route to India. At a stroke, da Gama redrew the economic map. Whereas spices and silks had previously been transported to the Levant by camel or caravel, and then loaded onto Venetian and Genoese ships for distribution around the Mediterranean, they could now be brought to Europe directly – with less risk and at a lower cost. This dealt a devastating blow to Venice's trade in pepper. With less cargo coming through Egypt, fewer galleys were sent to Alexandria – and prices at the Rialto shot up.[22] What was more, English and Dutch ships now had less need to pass through Venice; and slowly but surely, Lisbon began to challenge its position as Europe's pre-eminent port.[23]

The confused nature of the international situation wrought a peculiar change in Venice's relations with its Jews. Given the legacy of recent years, it was perhaps inevitable that the prevailing attitude was still one of hostility. Violent attacks were not uncommon. On 27 August 1502, a twenty-three-year-old man named Troiano Contarini was condemned to death for robbing and killing several Jews in Mestre.[24] Nor had the myth of 'blood libel' lost any of its potency. Just six days later, Jews in Venice's former colony of Ragusa (Dubrovnik) were accused of ritually murdering a 'poor old woman'.[25]

But the growing precariousness of Venice's situation beyond the *terraferma* also forced it to rely on Jewish aid more than it would perhaps have liked. Such was the cost of the Ottoman war – and so grave the banking crisis it provoked – that the government had to demand financial contributions far in excess of anything it had in the past.[26] On 2 January 1501, the Senate obliged Jews living in Venetian territory to pay 5,000 ducats each time it imposed a special tax known as a *decima* on its citizens, on the understanding that it would not ask for more than two *decime* a year.[27] Five months later, the Senate reaffirmed this, but added that, since the Christian population had already been burdened with four *decime*, the Jewish community would have to pay an additional 10,000 ducats to make it 'fair'.[28] From Venice's perspective, of course, this probably did not seem like an unreasonable demand. It has been calculated that, each year, this tax represented less than 1 per cent of the gross revenue that the Republic received from the city and its territories – and realized less than half the amount brought in by the tax on the meat trade.[29] But for the Jewish population, it was an extremely heavy burden. Though comparatively few in number, they were still 'by far the heaviest payers of direct taxation in the Venetian dominion'.[30] And the sums they provided each year were still enough to pay the shipbuilders in the Arsenale for a few weeks or keep a company of mercenaries in the field – neither of which Venice could afford to do without.[31]

So too, in the commercial field, Venice had need of Jews' help in its growing struggle with Portugal. A key role was played by Isaac Abravanel.[32] Born into one of Portugal's most illustrious Jewish families, Isaac had served as King Alfonso V's treasurer. After his patron's death, he had been forced to flee first to Spain, and then to Venice. Shortly after arriving in early 1503, he appeared before the Council of Ten offering to negotiate between Venice and Portugal. The Council jumped at the idea, and although it came to nothing, it was a sign of how much Venice was coming to rely on such itinerant figures.

Most of all, Venice had an acute need for Jewish moneylenders – both in subject cities and in the capital. On 14 January 1503, a generous ten-year *condotta* was therefore granted to the owners of three loan banks in Mestre: Asher, the son of Solomon, Abramo, the son of Fricele, and Marcuzo, the son of Jacob.[33] Of these, by far the most important was Asher. Better known in Italian as 'Anselmo del Banco' (literally 'Anselmo of the Bank'), the dynamic Asher Meshullam was the son of a banker from Camposampiero.[34] Working in Mestre alongside his brother, Chaim (Italianized as 'Vivian'/'Vita'), he built the family bank into the most successful of its kind – and grew enormously rich in the process.[35] Already among the most prominent figures in the Jewish community, he soon emerged as its unofficial leader – and, in the years to come, played a pivotal role in shaping its destiny.

According to the terms of the *condotta*, Anselmo and his colleagues would be allowed to come and go as they pleased, rent houses in Venice, and even have vaults set aside for their pledges. Though they were still forbidden to have a synagogue in Venice, they nevertheless had permission to get married, circumcise their children, and celebrate all the rites the Mosaic Law required. Most importantly, if the war on the *terraferma* caused them any difficulties, they would be allowed to take refuge in Venice and live there unmolested for as long as necessary. This last clause was probably intended as nothing more than a courtesy. Venice still had to be on its guard – especially against Cesare Borgia, whose conquests in the Romagna were growing by the day – but its affairs on the mainland were reasonably stable, especially in comparison with the Stato da Màr. Few patricians could have imagined that the clause would ever be invoked – or that it would have such far-reaching consequences.

*

Before long, however, the *condotta* had taken on a different hue. Peace having been accorded with the Ottoman Empire in August, Venice's attention was once again consumed by the affairs of Italy.[36] In the Regno, tensions between the French and Spanish had arisen almost as soon as the kingdom had been divided.[37] Conflict was all but inevitable; and what began as mere skirmishes soon escalated into open warfare. The French had the worst of it. On 28 April 1503, they were crushed at the Battle of Cerignola.[38] Forced to retreat to Naples, they braced themselves for a siege – but the writing was already on the wall. The Venetians were convinced the Spanish would soon take the whole kingdom.[39] And if they did, there was no telling what might happen to Venice's Apulian ports – or trade in the Adriatic.

Meanwhile, trouble was brewing in Rome. On 12 August, Pope Alexander VI and his son Cesare Borgia fell gravely ill after attending a dinner party. Though some thought malaria was to blame, others suspected poison.[40] Either way, the two men's condition quickly deteriorated. On the evening of 18 August, the pope was given the last rites; and before nightfall, he 'passed from this life into Hell'.[41] Cesare somehow clung on – but his position in the Romagna was now in peril. After the brief pontificate of the pliable Pius III, the conclave chose Giuliano della Rovere as the new pope. A strong-willed and warlike man, more comfortable in the saddle than in the pulpit, Julius II, as he was now known, had long nurtured a grudge against the Borgias. Days after a Spanish army defeated Louis XII's forces at the Battle of Garigliano, bringing French rule in Naples to an end, he had Cesare clapped in irons and shipped off to Spain as a prisoner.

A struggle for the Romagna now began. Venice was quickest off the mark. Still smarting from its losses in the eastern Mediterranean, the city was determined to compensate itself by absorbing as much of Cesare's state as it could – and was gratified by how easily this was accomplished.[42] In just a few breathless weeks, the Republic had already taken possession of Rimini, Forlì, Faenza, and a host of other towns along the via Aemilia.[43] More were expected to follow.

So rapid were Venice's gains, however, that her neighbours could not help being alarmed – Pope Julius II most of all. Given that the Romagna had traditionally been a part of the Papal States, he regarded Venice's expansionism as a direct threat to his own efforts to reassert control over the region. Once his position in Rome was secure, he set himself to driving Venice out of the towns she had acquired.[44] In 1508, Julius spied his opportunity. Furious at Venice's refusal to join an anti-French alliance, Emperor Maximilian declared war on the Republic instead – only for his forces to be quickly routed.[45]

It was a pyrrhic victory – not least for Venice's Jews. Despite the speed of the imperial retreat, the expedition had caused them considerable unease.[46] Over the past year, they had been taxed heavily – and the prospect of being asked to cough up even more money was simply too much to bear.[47] They were also worried about the safety of their businesses. The Senate attempted to reassure them by spelling out the conditions under which Jews could live in Venetian territory and clarified that only those with a letter from the doge could lend money.[48] But a palpable sense of anxiety nevertheless remained.

Even more worryingly, the failure of Maximilian's expedition convinced Venice's enemies of the need to unite against the Republic – exactly as Julius II had hoped. However strong their mutual enmities may have been, they all agreed that Venice's growing power threatened their own interests and could not go unchecked. On 10 December 1508, a league was formed at Cambrai.[49] Although this was ostensibly directed against the Turks, its true purpose was to curb the Venetians' 'love of conquest'. As the terms of the agreement made clear, the Republic was to be stripped of all its Italian possessions, until nothing remained of its land empire but a few islands in the lagoon.

Confronted with so formidable a threat, Venice tried to appease at least some of the league with promises of concessions. But the time for negotiation had passed. Realizing that war was now inevitable, the Republic scrambled to mobilize its forces. The treasury was ransacked, fresh mercenaries were hired, and press gangs scoured the *terraferma* for recruits. By the beginning of May 1509, Venice had assembled by far the largest army yet seen in the Italian Wars – and, in an age of massed battles, it was hoped that numbers alone might carry the day.

Yet the fortunes of war can rarely be calculated as easily as a statement of account. When the French crossed into Venetian territory, the Republic's commanders could not agree on how – or where – to make a stand. On 14 May, the French advance guard took the Venetians by surprise near Agnadello. Within hours, the army, in which such hopes had been placed, lay in ruins.

In a single day, Machiavelli later wrote, the Venetians 'lost what it had taken them eight hundred years to acquire'.[50] With terrifying speed, Venetian control of the *terraferma* collapsed.[51] While the French overran eastern Lombardy, the duke of Ferrara seized the Polesine, and imperial troops poured into Friuli and the Veneto.

Town after town fell to the invaders – often without so much as a sword being drawn in their defence. Only Treviso held out. The Venetians struggled to comprehend the scale – or the speed – of their losses. Amidst a storm of recriminations, many looked for a providential explanation. For Priuli, as for others, Agnadello was a sign that God had 'permitted and ordained the ruin of the Venetian empire'.[52] Drunk on its own prosperity, Venice had gorged itself on sins of the worst kind; and now it was paying the price.

Jews suffered more than most. Although Maximilian had offered to take Jewish communities north of Padua under his protection, his troops, hungry for plunder, were a constant menace. Even more dangerous, however, were their Christian neighbours. In the confusion of war, many townspeople took the opportunity to vent long-standing hatreds, settle perceived scores, or simply steal with impunity – often at the same time as attacks were made on the centres of Venetian administration. On 22 May, word reached Venice that the Brescians had 'opened the prison, plundered the armoury in the captain's *palazzo*', and 'robbed' (*sachizato*) the local Jews.[53] According to one estimate, some 30,000 ducats were stolen.[54] On 2 June, it was learned that the same had happened in Verona.[55] The next day, there was even worse news. In Mestre, Jews were reportedly in great distress;[56] while in Treviso, which had just risen in revolt, several armed citizens had ransacked the homes of the city's Jews.[57] Though nothing of value had been taken – most Jews apparently having taken the precaution of sending their movable belongings to Venice a few days earlier – the violence of the attack was hard to ignore.

Waves of Jewish refugees now flooded into Venice from the *terraferma*. Those who had signed the 1503 *condotta* came with the government's blessing. On 3 June, the Council of Ten gave Anselmo del Banco and his colleagues from Mestre permission to take up residence in the capital and store their pledges in a secure location. But a great many more came without such authorization. Most settled in the *sestieri* of San Polo and Santa Croce, where Venice kept its grain and salt, and where markets were usually held.[58] How many came is hard to gauge; but there were certainly more than Venice had ever seen before – and within a matter of days, their numbers were great enough to provoke angry complaints.[59]

Fearing that the sudden influx would cause a shortage of food, the government tried to expel those who had not been given permission to stay. But it seems that no command could overcome their fear of persecution. On 5 June, the Council of Ten ordered the Jews of Padua to return home.[60] Almost two weeks later, however, they were still refusing to leave.[61] Suddenly, Venice had the Jewish presence it had struggled so long to avoid – and was powerless to do anything about it.

*

By then, Venice's situation had become perilous. At the Corpus Christi procession – during which Christ's real presence in the Eucharist was celebrated by parading the sacrament around the city – a sombre, fearful mood took hold. As Sanudo reported, balconies overlooking the Piazza San Marco were closed; women were told to stay at home; and children were banned from entering the basilica.[62] A thousand troops lined the square, in case of invasion or coup. The procession itself, usually so full of pomp and ceremony, was sparse and muted. Besides those in office, only a few patricians were present, and even they were a sorry sight. Walking behind the consecrated host, Doge Leonardo Loredan was visibly trembling. For the first time since the War of Chioggia, it seemed like Venice itself might fall. According to the Vicentine writer Luigi da Porto, people wandered nervously about the streets, afraid that, at any moment, enemy ships might be sighted in the lagoon. Sorrow took the place of joy; women went into mourning; and men dared not go out without their weapons, 'such was the boundless dread which entered into their hearts'.[63]

Realizing the gravity of the situation, the Venetians quickly ceded the Romagnol towns to Julius II and the Apulian ports to Ferdinand of Aragon.[64] It was a clever sacrifice. Now that their principal goals had been achieved, neither the pope nor the king could see any point in crushing the Republic just so that Louis XII and Maximilian could carve up the rest of the *terraferma* between them. Without either breaking with their allies or making their peace with Venice, they quietly began reining in their campaigns. The league, which only days before had been on the brink of capturing the Serenissima, now faltered. Louis withdrew to Milan, leaving only a token force behind, while Maximilian struggled to hold on to his gains. Spying an opportunity, the Venetians now summoned their remaining strength. Patricians, usually so parsimonious, offered up vast sums for the defence of the *patria*; old soldiers were mustered into new detachments; and within days, the fightback had begun.[65] Encountering little resistance, they made rapid progress; and on 17 July, Padua was retaken. As Priuli later noted, Venice seemed to have risen 'from hell to paradise'.[66]

For Jews on the *terraferma*, however, the Venetian rally produced little improvement. In fact, it actually aggravated their position. As the Serenissima gradually reimposed its authority, townspeople accused any Jews who had not fled to the capital of colluding with the enemy – and of committing the most atrocious crimes in the Venetians' absence.[67] It was said that, even now, Jews were 'desecrating the Host, urinating in tabernacles', and murdering babies in their cradles.[68] Such accusations fuelled a resurgence of violence. Following the reoccupation of Padua, Jews again became the target of attacks. Once more, theft rather than physical harm was the principal aim. On 18 July 1509, a delegation led by Anselmo del Banco appeared before the Collegio, complaining about the 'cruelty inflicted' on the Paduan Jews – and especially about the destruction of pledges.[69] Recognizing the risk this posed to the credit market, if not the danger to Jews themselves, the Council of Ten sent their captains to the landward side of the lagoon, so that any goods of value could be taken to safety in Venice. But, as Sanudo noted, 'it was of little use'. In all probability, most movable goods in Padua had already been lost. Worst of all, the Council's decision did nothing to stop attacks elsewhere. Four days later, the *provveditore* had to use troops to restore order in Asolo and Castelfranco Veneto, near Treviso, after local Jews were 'put to the sack'.[70] On this occasion, the stolen goods were returned; but no one could be in any doubt about the jeopardy in which their businesses stood, despite – or rather because of – the restoration of Venetian authority.

Even Jews who had taken refuge in Venice suffered serious losses. Though many bankers had managed to transfer some of their assets to the city, this was evidently not true of all of them, and the disruption to their businesses was no doubt severe. This did not encourage them to return home, and it probably did not improve their standing in Christian eyes, either. According to both Priuli and Sanudo, they were treated no less harshly than before. Yet as the Venetian advance began to slow during the autumn, many patricians seem to have realized that, since the continued demands for the Jews to leave were plainly having no effect, it might well be wiser to accept reality and recognize their presence in the city. The Franciscans' disdain can easily be imagined; but there was simply no way the government could deal with the challenges caused by so many refugees – let alone derive any benefit from them – unless the reality of their residence was not acknowledged at some level. And as the Venetians' financial situation deteriorated, the need for some sort of dialogue was becoming acute.

When a Venetian fleet was destroyed at the Battle of Polesella on 22 December 1509, the truth of this was made apparent.[71] A little under two months later, Jews living in Venice protested that, in view of the losses they had sustained, they would be unable to pay the customary tax of 14,000 ducats.[72] Alarmed at the prospect of having its already strained budget reduced further, the Senate hastily came to an accommodation.[73] It agreed that, in light of the circumstances, *la università de li Judei* (the whole community of the Jews) would only have to pay 5,000 ducats – and three days later tasked Anselmo del Banco with the responsibility of collecting this sum with two other Jews of his choosing. Although, in true Venetian style, nothing was spelled out *too* clearly, this implicitly recognized not just a legitimate Jewish presence in Venice itself, but also the existence of an organized community, with structures and leaders of its own.

This proved a decisive step. By now, the Venetians' distaste for the Jews was unmistakable. Everyone knew they were only in Venice because of the war, and the Republic's faltering fortunes were only aggravating the tensions. Yet the pressures of war, and the difficulties of persuading the Jews to leave, had caused a shift in attitudes. Whereas in the past, patricians had debated whether Jews should be allowed to live in Venice at all, they were now beginning to ask themselves how Venice should deal with the Jews who were already there.

*

After the defeat at Polesella, the Venetians had to accept that they could not continue to fight alone. Even in its reduced form, the league was still too strong. Though little territory had been lost, the momentum had gone out of the Venetian campaign; and what had begun as a triumphant advance now became an unseemly retreat.

Within days of the battle, Ferrarese troops were swarming across the Polesine, and further attacks were expected to follow.⁷⁴ If Venice was to survive, it needed to make allies of its former enemies. The most obvious candidate was the pope. Having already begun distancing himself from the league, he was ripe for turning. It was no secret that his alliance with France had only ever been a matter of convenience; and now that he had gained everything he could reasonably expect from Louis XII, he was increasingly convinced that the king might be an obstacle to his wider ambitions. This gave Venice its opportunity. By agreeing to cede its rights in Ferrara to Julius – along with a host of other concessions – it succeeded in persuading him to break with Louis XII and conclude a peace.⁷⁵

This did little to dissuade Louis or his confederates from their course. In May 1510, they launched a two-pronged attack on Venetian territory; and, after being reinforced by Spanish troops, succeeded in capturing a number of key towns.⁷⁶ Nor, when Julius eventually launched a counterattack a few months later, did it do much to alleviate the situation. A revolt in Genoa came to nothing; the Swiss mercenaries whom he had paid to invade Milan turned back almost as soon as they had begun; and Bologna was gained, only to be lost again.⁷⁷ It was not long before Venice again found itself on the back foot. The following year, a lightning attack by Maximilian caught the Republic by surprise, forcing its commanders to fall back in disarray.

The alarm in Venice was acute. Coinciding with the Easter season – when Jews were traditionally 'blamed' for Christ's crucifixion – this caused hostility to rise once again. On 2 April, Fra Rufino Lovato preached a particularly violent sermon on the Campo San Polo, where many Jewish refugees had taken up residence. Blaming them for the city's suffering, he suggested that it would be a good idea 'to deprive them of everything they owned and put them to the sack'. Fearing that violence would soon follow, Anselmo del Banco and his brother Vivian immediately lodged a complaint. Straight away, Fra Rufino was reprimanded, along with a few others, in order to prevent any 'attack upon the Jews'.⁷⁸ But tensions were evidently running so high that the government could not afford to ignore the friars' complaints entirely. On 8 April 1511, Jews were ordered to leave the city within a month.⁷⁹ The only exceptions were to be those who had sought refuge under the terms of the 1503 *condotta*, and any others with special permission to remain. But no one could seriously have expected this to have any effect. As the government had already seen, such demands rarely carried much weight among refugees, especially in times of danger on the *terraferma* – and besides, this latest decree made it quite clear that some Jews had a *right* to be there. Certainly, very few left. Sanudo estimated that there were around 500 Jewish men and women then living in Venice, and there is no sign of any appreciable decline in their number in the months and years that followed.[80] The question of what else to do with them, however, was becoming hard to ignore. Now that the Venetian government had signalled that the Jews were there to stay – at least for the time being – it had to ask itself how the perceived 'danger' to Christians could be minimized, and how the city could profit most from their presence.

*

During the autumn, Maximilian continued to make gains at Venice's expense.[81] Following an outbreak of plague and civil unrest, almost the whole of Friuli fell to imperial forces; and in early October 1511, Treviso was besieged. But for Louis XII, the steady stream of successes proved costly. Though he had chosen not to campaign in Italy that season, his growing mastery of the north had begun to unsettle his other allies. Fearing that he intended to conquer the whole peninsula, Ferdinand of Aragon abruptly withdrew from their alliance – and instead formed a league with Venice and the pope. Known as the 'Holy League', this was ostensibly intended as nothing more than a defensive arrangement; but that it was directed against Louis was obvious. Soon, Ferdinand succeeded in persuading Henry VIII of England to join, and though Maximilian – who still hoped to seize more Venetian territory – was reluctant to commit, his attachment to Louis grew markedly cooler. Plans for a coordinated campaign were laid; and, for a while, the prospects of driving France out of Italy seemed to grow brighter.

Conveniently forgetting the decree of expulsion issued six months earlier, the Venetian government now made fresh demands of Jews in its territories. Two days before the Holy League was officially proclaimed in Rome, a new tax of 5,000 ducats was levied. Of this, two-thirds was to be paid by Anselmo del Banco and the other bankers living in Venice; the rest by those still residing outside the city. Clearly, while many Jews had still not fled the mainland, 'the greater part of their wealth had now become concentrated within' Venice itself; and this, the Venetian authorities were only too ready to exploit for their own ends.[82] Such an exaction cannot have been overly welcome, of course; but Jews in Venice could perhaps find some consolation in the fact that, for the moment, the capital seemed safe – and that, if the Holy League lived up to its promise, they might soon be able to put the disruption of recent years behind them.

Neither the Holy League nor Venice's Jews had reckoned with Louis' new commander. Then just twenty-two years old, Gaston de Foix was a dazzlingly gifted general, who combined extraordinary courage with a genius for exploiting his enemy's weaknesses. He confounded the League's forces with his speed and decisiveness. After first repelling a Swiss attack on Milan, he foiled the pope's attempt on Bologna and massacred the Venetian garrison which had just retaken Brescia.[83] On 11 April 1512, he then inflicted a crushing defeat on a combined Spanish and papal army at the Battle of Ravenna – albeit at the cost of his own life.[84] Within days, almost the whole of the Romagna had surrendered to the French. All Italy lay at Louis' feet. Puffed up with pride, he ordered the army to march on to Rome – and many Spaniards feared that Naples itself might soon be in danger.

But Louis' victory proved hollow. Though the League's forces had been badly bruised, Julius was not willing to give up so easily – and soon succeeded in rallying his allies for the coordinated counter-attacks they had always planned.[85] The French were in no state to resist. Exhausted by weeks of hard fighting, and still reeling from the loss of de Foix, they struggled to hold their ground. Before long, they were being pushed back on all fronts. In late May, Swiss and imperial troops entered Verona; the Venetians retook Cremona and Bergamo; and papal forces advanced almost unopposed down the Adriatic coast.[86] By June, Milan itself had fallen to the Swiss. Hemmed in on all sides and perilously short of money, Louis bowed to the inevitable. He gave orders for Lombardy to be abandoned; and within a matter of weeks, the remains of his once-triumphant army had limped back over the Alps to France.

It had taken less than three months for French rule in Italy to collapse. Even the Holy League was taken aback. Anticipating a much longer campaign, its members had not bothered to discuss what to do with Louis' territories once he had been defeated.[87] The duchy of Milan quickly became a sticking point. Naturally enough, the Milanese themselves wanted things to go back to how they had been before Charles VIII's invasion, and chose Ludovico Sforza's nineteen-year-old son, Massimiliano, to be their duke. Ideally, they would have liked the duchy to have returned to its old borders, too; but Venice wanted everything it had held before Agnadello. In this, however, the Republic was opposed by Maximilian, who was demanding Bergamo. Ferdinand and Julius urged the Venetians to let the emperor have his way. When they refused, the pope then threatened them with excommunication, and Ferdinand's army seized Brescia – closing off the road to the disputed city.

Suddenly, Venice felt itself under threat. Now that Louis XII had been driven out of Italy, the Holy League seemed to be turning on the Republic. The death of Julius II on 21 February 1513 did little to lessen the tensions. His successor, Giovanni de' Medici – who took the name Leo X – was more subtle and flexible; but his preoccupation with his family's aggrandizement left no doubt that he, too, would oppose Venice's interests, at least for now. In one of those strange twists which make the Italian Wars so bewildering to modern eyes, this perilous confluence of events persuaded Venice to seek help from its old enemy, Louis XII; and in March 1513, a new treaty was signed.[88] Venice agreed to help Louis recover the duchy of Milan; and in return, it would get most, albeit not all, of what it wanted.

A few weeks later, a new French campaign began.[89] Uncertain of the new pope's commitment, the Spanish pulled back from Lombardy, and the western parts of the duchy of Milan were soon overrun. Only the Swiss stood between France and their goal. Outnumbered, and lacking both artillery and horse, they had encamped in Novara – and there was every reason to suppose that they could be dealt with relatively easily. But as the French approached Novara, they were surprised by the Swiss and routed.[90] Before the survivors had time to regroup, the Spanish swept back in; and together with the Swiss, drove the French out of Italy once again. The Venetians were crestfallen. As soon as news of the defeat became known, their army retreated with shameful speed and braced itself for further assaults.

Venice was not without hope, however. Despite the loss of its only ally, its army was largely intact; and the events prior to Novara had shown that its enemies were far from united. If it could hold its nerve and keep the money flowing, it might yet hold out. And if it could do that, there was a decent chance it could come to some agreement with Pope Leo X, who had remained surprisingly aloof from recent events. In the spirit of solicitation, rather than recrimination, the government therefore renewed the Jews' *condotta* when it expired in July.[91] The new agreement, negotiated by the redoubtable Anselmo del Banco, was nothing if not favourable. The Jewish community undertook to pay an annual tax of 6,500 ducats. As with the tax which had been levied in late 1511, it was agreed that Anselmo would pay 2,000 ducats; while Abramo, son of Fricele – who had also signed the *condotta* of 1503 – would contribute a further 2,000. The remaining 2,500 ducats would come from the rest of the community. Anselmo would act as their guarantor and was empowered to collect payments from individuals. In return, the Council agreed to extend the *condotta* and to allow Jews to go on lending money in the city of Venice for another five years. It still reserved the right to impose further forced loans; but the new *condotta* nevertheless consolidated the Jews' position in the lagoon – and strengthened Anselmo's now-acknowledged position as the head of the *università*. Yet the problem of what to *do* with the Jews was only growing more acute.

*

At first, Venice's optimism appeared to be well founded. By the time the *condotta* was signed, the Holy League was already suffering from a lack of direction.[92] A half-hearted attempt to lay siege to Padua was abandoned after just eighteen days. With supplies running low, the combined Spanish and imperial army then pushed further into the Veneto – more for the sake of venting its commanders' frustration than achieving any particular goal. Mestre, Fusina, and Marghera were burnt, and Venice itself was shelled. But further than this it could not go. Running short of food, and deep in enemy territory, its position soon looked desperate. Just days later, the Spanish commander, Ramón de Cardona, felt obliged to order the retreat. At once, the Venetians seized their chance. Mustering all their strength, they gave chase, determined to catch Cardona's forces before they could reach the safety of their winter quarters. Victory seemed to be theirs for the taking. Writing from Creazzo on 6 October, the *provveditore generale*, Andrea Loredan, wrote confidently of their *indubitata vitoria*;⁹³ and even the Venetian commander, Bartolomeo d'Alviano – not known for his hyperbole – regarded it as a certainty.⁹⁴

When the Venetian army encountered the League's forces at Schio, just north of Vicenza, however, the foolishness of these predictions quickly became clear.⁹⁵ Shrouded in mist, d'Alviano's troops, most of them untrained volunteers, were easily outclassed by Cardona's battle-hardened professionals. '[I]n less than half an hour,' wrote the future doge, Andrea Gritti, 'these good men were routed.'⁹⁶ Those who could, fled. But while some made it back to Vicenza, many more were butchered by the pursuing Spaniards within sight of the city.

When word of the disaster reached Venice, late on the night of 7 October, 'all those who were in the Senate were like dead men'.⁹⁷ It seemed almost impossible to believe. The only explanation that anyone could offer was that God – or perhaps Fate – was punishing the Venetians for their sins.⁹⁸

Stoically, Andrea Gritti urged the Senate not to despair; but most could not help it. After the battle, what remained of the Venetian army quickly disintegrated. Some were too weary, or too badly wounded, to fight; others simply deserted. Meeting little resistance, Cardona seized Vicenza, then settled in for the winter in the Polesine.⁹⁹ Meanwhile, Maximilian swept into Friuli. But though the fighting continued for much of the following year, the usual problems of supply prevented either Cardona or the emperor from making further gains. Little by little, the conflict degenerated into a series of inconclusive skirmishes, which achieved nothing beyond driving the two sides to exhaustion.

Then, just as Venice's spirits were at their lowest, news arrived that Louis XII had died early on the morning of 1 January 1515¹⁰⁰ – worn out, it was said, by his young wife, Mary Tudor.¹⁰¹ He was succeeded by his cousin, Francis of Angoulême. Young and dashing, the new king immediately announced his intention of mounting an expedition to Italy and opened negotiations with potential allies – including Venice.¹⁰² This was a welcome prospect, to say the least. But the Venetians were cautious by nature, even in their despair. They would not conclude a new agreement quickly; and until they did, they would have to continue their struggle alone.

Tired of a fruitless war, and worn down by shortages and overcrowding, the Venetians began to grow restless. They were tormented by the thought that Heaven had turned against them. When Lent came around, processions were held every other day in the hope of assuaging God's wrath. Yet if the Venetians wanted forgiveness for their sins, they were even keener to attribute blame. Inevitably, fingers were pointed at the city's Jews. Despite all evidence to the contrary, they were first accused of not paying their fair share towards the war effort. On 23 March, Antonio Tron put forward a proposal to force Jewish *strazzaruoli* (second-hand dealers) to pay the *decima*, as in the past. Thanks to the intervention of Anselmo del Banco – who, according to Sanudo, had 'great power' – the Council of Ten voted this down, perhaps fearing that it risked driving *strazzaruoli* out of business just when the city needed to keep the supply of credit flowing.[103]

Rather than tempering criticism, this only inflamed the Jews' opponents further. On Good Friday, a Franciscan preacher at the Frari, outraged by their supposed wealth, demanded that their property be 'confiscated and used for the defence of the State'.[104] The same day, Sanudo complained that, contrary to their usual practice of remaining hidden from view during Holy Week, Jews were to be seen 'everywhere' in the city. Unable to conceal his disgust, he condemned this as a 'dreadful occurrence' – and insinuated that, if there were any justice in the world, such exposure would have been severely punished.[105]

Yet, after many years of war, even the Jews' fiercest critics had come to recognize that they were necessary – even essential. Although Sanudo, for example, grumbled about the 'great number' of Jews living in the city, he grudgingly noted that it was impossible to say anything 'because, on account of the war, they are needed'.[106] The Venetian economy simply could not do without them.

A new solution to Venice's 'Jewish problem' now presented itself. If Jews could neither be expelled nor be allowed to go on living freely, the only other option was to confine them. On 23 April, Giorgio Emo, a leading member of the Collegio, proposed that Jews then living in Venice should be removed to the island of Giudecca.[107] This was not a new idea, of course. Back in the fourteenth century, the Senate had made plans for a separate Jewish quarter and had even begun scouting for a suitable location.[108] But this was the first time anyone had mentioned it since then – let alone in relation to Giudecca. As Emo saw it, the advantages were clear. On Giudecca, Jews would be close enough to the Rialto to engage in trade, but too far away to lead Christians into error – or to cause offence with their 'arrogance'.

Understandably, the Jews were appalled. Rushing off to see the Collegio straight away, Anselmo del Banco and his brother Vivian pointed out that, if the Jewish community was moved to Giudecca, it would almost certainly be attacked by the mercenaries billeted there.[109] The effect this might have on moneylending hardly needed saying. If Jews were to be moved anywhere, Anselmo and Vivian suggested, they should be sent to Murano, about a kilometre north of the city. It was a clever ruse. Although it *seemed* like a reasonable suggestion, not too dissimilar to Emo's original proposal, it was plainly unacceptable. Murano, as everyone knew, enjoyed a high degree of autonomy.[110] It had its own council, it lived according to its own laws, and it even minted its own coins. If the Jews were moved there, they would be safe from attack and would still be able to access the Venetian market. Indeed, given that many wealthy patricians had villas on Murano, Jewish moneylenders could even afford to let clients come to them. But they would nevertheless be living in a separate jurisdiction – with potentially far-reaching implications for both future *condotte* and, more importantly, taxes. The Collegio took the hint. After much discussion, it decided to let Emo's proposal drop.

No one seems to have objected to the idea of confinement in itself, however. It was, in many ways, the solution they had all been looking for. Both moderates and hardliners could agree that it offered a neat way of balancing Venice's financial needs with fears of 'contamination' – in the short term, at least. All that was needed was to find a more suitable location. In a city as crowded as Venice, this would be no easy matter. To set aside a quarter big enough to house the entire Jewish population would take more political determination than the government was then willing to muster. But it would not take much for that to change.

*

The ground was already beginning to shift. While Franciscan preachers were venting their spleens against Venice's Jews, a new agreement was finally concluded with Francis I. Venice would help Francis recapture the duchy of Milan; and, in return, Francis promised to help

Venice recover all the lands then occupied by Maximilian. Within weeks, preparations were already in full swing.[111] Intending to lead the campaign himself, Francis assembled an army 100,000 strong. This startled the Holy League out of its torpor. To defend Massimiliano Sforza's domains, four armies were hastily put into the field. Together, they were a formidable enemy – and, had they fought in concert, they may well have prevailed. Yet each had its own priorities. The pope, wary as ever, was interested only in protecting Piacenza and Parma, while Cardona focused on holding Verona, and the emperor dawdled in Friuli. This left the Swiss and the Milanese to guard the Alpine passes into Lombardy alone. Obliged to spread themselves out across many valleys, their handicap was easily exploited. While some of the French army came by the Susa pass, the greater part went by less familiar routes – catching the Milanese unawares. At Villafranca, their commander was taken prisoner and their cavalry captured. The Swiss pulled back from the passes, hoping to regroup; but the French, having now seized the advantage, pressed on, heedless. Novara was taken; and after an attempt at negotiation failed, Francis swung south to prevent any Spanish or papal reinforcements from coming to Milan's aid. He pitched camp at Marignano, some 16 kilometres south of the city, and asked the Venetians to join him. Before they could arrive, however, the Swiss took him by surprise. Though barefoot, dressed in rags, and short of both cavalry and artillery, they were fearsome warriors – and Francis' troops soon found themselves giving ground. All day and into the night the battle raged, only halting when it became too dark to see. When the fighting resumed the following morning, the Swiss seemed to have victory within their grasp. But just as the French were losing hope, Bartolomeo d'Alviano appeared at the head of the Venetian army. Riding headlong into the fray, he overwhelmed the Swiss wing – and carried the day.

As the French commander Giangiacomo Trivulzio later observed, it had been an encounter 'not of men, but of giants'.[112] No one could say exactly how many had been killed. 'Some put the number of Swiss dead at fourteen thousand, others spoke of ten, the most moderate of eight ... [O]f the French dead ... estimates likewise varied.'[113] But of the battle's import, there could be no doubt. Nothing now stood between Francis and Milan. Realizing that all was lost, Massimiliano Sforza quickly relented; Pope Leo X asked for terms; and the whole of Lombardy lay at France's feet. Venice erupted with joy. Convinced that victory had come from God, the Senate 'voted to distribute grain to the poor in thanksgiving', and Doge Leonardo Loredan ordered bells to be rung throughout the Veneto for three days.[114] No doubt the city's Jews breathed a sigh of relief, too.

Yet no sooner had the celebrations ended than the Venetians' delight turned to a gnawing anxiety. Through their ambassador at Rome, they learned that Francis had 'made no mention' of Venice in the draft agreement he had presented to the pope.[115] What this might mean was unclear; but it was hard to avoid the suspicion that Francis, having now achieved his goal, might be preparing to renege on his promises to the Venetians. His conduct over the following months did little to reassure them. Although the king had previously agreed to help them recapture Brescia and Verona, he was slow to send troops – and did nothing to overcome the tensions between French and Venetian commanders.[116] By the beginning of winter, the two cities were further from being retaken than ever. Yet Francis only seemed to grow more indifferent. When, in December, he met the pope in Bologna, he once again failed to address Venice's interests – much to its ambassador's distress.[117]

Glumly, the Venetians realized that their hope in Francis had been misplaced. Now that his relations with the pope had been put on a stable footing, and Milan's southern border was secured, he saw no reason to remain in the duchy any longer. Resolved to reconquer the kingdom of Naples, he set off for France to begin preparations, leaving Charles de Bourbon to govern Lombardy on his behalf.[118] Though some troops were left to help the Venetians, they were barely more than a token force – and fell far short of what was needed. Venice's position quickly began to weaken. Already, in early January 1516, the siege of Brescia was in jeopardy. As Sanudo reported, 'there was a great shortage of everything'.[119] In Verona, things were no better.

In this, the emperor Maximilian spied the opportunity he had been waiting for. Taking advantage of Francis' absence and the Venetians' disarray, he now set out to seize the duchy of Milan for himself. In early March 1516, he led his army south from Trent. Skirting the banks of Lake Garda, he passed Verona, and, after pausing briefly to lay siege to the fortress of Asola, pressed on towards his goal, meeting little resistance as he went.[120] The Venetians were shocked.

Regardless of whether or not Maximilian succeeded in taking Milan, his invasion posed a clear threat to the Republic's possessions on the *terraferma*.[121] He had to be stopped – and quickly. But how? Since the death of Bartolomeo d'Alviano, in October 1515, Venice had struggled to find a general it could rely on; its forces were gravely depleted; and its treasury was empty.[122] Worst of all, the French seemed unwilling to put up a fight. Now that Francis' attentions had shifted to Naples, neither he nor Bourbon could see any point in wasting resources on a potentially fruitless defence. On 13 March, Sanudo reported that the whole of Venice was in despair because of the 'dreadful news' that the French were going to retreat, rather than give battle.[123]

As Lent wore on, a sense of foreboding began to take hold. News of Maximilian's progress was scarce; but the refugees who came pouring in from the *terraferma* only added fuel to popular anxiety. Having fled from cities which had already suffered much in recent years, they made no secret of their dissatisfaction with the government – sparking fears of civil unrest in the event of an imperial victory. On 24 March, the Council of Ten was so jittery that it ordered its captains to confiscate weapons from any foreigners they found milling around the Piazza San Marco.[124]

When information finally began to trickle in, the following day, it did nothing to allay public fears. It was reported that, two days earlier, Maximilian was encamped near Caravaggio, less than 10 kilometres from the French army – and within striking distance of Milan itself.[125] No one knew what the French would do next, or even if they had already fled across the Adda; but the mere proximity of the two forces was enough to set the Great Council's nerves on edge.

While patricians fretted over Maximilian's advance, mendicant preachers throughout the city delivered the usual Easter sermons – no doubt peppered with diatribes against the Jews. In the Campo San Polo, where many Jews lived, Fra Rufino Lovato spoke before an 'enormous crowd', after which a masquerade was put on, featuring a bishop baptizing a Jew and his sons.[126] Compared to the fire and brimstone of previous years, this was fairly tame stuff, of course. Though there was some grumbling about the 'dangers' of having Jews in the city, there were no complaints about Jewish 'arrogance', no demands for the confiscation of property – in fact, no demands of any kind. But it was enough to breathe new life into calls for the Jews' segregation.

On 26 March, Zaccaria Dolfin, a respected member of the Collegio, put forward a proposal similar to that which Giorgio Emo had tabled the year before.[127] Like the mendicants, he began by pointing out that the Jews' presence in the city was the source of all Venice's afflictions. Since they could neither be expelled nor be confined to an outlying area, like Giudecca or Murano, he therefore suggested that they should be sent to live on an island in Cannaregio known as the *geto nuovo*.[128]

It had never been an appealing place.[129] In the fourteenth century, it had been nothing more than a marshy patch of land, rented by local fishermen. Just across the canal, however, was the communal copper foundry (*geto del rame*). Working around the clock to produce bronze for Venice's cannons, the foundry was insufferably noisy and dirty. For security reasons, it was carefully walled off from the surrounding area. The only point of access was a gate on the *fondamenta* of Cannaregio. But in time, the island was linked to the foundry by a wooden bridge, so that it could be used as a dump. For this reason, it soon came to be known as the 'terrain of the ghetto' (*terren del geto*).

At the beginning of the fifteenth century, an attempt was made to vary the island's use slightly. The ground was strengthened; a wooden hut was built for one of the master cannon-founders; and at least some pieces of artillery may have been cast there. But by then, the foundry was getting short of space. Unable to keep up with Venice's growing appetite for guns, it was transferred to the Arsenale; and in 1434, both the *geto* and the *terreno* were sold off. The new owner, Marco Ruzini, immediately began redeveloping. The old foundry was demolished, and a whole street of new buildings went up. The island, by contrast, remained as it was. Since the foundry's relocation, it had become a grassy meadow, where young nobles practised their archery and boys set traps for birds. To earn at least some money from it, Ruzini rented it out to textile workers, who laid out their clothes to dry in the sun. This was not uncommon in that part of Venice, but nor was it the best commercial use of the land. In 1455, the island was purchased by two brothers, Costantino and Bartolomeo da Brolo, who were eager to exploit its potential. Twenty-five houses were built around the edge, leaving a large square in the middle. Three wells were then dug, each emblazoned with the family crest; a second bridge was added, linking the island with the Fondamenta dei Ormesini to the north; and there may have been plans to construct a church as well. By the time everything was finished, the island stopped being called the *terren del geto* – and became known as the Ghetto Nuovo instead.[130]

By 1516, it had become a typical working-class area. The houses were cramped and shoddily built; and the da Brolo had made few concessions to their tenants' comfort. For Dolfin, it could hardly have been better. There was everything he needed to keep the Jews segregated. Surrounded by canals, and girded by high buildings, it was already 'like a castle' (*castello*) – but, as he pointed out, it could easily be 'closed off' from the rest of the city even further 'with a wall and drawbridges'.

The Collegio were taken with the idea. After talking it over with the Ghetto's current owners, they summoned Anselmo del Banco and 'two other Jewish leaders' to inform them of Dolfin's plan.[131] Anselmo was every bit as outraged as before – if not more so. What Dolfin was proposing was unjust, he claimed. The safety and prosperity of Jews depended on them being among Christians. If they were forced to move to the Ghetto, he argued, their houses would be robbed, and their businesses would be ruined. It was also bad for Venice. Adopting a more threatening tone, Anselmo pointed out that, since 'poor Jews' would not want to live under such disadvantageous conditions, they would leave the city – meaning that he would have no one left to tax, and no means of meeting his obligations to the Venetian state. It would be far better, Anselmo concluded, to let the Jews stay where they were for the moment and then return home once Venice's territories on the mainland were reconquered.

As soon as Anselmo left the palace, Dolfin jumped to his feet again, demanding that his proposal be put before the Senate. Enough members of the Collegio were on his side for this request to pass, but the Senate's support was far from guaranteed. Now that Dolfin's proposal had been tabled, Anselmo and his brother would be lobbying furiously, just as they had the year before – and Maximilian's campaign was not yet so terrifying that the more moderate senators could be counted upon.

All eyes now turned to Lombardy. Almost immediately, the news began to darken. Shortly after the Collegio's meeting broke up, a courier brought word that thousands had died in battle and that Milan was 'in disarray' (*sotosopra*).[132] Since this was just a rumour, little faith was put in it. The next day, however, it was reported that

Bergamo had 'gone over to the enemy'.[133] On 28 March, the Venetians were informed that the French had retreated and that the emperor was in hot pursuit. Even if the Swiss had not entered Milan, as some sources claimed, it would surely not be long before the city fell.[134]

Any doubts that senators may have had quickly dissipated. On the afternoon of 29 March, Dolfin's proposal was passed by a large majority.[135] '[I]n order to avoid many disorderly and unsuitable situations', all Jews then living in Venice, as well as any who arrived later, were to go immediately to the 'group of houses . . . in the Ghetto, near the church of San Girolamo'.[136] Since they were forbidden to own property in Venice, they would be obliged to rent accommodation from Christian owners for one-third more than the going rate. Access would be strictly limited.[137] Two high walls would be built to close off the sides looking out onto canals; quays and canal doors would be sealed; and stout gates would be placed at either end of the bridge leading to Cannaregio.[138] These would be opened in the morning, at the ringing of the *marangona* bell, and closed in the evening at sunset by four Christian guards. These guards would be paid by the Jews themselves and be required to live alone in the Ghetto to avoid any distractions. They would be provided with two boats – again paid for by the Jews – with which to patrol the canals around the Ghetto 'day and night'. There would be no synagogue; and anyone found in the city outside the permitted hours would be heavily fined.

Anselmo and the other Jewish leaders were probably hoping this would soon be quietly forgotten, like so many other decrees before. After all, it wasn't so long ago that the Senate had ordered the whole Jewish population to leave the city. And what had come of that? This time, however, the Senate was serious. On 1 April, city criers read the decree in public, and ordered all Jews to move to the Ghetto within ten days.[139] Some banks and second-hand dealers dragged their heels, and the banks even persuaded the Collegio to grant them a further extension.[140] But eventually, even they had to bow to the inevitable. By 25 July, everyone – even the great Anselmo del Banco – was there.[141]

The Ghetto Nuovo had been born.

4

'Under the Protection of the Lord'

(1516–1541)

The Ghetto's existence was nevertheless precarious. As the Senate's decree made clear, it was only ever intended to be a temporary expedient, and plenty of Venetians were anxious to be rid of it. When Maximilian's campaign collapsed, just weeks after it had begun, their impatience only grew.[1] Now that the worst of the fighting was over, and Venice had recovered most of the lands it had lost on the *terraferma*, the justification for the Ghetto's existence seemed to be seeping away. Granted, a formal peace had yet to be concluded. Venice's finances were still a mess, and it would take time for the Veneto to be completely pacified. But the expectation that, sooner or later, the city's Jews should be made to leave was getting hard to ignore.

For the moment, there was little the Venetian government could do. Although the Ghetto had been established by a Senate decree, the *condotta* of 1513 had guaranteed certain Jewish bankers a right of residence in time of war. As long as the *condotta* remained in force and hostilities continued, even on paper, the government could not legitimately deprive Jews of their homes in the Ghetto. The most it could do was make life unpleasant for them in the hope that some would leave of their own volition.[2] With a few minor exceptions, all requests for the easing of restrictions were refused – and a host of fresh impositions introduced.[3] Amidst a storm of protests about 'dishonest' Jewish moneylenders, harsh new financial demands were made.[4] Clothing rules were tightened, too: doctors were banned from wearing the wide-sleeved 'ducal' robes that were the mark of their profession, and all Jews were required to wear the yellow hat – a visible mark of their exclusion from Christian society.[5]

When, in July 1518, the *condotta* expired and Venice signed a truce with Maximilian, the Jews' opponents jumped at the chance to take more decisive action. Encouraged by the fiery sermons of Fra Giovanni dell'Angiolina, a small group of patricians began agitating for the *condotta* not to be renewed – and for the cancellation of any other agreements which might have allowed Jews to remain in the city.[6]

They were, from the outset, an uncoordinated bunch. Though most had served in the Collegio – the nearest thing Venice had to a cabinet – they had little in common beyond their dislike of Jews. They had neither a leader nor a common strategy. But what they lacked in organization, they more than made up for in vehemence. As so often in the past, their arguments centred on moneylending and providence. However much Venice might have needed credit, Gabriele Moro noted, usury was a sin – pure and simple. It didn't make the slightest difference that Cardinal Bessarion had sanctioned it fifty-odd years ago.[7] Not even the pope 'had the power to grant [Jews] permission to lend' at interest.[8] On this, God's law was clear, and anyone who broke it was invariably punished. King Alfonso of Naples had 'lost his kingdom' after giving refuge to Spanish exiles, and the duke of Milan had been 'driven from power because he favoured and protected the Jews'.[9] If Venice renewed the *condotta*, Moro warned, it would surely suffer the same fate. If Venice *expelled* the Jews, by contrast, it would doubtless be showered with good fortune. 'God will make this Republic flourish', Piero da Ca' da Pesaro promised, 'just as He did for the king of Portugal, who having driven them out, discovered and sailed around India' – growing fabulously rich in the process.[10]

This was hardly sophisticated stuff, and many patricians remained unconvinced. But it struck a chord, nonetheless. On 11 July, while debates about the *condotta* were still ongoing, the Heads of the Ten voted to close all Jewish *strazzaria* shops, on the grounds that they were taking business away from their Christian competitors.[11] This was a heavy blow. Although the name *strazzaria* literally means 'rag trade', the trade in second-hand goods was anything but downmarket. Even before the Ghetto had been established, it had grown to encompass everything from furniture and linen to jewellery, tapestries, and medallions – and was so profitable that it may already have rivalled banking.[12] Without it, the Jewish community would struggle to make ends meet.

Understandably, the decision provoked an angry response. That same morning, Anselmo del Banco and Abramo, the son of Fricele – the owners of the two largest Jewish banks – announced that they would close all their branches within six months.[13] They probably never intended to follow through with this, of course. More likely, it was just a threat. Although Anselmo and Abramo may have heard about Moro's attack on usury, they knew that Venice was still reliant on Jewish loans. Given how fragile the Venetian economy was just then, they were gambling that the prospect of another credit crunch would frighten the government into revoking the Ten's decree – and perhaps even persuade it to renew the *condotta*.

It seemed like a safe enough bet at first. When the issue of the *condotta* was next debated, on 10 November 1519, many patricians argued that Jewish banks were too important for Venice to risk losing.[14] Though not a member of the Senate, Marin Sanudo noted that Jewish moneylenders were as vital to a city as bakers. While it was all very well to have misgivings, he argued, it would be madness to let them leave when there was no one to take their place. The following spring, a proposal was therefore tabled to renew the *condotta*, on deliberately attractive terms.[15] Had it passed, Jews would not only have been able to go on lending money, but also have been allowed to deal in *strazzaria* again, exactly as Anselmo and Abramo had hoped.

But the two bankers had underestimated their enemies' resolve. While it was true that Venice currently had no alternative to Jewish moneylenders, the establishment of a *monte di pietà* offered a ready solution. In principle, nothing could have been easier – and in Antonio Tron, it found its most effective advocate. An old and well-respected figure, he realized that to overcome his colleagues' scepticism, he needed to show that a *monte* could replace Jewish banks without costing too much money or causing too much disruption.[16] On 10 February 1520, Tron outlined his plan.[17] To keep credit flowing, he proposed that the *condotta* be extended for a further year. Meanwhile, indirect taxes on wine and cornmeal would be diverted to floating the *monte*. Once its coffers were full, Tron explained, Venice would have no more need of Jewish bankers and could expel them whenever it liked.

As yet, Tron did not have a majority, but he was tantalizingly close – and was gathering momentum by the day.[18] A few weeks later, the heads of the powerful Quarantia al Criminal threw their weight behind him. By early March, he could have been forgiven for thinking that a *monte* was now within reach. All that remained was to decide how much Jewish bankers should pay for an extra year's grace, and what other terms should be revised.

For a time, the Jews' future hung in the balance. However painful the loss of *strazzaria* must have been, the thought of losing their homes must have been even harder to bear. For all the indignities they had suffered, all the discomfort endured, the Ghetto was still their refuge. There, at least, they had been safe. By contrast, the mainland, still scarred by war and already studded with *monti*, presented a forbidding aspect. Even if they were spared the violent antipathy of locals, the prospects for business were far from encouraging. As the days ground on, a dark, ominous future seemed to loom before them.

Tron's plan was still too radical for many patricians' tastes. When the 'Jewish question' was next debated, it came in for some heavy criticism. Some simply mistrusted *monti di pietà*. As Andrea Trevisan argued, they were an invitation to fraud. No matter how carefully the statutes were designed, the funds would inevitably be misappropriated, either by dishonest administrators or by unsuitable borrowers. Instead of helping the needy, he explained, a *monte* would merely facilitate 'corrupt intrigues and . . . evil-doers'.[19] Others thought the timing was wrong. War was once again on the horizon. Shortly after the *condotta* had expired, the emperor Maximilian had died and had been succeeded by his nineteen-year-old grandson, Charles V.[20] Having inherited not only the Spanish kingdoms and the Habsburg territories in Austria and the Low Countries, but also the Valois duchy of Burgundy and the kingdoms of Naples and Sicily, Charles was in a position to intervene more forcefully in Italian affairs than any emperor since Frederick II – and had already begun preparing for an expedition against Milan. What was worse, the Ottoman sultan, Selim the Grim, was also rumoured to be planning a campaign in the western Mediterranean.[21] Where he might strike no one knew, but Croatia seemed the most likely target – close enough to Venice's own possessions to be a source of serious alarm. Now was clearly not the time to take risks. Venice needed every penny it had to fit out new warships and ready its defences. It simply could not afford to divert taxes away from the Arsenale – much less trust the credit market to a new and potentially corrupt institution.

In the face of such sustained opposition, Tron's support collapsed.

On 3 March, his proposal received just eleven votes – even less than a hare-brained scheme to ban usury altogether, while allowing the Jews to live in the Ghetto anyway.[22] For the moment, at least, the *monte* was a dead letter. This left the Senate with a stark choice: it would have to either let the Jews remain in Venice or expel them *tout court* – in the knowledge that there would be nothing to take their place. For most, it was hardly a choice at all.[23]

*

On 16 March 1520, the Senate finally agreed to renew the *condotta* for another five years.[24] As Anselmo and Abramo hoped, Jews would be allowed to remain in the Ghetto. The ban on *strazzaria* was reversed and, although no new banks could be founded, all those which were currently operating could continue much as they had before the crisis of 1509. Interest rates were capped at the relatively generous rate of 15 per cent, and the familiar rules about the sale of pledges still applied.

At the same time, an effort was made to make the mainland less forbidding – and to facilitate the recovery of larger firms which had lost money because of branch closures in subject cities. Unlike in Venice itself, banks on the *terraferma* would be allowed to charge interest at up to 15 per cent on pledges and 20 per cent on notes. Given the state of the international situation, the Senate also promised that, in the event of war, Jewish bankers on the mainland would be able to bring their pledges to Venice for safekeeping – just as it had done in 1503.

But this all came at a cost. In return, the Jews would be obliged to pay an annual tax of 10,000 ducats. As the *condotta* explained, almost half of this would be earmarked for the Arsenale and the fleet. In addition, the community was required to hand over 4,000 ducats in advance to help cover the most pressing naval expenses. This would, of course, be deducted from future tax payments; but as the Senate carefully reserved the right to demand further such contributions down the line, there was no guarantee that the final bill might not be significantly higher – especially in the event of war.

This was a steep increase on what had previously been demanded – too steep, in fact, for many Jews to bear. On 20 March, Anselmo del Banco protested that, after the privations of recent years, the community would almost certainly not be able to pay.[25] He begged the government to be more reasonable. They were *willing*, after all. When the will and the means are at odds, he reminded the Collegio, it is the will that counts in the end. His words fell on deaf ears. The Senate's decision was final – and the Collegio saw no reason to negotiate. The Jews would have to take it or leave it, the vice-doge shrugged.

They didn't exactly have a choice. Having already threatened to close their banks once, they could hardly do so again, and they had nothing else to bargain with. On 2 May, after more than five weeks' hesitation, they reluctantly accepted the Senate's terms.[26] It was far from ideal, but the Ghetto's future was assured – at least for a while.

*

Almost immediately, Jewish life began to recover some of its former vitality. On the *terraferma*, Jewish banks were quickly reopened. By the spring of 1520, branches were already active in Montagnana, Portobuffolè, Portogruaro, Conegliano, Verona, and Crema, while Anselmo's brother, Vivian, was lending in Padua again.[27] In Venice itself, a period of comparative calm ensued. Although there was some quibbling over the payment of the money which had been earmarked for the Arsenale in September 1521, relations between the Venetian government and the Jewish community seem to have reached an equilibrium of sorts.[28] The intermittent bouts of violent hostility that had so marred previous years abated. Apart from some brief protests over the baptism of a fifteen-year-old boy, which many Jews feared had been procured by force, there were few – if any – altercations;[29] and in foreign correspondence, it became a matter worthy of remark when a monarch regarded Jews with anything other than tolerant indifference.[30]

When the *condotta* was next discussed three and a half years later, its renewal aroused little debate. More so even than before, the threats facing Venice were severe. Although the Ottoman sultan Selim the Grim had died before he could launch his planned campaign, his successor, Suleiman 'the Magnificent' was proving no less resolute in his pursuit of imperial expansion.[31] In 1521, his armies had captured Belgrade, and the following year, the island of Rhodes was taken, too. In itself, Rhodes was of little consequence, either militarily or politically, but its position, halfway between Crete and Cyprus, caused Venice to fear for her possessions in the eastern Mediterranean.[32] And that was not all: in autumn 1521, Emperor Charles V had finally launched his long-expected attack on Lombardy.[33] Meeting little opposition, his forces had quickly driven the French from Milan. A few weeks later, news arrived that Pope Leo X had died and that the emperor's former tutor had been elected to succeed him. The Venetians were forced to accept Charles' proposal of an anti-French alliance with unseemly, but understandable, haste – in the full awareness that, if Francis I tried to reclaim his lost duchy (as seemed likely), they might soon be called upon to fight.[34] With a fleet to keep in trim and a land army to supply, Venice's need for Jewish bankers was acute. Only they could supply the taxes, loans, and credit upon which her fortunes in the field would depend. When the Senate voted, on 2 September 1523, scarcely a voice was raised in opposition, and the bill to extend the *condotta* by a further four years was passed by a huge majority.[35]

The following month, the government granted the Jewish community even more concessions. Although a request for a halt to the boat guarding the Ghetto at night was denied – presumably because of lingering fears of social 'contamination' – Jewish bankers were given permission to set up banks in parts of the *terraferma* where they did not currently operate, greatly expanding their markets and potential profits.[36]

This did not mean that the Jews' enemies had given up.[37] Even before the *condotta* was renewed, a fresh attempt was made to secure the establishment of a *monte di pietà*. This time, the impetus did not come from Antonio Tron, nor was it inspired by Franciscan preaching. Instead, it issued from a third group, associated with a recently founded Venetian charity known as the Ospedale degli Incurabili (Hospital of Incurables). This owed its origins, at least in part, to the Compagnia del Divino Amore (Company of Divine Love), a Genoese confraternity known for combining an ascetic piety with unstinting work on behalf of the disadvantaged.[38] This took various forms; but having already provided for public health, the governors of the Ospedale felt it was time to turn their attention to the care of Venice's poor. Their approach – and motivation – was markedly different from Tron's. During the Senate debates, they avoided attacking the Jews openly and made no calls for expulsion. Nor did they try to present the *monte* as a substitute for Jewish banking. As many cities on the mainland had already found, *monti di pietà* could exist *alongside* Jewish banks – one offering small loans to the 'working' poor at low or no interest, and the other serving anyone else who happened to need credit on a commercial basis. Notably, since the proposed *monte* was intended to supplement rather than replace Jewish lenders, its capital requirements would be somewhat lower than Tron had envisaged, holding out the possibility that the necessary funds could be raised from private individuals, rather than tax revenues.

This was almost perfectly tailored to appeal to the principles and prejudices of the Venetian patriarchate. Moderate in vision and parsimonious in design, it assuaged the concerns of those who had opposed Tron's proposal three years earlier. If it did all that was promised, it would place no burden on the public purse; it would leave the Arsenale undisturbed; and the credit market would be enlivened, rather than interrupted. At the same time, it was potent enough to satisfy the anti-Jewish lobby. Some may have hoped that once it was operational, its functions could be expanded to the point where Jews would eventually be crowded out of the market. Either way, it was a promising beginning.

On 27 March 1523, the Senate voted overwhelmingly in favour of a *monte di pietà*,[39] and the following year, the governors of the Ospedale presented their draft statutes to the Collegio. These were familiar enough fare. But great ingenuity had gone into assuring the *monte*'s financial independence. Rather than relying on donations – which was perhaps the most obvious course – it was proposed that the necessary funds be raised from private loans and deposits, which could be repaid on request. To allay any concerns investors may have had, the governors would personally guarantee sums up to 1,000 ducats and promised to keep 25 per cent of the *monte*'s funds on hand, in cash, at all times. Most likely, no interest was to be offered; but as a haven – for both savings and the soul – the *monte* was almost ideal. And since the scheme cost no one a penny in the long term, least of all the Venetian state, no one could really object. A pall fell over the Ghetto.

This was when the Council of Ten stepped in. Wielding the full force of its authority, it reversed the Senate's decision and cancelled the entire project. Those who had proposed the statutes were hauled before the Heads of the Ten and told – 'with stern, severe, and well-chosen words' – to let the matter of the *monte di pietà* drop. Henceforth, no one was 'to propose' or even 'speak of . . . a *monte di pietà*' again without the Council's unanimous consent.[40] Any copies of the statutes were to be handed over and sealed in the Council's archives, and those patricians involved were never to reveal that they had been summoned, let alone reprimanded. It was to be as if the whole thing had been just a bad dream.

Why the Council of Ten did this is something of a mystery. Perhaps the Council's members feared that, in time, the *monte* might become a financial behemoth, independent of government control yet exercising an authority over the poor to rival that of the state itself. Or maybe they worried that the *monte* might have functioned as some sort of tax evasion scheme. Although it was not unknown for civic bodies to raid the funds of local *monti* in times of crisis, it had often proved extremely difficult. If Venice's position worsened, it was possible that the rich would invest money in the *monte* simply to 'hide' it from the government's prying eyes. Each of these possibilities may have carried some weight, but uppermost in the Council's minds was probably the same fear of corruption that had scuppered Tron's scheme a few years before.

Whatever the reason, the Council's decision doomed the *monte* for ever. Though the Council could have granted the governors of the Ospedale permission to revive the project in future, the severity of its threats, coupled with the traditional conservatism of its members' outlook, made that unlikely. For the moment, the dominance of Jewish lending seemed assured.

*

This did not mean that tensions had lessened. While the *monte* was being debated, an ugly dispute had been brewing in another corner of the Venetian government, which revealed the persistence of anti-Jewish feeling. In July 1523, the Polish ambassador had accused Jacob Meshullam – the son of Anselmo del Banco – of cheating a Polish Jew out of a diamond which belonged to the *voivode* (governor) of Cracow.[41] Jacob naturally protested his innocence: although he *did* have such a diamond in his possession, he claimed that he had purchased it legitimately and had witnesses who could back him up.[42] It was a plausible enough story. In recent years, Poles had often bought and sold jewels in Venice through Jewish dealers.[43] It was quite possible that the voivode, or his agent, had simply got a bad deal and that the ambassador was misrepresenting the transaction on the king of Poland's orders.[44] The Venetian authorities were nevertheless chary of giving him too much credence. For one thing, Jacob had form: a few years before, he had got into trouble over a sapphire he claimed to have won from Piero di Andrea Bragadin in a game of cards and had only managed to extricate himself after bribing another patrician to lie under oath.[45] For another, the king of Poland was not a person Venice could afford to brush off lightly. Since Suleiman the Magnificent's attack on Belgrade, he had become a natural – even necessary – ally in Venice's struggle against the Ottoman Empire; and when his wife inherited the port of Bari, in February 1524, her favour also became a factor in the Republic's commercial future.[46]

Over the following months, the case was passed from council to council, drawing ever more exalted patricians into the fray. Hearings were postponed and, as time wore on, tempers began to grow short.[47] Some still had doubts about whether the diamond had *really* been swiped, but more than enough were convinced of Jacob's guilt to convict him. Most of the Quarantia's members probably felt that proof was of less moment than political expediency – and that the fate of a miscreant Jew was a small enough price to purchase a king's goodwill. That Jacob was Anselmo del Banco's son no doubt made the decision easier. For some, it may even have been the inspiration. After recent disappointments, the temptation to visit on the son the 'sins' of the father may simply have been too great to resist.

After some debate, Jacob was sentenced to return the diamond, pay a hefty fine, and have both his eyes put out.[48] This may have been intended merely as 'blackmail', since Jacob was later allowed to pay a further 2,000 ducats – most likely for the upkeep of the Arsenale – in return for his sight.[49] But even as a threat, it was a potent reminder that, though the battle over the *monte* may have been won, the Jews' enemies were still spoiling for a fight. All they needed was an excuse.

*

In the event, it was Charles V who provided it. For the past two years, Venice had stood by the emperor out of necessity, rather than conviction. When Francis I launched his long-expected campaign to retake Milan, therefore, it was slow to answer Charles' call – and even slower to risk troops in his defence. The moment Francis seemed to gain the upper hand, Venice stopped fighting altogether.[50] Without explicitly renouncing its alliance with Charles, it signed a non-aggression pact with Francis – and resolved to sit out the rest of the conflict in peace, confident of a French victory. It was a grave miscalculation. At the Battle of Pavia, on 24 February 1525, the French army was annihilated and the king himself taken prisoner.[51]

Venice was now in serious danger. Even though Charles claimed to see no benefit in punishing the Republic for its perfidy, his mastery of northern Italy posed an undeniable threat to its possessions on the *terraferma*.[52] Sooner or later, it would have to fight him. If it was to stand any chance, however, it would need allies. Over the summer, talks were opened with the new pope, Clement VII, about forming a new anti-imperial league. Approaches were even made to the Ottoman Empire.[53]

When Francis I was eventually released, the following year, Venice's diplomatic efforts bore fruit. Repudiating the promises Charles had extracted as the price of his liberty, the king immediately joined Venice and the pope in their league.[54] Known as the League of Cognac, its goal was to force the emperor from northern Italy – either through negotiations or, if necessary, by force of arms.

War was now inevitable. More so than for many years, Venice needed ships, soldiers, and supplies. Most of all, it needed money. As ever, the Jews were among the first to be tapped. On 10 March 1526 – while negotiations were still ongoing – the Savii del Consiglio (who oversaw the execution of the government's resolutions) ordered the Jewish community to pay a special tax of 10,000 ducats.[55] They were well within their rights: the *condotta* had provided for circumstances just such as this. But for Venice's Jews, it was too much. A week later, Anselmo del Banco went to lodge a complaint.[56] He announced that, in light of the Savii's demand, Jewish bankers had no choice but to shut up shop. For the next year, until the *condotta* expired, no more money would be lent. This was exactly the same tactic he had used back in 1518, when the Heads of the Ten had closed the *strazzaria*. And given that the *monte* was now a dead letter, he probably felt confident it would force the government into backing down.

Anselmo's timing could hardly have been worse. Just three months after his protest, the League launched its campaign.[57] At first, everything went smoothly. Taking advantage of disagreements in the imperial camp, the League swept into Lombardy. But just as the League was gaining in confidence, Charles suddenly turned the tables. By tricking the pope into making a premature attack on Naples, he forced Clement to accept a truce. Thus robbed of the pope's support, the League faltered. While its members debated what to do, Charles' army was reinforced by a large contingent of German landsknechts (mercenaries), and by late February 1527, he was ready to mount a new offensive. Where he would target, no one could say; but wherever it was, Venice would surely stand to lose.

In this atmosphere of growing alarm, Anselmo's gambit backfired. The Jews' enemies were roused to fury; and even more moderate patricians appear to have taken umbrage. In mid-March, Gabriele Moro – who had led calls for expulsion back in 1519 – persuaded the Senate to pass a decree ordering the Jews back to Mestre.[58] Once their grace period expired, they would be forbidden to lend money in Venice itself and would only be allowed to spend a maximum of fifteen days in the city each year. To prevent any accidental 'contamination', Jews would also be required to wear a yellow *baretta* at all times.[59] An act of pure spite, this 'seemed designed to get the worst of every world'.[60] Although it stopped short of *banning* Jews from lending, it made it more difficult for borrowers to secure a loan and did nothing to improve credit for the poor. Financially speaking, it would leave everyone – Christian and Jew – worse off. But that was beside the point. For Moro, the only thing that mattered was that Venice would finally be rid of the Jews – and the Ghetto would be no more.

*

Though Charles V had created this crisis, he would also inadvertently help to diffuse it. By the time Moro's bill was passed, the imperial army had been beset by troubles. Angry at the lack of food and pay, the German landsknechts had mutinied and set their minds to plunder.[61] Leaving Lombardy, they turned south and pushed into Tuscany.[62] Behaving more like rapacious thugs than trained soldiers, they tore through the countryside, raping and killing as they went.[63] The League threw everything into defending Florence. Fresh levies were raised; France and Venice were asked to send reinforcements; and the duke of Ferrara was pressed into the League's service. But nothing could stop the landsknechts now. Hungry for gold, and fired by their Lutheran faith, they simply turned away – and made for Rome.

Early on the morning of 6 May, 'imperial' troops scaled the city walls under cover of fog.[64] Quickly overpowering the defenders, they put Rome to the sack. Women and men, rich and poor, old and young were slaughtered indiscriminately; ambassadors and priests were taken hostage; and every treasure was looted. Some 30,000 homes were destroyed, and as many as 10,000 people were killed.[65] As one eyewitness remarked, 'Hell itself [was] a more beautiful thing to behold.'[66]

Only with great difficulty was Charles V able to regain control of his troops; but there was no denying that his position had been greatly strengthened by the mutiny.[67] The pope, having only narrowly escaped with his life, soon capitulated, robbing the League of its principal architect, and leaving the emperor a free hand elsewhere. In Venice, fear took hold. Though Charles' forces in Lombardy still lacked money and supplies, it was expected that, before long, 'the emperor's flag [would] fly above the Piazza San Marco'.[68] Food was also running short: just two weeks after the Sack of Rome, Sanudo reported that 'flour is expensive [and] there is no meat in the butchers' shops';[69] and by June, a Brescian citizen complained that it was impossible to find bread or fodder anywhere.[70]

It was painfully apparent that Venice needed the Jews after all. Despite Anselmo del Banco's threat the previous year, at least some Jewish banks were still operating. But unless more credit was made available soon, people would surely starve. Just then, Venice's forces in Lombardy were laying siege to Pavia, and a new fleet was being prepared for an attack on Naples. If the Republic was to stand any chance of pushing Charles V back, more money would have to be raised. On 7 October, a forced loan of 10,000 ducats was therefore demanded from the Jewish community to help pay for armaments, provisions, and hemp.[71] The Jews were in no mood to listen, though. Since their *condotta* was due to expire the following September, and the government had failed to offer them anything in return, they saw no reason why they should help the Venetians, even in their hour of need. Having caught wind of what was afoot, they closed their banks before the loan was requested and refused to lend a ducat more.[72]

It was foolish – even arrogant – of the Venetians to expect aid from the very people they had so recently spurned. As the famine dragged on, they were quickly disabused of their illusions. In November, Venice was gripped by freezing weather. As Sanudo noted, 'the extreme cold . . . caused the deaths of several tramps and galleymen staying under the porticoes in Piazza San Marco and at the Rialto'.[73] It also gravely exacerbated the famine. By the middle of December, prices were so high that 'every evening' children roamed the streets, crying 'Bread! I am dying of hunger and cold'.[74] Now seriously alarmed, the government belatedly scrabbled for a solution. What little grain was left on the mainland was hastily brought to the capital, and coarsely made loaves were distributed to the poor once a week.[75] It was too little, too late. Waves of starving *forestieri* were already flooding into the city. 'So many have come here from the countryside around Vicenza and Brescia that it is stupefying', wrote Sanudo on 20 February 1528.[76] It was impossible to help them all. 'Give alms to 200 and as many again appear', he explained:

> You cannot walk down a street or stop in a square or church without multitudes surrounding you to beg for charity: you see hunger written in their faces, their eyes like gemless rings, the wretchedness of their bodies with skins shaped only by bones . . . Certainly all the citizens are doing their duty with charity – but it cannot suffice . . .[77]

In a bid to combat vagrancy, the Quarantia voted to register the poor, build makeshift shelters for the sick and infirm, and provide subsistence for as long as the famine lasted.[78] In the cramped conditions that were provided, disease quickly spread – and by summer, typhus was running rampant.

Previously acute, Venice's need for the Jews now became urgent. Even their most fervent opponents seem to have recognized that, in the absence of an alternative source of credit, their services were indispensable. There was no question of them being sent back to Mestre now. Indeed, every effort was made to encourage them to stay. In July 1528, *strazzaruoli* were given permission to remain in the city;[79] and two months later, the Council of Ten formally revoked Moro's infamous decree.[80] In its place, a new five-year *condotta* was confirmed, on more generous terms than before. Jews would be allowed to go on lending money at the same rates as before, and the basic annual tax was reduced to half its previous level, while the rents payable for banks in Padua and Mestre remained unchanged. This was still a large sum – easily as much as Venice expected some subject cities to pay. And it could still demand additional subventions, either as loans or as outright gifts. But taken as a whole, the terms more than met the Jewish community's needs. Not even Anselmo del Banco could object.

*

As so often before, a crisis had saved the Jews from expulsion – and, like all others before, it eventually passed. Undone by the defection of Genoa, Francis I was forced to ask for terms; and a peace – negotiated by the king's mother, Louise of Savoy, and the emperor's aunt, Margaret of Austria – was duly signed at Cambrai on 3 August 1529.[81] A few days later, Charles V set off for Italy in person. After being reconciled with Pope Clement VII in Bologna, he received the imperial diadem from the pontiff's own hands. By then, the famine in Venice was already abating.[82] With the onset of warm weather, abundant harvests once again resumed; the typhus epidemic receded; and the refugees in whose cramped quarters it had first spread finally returned home.

The Venetians could well have been forgiven for feeling cautiously optimistic. Apart from their ports in Apulia and a few towns in the north – which they had been obliged to return to the emperor and the pope – they had emerged from the conflict with their territorial possessions almost intact and with remarkably little blood having been spilt in battle. With Italy now at peace, Venice could set her mind to restoring her former prosperity – and, in time, to reassessing the Jews' place in city life.

But something had changed. The long years of war had weakened Venice, perhaps even more than she realized. Though the city still boasted an 'empire', of sorts, she no longer commanded the same authority she once had. Francis I – previously her strongest ally – had thrown her over to secure a separate peace, and when she eventually concluded her own treaty with the emperor, she could only meekly accept the terms he dictated in his triumph. Her armies had been exposed as ineffective, even cowardly; her treasury was all but empty; and her resolve – as anyone could see – was dubious at best.

The fragility of Venice's position was soon made vividly apparent. Within months of the Treaty of Cambrai, Francis I had resolved to take up his claims in Italy again and was already plotting how best to take advantage of Charles' growing difficulties with his Lutheran subjects. Meanwhile, Suleiman the Magnificent was making rapid gains in every direction. Though the siege of Vienna had come to nothing the previous year, he was pressing his advantage in Hungary and the Balkans, while his fleet harassed shipping in the Adriatic with growing confidence.

While these two worries remained distinct, Venice was able to avoid being drawn into a major conflict, albeit at the cost of some minor humiliations. When the duke of Milan died in 1535, however, Venice's balancing act was cast in jeopardy.[83] Since the duke had left no heirs, both Charles V and Francis I had felt justified in claiming the duchy for themselves. Venice first tried to mediate; then, when negotiations failed, quietly withdrew in the hope of sitting out the war. Francis had other ideas. Much to the outrage of Christian commentators, he concluded an anti-Habsburg alliance with Suleiman the Magnificent. For the Venetians, this was worrying enough. But when Suleiman proposed that they, too, should join the campaign, their alarm was acute.

The Venetians were faced with an impossible choice. They could not accept Suleiman's offer without strengthening the Ottomans' hand in the Mediterranean, but could not decline without making themselves the target of his ire. Playing for time did not help: Suleiman, taking their hesitancy for rejection, launched an attack on Corfu – a key stopping-off point on Venice's eastern trade routes. Thanks to a combination of bad weather and good luck, the sultan's assault was fended off; but before the Venetians could celebrate, Suleiman had already turned his fury against the Aegean. The ports of Nauplion and Malvasia – Venice's last remaining possessions in the Peloponnese – fell, followed by a clutch of its island outposts.

With few resources and no allies to draw upon, Venice had no option but to sue for peace. But if it was hoping for clemency, it was sadly mistaken. Recognizing the Venetians' frailty, Suleiman foisted on them a treaty more shameful than merely unequal. Not only would he keep everything he had seized, but he also demanded astronomical reparations and imposed harsh new constraints on Venetian ships in Ottoman waters. Venice was in no position to refuse.

Nevertheless, Venice's losses were far from fatal. Even in victory, Suleiman still regarded it as a serious rival in the eastern Mediterranean. Nor, indeed, did the war make further conflict inevitable.[84] Both parties stood to gain from peaceful trade. But it proved beyond any doubt that the Republic's star was now in decline – and that its fortunes would henceforth depend on others' favour.

This frailty cemented the Ghetto's future in the longer term. Now that Venice's malaise had been laid bare, it would prove nearly impossible to seriously challenge the necessity of the Jews' presence ever again. In the face of growing fiscal and commercial uncertainty, the chauvinism of the past lost much of its force, and old pieties were set aside in the interests of state. Only the Jews could offer the unique combination of taxes, loans, and cheap credit that the Venetians so needed; and though their contribution to the exchequer probably never amounted to more than a few per cent of the city's annual income, the faltering Republic could not afford to do without them.[85] The *condotta*, which had so recently provoked such friction, now became a mere formality. In 1533, the *capitoli* – that is to say, the terms of the agreement – were reconfirmed for another five years, almost without dissent, and in 1537 for a further ten – with the provision that the advance payment should go towards the defence of Nauplion and Corfu.[86]

In the years after the Treaty of Cambrai, there were still occasional flashes of severity – even resentment – in government circles. Requests for exemptions to clothing rules were haughtily refused;[87] complaints about the tax burden were dismissed, almost out of hand; and fresh demands for money were made.[88] In July 1532, the conversion of a Christian woman to Judaism also caused an ugly scandal, which resulted in the Quarantia al Criminal sending their captains into the Ghetto.[89] Nor, among Venice's Jews, was there any lack of spleen. Even before the Ottoman war broke out, angry complaints were voiced about both the sums exacted and the financial difficulties in which some Jews found themselves.[90]

But the bitterness which had so marred Christian–Jewish relations in recent years seemed to have eased. Jewish banking ceased to be the occasion for vitriol. Attacks on usury were rare, even at Easter: if Sanudo is any guide, the only accusation against a Jewish moneylender in the period 1529–33 was made by a Jewish convert.[91] Though genuine warmth was still lacking, there was a measure of respect, even affection. When Anselmo del Banco died, in April 1532, Sanudo hailed him as '*uno gran hebreo*' and described the scale of his funeral cortège with undisguised admiration.[92] Even old grievances were set aside. On 15 July 1533, Anselmo del Banco's disgraced son, Jacob Meshullam, was baptized at the church of the Frari in the presence of Doge Andrea Gritti. Taking the name 'Marco Paradiso', he counted among his godfathers none other than Gabriele Moro, who had tried so hard to expel Venice's Jews only a few years before. Despite his past 'crimes', he was created a knight of St. Mark; and the pope himself issued a *breve* allowing him to keep his wealth – provided, of course, that he returned any money he had earned by charging interest.[93]

*

Now that the Jewish community had been set on a more stable footing, life in the Ghetto began to change. Housing was, admittedly, no better. In most cases, it actually got worse. Space had always been limited, so to meet the demands of a growing population, buildings underwent a 'a rapid . . . process of fragmentation'.[94] Apartments were divided into smaller units; rickety attic extensions were built, often by tenants themselves; and even rooms on the ground floor, previously used by shops or ateliers, were pressed into service as accommodation. A building which had accommodated a single Christian family in 1514 housed four or even five Jewish families by 1521, and over the next fifteen years, the number increased even further.[95]

Not all accommodation was of the same quality, of course. Some properties were larger and more comfortable than others. Even at this early stage, apartments below the attic, but above the water, were presumably more desirable. Who lived where was officially decided by the Ufficiali al Cattaver – the magistrature with responsibility for overseeing public expenditure, trade, and property – and by the 1530s, the allocation of lodgings was already beginning to reflect social differences in the Jewish community. Whereas Simon, who worked for Anselmo del Banco, and two Jews who sewed bonnets lived in poky garrets or rooms at the back of shops, Damian the physician and Aaron the innkeeper received more commodious homes on upper floors.[96]

There were also some restrictions on everyday activities. Since the *campo* still belonged to the da Brolo family, they controlled access to the Ghetto's three wells and specified where animals could be slaughtered or meat butchered.[97]

The Ghetto began to flourish, nonetheless. To satisfy Jewish dietary requirements, a host of new facilities quickly appeared.[98] By the late 1530s, there were already several kosher butchers, a bakery, cheese shops, and a tavern where Jewish travellers could stay. Though these were probably situated just outside the Ghetto walls and served a large Christian clientele, their produce was certified kosher. Synagogues – known in Venetian as *scuole* – began to spring up too.[99] In 1528–9, the Scuola Grande Tedesca was built on the southern side of the *campo*; and four years later, a certain Schlomo donated 180 ducats for the construction of the Scuola Canton, just a few doors down, in a corner (*canton*) owned by the Erizzo family.[100] Given the Venetians' horror of Jewish worship, care was taken to ensure that, from the outside, each looked as nondescript any other building. Inside, though, they became focal points not just for prayer, but also for education, social activity, and community gatherings.

The cultural life of the Ghetto, too, grew in confidence and variety. Thanks in part to the influx of scholars from the mainland, Venice quickly became the leading centre of Hebrew publishing – not just in Italy, but in the whole of Europe. Already, in the late fifteenth century, Christian humanists had shown enough interest in the study of the Hebrew language for Venetian printers to experiment with the use of Hebrew type. Leading the way was Aldus Manutius. In 1498, he had included five words from Psalm 65.2 in his edition of Angelo Poliziano's *Opera*; and the following year, a few lines in Hebrew found their way into the *Hypnerotomachia Poliphili*. Encouraged by this, he then sent Conrad Celtis some sample pages from a proposed polyglot Bible, and even printed a clear, if rather rudimentary *Introductio utilissima hebraice discere cupientibus* ('A Very Useful Introduction for Those Wishing to Learn Hebrew').[101]

But not until Daniel Bomberg's arrival in Venice did Hebrew publishing come into its own. The son of a wealthy Antwerp burgher, Bomberg had come to Venice to pursue a career in trade, perhaps as the representative of his father's firm.[102] He had not been in the city long before he came across Fra Felice da Prato. A former Jew, Felice had converted to Christianity well into his forties.[103] He became an

Augustinian friar, studied at the University of Padua, and in time moved to Rome, where he taught Hebrew to leading members of the Curia. How he and Bomberg met is not clear; but it is certainly tempting to believe that it was as teacher and pupil. Whatever the case, on 5 September 1515, they published their first book together – Felice's Latin translation of the Psalms. Although the marginal notes contained a few words in Hebrew, this was not a Hebrew book per se. Nor, indeed, was Bomberg's role particularly striking: he merely put up the money for the book to be printed. But within weeks, he and Felice were already planning to set up their own Hebrew printing house, and in December 1515, the Senate granted them a privilege, allowing them to publish whatever works 'God may allow [them] to print'.

This was significant in more ways than one. A few years earlier, Gershon Soncino, arguably the foremost Hebrew printer of his day, had also applied for the right to print in Venice, only to be turned down.[104] It is possible that Bomberg was simply regarded as a safer bet by the Venetian authorities: even though he set out to cater almost exclusively to a Jewish readership, the fact that he was a Christian – and a merchant – is likely to have reassured them. According to the terms of his privilege, Bomberg was given a complete monopoly of Hebrew printing in Venice. For a period of ten years, no one was allowed to publish, import, or sell any other Hebrew works. It was a recipe for success – and Bomberg exploited it to the full.

Less than a year later, on 30 November 1516, their first Hebrew work rolled off the press: an edition of the Pentateuch, prepared by Felice da Prato, together with the five Megillot and Rashi's commentaries. By the time it appeared, however, Felice was already at work on the Rabbinical Bible (*Mikraot Gedolot*). Printed between 1517 and 1518, this sumptuous, four-volume work contained not only the usual commentaries, but also the Masoretic notes, showing the correct pronunciation and interpretation of the text. In a nod to Bomberg's Christian faith, it was also 'the first Hebrew Bible to use chapter numbers . . . as well as to divide the books of Samuel, Kings, and Chronicles into two books each'.[105]

Before the Rabbinical Bible was completed, however, the Senate revoked all existing privileges, perhaps in a misguided attempt to impose some order on the publishing trade. Bomberg was therefore obliged to apply for a new privilege. Fortunately, this was approved by a thundering majority. Bomberg was now able to expand his operations. The following year, he hired Baruch Adelkind and his sons to help with compositing and corrections. Of this extraordinary family, the most outstanding was Cornelio, who swiftly became one of Bomberg's closest collaborators. At the same time, he also recruited a series of noted Hebrew grammarians. With their aid, he embarked on the publication of the complete text of the Babylonian Talmud. As Joshua Bloch noted, this was 'an epoch-making event in the history of Hebrew printing'.[106] Prepared by Hiyyah Meir ben David, a judge in the city's rabbinical court, its arrangement of the major commentaries established a standard which remains largely unchallenged even today. Indeed, such was its fame and influence that Henry VIII of England even purchased a copy to help with his divorce from Catherine of Aragon.[107]

Over the next twenty-five years, Bomberg's press worked with feverish intensity. Somewhere between 200 and 250 titles appeared under its imprint, collectively reflecting the diversity of the Jewish community's interests and the vibrancy of its thought.[108] First, in 1523, there came the *editio princeps* of the Jerusalem Talmud. Then, under pressure from eager clients, he prepared a new four-volume edition of the Rabbinical Bible, even more magnificent than the first.[109] Granted, it was not all plain sailing. When his original privilege expired in October 1525, the Senate refused him permission to go on printing Hebrew books until he handed over 500 ducats as a sweetener the following March.[110] Given the vast expense of producing works like the Babylonian and Jerusalem Talmuds, he sometimes ran into serious financial difficulties, and there were occasional unexplained pauses in production (1533–7, 1539–43).[111] But apart from that, his efforts were unstinting. Almost no area of Jewish literature escaped his attention. He produced liturgical works, halakhic *responsa*, grammatical studies (including a path-breaking study of Hebrew vowels), philosophy, and even the first Karaite book for communities in Central and Eastern Europe. Everything he touched was of the highest quality – so much so that when, in 1537, the Senate attempted to clamp down on substandard books by imposing fines on any publisher who used paper that blotted, Bomberg appears to have been completely unaffected.[112]

Bomberg was too successful not to inspire imitators.[113] By the time of his death, in 1549, at least three further Hebrew presses had been established. Of these, the most important was that founded by Marco Antonio Giustiniani. Based in the Calle delli Cinque alla Giustizia Vecchia, not far from the Rialto, the Giustiniani press benefitted from the collaboration of Cornelio Adelkind, and made no secret of its desire to emulate – if not exceed – the excellence of Bomberg's work. The following year, Alvise Bragadin opened another press, and a period of fruitful, if not always cordial, rivalry with Giustiniani began. Vying to produce the finest edition of the Mishneh Torah, they appealed not only to leading rabbis, but even to the pope – a clear indication both of the importance attached to Hebrew scholarship, and of the immense value of the market for Hebrew books. And as the Ghetto became more firmly rooted in Venetian society, the pace of competition only quickened.

*

Daily existence in the Ghetto left a great deal to be desired. Few, if any, families were allowed to live in the Ghetto Nuovo; prejudice was still rife; and though restrictions on trade were less onerous than in the past, Jewish businessmen still chafed against them. Nevertheless, compared to how it could have been, it was something of a blessing. Indeed, by 1541, many of Venice's Jews had started to believe that, after so many tribulations, they were at last living 'under the protection of the Lord'.[114]

PART II

The Golden Age

5

Expansion

(1541–1553)

Now a more permanent feature of Venetian life, the Ghetto Nuovo quickly began to grow, swelled by a stream of new visitors. As in previous years, many were from the Italian mainland. But a growing number now came from the Iberian Peninsula. They fell into two main groups. Some were Spanish Jews, who had been expelled from Castile and Aragon after the conquest of Granada. Others were 'crypto' Jews, mostly from Portugal. Also known as 'Marranos' (a pejorative term, thought to derive from a word meaning 'pig'), they had been forced to convert to Christianity in the late fifteenth century.[1] For a time, many had managed to live a double life. While adhering to Christian ways in public, they had continued to practise their Jewish faith in private.[2] But as converts, they were under constant suspicion – and when the Inquisition was introduced into Portugal in 1536, many had chosen to flee rather than face persecution.[3]

For Marrano refugees, the attraction of Italy was understandably hard to resist – so much so that a good many travelled there directly. But others feared that if their place of birth became known, they would be able neither to remain Christians without arousing suspicion, nor to resume their Jewish faith openly without risking harsh punishments for apostasy. Indeed, back in 1497, Venice itself had ordered any Marranos arriving from 'Spain or elsewhere' to leave without delay – and made it clear that it would severely punish any Christian caught doing business with them.[4] To avoid this problem, Marranos first made for the Ottoman Empire. As early as 1532, Marrano businessmen, like the Antwerp-based spice merchant Diogo Mendes, were regularly helping to smuggle their co-religionists to Constantinople, Salonika, or Cairo, via the Low Countries.[5] Once safely under the sultan's protection, they shook off their former lives, and then went on to Italy in the guise of Ottoman – rather than Portuguese or Spanish – subjects.

By necessity, as much as by inclination, they were a mercantile people, endowed with a buccaneering spirit and a keen eye for opportunity. Having been prominent figures in Mediterranean trade long before their flight, they lost no time in using their 'money and international connections to build up imposing financial empires in the East' – and in establishing themselves as vital intermediaries in the lucrative trade with the West.[6]

The Venetians were quick to recognize the value of such 'Levantine' Jews. In the decades since the foundation of the Ghetto Nuovo, the city's prosperity had been severely damaged. The recent war with the Ottoman Empire had taken a heavy toll on its commerce with the eastern Mediterranean. Between 1537 and 1541, the Levantine galleys had been suspended; and large ships of every kind had been decommissioned for want of business.[7] By the time peace had been concluded, some Venetians doubted whether it would ever be possible to restore eastern trade to its former prosperity.[8] If the city was to survive as a major trading power, it needed to attract more foreign merchants and boost the value of goods passing through its quays. And in Levantine Jews, the Venetians spied the solution. In contrast to the German and Italian Jews already living in the Ghetto Nuovo – who had never had much taste for overseas business – the Levantines were not only in a position to revitalize trade with the Ottoman Balkans, but, as a result of their maritime wanderings, had also built up a network of valuable contacts throughout the Mediterranean. By 1541, they already controlled much of the trade along certain routes. As the Cinque Savi alla Mercanzia noted that summer, 'the greater part of the merchandise which comes from upper and lower Romania' – what is today northern Greece and Bulgaria – was in the hands of Levantine Jews.[9] It was only logical to encourage them further.

Unfortunately, the Venetians were not the only ones to recognize the Levantines' potential. Although the states of southern Italy, being under Spanish rule, remained staunchly hostile to any Jewish presence, those in the north were already clamouring to welcome them. In 1534, Pope Paul III tried to persuade Portuguese Marranos to settle in Ancona by 'granting them safeguards against . . .

prosecution' and exempting them from any obligation to pay taxes or wear distinguishing clothing.[10] Four years later, Duke Ercole II of Ferrara invited 'all Spaniards and Portuguese . . . whether Christians or infidels' to live and trade freely in his lands, with the assurance that they could go on practising whatever customs they had before.[11] And in 1551, Cosimo de' Medici – who hoped to expand Livorno's trade with the Near East – likewise offered them residence in Tuscany.[12]

It was clear that, if Venice was to compete, it would have to do something to make itself more attractive. On 2 June 1541, the Senate therefore voted by an overwhelming majority to grant 'itinerant Levantine Jewish merchants' (*hebrei mercadanti levantini viandanti*) generous tax breaks, and to provide them with improved accommodation in the city itself.[13] The only problem was the lack of space. As the Levantines' representatives pointed out, the Ghetto Nuovo was already painfully overcrowded. There were no more than thirty or so buildings as it was; and while every effort had been made to maximize the habitable area, there simply wasn't enough room for the new influx. After a brief investigation, the Senate therefore agreed to let them live in a narrow strip of land between the Ghetto Nuovo and Cannaregio, known as the Ghetto Vecchio (the Old Ghetto). It wasn't much. There were only a few short, squat buildings, a tiny square, and a scraggy little garden. But it was still enough to house a reasonable number – and that was all the Senate and the Levantines needed.

Life in the Ghetto Vecchio wouldn't be easy, though. However much the Venetians may have needed the Levantines' commercial acumen, they had no intention of allowing the new arrivals to 'contaminate' their Christian neighbours. Like the Ghetto Nuovo, the Ghetto Vecchio was to be sealed.[14] There were to be only two gates: one opening onto Cannaregio, the other leading to the Ghetto Nuovo. Doors belonging to Christian houses outside the Jewish area were walled up, balconies were prohibited, and guards were posted at the Cannaregio entrance to prevent anyone from coming or going other than at the permitted times.[15]

There was no question of the Levantines making themselves comfortable. Indeed, the Senate seems to have gone out of its way to keep them both separate and transient. Unlike the Jews of the Ghetto Nuovo, they were only visitors. As Ottoman subjects, they had no right of residence. They could stay for no more than four months at a time – and, though this was later extended to two years, they were strictly forbidden to bring their families. Even then, their activities were to be tightly controlled. While in Venice, they were only permitted to engage in trade. They could neither lend money nor deal in second-hand goods – which, until then, had been the lifeblood of Venice's Jewish community. And since they had no formal agreement with the Venetian government – no *condotta* – there was nothing to stop the Senate throwing them out whenever it liked.

At first, no more than a handful of Levantines came to the Ghetto Vecchio. At one point, so many of the houses were empty that the 'German' Jews were even given permission to live there.[16] Yet the Levantines' arrival fundamentally changed the character of Jewish life in Venice. There were now two separate communities living side by side – each with its own language, customs, and religious practices. Whereas most of the Italians and 'Germans' were Ashkenazim, the Ladino-speaking Levantines tended to be Sephardim. To Venetian eyes, the differences may have seemed subtle; but they were nevertheless important. Dietary requirements – known as *kashrut* – were often stricter for the Sephardim than for the Ashkenazim; Hebrew words were pronounced differently; and each community followed its own distinctive liturgy. This meant that a new synagogue was needed. Just a few years after the Ghetto Vecchio was established, the Scuola Levantina was founded in the square. So too, new butchers and new ovens were required, new books had to be printed, and a thousand other adjustments had to be made. Inevitably, some tensions arose. Harsh words were exchanged, and on at least one occasion, a minor dispute erupted into a public brawl. But in the daily back and forth between Germans and Levantines, a richer culture was born, endowing the community with a fresh vibrancy – and transforming the Ghetto into a microcosm of the Jewish world.

*

While the Levantines settled into life in Cannaregio, Venice's broader attitude towards religious minorities was undergoing a sea change. Since the end of the war with Suleiman the Magnificent, Venice had done its utmost to stay out of Italian affairs. Desperate to avoid being drawn into another futile conflict, it had distanced itself from both Emperor Charles V and Pope Paul III. In doing so, however, it had also turned its back on their attempts to defend Catholicism against the Protestant Reformation. This freed Venetian merchants from religious constraints, and within a year of the Ghetto Vecchio's establishment, the city had become a haven for exiled dissenters. 'Heretics' were everywhere. Lutherans 'took over' the bakers' guild;[17] Anabaptists found work as artisans;[18] and Calvinist views could occasionally be heard in church.[19] By 1542, Venice had become so receptive to dissent that Italian reformers like Bernardino Ochino even hoped that it might soon repudiate Catholicism altogether.[20]

Jews, too, benefitted from this new spirit of tolerance – especially the Levantines. Exactly how far they had revitalized Venice's trade with the Balkans is hard to say, but the government was more than happy to let them stay on. Over the next few years, the Senate renewed their customs exemptions three times without so much as a murmur of opposition. Most likely, it also extended their right to lodge in the Ghetto Vecchio at the same time. The German Jews were also treated with more indulgence: now that their economic value had been proved, their material environment became the object of concern. In October 1542, Leonardo Minotto set aside 'no less than 3,000 ducats' in his will to improve the Ghetto Nuovo.[21] Even the Marranos began to get a little more sympathy. When, in March 1544, Brianda, the widow of Diogo Mendes, sought permission to settle in Venice with her sister Gracia, the city welcomed them with open arms. As the heirs of the vast Mendes fortune, they were just the people to bolster the Venetians' commercial recovery – and the government saw no need to bother them with questions about their private beliefs.[22]

*

Not everyone was happy, though. The papal nuncio, Giovanni Della Casa, was horrified.[23] A tall, wiry Florentine with a long beard and a piercing gaze, he had watched the growth of Venice's Jewish population with growing alarm. Like his colleagues in the Curia, he suspected that the Levantines' commercial skill had blinded the Venetians to how dangerous they really were. It was common knowledge that, while the Levantines were 'officially' Jews, many had previously been Christian. And if a Christian convert could revert to Judaism, Della Casa reasoned, what was there to stop that person persuading other Catholics to renounce their faith, as well?

The Church had already begun to take a harder line against Levantines in the Papal States. While Pope Paul III was still keen to attract Jewish merchants to ports like Ancona, he had come to feel that it would be better if they converted – or rather, *returned* – to Christianity. Wherever possible, he preferred to use persuasion. In the bull *Cupientes iudaeos*, the pope promised that converts could keep property, become citizens of wherever they were baptized, and receive a good Catholic education.[24] If this didn't work, however, there was always persecution. On 21 July 1542, the pope approved the establishment of a Roman Inquisition.[25] Its function was to protect the Christian religion from the corrupting effects of heterodoxy and assure its dominance over an increasingly diverse society. Understandably, it was mainly concerned with Protestants, but it was also tasked with seeking out and punishing any Jews who had renounced their baptism, or Marranos who had secretly reverted to the Jewish faith.

Della Casa's task was to extend this policy to Venice. As the Roman Inquisition's official representative in the lagoon, he was charged with overseeing the repression of heresy throughout Venetian territories.[26] In this, he proved remarkably zealous. Within months of his arrival, he had already opened proceedings against a number of well-known troublemakers, mostly in holy orders. But there was only so much he could do. From the first, the Venetian government had been deeply mistrustful of his motives. While they were happy enough for Della Casa to discipline errant priests, they feared that if the Roman Inquisition was given a free hand, Venice's sovereignty would be threatened. As time wore on, their suspicions only grew.

By the spring of 1547, however, Venice's resolve had begun to falter. Following the death of Francis I's son, Charles, the fragile peace between France and the Empire had collapsed; and, as Italy hurtled once again towards war, the pope had urged Venice to join him in an anti-imperial alliance.[27] The Venetians, of course, refused. But isolation came at a price. In a bid to force the Republic's hand, both sides had pressured the government to abandon its policy of toleration. While the ageing Cardinal Jacopo Sadoleto fulminated against the 'Lutheran plague' poisoning the city, the emperor's ambassador warned Venice against consorting with heretics and hinted grimly at the retribution it would suffer if it did not change its ways.[28] Eventually, the Venetians caved in. Though still unwilling to allow a 'foreign' body jurisdiction over its affairs, it reluctantly accepted that tighter religious controls were now needed.

On 22 April 1547, Doge Francesco Donà and his councillors voted to establish a Venetian Inquisition – 'for the honour of our holy Mother Church'.[29] Like its counterparts elsewhere, its remit was broad. It was given full authority to both pursue and prosecute heretics in the capital, and to oversee the work of local inquisitorial courts on the mainland and overseas. Its powers were equally sweeping. Not only was it free to decide how to proceed, and against whom, but it also had the right to use torture in interrogations; and if it chose, it could even request the death penalty.[30] This, understandably, made some patricians a little queasy, so to limit the possibility of ecclesiastical overreach, three laymen were appointed to serve on its tribunal, alongside the Franciscan inquisitor and the papal nuncio, Giovanni Della Casa.[31] Known collectively as the *savi all'eresia*, they were answerable to the Venetian government, rather than the Church, and could, in theory, block any investigation that trespassed too far on Venice's prerogatives. But in the public mind, their involvement only served to bolster the Inquisition's authority further.

Della Casa was exultant. 'God has shown the greatest favour in allowing me to introduce the Inquisition into this dominion peacefully and without any upset', he crowed.[32] Here, at last, was the opportunity he had been waiting for – and he wasted no time in swinging into action. Almost from the first, Levantines were among his targets. Of the 1,565 cases heard by the Inquisition over the following decades for which records survive, almost 5 per cent concerned people of Jewish birth or descent.[33]

To start with, at least, most of the accused were Marranos, who were suspected either of reverting openly to the faith of their fathers, or of maintaining more subtle ties to Jewish life. But a good many cases were also brought against Jews and recent converts to Christianity. Although rarely charged with apostasy, they could be arraigned for more discreet forms of 'judaizing', such as owning books contrary to the Christian faith, insulting a Catholic priest, living outside the Ghetto, attempting to convert a Christian to Judaism, and – in one particularly unusual case – digging up the corpse of a Jewish women to send it to Galilee.

The Inquisition was no blunt instrument, however. Whether from prudence or simple pragmatism, it was careful to avoid arbitrary decisions and, wherever possible, followed a standard procedure. By the standards of the day, in fact, its investigations 'could be considered fair-minded, with accurate and reasonable verdicts'.[34] Questions were probing, but rarely mendacious; evidence was preferred to insinuation; and confessions were often met with clemency. Moreover, punishments were no harsher than those handed down by Inquisitions elsewhere – and were, in many cases, a good deal more restrained than those favoured by the civil courts. In the twenty-five cases for which the outcome is known, not a single capital sentence was passed. Two people were banished for life, three received 'spiritual punishments', six were sent to the galleys, and nine were released.

Yet that Jewish life was more vulnerable than before is not in any doubt. Only recently a haven for heterodox beliefs, Venice was now seized by a creeping suspicion; and those it had once welcomed as commercial partners, it now regarded with misgiving. Although the accused probably never accounted for more than a small percentage of the population, for many Jews, the city streets must nevertheless have acquired a threatening aspect. Anonymous denunciations issued from darkened corners; watchful eyes peered between closed shutters; and mere whispers gained a sinister strength.

The poor were at greatest risk. As the trial testimonies reveal, poverty was often cited as the principal motive for 'sin'. On 10 April 1548, Giacomo Francoso, a stocky youth from Sarzana, was sentenced to twenty years in the galleys for having been baptized as a Christian no fewer than four times – purely for the gift of money which godparents customarily gave new converts.[35] As he frankly admitted, his clothes were in tatters, and it was the only way he could think of to replace them. On other occasions, precarity itself exposed the accused to investigation. One summer night in 1549, Francisco Oliviero was leaving the house of a courtesan in Santo Stefano when he was attacked by a gang of roughs and badly wounded.[36] Fearing for his life, he called for a priest to hear his confession. This done, he was taken to the house of Paolo Peruta at San Marcuola. Two days later, Francisco had himself carried into the Ghetto Vecchio to be cared for at the inn. This immediately attracted the Inquisition's attention. Who was this young man? Was he a Christian? Or a Jew in disguise? The priest had simply assumed that, since he was found wearing a black hat and sword, he must have been a Christian – perhaps a Spanish Marrano; but the accounts of other witnesses were less encouraging. According to the innkeeper, Bondi di Vitali, the wounded man had signed in under the name 'Joseph the Jew'. He had been visited by his Jewish brother, Davide, and though he occasionally wore Christian clothes, he was anxious not to be buried in a Christian cemetery. Several other witnesses appeared to confirm this. Despite a few private doubts, they had all seen him in a yellow hat – sometimes even in the Ghetto itself. Francisco, who had since been arrested, was bewildered. Although he had indeed been circumcised by his father, he insisted that he had been baptized as a child and had 'always lived as a good Christian'. He claimed that he had only gone to stay in the Ghetto because he was poor and had relatives there who could help him. He had never observed Jewish rituals – and had certainly not worn Jewish clothes. The only reason the so-called witnesses had said otherwise, he railed, was because *they* were the ones who had attacked him in the first place. The Inquisition was unconvinced. Satisfied that Francisco was indeed a Jew, it found him guilty of having sexual relations with a Christian woman and of confessing to a priest 'like a Christian'. It sentenced him to four years in the galleys.

But it was not only the poor who felt the Inquisition's ire: the wealthy were indicted almost as frequently. Though their value to the Venetian economy may have shielded them a little, it could not hide them from the Inquisition's gaze altogether. Indeed, at times, their riches actually invited the Inquisition's attention – occasionally even with the government's complicity. The most striking – and poignant – case centred on the Mendes family. Shortly after the Inquisition was established, a dispute over money led Brianda Mendes to accuse her sister, Gracia, of practising Judaism in secret.[37] At this, the Venetian government spied an opportunity to seize the legendary Mendes fortune for itself. While Gracia was being interrogated by the Inquisition, an embargo was placed on the family's assets. Gracia had seen this coming, though. Shortly before being arrested, she had taken the precaution of transferring some of her money to Constantinople. When this became known, it caused a scandal in Venice. But as Gracia had no doubt intended, it also piqued the sultan's interest. At the urging of her associate, Moses Hamon, Suleiman took Gracia under his protection and dispatched an envoy to Venice to secure her release. This forced the Venetians' hand. Unwilling to risk an international incident, the government reluctantly granted her permission to leave under safe conduct for Ferrara, where she was received as a practising Jew. After an ugly affair, in which Gracia's nephew, Joseph Nasi, was condemned to death *in absentia* for trying to kidnap his cousin,[38] she finally accepted the Senate's help in putting an end to her dispute with Brianda – and left to begin a new life in Constantinople. For the Inquisition, however, the story was far from over. In Gracia's absence, her agents, Agostino Enriques and Odoardo Gomes, traded accusations with Brianda's; and, in a crowning irony, Brianda herself was eventually expelled from Venice after confessing to being a 'secret' Jew – albeit not before handing over vast sums of money to procure her retainer's freedom.

*

While the Inquisition was gathering pace, a fresh wave of anti-Jewish feeling spread across the mainland. Driven by the spirit of the Counter-Reformation, subject towns saw no distinction between the recent Levantine arrivals and established settlements; and within months, Jewish lending once again came under attack.[39] On 5 November 1547, Crema persuaded the Venetian government to recognize the monopoly granted to its *monte di pietà* – effectively driving Jewish moneylenders out of business. The following month, Verona received permission to ban Jewish usury after the expiry of the current *condotta*. A similar measure was approved in Padua. More worryingly, there were renewed outbreaks of violence. On 22 November, a pogrom erupted in Asolo. Three years before, following another spate of attacks, the Council of Ten had ordered the citizens to protect local Jews, but in the heat of resentment, such warnings were quickly forgotten. Fourteen Jews were killed. Many more were injured. Houses were ransacked, and pledges held by Jewish bankers were stolen – or more likely, 'reclaimed' by those who had pawned them.

Even in Venice itself, attitudes grew more hostile. When the Senate discussed the renewal of the German Jews' *condotta*, in December 1548, there were calls for harsher terms to be imposed.[40] Some of the more reactionary patricians even wanted to ban usury altogether – and, for the first time in many years, they were given a sympathetic hearing. But even in the charged atmosphere stirred up by the Inquisition, that was going too far. The Senate eventually contented itself with raising the Jews' annual tax while reducing their interest rates. From then on, Jews would have to pay 10,000 ducats a year and charge no more than 12 per cent. This was significantly less than bankers had grown used to asking – and would certainly have come as a shock. As they must have known, there was no financial justification for this. Since Venice was then at peace, there was no fleet to be maintained, nor troops raised; and for once, the treasury had no urgent need for funds.[41] True, the Jews could tell themselves that at least no further restrictions had been placed on them. They were still allowed to sell second-hand goods, engage in trade, and buy and sell books. But this can hardly have made up for their lost income or given them much hope for the future.

Worse still was the treatment of the Marranos. On 8 July 1550, just as the affair of Gracia Mendes was reaching its peak, the Senate voted to expel the entire population, just as it had over fifty years before.[42] Following the expulsion of the Marranos from the Netherlands, the previous year, a large number of migrants had recently flooded into the city. One clerical observer professed to have counted around 10,000, whereas a more reasonable estimate put the figure at no more than 300.[43] Either way, it proved too much – and, coupled with a growing resentment of the Marranos' prosperity, prompted many patricians to regret their erstwhile policy of tolerance.[44] Having once been seen as a pardonable necessity, Marranos now came to be regarded as 'worse than the Jews' – a tribe of godless dissemblers, whose instinctive disregard for truth threatened not just religion, but the very fabric of commerce itself.[45] They had to go. All Venetians who had dealings with Marranos were ordered to break off relations immediately, and it was hoped that Venice would soon be free of a pernicious menace.

In its frenzy, however, the Senate had forgotten why it had welcomed the Marranos in the first place. They were too much a part of the Republic's economy to be so easily dispensed with. By the end of August, Venetian merchants were complaining that their businesses were now at risk.[46] Over the past few years, they had come to rely on Marranos for their supplies of wool, silk, cloth, wine, oil, pepper, sugar, and countless other essential goods. If they were to obey the Senate's decree, they would have to either conjure up new trade routes out of thin air or shut up shop altogether. Reluctantly, the Senate had to acknowledge that they had a point. It claimed the intention had been to stop Marranos from living in Venice and its territories, rather than to ban trade with Marranos living overseas. But the damage had been done. As Marranos left the city, vital trading links were lost and vast fortunes removed. Just months later, the bank of the procurator Antonio Priuli collapsed 'through the withdrawal of Portuguese deposits' – gravely harming the commercial credit market and undermining confidence just when a steady hand was needed.[47]

Rather than giving the Venetian government pause, the upset of the Marranos' expulsion only caused it to redouble its efforts against the Jews. There was no real logic to this: Venice's economic interests argued strongly for restraint. But anti-Jewish feelings were running too high not to take priority. Over the warnings of more moderate patricians, the campaign against Jewish banking that had begun a few years earlier was extended.[48] New *monti di pietà* were approved in Rovigo and Badia Polesine; and local governors were empowered to punish with heavy fines, imprisonment, or galley service any Jews guilty of lending without permission. Most importantly, Christians were also banned from buying debts owed to Jewish bankers and collecting the money themselves. Ostensibly, the reason for this was pastoral. As the legislation explained, the whole point of allowing Jews to lend money at interest was to save Christians from the sin of usury; but by trading in debt, they were just getting mired in it again. The real reason was probably financial, though. In prohibiting the practice, the Senate was preventing Jewish lenders from recouping money on bad loans – in effect, forcing them to keep more liabilities on their books, and pushing them further towards the red.

Where this would lead was anyone's guess. But the brief honeymoon period after the foundation of the Ghetto Vecchio was certainly over – and both Venice and its Jews would have to pay the price.

6

The Great Fiction

(1553–1589)

On the morning of 21 October 1553, the new papal nuncio, Ludovico Beccadelli, watched as a great bonfire was lit in the Piazza San Marco.[1] A hunched old man with a wispy beard and a faraway look in his eyes, he had likely been looking forward to this moment. For the past few days, armed guards had been scouring the city, searching for copies of the Talmud and any other Hebrew books harmful to the Christian faith. No corner had been left unexplored. The Ghetto had been raided. Printers' workshops had been smashed up. Even the libraries of Venice's leading humanists had been searched. And now, as the flames licked higher, Beccadelli could be forgiven for feeling a glow of satisfaction.

As he wrote later that day, it was *'un bel fuoco'* – 'a good fire'.[2] At a stroke, the Hebrew book trade was decimated. The Giustiniani press, which had published its great Babylonian Talmud only two years before, was virtually ruined. The paper and printing materials alone had cost 3,000 ducats, but the true losses may have been eight times higher.[3] Other printers were left penniless. Many fled. Some managed to set up shop in Cremona, Ferrara, Mantua, and a few other places. Most never returned.

Beccadelli took no pleasure in the destruction of books per se. Like his friend and predecessor, Giovanni Della Casa, he was more of a scholar than anything else – and was, by nature, a gentle soul.[4] A portrait by Titian, painted in 1552, shows an almost grandfatherly figure, weighted down by responsibilities he neither wanted nor particularly enjoyed.[5] All who knew him could testify that he was kind and deferential, almost to a fault – certainly no book-burning zealot.

Yet in the bonfire, Beccadelli still found cause for celebration. A new phase in Venice's relations with both the papacy and the Jews had begun. As he knew, the Venetian government had not been averse to burning books in the past – especially if they happened to be Protestant – but it was telling that, in this case, the initiative had come from Rome.[6] Back in August, the pope had ordered the destruction of all Jewish books in the city, and later extended this to the rest of Italy.[7] Far from hesitating – as they might have done not so very long ago – the Venetians had hurried to do his bidding. Since the expulsion of the Marranos, they had been growing steadily more receptive to the papacy's anti-Jewish rhetoric; now that the Italian Wars were drawing to a close, they could see no danger in answering Rome's call, especially as the pope's policy happened to coincide with the wishes of most citizens. Before any other Italian state had a chance to act, the Council of Ten approved the action.[8] As Beccadelli noted, not a single voice was raised in opposition; and the bonfire was entrusted not to the Inquisition, but to a secular magistracy – a clear sign that, from now on, wherever the pope led, the Venetian state would follow.

*

Such servility came at a fateful moment. Following the election of Pope Paul IV, on 23 May 1555, the papacy's policy towards Jews grew suddenly – and dramatically – more aggressive. The new pontiff, a harsh, uncompromising man known for his austerity, made no secret of his distaste for tolerance and lost no time in making Jewish lives a misery. One of his first acts was to promulgate the bull *Cum nimis absurdum*. This set out to 'destroy the prosperity of the Jews in the Papal States' and achieve a complete separation between Jewish and Christian populations.[9] The following year, twenty-four Portuguese Marranos who had reverted to Judaism were burnt at the stake in Ancona,[10] and in 1559, the *Index Librorum Prohibitorum* (Index of Forbidden Books) was issued, banning anyone from printing – or even reading – 'the Hebrew Talmud and all its glosses, annotations, interpretations, and expositions'.[11]

Venice had already anticipated some of this, of course. Many of the measures outlined in *Cum nimis absurdum* – segregation, distinguishing marks, a ban on Jewish property owning – had been introduced almost forty years before. Yet while the bull had little impact on Venetian legislation, the Republic was nevertheless eager to share in the spirit of the pope's reforms and saw in his attacks an invitation to extend its campaign against Jewish moneylending.[12]

The first priority was to expand the number of *monti di pietà*. Over the next two years, a raft of new foundations was approved: some in large subject cities like Bergamo, but most in smaller towns between Treviso and Udine, where biting poverty had so far supplied steady demand for Jewish loans.[13] More important, however, was the need to enlarge their operations. As charitable institutions, *monti* had until then derived their working capital principally from donations. This had inevitably placed a limit on their growth. After all, how many businessmen are ready to hand over their cash for no return? To solve this problem, the Venetian authorities cannily decided to let *monti* 'offer depositors a modest rate of interest'. It was rarely above 4 per cent, but this was enough to attract Christian investors looking for a safe haven – and, provided that *monti* made loans at around 6 per cent, it allowed them to greatly expand their lending capacity. Now, with full coffers, they could finally lend to people other than the deserving poor – and thereby challenge Jewish moneylenders on their own ground. In fact, given that their rates were much lower, they could even drive them out of business.

Soon enough, many towns on the mainland felt confident enough in *monti di pietà* to do without Jewish moneylenders altogether. One after another, long-standing agreements were cancelled – or, more often, simply allowed to lapse.[14] Fortunately, this led to few calls for expulsion. Only in Udine did tensions run so high. An effort was nevertheless made to curb the Jews' other economic activities, and many towns tried to restrict them to the second-hand trade.[15] Dealing in cloth, silk, velvet, or gold was strictly forbidden; and on 28 May 1554, the Senate even ordered Jewish manufacturers throughout the *terraferma* to shut up shop within a month.[16]

The effect on Jewish life was catastrophic. Banks, ruined by the reform of the *monti di pietà*, collapsed; businesses folded; and families lost their livelihoods. Facing an uncertain future, many saw no point in staying. Entire communities packed up and left – so much so that, within a few years, there were no Jews to be found either in the towns of Castelfranco Veneto and Montagnana, or even in the city of Crema. For those who remained, their departure came as a heavy blow. After all, the community's annual tax bill still needed paying;

and with many of its largest taxpayers having 'either emigrated or gone bankrupt', it was going to be difficult – if not impossible – to make up the shortfall.[17]

When the Jews' *condotta* came up for renewal in November 1558, the Senate showed them a little clemency.[18] The annual tax was reduced to 8,000 ducats, and the few banks remaining were allowed to continue operating on much the same terms as before – albeit under tight supervision. But the burden this placed on the community was still much too high. Seven years later, when the time for renegotiation came round again, Jewish representatives protested that their situation was even worse than before. Even lending at the maximum allowable rate, the remaining bankers were losing money hand over fist. To show how bad things were, the representatives presented a list of the eleven banks which had operated under the terms of the 1548 and 1558 *condotte*. Since then, most had gone bankrupt, or otherwise 'come to grief'. If these figures were correct, this meant that, in the space of less than twenty years, the 'taxpaying capacity' of the Jews in Venice and its dominions had fallen by almost 70 per cent. The community would struggle to pay half of what was asked – let alone 8,000 ducats. Surely the Senate could make some allowances?

The Senate was unmoved. Moderate voices were now in the minority; and many of those who had previously voted to help the Jews had been spooked by the banks' instability. What worried them was not just that the Jews might not be able to pay their taxes, but the thought that *they* might lose money, too. For some time, Jewish banks had relied on Christian investors for their capital. Until recently, this hadn't been a problem. The returns had generally been healthy; and given that investors received interest from Jews, rather than other Christians, no one could claim that they were profiting from usury. But now that the banks were teetering on the brink of collapse, many patricians were frightened they might lose their investments. They wanted the Jewish community to guarantee their deposits in the event of a failure – and refused to support the renewal of the *condotta* on any terms until such an assurance had been given.

This was no bluff. When a draft was put to the vote on 6 August 1565, it was rejected by a wide margin.[19] Quite suddenly, the Jews were stripped of their right to live in Venice. They were given one year to wind up their affairs – and then they would have to go. During that period, they were forbidden to either lend money at interest or sell second-hand goods. This was blackmail of the most brutish kind, most likely designed to force the Jews' hand rather than expel them per se. But for a few, nail-biting months, the Ghetto's future hung in the balance.

While the Jews scrambled to come to terms, the crisis in the banking sector began to spiral out of control. By preventing Jewish banks from operating, the Senate inadvertently added to the uncertainty of their position – leading skittish investors to withdraw their capital. What began as a trickle soon became a flood. This severely undermined the banks' solvency and put their survival in even greater jeopardy.

Eventually, a compromise was reached. On 16 March 1566, the Senate approved a new *condotta*.[20] Much to the Jews' relief, the Ghetto's existence was confirmed, moneylending was restarted, and the tax burden was lowered to a more manageable level. But in return, they had to pay a heavy price. Not only did the Senate slash interest rates to a new low, it also imposed tighter constraints on Jewish banking. It stipulated that there must be at least five Jewish bankers operating in the Ghetto at any time. In an effort to limit the fallout from any bankruptcies, it also banned Jewish bankers from owing money to Christians. From now on, Jewish banks would be dependent on other Jews for investment, many of whom were already extremely hard up. Even if they managed to weather the current storm, they would no longer be able to go on lending as they had before – or recover so easily from any future crises.

*

The Venetians were just getting started. Not long after the new *condotta* was confirmed, Suleiman the Magnificent died while campaigning in Hungary. Throughout his forty-six-year reign, he had been a constant thorn in Venice's side. Now he was gone, the Venetians could be forgiven for breathing a sigh of relief. His successor, Selim II, seemed to be cut from a quite different cloth. Known rather unkindly as 'the sot', he was a worldly, even epicurean figure, more at home in the harem than in the harness – and, at first, the Venetians saw no cause for concern. Quite the opposite, in fact: Selim went out of his way to assure them of his goodwill, and, in any case, the Ottoman army was still too busy fighting the Habsburgs to be much of a threat. But it was folly to underestimate him. Despite his unprepossessing bearing, Selim burned with the same restless ambition as his father, and recognized in Venice a rival whose destruction was long overdue. As soon as his throne was secure, he turned his attention towards Cyprus. It was an obvious target.[21] Its wealth was legendary. Under Venetian rule, it had become 'the Republic's richest overseas colony' by far,[22] exporting vast quantities of salt, sugar, cotton, and wine. More importantly, it occupied a strategically vital location. Less than 70 kilometres from the Anatolian coast, it was the key to Venetian trade with the Levant and posed a glaring obstacle to further Ottoman expansion in the eastern Mediterranean.

For a time, the Venetians believed that war might still be avoided. There had been threats like this before. Provided they didn't rise to Selim's provocations, there was a chance that diplomacy might yet defuse the crisis. So when a powder magazine mysteriously exploded in the Arsenale on 13 September 1569, the government said nothing – even though the finger of suspicion pointed squarely at Ottoman saboteurs.[23] But the time for delicacy was already long past. Early the following year, Selim arrested Venetian merchants in Constantinople.[24] This was too much for the Senate to shrug off. In retaliation, it ordered the detention of all Turkish subjects in Venice. This gave Selim the excuse he had been waiting for. On 28 March 1570, his ambassador informed the Collegio that, if Venice did not surrender Cyprus willingly, he would take it by force.

With war on the horizon, the Venetians hastily began casting around for help. Most European powers refused, but in Pope Pius V and Philip II of Spain, Venice found ready allies. Together, they assembled a great fleet of more than 200 ships: more than enough, in principle, to meet the Ottoman threat. At Philip's insistence, however, command was given to his great-nephew, Gian Andrea Doria – a pompous braggart with little talent for leadership. Not long after the fleet set sail for Cyprus, news arrived that Nicosia had fallen. The Venetians wanted to rush to its aid, but the cowardly Doria saw no point in carrying on. Over howls of protest, he ordered the fleet back to port. Cyprus was now on its own.

The very same day, the Ottoman fleet laid siege to Famagusta. Led by the formidable Marcantonio Bragadin, the city held out for almost a year. By the following summer, however, its strength was exhausted. On 1 August 1571, Bragadin sued for peace – hoping that the Ottomans would have mercy on the city. He was cruelly mistaken. When he arrived at the Ottoman camp, Selim's general had him clapped in irons, and Famagusta was sacked. Two weeks later, Bragadin – already gravely ill – was paraded around the ramparts with baskets of rocks on his back, before being hoisted up the mast of a Turkish galley and flayed alive in the town square.[25]

By then, a second relief expedition was already underway. After the disasters of the previous year, the pope had persuaded Philip II to join him and the Venetians in a new Holy League against the Ottoman Empire. This time, there was to be no messing around. Overall command was given to the dashing Don Juan of Austria; and by mid-August, the combined fleet was ready to sail from Messina. The Ottomans – having just finished mopping up the last pockets of resistance on Cyprus – now decided to try their luck. Realizing that Venice was practically undefended, they sailed into the Adriatic and made for the lagoon. When they saw the Christian fleet approaching, however, they quickly turned back and headed for Greece, where they would have the advantage – or so they thought.

On 7 October 1571, the two enemies met off Lepanto in the Gulf of Patras. The fighting was fierce, and at first, it seemed as if the Ottomans were gaining the upper hand. But in the end, Don Juan secured a crushing victory. The Ottoman fleet was decimated: 113 ships were sunk and 117 captured. Its commander, Ali Pasha, was killed, and more than 8,000 Turks were taken prisoner. The plunder, understandably, was colossal.

When news of the battle reached Venice on 18 November, the city exploded with joy.[26] Cheering crowds filled the squares; merchants decked out their shops with gold brocade; and a great triumphal arch was erected over the Rialto. As night fell, torches and candles blazed from every window; musicians played on street corners; and, in a delirium of wine and wonder, the dancing went on until dawn. Never had such a celebration been seen – or such a battle won. As the Spanish historian Fernando de Herrera later put it, Lepanto was simply 'the greatest victory the heavens ha[d] ever seen'.[27]

Such exuberance was perhaps excessive. In purely strategic terms, Lepanto had changed little. The Ottomans, though beaten, had not been driven back. Cyprus was still in their hands, and its recovery was, if anything, even more remote than before. Yet for the Venetians, the battle's significance could not be weighed in so fine a balance. For the past 200 years, the Ottomans had carried all before them. There was nothing they had set their eyes on that they had not seized, no ambition they had not satisfied. Now, all that was at an end. The myth of Ottoman invincibility had been shattered. And though Lepanto may not have marked the end of the war, the Venetians could fight on with renewed confidence – and the conviction that God was with them.

For Venice's Jews, Lepanto was less of a triumph. Ever since the *condotta* had been granted, they had been under growing pressure from the secular authorities. In September 1568, the Esecutori contro la Bestemmia (responsible for the suppression of heresy and other moral offences) ordered the destruction or correction of thousands of Jewish books, especially those published by 'foreigners' and 'Levantines'.[28] The outbreak of war had only made things worse. Even before hostilities had begun, the Venetians had held them responsible. The driving force behind it all was said to have been Joseph Nasi. After being sentenced to death by the Council of Ten for kidnapping his cousin more than a decade before, he had fled to Constantinople, where he had become one of the sultan's most trusted advisers. As a reward for his services, he had even been created duke of the former Venetian colony of Naxos. He was known to have been instrumental in convincing Selim to attack Cyprus, no doubt in the hope of being made either its king or, at the very least, its *beylerbey* (viceroy).[29] In February 1568, he was linked to a plot to blow a hole in the walls of Famagusta in preparation for a Turkish attack; many Venetians suspected that he had been behind the explosion at the Arsenale, too.[30]

But *all* Levantines were under suspicion – not just Nasi. Since they were technically Ottoman subjects, they were all treated as potential collaborators. This was particularly true of Marranos, who were thought to be duplicitous by nature. Shortly after the war broke out, a certain Righetto (alias Enriques Nuñez, alias Abraham Benvenisti) had been brought before the Inquisition on a charge of judaizing.[31] Under questioning, he confessed that he had only adopted 'a Christian identity from motives of self-preservation' and made no bones about his lack of belief.[32] Before he could be sentenced, however, he escaped from prison and took off to Constantinople, where he openly resumed his Judaism and joined the circle of Joseph Nasi. This last fact was particularly alarming. Prior to being handed over to the Inquisition, Righetto had also been investigated by the

Council of Ten for allegedly spying on Nasi's behalf – and here, it seemed, was the 'proof'.

Righetto's case was '[i]n no sense . . . a *cause-célèbre*'.[33] Even if he really had been passing information to the Ottomans, he was too insignificant a figure to have done any real harm. Nor, indeed, was he typical. Yet his guilt, if only by association, nevertheless reinforced the belief that Levantines – Marrano and Jew alike – were enemy agents, working against Venice's interests from within. More importantly, it also seemed to justify the government's decision, in early 1570, to detain the Levantine Jews along with all the other Turkish merchants in Venice – and to keep them locked up for the duration of the war.[34]

After the victory at Lepanto, the Venetians decided the time had come to take more decisive action. 'As an act partly of revenge, partly of thanksgiving', the Senate voted, on 18 December 1571, to expel Jews not only from Venice itself, but from *all* Venetian territories.[35] In the heady excitement of the moment, it seemed clear that economic sanctions no longer reflected either the magnitude of God's favour or the enormity of the Jews' supposed crimes. As some patricians noted, to retain the Ghetto would have been unjust, ungrateful, even impious. Only the complete dissolution of Jewish life would suffice.

*

No sooner had the Senate's decree been passed, however, than its absurdity became apparent. While the Venetians were keen to press on with the war against the Ottoman Empire, their support was melting away. Following Pope Pius V's death in May 1572, Spain withdrew from the alliance, claiming that the Turks had been punished enough. Unable to carry on alone, Venice had no choice but to sue for peace. The terms were humiliating. Venice agreed to surrender all claims to Cyprus and to pay the sultan 300,000 ducats in reparations. The sense of shame was acute. Lepanto had seemingly been for nothing. Worse still were the economic consequences. During the war, Venice had lost most of its merchant fleet.[36] This severely limited the range of its activities. Having already retreated from the Atlantic and the Black Sea, its ships were now forced to retire from the Mediterranean and confine themselves to the narrow waters of the Adriatic. Yet even there, Venice found itself at a disadvantage. During the war, much of the trade entering Italy from the East had been diverted to the papal port of Ancona, some 225 kilometres further south.[37] Coupled with competition from French, Dutch, and English shipping, this contributed to a slump in key commodities – and dealt a heavy blow to Venice's prospects.[38] As one scholar has put it, the 'good old times' seemed to be over.[39]

It would have been madness to expel the Jews at such a moment. Even in their enfeebled state, Jewish banks were still vital to the credit market; while Jewish merchants were among the few commercial agents with the connections – and wherewithal – to capitalize on remaining trade routes. However intense popular hostility may have been, Venice could not afford to 'sacrifice its own commercial and economic interests' merely for the sake of 'religious considerations'.[40] Already, Venice's rivals were lining up to entice Jews and Marranos away.[41] If the Republic was to avoid sliding into irrelevance, it needed not just to stop them leaving the city, but to encourage more to come.

The government's first step was to grant a new *condotta*.[42] This was designed to allow Jews to go on living in the Ghetto, while lending money on terms which even the most hostile patricians could accept. Its key innovation was to transform Jewish banks from profit-making businesses into something more like *monti di pietà*. From then on, Jews would be required to set aside 50,000 ducats for small loans to the poor. This sum was to be raised exclusively through taxes levied on the Jewish communities in the Ghetto, and interest rates were to be reduced to 5 per cent – just enough for banks to cover their expenses. This was, no doubt, a heavy burden for Jews to bear; but since they were tacitly encouraged to pursue other commercial interests on the side, they likely regarded it as a price worth paying. At the very least, it finally put an end to debates about the legitimacy of Jewish lending and safeguarded the Ghetto's future.

The second step was to make Venice more attractive to Jewish merchants. In December 1573, the Ten voted to grant safe conducts to Spanish and Portuguese Jews, and to anyone else of Jewish descent who wanted to settle in Venice.[43] It guaranteed that, provided they declared themselves to be Jews on arrival, lived in the Ghetto, and wore the yellow signs, they would be protected from religious harassment for as long as they remained in the city. This represented a gigantic shift in government thinking. Whereas, in the past, it had been careful to deal only with Levantines, whose origins were conveniently masked by their Ottoman guise, it was now appealing directly to Iberian Jews – in the full knowledge that most of them were Marranos who had cast off their Christian faith.

But in this lay a problem. While the Council of Ten may have been willing to overlook the uncomfortable background of any new arrivals, the new nuncio, Giovanni Castagna, was not.[44] Early the next year, he lodged a formal protest, accusing the government of encouraging apostasy, and demanding that it stop immediately. This was a bold request. As Castagna must have known, the pope had recently granted Jews similar concessions in his own territories – and any fool could see how pressing was the economic need. But the Venetians felt they could hardly refuse. However much international trade was struggling, few patricians were willing to risk an open breach with the nuncio just then. When the bill came before the Senate, it was reluctantly rejected.

This didn't mean that Venice was closing its doors altogether, of course. If Spanish and Portuguese Jews wanted to come to the city, even without a safe conduct, officials didn't *have* to ask them where they had come from – and they didn't *have* to say, either. As long as no one made a fuss, the thinking seems to have gone, the nuncio wouldn't be any the wiser. Granted, the numbers of Jewish arrivals wouldn't be as high; but given enough time, such a policy might well have worked.

Unfortunately, time wasn't something Venice had. In 1575, the city was struck by the plague. In the words of one modern historian, '[i]t was a visitation as dramatic and terrifying as the Black Death over two centuries before'.[45] Although several eminent doctors confidently claimed that it would only affect the lower classes, it ripped through Venetian society with undiscriminating speed. Soon, the Lazzaretto Vecchio was so full of the sick and the dying that 'it seemed like Hell itself'.[46] In a desperate effort to contain the infection, old galleys were hastily converted into floating hospitals and towed out into the lagoon, and houses suspected of harbouring the plague were placed under quarantine. But nothing seemed 'able to stop . . . the furious pestilence'.[47] As one Jewish scribe put it, the city – once 'thought to be the perfection of beauty' – now became 'desolate'.[48] The mortality was appalling. According to the notary Rocco Benedetti, so many died that the stench of burning bodies became too much to bear.⁴⁹ Shops drew down their shutters; inns closed; even '[a]dministration became chaotic'. Trade virtually collapsed. A blockade was imposed on any city where an outbreak had been reported, which, given that most of Italy had been overrun, effectively cut Venice off from mainland markets. Unemployment shot up. Never had Venice seen such poverty. Realizing the scale of the crisis, the government scrambled to raise funds for poor relief; but even if this softened the blow a little, it did nothing to alleviate the desperation of most people.⁵⁰

By the time the plague finally abated two years later, Venice was in a pitiable state. According to Cornelio Morello, an official at the Provveditori alla Sanità, at least 50,000 people died – around 30 per cent of the total population.⁵¹ Few families had escaped unscathed. Many had been 'wiped out altogether'.⁵² The city wreathed itself in grief, scarcely daring to believe that the horror might be at an end. As Andrea Morosini remarked, all courage had turned to fear, all hope to despair.⁵³

In time, the first shoots of recovery began to appear. In the spring of 1577, the Senate commissioned Andrea Palladio to build a new church on the island of Giudecca, in thanks for Venice's deliverance. Among the labouring classes, standards of living began to rise. Now that there were fewer workers competing for jobs, the survivors were in a far stronger position than before.⁵⁴ Employment and wages quickly rebounded. The damage to Venetian commerce was less easily repaired. Trade routes, already few and fragile, had been abruptly severed; businesses had foundered; and confidence, once lost, could not readily be regained.

More so than ever before, Venice needed new opportunities. Happily, Daniel Rodriga – a Levantine Jew, most likely of Portuguese origins – had the solution. In early 1577, shortly after the plague was officially declared over, he put forward a proposal to establish a new port – or *scala* – at Spalato (modern Split) on the Dalmatian coast.⁵⁵ His idea was that goods could be brought overland from the Balkans, then loaded onto ships at Spalato and taken across the Adriatic to Venice. This would dramatically reduce not only the risks of piracy, but also the cost of shipping to Venetian merchants.⁵⁶ Even more importantly, being further north, it would divert trade away from Ragusa (Dubrovnik) – and hence cut the volume of goods sent to Ancona. At a stroke, it would tilt the balance of power in the Adriatic back in Venice's favour. All Rodriga wanted in return, he said, were a handful of privileges for merchants of any nation then living in Venetian territory. He was careful not to mention any *specific* merchants; but from what followed, it is clear that he had Levantine and Iberian Jews in mind.[57]

This was just what Venice needed. Recognizing the potential of Rodriga's proposal, the Senate quickly agreed to establish a *scala* at Spalato – and no doubt revelled in the thought of the riches it might bring. If Rodriga was expecting any gratitude, however, he was cruelly disappointed. The Senate refused to grant any new concessions, least of all to Jews. From a commercial perspective, this made little sense. The Senate did not seem to realize that, if it did not give Jewish merchants the freedom to capitalize on their connections in both Italy and the Ottoman Empire, the new port would struggle to reach its potential.

Ostensibly, the reason for the Senate's refusal was political. Venice had never granted commercial privileges to non-citizens before – and there was no reason to break with tradition now. It might even have been dangerous: as the Cinque Savi alla Mercanzia pointed out a little later, it was likely – even probable – that Rodriga's Jews would quickly dominate new trade routes between Venice and the Balkans.[58] Given that many were Turkish subjects, the thinking went, there was a risk that, if another war with the Ottoman Empire broke out, they would turn against Venice – taking a good portion of its trade with them. The *main* reason, however, was religious. No matter how intense Venice's economic need, it could not grant concessions to any Jews who might be apostates without running afoul of the nuncio.[59] Unless it could find some way of getting around this issue, its hands were tied.

Undeterred, Rodriga tried again. At some point before 21 June 1579, he petitioned the Venetian government for permission to bring around fifty Jewish families to Venice.[60] He promised that each would contribute at least 100 ducats to the state treasury in customs duties each year – and asked only that they be granted the same privileges as the Jewish merchants and bankers already living in the Ghetto. When this was rebuffed, he tried a third, then a fourth time. On each occasion, he changed his proposals a little, in the hope of mollifying concerns or playing on the sympathies of newly elected officials. In 1584, in fact, he could hardly have petitioned for less, requesting only safe passage for married Jews who were living in Venice without authorization. But each time, he received much the same response. Either the Cinque Savi 'deferred' their decision until a later date – or they rejected his proposals out of hand.[61]

The pressure on Venice was rising. Despite steady growth in some sectors, such as wool and silk production, the city's economy was taking another turn for the worse.[62] In 1584, the Pisani-Tiepolo bank collapsed, forcing the government to create a state-run bank – the Banco della Piazza – simply to 'keep money safe' and enable businessmen to make transfers.[63] Ship production faltered. In 1589, Bernardino Rosso still hadn't sold his latest ship after three years and had to petition for government subsidies just to keep his business afloat.[64] To cap it all, piracy in the Adriatic became more frequent.[65] Inevitably, with food now harder and more expensive to import, the cost of living increased and the real wages of many labourers faltered.[66]

Rodriga seems to have sensed his opportunity. Early in the summer of 1589, he submitted a new proposal for a charter (*condotta*) of privileges.[67] This was bolder and more ambitious than any of his previous schemes. It requested that 'Jewish, Levantine, Spanish, and other merchants' should be allowed to live securely with their families anywhere in the Venetian state, with the freedom to come and go without molestation, and to trade throughout the Adriatic; that they could live and worship as Jews, without being subject to investigation by any magistracy, secular or ecclesiastical, even 'if they had lived ... according to another religion elsewhere'; that, in case of a war with the Ottoman Empire, they would not be detained or otherwise imprisoned, or suffer any reprisals against their families or property; that, although they would pay the usual customs duties, they would not be required to contribute towards the upkeep of Jewish banks in the Ghetto and would devote themselves entirely – and exclusively – to trade; and, finally, that they would be given a quarter of their own in Spalato, where they would be allowed to live with their families and enjoy all the same privileges.

It was almost impossible to say 'no'. On 20 June 1589, the Venetian government agreed to send Rodriga's proposal to the Cinque Savi alla Mercanzia for their opinion; and a week later, a report was submitted.[68] It could hardly have been more positive. Given 'the state of trade at present', the preamble read, there was no doubt that Venice's economy would be strengthened if more merchants came to live in its territories – or that certain guarantees and privileges would have to be made if they were to be tempted away from other states.[69] Rodriga's request was therefore approved, almost without alteration. Indeed, in a striking volte-face, the Cinque Savi even noted that the settlement of Jews in Spalato would be 'very useful for promoting the port . . . and facilitating' its trade with Venice.[70] The only significant qualification concerned religion. Since the Cinque Savi were responsible only for trade, they declined to make any recommendations about Rodriga's request for ecclesiastical immunity. This meant that, in principle, the Inquisition would still be free to investigate any Iberian Jews it suspected of apostasy. Such caution was perhaps pardonable. Anything else would surely have aroused the nuncio's ire. But, as Rodriga must have realized, it threatened to deter many former Marranos from coming altogether – potentially derailing the whole project.

The government had gone too far to turn back now, though. Later that afternoon, the Senate approved a new *condotta* by a huge majority, and in doing so, made one small – but vital – alteration.[71] Realizing that the nuncio's only real problem with Iberian Jews was that they *came from* Iberia, the Senate decided to refer to them as 'Ponentine' (Western) Jews instead. This was a patent fiction, but it was enough to conceal their true origins – and to mask their presumed apostasy from the Inquisition's gaze, after a fashion.

Provided they wore the yellow *baretta* and paid 'the usual customs duties', 'Levantine and Ponentine Jews' would be allowed to live with their families in the Ghetto for a period of ten years, during which time they were encouraged to trade as much as they possibly could. They would have the right to elect their own officials and tax themselves as required; they were promised a safe haven in times of war; and they would be answerable for their commercial affairs only to the Cinque Savi alla Mercanzia. Rodriga – now recognized as 'consul' (*Console*) of the Jews – was triumphant.[72]

This marked a dramatic shift in Venice's relationship with its Jews. Under the terms of the new *condotta*, Iberian Jews now enjoyed a degree of equality far greater than in many other parts of Europe. Though they were still not on 'an equal footing' with Venetian citizens, Levantine and Ponentine merchants benefitted from commercial privileges no other foreigners had ever been granted.[73] They were, more importantly, free to be Jews. However much churchmen like Castagna and his successors might protest, Marranos could resume their faith with some impunity; and all Jews could worship without fear or hindrance. The price of this (relative) freedom was still confinement; but thanks to the Senate's great fiction, the bonds seemed to be loosening at last.

7

The Golden Age

(1589–1630)

By the time of Daniel Rodriga's death in 1603, the Ghetto was entering its golden age. Although in many other parts of Italy, the fierce glare of the Counter-Reformation had caused anti-Jewish policies to harden, in the lagoon, pragmatism had eclipsed prejudice, and mere tolerance was beginning to shade off into a benign acceptance.[1] Within the bounds of an increasingly porous confinement, everything possible was done to nurture Jewish life. Religious freedom was assured for all professed Jews; commerce was encouraged; and, shy of citizenship itself, every legal protection was accorded to the Ghetto's inhabitants. Only rarely were flashes of the old hostility glimpsed in government policy, and even those seemed to lack conviction. Assured of their safety, and attracted by almost unmatched opportunities, Jews flocked to the city from far and wide – so much so that, within thirty years or so, the population had almost tripled.[2]

Such remarkable stability had been made possible by a transformation in Venice's relations with the papacy. Already strained when the Senate approved Rodriga's charter, these quickly deteriorated in the wake of a dramatic – and irrevocable – decline in the Serenissima's economic fortunes. Granted, the danger seemed slight at first. In the decade or so after 1589, Venetian trade and manufacture were showing signs of recovery. Imports from the Levant shot up to almost three times their previous level; spices flooded in from Alexandria and Beirut; and fresh supplies of cotton and silk boosted the already thriving cloth industry.[3] Yet these sprigs of hope belied a deeper – and more lasting – sickness. Nowhere was this more evident than in the merchant marine, which, until then, had been the pride and foundation of Venice's commercial prowess. Shipbuilding, already struggling in the aftermath of the plague, was now sliding into a crisis so severe that, by the end of the century, Venice was actually 'buying more ships abroad than she built at home'.[4] This left a void which the English, the French, and the Dutch were more than happy to fill. With more ships, better manned and more vigorously defended against pirates, they were now vying for dominance of Mediterranean trade – much to the alarm of Venetian merchants.[5]

This underscored how necessary – indeed, essential – the Levantine and Ponentine Jews were. Though a few patricians were still concerned about entrusting so much of Venice's trade to foreign nationals, most recognized that Jewish merchants were vital to the Republic's commercial fortunes.[6] Fearing, rightly, that Italian princes like the Grand Duke of Tuscany were already anxious to lure them away, Venice therefore hastened to assure them of its goodwill.[7] On 20 June 1590, the Senate approved a slew of new privileges demanded by Rodriga, including an undertaking to set aside new living quarters if there was not enough space in future;[8] and eight years later, their *condotta* was renewed, with only rare voices being raised in opposition.[9] Though, in contrast to the previous charter, this now required the Jewish merchants to contribute to the upkeep of the Tedeschi banks in the Ghetto Nuovo, its terms were once again remarkably generous. As the preamble stated:

> At this time, even greater are the reasons which on other occasions induced this Council to permit the residence of Levantine and Ponentine Jewish merchants in this city and their trade in the places of our state, principally for mercantile trade which is so important to the public service . . .[10]

Beyond the constraints set out in the charter itself, nothing was allowed to interfere with Jewish commerce – even the Church. There was no open breach, of course; but a quiet independence began to creep into Venice's dealings with the ecclesiastical authorities. Though the papal nuncio continued to protest about the presence of Marranos in the city, the Venetian government greeted his appeals with polite disinterest. The Inquisition, too, was slowed. As one observer noted, discreet but 'insuperable difficulties' always seemed to get in the way of its proceedings – even in the most blatant cases of apostasy. In the last decade of the sixteenth century, 'just one sentence was recorded for the crime of judaizing'.[11] By 1599, an inquisitorial dossier could claim – with only slight exaggeration – that Venice had become a 'free city' (*città libera*), in which no one, Marrano or Jew, need fear the Inquisition's gaze.[12]

*

Alone, however, even Jewish merchants could not arrest Venice's economic decline. Over the past few years, the Ottoman Empire had been experiencing a severe monetary crisis. In an effort to impose some stability, the currency was abruptly devalued in early 1600.[13] This gave European coins – even debased or counterfeit coins – an 'unusual value in eastern markets'.[14] English, French, and Dutch merchants, who could command a ready supply of hard cash, were hence able to buy goods at 'unusually low prices'. For the Venetians, however, the devaluation came at exactly the wrong time. Just then, Venice was extremely short of coins, and had foolishly taken the recovery of its manufacturing sector as a sign that it should focus on trading in its own products. The result was sudden and devastating. Foreign merchants snapped up all the goods that the Venetians had previously shipped from Beirut, Smyrna, and Alexandria. Coupled with a peace treaty between England and Spain in 1604, which allowed English ships to pass more easily through the Strait of Gibraltar to northern markets, this contributed to a catastrophic decline in Venice's struggling maritime trade. Over the next few years, the volume of goods passing over the Serenissima's quays dropped by an estimated 40 per cent – more, perhaps, than even the most pessimistic had feared.[15]

The sudden collapse of trade forced the Venetians to shift their attention towards the land. Though somewhat peripheral to Venice's traditional outlook, it was now recognized that agriculture, if managed properly, 'might be made to supply the income which the sea could no longer provide'.[16] Already, some of the more forward-looking patrician families had begun to transfer their investments from the fleet to the fields; and the opportunities afforded by rising grain prices were proving hard for even the most conservative to resist.[17] If this trend continued, it had the potential to boost Venice's tax revenues, overcome a growing shortage of food, and revive domestic trade, all at the same time.

There was only one problem. Much of the land on the *terraferma* was then in ecclesiastical hands. According to Cardinal Roberto Bellarmino, the Church owned at least 25 per cent of the estates in the Venetian *dominio* and was looking to acquire even more.[18] This obviously reduced the amount of land available for purchase by laymen. But what made it even more troubling was that ecclesiastical lands were also exempt from taxation and generated revenues that were sent to Rome, rather than remaining in the local economy.

Clearly, if Venice wanted the *terraferma* to be the panacea it so desperately needed, something would have to be done. But what? Opinion was divided.[19] Some of the more established members of the government – known as the 'Old' (*vecchi*) – argued for caution. They believed that if Venice trusted to its traditional policy of neutrality and avoided antagonizing the Church too much, some sort of arrangement might yet be found. Others preferred a more confrontational approach. Known, inevitably, as the 'Young' (*giovani*), they could see no point in clinging to the past. Times had changed, they argued: unless Venice changed with them, its wealth and prestige would be lost forever. Like it or not, that meant tackling the papacy's challenge head-on.

Had the papacy shown even a little restraint, caution might still have carried the day; but the annexation of Ferrara, followed by an ill-judged attempt to seize control of a Venetian subject town, convinced the government that a more assertive policy was now required. Between 1603 and 1605, the Senate passed a series of laws banning any new churches from being built anywhere in Venetian territory without the government's permission and preventing the Church from acquiring any more land through bequests.[20] As the Venetians were keen to point out, neither of these pieces of legislation was altogether new. They merely extended to the *terraferma* restrictions which had previously applied only in the capital. But the Curia could not help seeing them as a direct assault on the Church's interests – which, of course, they were.

Tensions were rising fast. What had begun as a matter of landholding was fast becoming a question of whether Venice – or the Church – exercised ultimate authority. The Venetians still wanted to avoid an open breach if they could.[21] It was hoped that, now the Senate had taken a stand, the Republic would be in a stronger position to negotiate a favourable settlement. When the Council of Ten ordered the arrest of two clerics in October 1605, however, any possibility of a diplomatic solution was confounded. They were a tawdry, unpleasant pair, scarcely worth the trouble they were to cause. One, Scipione Saraceni, was accused of public indecency; the other, Marcantonio Brandolino, of sorcery, incest, and murder.[22] There was no doubt they were guilty, but for Pope Paul V – who had been elected just a few months before – all that was irrelevant. The only thing that mattered was that they were in holy orders. A 'true pope of the Counter-Reformation', he believed that he had been chosen by God to defend the Church's supremacy in all matters touching the spirit.[23] To his mind, it was intolerable – even heretical – for the Venetians to have arrested Saraceni and Brandolino. As clerics, they could only be tried by an ecclesiastical court – regardless of their supposed crimes. Unless Venice released them immediately, he thundered in consistory, it would be excommunicated.

At this, the Venetians balked. The new doge, Leonardo Donà, was a leading member of the Young, and had been chosen precisely because of his determination to uphold the Republic's sovereignty, come what may.[24] Though pious to the point of austerity, he valued the authority of his own conscience above that of the Church, and had no fear of excommunication. He refused to hand over the clerics; and so, at the beginning of May 1606, Venice and all its territories were placed under interdict.

A war of pamphlets now broke out. Of Venice's polemicists, the most effective was Paolo Sarpi, the state theologian. A Servite friar, then well advanced in years, Sarpi was a brilliant, broad-minded scholar who had twice been denounced to the Inquisition for his unorthodox views and dalliances with heretics.[25] After republishing the anti-clerical works of Jean Gerson, he penned an anonymous tract arguing that, in all temporal matters, the Church should be subject to the secular authorities. This was swiftly placed on the Index of Forbidden Books, prompting him to respond with further, even more excoriating tracts – including an attack on benefices that many feared might spark a second Reformation.[26] On his advice, the Venetian government disregarded the interdict and forced priests to administer the sacraments. But it seemed increasingly likely that the dispute would have to be settled by force of arms. After some hasty diplomacy, Venice allied with France and Paul V with Spain – and before long, large armies were readying for battle.

When the crucial moment came, however, the two sides hesitated. For all their fiery rhetoric, they each had too much to lose from war. A peace was therefore brokered. Though Venice refused to admit any fault, it agreed that, if the pope lifted the interdict, it would surrender the two clerics to the king of France, who would then hand them over to the pope on his own authority. The legislation limiting the papacy's acquisition of new lands 'was not repealed' but 'neither was it enforced', and the Venetian government's right to treat errant clergymen just like any other citizens was quietly – if grudgingly – acknowledged.[27] This fell far short of what Sarpi would have liked; but for the Venetians, it was a victory of sorts.

*

For the Jews of Venice, it was little short of a triumph. Any lingering doubts about their economic utility had been dispelled, once and for all. Still reeling from the collapse in maritime trade, Venice was now prevented from recovering its losses on the *terraferma* to quite the extent it had hoped. Unless the Republic could reach an agreement with its commercial rivals – a proposal to which the Old were implacably opposed – it could not hope to address, much less overcome, the decline in its fortunes without the help of Jewish merchants.[28] It also needed their help to combat the risk of poverty. Though the English traveller Thomas Coryat claimed to have seen a 'great abundance . . . of victuals' during his visit to Venice in 1608, the unsatisfactory resolution of the struggle still left the city prone to fluctuations in both prices and real wages.[29] If it was to withstand any future shocks, it therefore had to be sure that the poorest still had access to credit – which it could only achieve by relying more heavily on the Jewish loan banks.

On 21 June 1611, the Senate therefore renewed the charter of the Levantine and Ponentine Jews by a large – albeit not overwhelming – margin.[30] It would have done so sooner, but for a jurisdictional dispute between the Cinque Savi alla Mercanzia and the Ufficiali al Cattaver (also known simply as the 'Cattaveri').[31] For the most part, the terms were the same as in 1598. But there were a few significant changes. In the first place, the safe conduct was now extended to all Levantine or Ponentine Jews who had arrived in Venice before 1589, or who might come there in future – a measure clearly intended to help retain long-standing residents and attract new arrivals. In the second place, all Levantine and Ponentine merchants were now definitively required to contribute to the expenses of the loan banks run by the Tedeschi Jews in the Ghetto Nuovo. Only visiting merchants lodging in the Ghetto Vecchio and the Jews of Corfu were exempt.

This was not an uncontroversial decision. When the idea had first been proposed, more than a decade before, the Levantines and Ponentines had protested in no uncertain terms. In March 1607, Joshua Ferro – who had succeeded Daniel Rodriga as their consul – argued that they already paid more than 50,000 ducats in import duties and did not need burdening with any more impositions.[32] But the Senate evidently felt it necessary to guarantee the banks' stability. Since the banks were forced to lend at very low rates of interest, they were continually at risk of running a loss, and since their funds were raised only from taxes on German Jews, there was a limit to how far they could sustain this.[33] It is possible that some additional capital was raised from abroad, but the Senate reasoned that the only way of ensuring their liquidity was to have the Levantine and Ponentine Jews contribute as well – so that trade would effectively subsidize lending.

This had two important effects. Firstly, it made the Ghetto a more permanent component of the Venetian economy. Now that banking and trade were inseparable, it would be difficult, if not impossible, for the government to interfere with either without damaging the other – not to mention its own interests. Secondly, the sharing of responsibilities welded the Jewish communities together as never before. Whereas, in the past, Germans, Levantines, and Ponentines had each operated more or less independently of one another, the fact that responsibility for the banks now fell on all residents of the Ghetto meant that a much greater degree of co-operation was necessary. To meet this need, the Università degli Ebrei was hence set up to act as a 'mechanism for joint decision making'.[34] Although each community continued to negotiate its own *condotte* and administer its own religious affairs (including synagogues, ritual baths, and charity funds), the Università came to serve as the Ghetto's semi-official government, collecting centralized taxes, arbitrating in disputes, and administering its own business.

The Università consisted of two main bodies: the Large Assembly and the Small Assembly.[35] The Large Assembly was effectively the 'lower house'. It was open to any male resident who paid at least 12 ducats a year in tax and was principally responsible for choosing members of the Small Assembly. As the Ghetto's main executive body, it handled most of the community's day-to-day affairs. It was assisted by two smaller committees, responsible for banking and tax assessments. None of these bodies was ever truly 'representative'. Surviving records show that, in 1607, only about 11 per cent of the Jewish male population voted in the Large Assembly. Nor was it free from divisions. As was only to be expected, the banking committee was split along ethnic lines. Nor, indeed, was it even stable. During the period 1607–24, the size and function of each body changed radically. Yet the Università was an undeniably *collective* enterprise. Once called into being, it held the disparate groups together – and from many people, forged a single Ghetto.

*

Venice's struggle with the papacy also made the Ghetto safer than ever before. Now that the Republic had asserted the supremacy of its own authority, it was free to extend its protection to both Jews and Marranos without fear or restraint. This did not mean that religious hostilities had altogether disappeared. From time to time, there were still some outbursts of official antisemitism, chiefly motivated by fears of social contagion. Shortly before the interdict was imposed, the Cattaveri ordered certain doors in the Ghetto Vecchio to be walled up, 'low balconies' to be fitted with iron bars, and a new wall to be built to stop Jews from leaving.[36] A little over a decade later, the Cattaveri again warned about the danger of balconies, and commanded Jewish residents to respect the laws which had been designed to protect neighbouring Christians from 'infection'.[37] But such actions tended to be the exception rather than the rule, and were vigorously opposed both by the Jewish community itself and by other organs of the Venetian government.[38] Provided there were no egregious affronts to Christian sensibilities, *ragione di stato* was given precedence over religious scruples, and every effort was made to shield those of Jewish origin from ecclesiastical prosecution. Whereas previously, the government had been content merely to put difficulties in the way of inquisitorial investigations, it now embarked on a more systematic policy of obstruction, which could sometimes border on the aggressive.[39]

The basis of the Venetians' position was summarized by Paolo Sarpi. In late 1616, he wrote a *consulto* denying the Inquisition's right to investigate anyone of Jewish descent.[40] Since the Holy Office had authority only over 'the baptized', he began, it plainly had no jurisdiction over Jews.[41] Nor could it judge judaizing Marranos. Although, as Christian apostates, they technically fell within its purview, Sarpi noted that all those then living in Venice had received safe conducts allowing 'them to come and live with their families . . . in the Ghetto . . . and *to exercise their rites and ceremonies without impediment*'.[42] These safe conducts had been granted according to the law and were hence inviolable. More importantly, Sarpi argued, they also served the interests both of Venice and of Christendom itself. Anyone could see that, if Venice did not offer them its protection, they would simply take their great 'wealth and industry' to 'the lands of the Turks'.[43] And since various popes had given similar assurances to Marranos in their own territories in the past, the Venetians had a clear precedent.

A typical case occurred in the summer of 1608. Towards the end of May, the papal nuncio, Berlinghiero Gessi, learned that two Portuguese Marranos, Antonio Rodrigues and Manuel da Costa, had gone to live in the Ghetto as Jews, after previously living in Venice as Christians.[44] In the Ghetto, they took the names Iosef and Moise Masaod. This naturally aroused the Inquisitor's suspicion; but when he raised it at a meeting of the Holy Office, the lay *assistenti* refused to take any action, apparently on the grounds that it would have an adverse effect on trade. Gessi was usually quite restrained in his dealings with the Venetian government, but this was clearly unacceptable.[45] The following month, he asked the Collegio to open its own proceedings instead. To his alarm, the doge, Leonardo Donà, refused. Donà pointed out that the Masaods had come to Venice under safe conducts which protected their previous lives from investigation, and that these had to be respected.

Undeterred, Gessi tried again a week later – and three more times over the summer. Each time, he met with the same response. The doge was intransigent: there was no way Venice could break the safe conducts. Even if it could, Donà asked, what good would that do? If the government started digging into the Masaods' past, the doge argued, the whole Ghetto would be in uproar. A good many merchants would probably leave for Constantinople, too. And supposing the Masaods did turn out to be apostates? Surely it was better that they lived openly as Jews in the Ghetto than falsely as Christians in the city? Granted, this wasn't ideal, but even if Venice couldn't claim to have acted perfectly, then it had at least chosen the lesser evil. Besides, the doge added, there were plenty of Marranos in Ancona – and the pope didn't seem to mind. This rattled Gessi. In a series of testy exchanges, he replied that, while there were certainly Jews in Ancona, there weren't *any* Marranos, and that *no* pope would ever have tolerated apostasy. Clearly furious, he resolved to bring the Masaods' case before the Holy Office again, perhaps hoping to use his authority to force it through; but just as the Inquisition was about to meet, one of the *assistenti* quietly slipped him a copy of a papal bull issued by Julius III clearly stating that the Marranos of Ancona were not to be bothered. With that, the whole affair was dropped.

No less striking was the case of Simon Gomez, some eight years later.[46] Much like the Masaods, Gomez and his family were Portuguese Marranos who had lived as Christians in Pisa for some years before coming to live in Venice as Jews. Not long after his arrival, however, the Pisan Inquisition got wind of his apostasy and asked its Venetian counterpart to take him into custody. Once again, Gessi took the matter up. He argued that, if the Holy Office did not send Gomez back to Pisa, it would only encourage more judaizing Marranos to come. The *assistenti* were not so sure, and asked Paolo Sarpi for his advice. This was uncompromising.[47] Sarpi repeated that the safe conduct granted to the Gomez family was inviolable and had a precedent in the papacy's own policy towards the Marranos in Ancona. He also noted that neither Gomez nor his family had been accused of committing any crime in Venice itself. Indeed, as far as he could tell, they were living quietly in the Ghetto, 'wearing the red hat and not causing any scandal'. As such, Sarpi reasoned, allowing anyone to investigate them for their past would not only be a betrayal of the promise they had been given, but would also 'open the door to innumerable troubles' and cause all manner of confusion, without delivering any tangible benefit. The Venetian government seems to have agreed. Nothing came of the case – and Gomez was presumably left in peace.

*

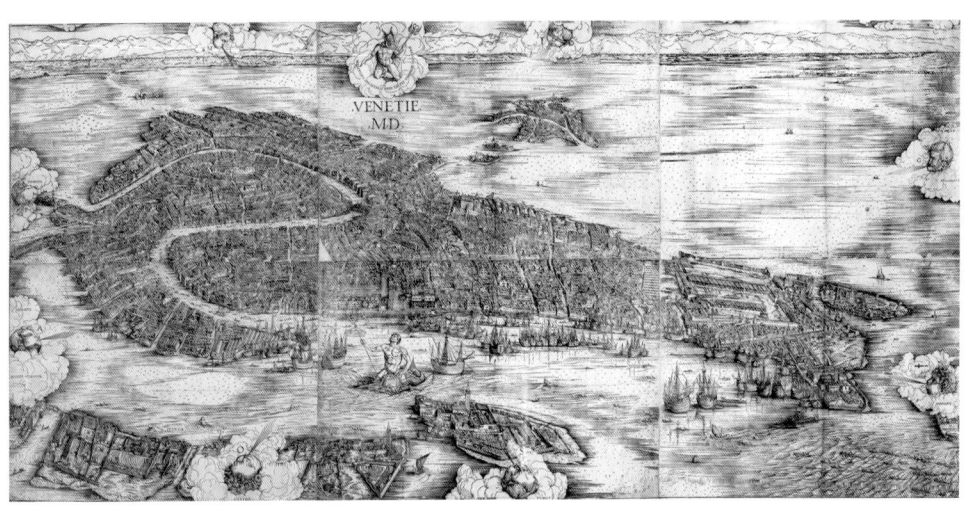

1. Jacopo de' Barbari's *Veduta di Venezia* (1500), a depiction of Venice as it would have appeared shortly before the Ghetto's foundation.

2. The martyrdom of Simon of Trent as shown on a broadsheet printed in 1475.

3. A portrait of Doge Leonardo Loredan by Giovanni Bellini, 1500.

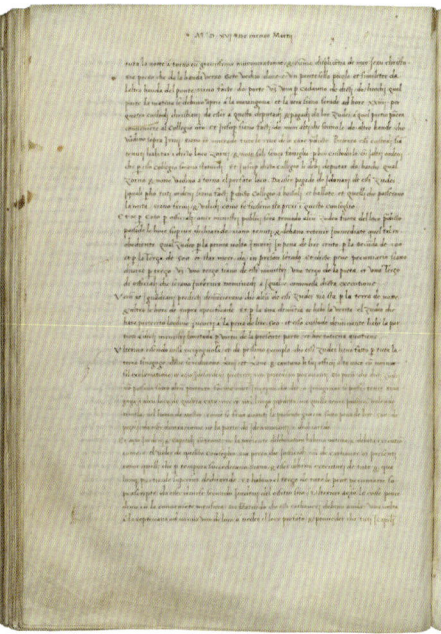

4. The senate decree establishing the Ghetto Nuovo in March 1516.

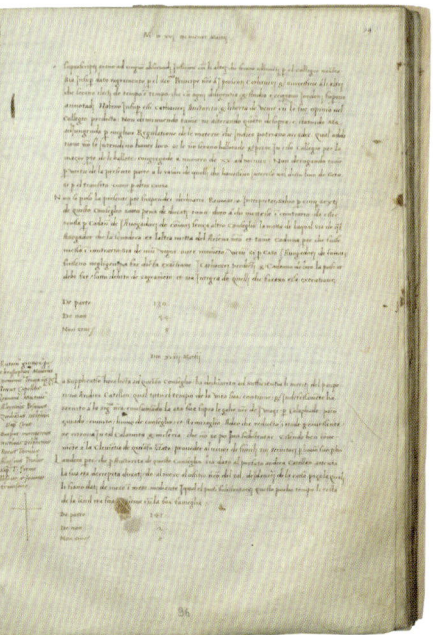

5. The Campo del Ghetto Nuovo. The well in the foreground still bears the arms of the da Brolo family, who owned the island when the Ghetto was founded.

6. Bricked-up windows and quays along the Rio di Ghetto Nuovo.

7. Facade of the Scuola Italiana. The cupola (rounded dome) above the bimah – the raised platform used for Torah readings – can be seen peeking out from between the rooftops.

8. View of the Scuola Canton from the Campo del Ghetto Nuovo.

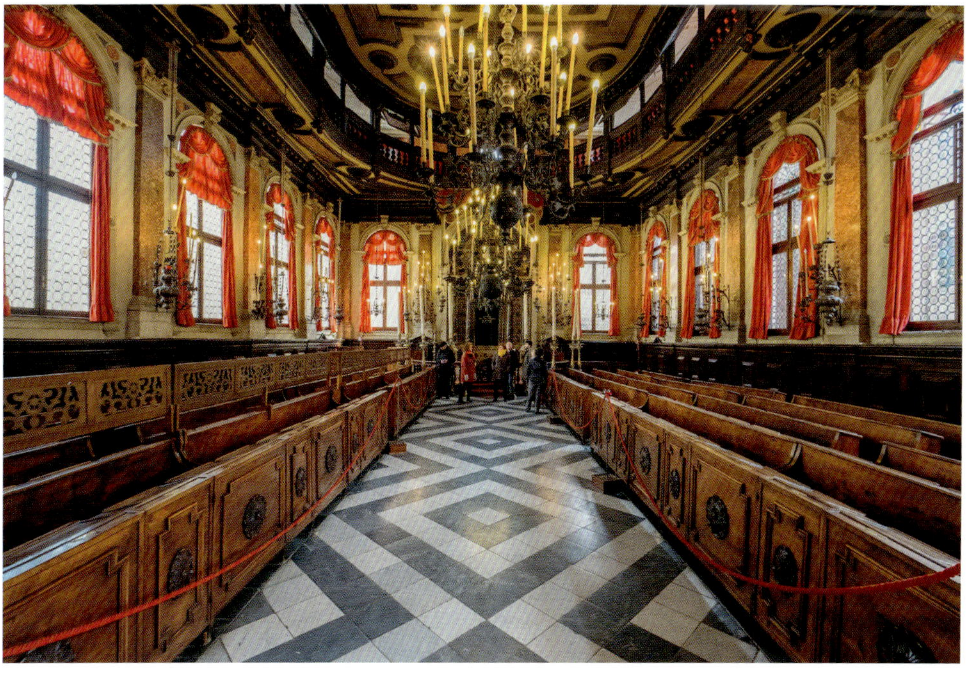

9. Interior of the Scuola Spagnola (or Ponentina).

10. Portrait of Ludovico Beccadelli by Titian, painted in 1552, the year before Beccadelli oversaw the burning of Jewish books in the Piazza San Marco.

11. A portrait of Leon Modena, shown here as a detail from the title page of the 1638 edition of his *Historia de' riti Hebraici*.

12. Portrait of a young woman thought to be Sara Copia Sullam, attributed to the artist Antonio Lagorio.

13. Title page of Sara Copia Sullam's 1621 *Manifesto*, a masterpiece of wry condescension in which she rebutted accusations that she had denied the immortality of the soul.

14. Santa Maria della Salute, commissioned by the Venetian government at the height of the plague of 1630–1.

15. The Banco Rosso, one of the three Jewish loan banks in existence by the end of the sixteenth century, as it appears today.

16. An eighteenth-century drawing of a Jewish body being carried by gondola to the cemetery on the Lido.

17. A drawing of the Canale degli Ebrei from July 1688. The canal was cut so that Jewish funeral boats could avoid being pelted with stones by boys standing on the bridge of San Pietro.

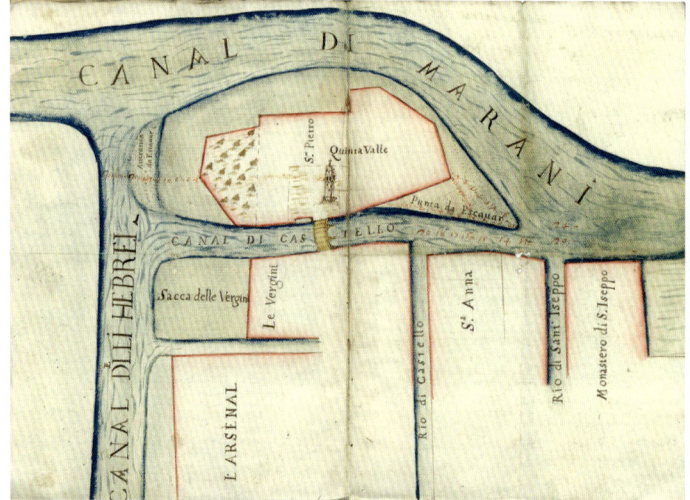

18. The Jewish Cemetery on the Lido.

As the Inquisition's influence waned, life in the Ghetto thrived. Buoyed by prosperity and migration, the population began to rise steeply. Thomas Coryat was likely exaggerating when he claimed that there were 'betwixt five and six thousand' Jews in Venice by 1608, but he was probably not far off.[48] One modern estimate puts the figure at around 3,000 – and it had almost certainly risen even higher by 1630.[49]

This put considerable pressure on housing. Within a few years of the interdict, buildings in the Ghetto Nuovo were so overcrowded that some Tedeschi Jews were reported to be abandoning their assigned lodgings and inveigling themselves into other people's houses, presumably in the Ghetto Vecchio.[50] Illicit 'improvements' were common: families built rickety balconies, or even entire storeys, onto their apartments, usually without their landlords' permission. In 1604, Daniel Rodriga's family, who were still living in the house Daniel had first rented from Camilla Minotto almost thirty years before, were stopped just before they could start 'enlarging' the property; another man, Jacob Saracin, had already smashed through his attic wall by the time the Venetian authorities intervened – much to the dismay of his neighbours.[51]

With so many people living in such close proximity, hygiene became a pressing concern. By 1609, so much waste was being produced that it posed a danger to public health. A Brescian landowner named Iseppo Paolini put forward a plan to dig a new refuse pit in one of the squares, most likely in a corner of the Campo del Ghetto Nuovo.[52] This was to be equipped with five decent-sized openings and was intended to be emptied on a regular basis. Access points were another major issue: by 1613, the Agudi bridge had to be completely rebuilt – apparently by the residents themselves – to prevent it collapsing under the weight of everyone who came in and out of the Ghetto every day.[53]

Shops, too, began to multiply.[54] There were already kosher bakeries in each of the two ghettos and a good number of butchers, greengrocers, oil sellers, and wine merchants. Most of these tended to cater to a specific community – Levantine Jews almost never bought food from 'German' shops, and vice versa – but there were still a few food shops which sold to everyone (as the locals put it, *senza pregiudizi* – 'without prejudice'). At least one, owned by Fidela Scaramella, was even run by a Christian.[55] There were also tailors, barbers, booksellers, hatters, wood carvers, quack doctors – even a nurse for Jewish children.[56] And new shops were opening their doors all the time.

Religious life, enlivened by the growing sense of permanence and self-confidence, became richer and more vibrant. During his visit, Coryat counted at least seven different synagogues: five in the Ghetto Nuovo (the Scuola Grande Tedesca, Scuola Canton, and Scuola Italiana, plus the smaller Scuola Luzzatto and Scuola Coanim) and two in the Ghetto Vecchio (the Scuola Levantina and Scuola Spagnola or Ponentina). A third, the Scuola Mesullamim, was added before 1635. Several of these underwent extensive renovations.[57] At the Scuola Italiana in the Ghetto Nuovo, new brickwork was added, a women's gallery was installed, and a cupola was opened in the ceiling above the *bimah*.[58] It can still be seen today, peeking out from between the rooftops. A short time later, the Scuola Spagnola (or Ponentina), was completely remodelled to accommodate its growing congregation.[59] In 1612, a new plot of land was purchased; a nearby well was filled in; and some neighbouring buildings were knocked down. The following year, a committee was appointed to oversee the construction, and over the next few decades, leading Christian artists were commissioned to decorate the interior in a style which would have done honour to the grandest of Venetian *palazzi*. Great pilasters of fake marble flanked the windows; a vast *aron* was built; and – unusually – a rail was placed around the ark. As in the other synagogues, the effect was enhanced by an abundance of liturgical objects donated by pious worshippers, including gilt crowns, silver *yadim* (ritual pointers), rich brocade curtains, fine pewter pitchers and basins, and much more besides.

Visitors could scarcely believe the magnificence. Coryat marvelled at the 'great company of candlesticks in each Synagogue' – and was quite taken aback by the elegance of the worshippers.[60] The men were as handsomely turned out as they were devout, while the women, seated high above in a 'loft or gallery', were glamorous, almost to a fault. Some, indeed, were 'so gorgeous in their apparel, jewels, chaines of gold, and rings adorned with precious stones, that some of our English Countesses do scarce exceede them'.[61] Alongside the formal religious life of the synagogues, kabbalah – a form of Jewish mysticism – flourished. Back in 1575, Rabbi Menahem Azariah da Fano had introduced public lessons after the morning service; and since then, their importance had steadily grown – to the point where they rivalled the *yeshivas* as a venue for religious learning, especially for those who lacked knowledge of the Talmud. Stressing the need to seek out new paths to the divine, even in everyday life, these were popular in focus and inclusive in nature. Unlike Talmudic study, they were open to both women and men; while preaching took place 'in those special vernaculars that . . . would later give rise to the various *judesmos*, such as Yiddish or Ladino, and the varieties of Judeo-Italian'.[62]

Cultural life, too, burst into flower, fuelled in part by the growing diversity of social and religious experience. Jewish poets, philosophers, and playwrights launched into a flurry of creativity; Jewish printers operated presses in defiance of the ban imposed in 1548; and Jewish music and dancing took Venice by storm. Well before the interdict, the Venetian government had exempted certain performers from the long-standing prohibitions on mixing with Christians. In November 1590, a troupe of Jewish musicians were granted a licence to put on *una opera premeditata*; while in January 1597, a man called Iseppo was given permission to perform in patrician houses with two other lute players during the carnival season 'until the sixth hour of the night'.[63] In the decades that followed, attitudes relaxed still further. This did not mean that *all* forms of music were accepted – in June 1613, a Jewish singer called Rachel was banned from going around the city in a gondola without the Cattaveri's permission, on account of her scandalous behaviour[64] – but such examples were increasingly the exception rather than the rule. Indeed, by then, music was already forging a close bond between the Jewish and Christian worlds. In 1611, the Small Assembly voted to put on a suitable dance performance to please the doge 'on the day of his festivities', while in 1617, dance-master Camillo Rieti was authorized to teach in Christian homes.[65]

Life in the Ghetto was not always rosy. Although some Jews were rich enough to impress visitors with their dress, poverty was not unknown. After the interdict, the Inquisition prosecuted a licensed beggar who had himself baptized several times over, just for the money, and a poor Polish woman who was scraping a living as a nurse after spending many years as a slave in southern Italy.[66] They were clearly not alone. By the early seventeenth century, the Ghetto housed several charities which had been set up to support poorer members of the community. There were many confraternities devoted to giving alms, providing dowries for poor maidens, clothing the needy, and paying for the release of prisoners, among other charitable efforts.[67]

The presence of so many people in the Ghetto inevitably caused tensions. Neighbours were constantly bickering, and different communities regarded each other with mistrust, even hostility. One shopkeeper, whose establishment was supposed to sell produce *senza pregiudizi*, complained that the rivalry between Sephardim and Ashkenazim was so intense that 'it was not even safe to stay at home'.[68] Violent crimes were far from uncommon. Even visitors were sometimes threatened. One day in 1608, Coryat was debating the divinity of Christ with a rabbi in the Campo del Ghetto Nuovo when he suddenly found himself surrounded by 'forty or fifty Jewes', who wrongly believed he was insulting their religion. Afraid they might hurt him, Coryat began edging towards the bridge – where, by a stroke of good luck, he was rescued by the English ambassador, Sir Henry Wotton.[69]

Yet the Ghetto was no more prone to disorder than any other part of the city – and these incidents did nothing to interfere with the wider efflorescence of Jewish society, or its integration into Venetian life.[70] Quite the opposite: precisely because there were such tensions, there was a strong incentive for community leaders to resolve them peacefully, or at least to minimize their effects. This not only strengthened Jewish self-government, but also fostered closer co-operation with the Ghetto's Christian neighbours. It was not unknown for the head of a family to attempt to resolve a dispute by calling on a patrician to mediate or to witness an agreement.

*

One of the Ghetto's most prominent residents was Leon Modena. A rabbi by vocation, a cantor by profession, and a gambler by habit, he was a prolific author of books in both Hebrew and Italian. Of these, perhaps the most intriguing is an autobiography – the *Hayyei Yehuda* ('Life of Judah').[71] Covering a period of some thirty years – from the death of his eldest son in 1617 to shortly before his own in 1648 – it offers a remarkably vivid portrait, not just of one man's life, but also of the Ghetto itself.

Modena was born in Venice on 23 April 1571.[72] His father, a pawnbroker and merchant, came from a French family which had probably fled to Italy after the persecutions of the fourteenth century, while his mother was from Apulia. His ancestors had settled first in Viterbo, then in Modena, where they grew so rich that they adopted the city's name in gratitude. One branch later moved to Bologna, before finally putting down roots in Ferrara. Shortly after Modena's mother fell pregnant, Ferrara was struck by an earthquake, forcing his parents to take refuge in Venice; eight months later, they returned home, baby in arms. As Modena was fond of telling people, he was a precocious child. At the age of two and a half, he 'recited the Haftarah in the synagogue'; at three, he could 'translate the weekly Torah portion' into Italian; at twelve, he rendered some of the more pornographic sections of Ariosto's *Orlando Furioso* into Hebrew; and at thirteen, he was already writing his own poetry.[73]

In the summer of 1590, Modena returned to Venice to marry his cousin Esther. The match had been arranged by his mother, and the whole family were looking forward to the celebrations. When they arrived, however, they found Esther confined to her bed. No one thought it was anything serious, but 'her illness grew worse by the day' – until, a week later, 'at the hour of the Sabbath bride, [she] departed . . . for eternal life'.[74] Modena was distraught. But under pressure from his relatives, he was eventually persuaded to marry Esther's sister, Rachel, in her stead.

It was not an easy relationship. Rachel, too, had fragile health. During their years together, she suffered from regular bouts of fever, gout, and *petechiae* (red or purple spots). Modena feared for her life on at least one occasion.[75] She was also prone to mental illness – so much so that he later despaired of her sanity. This put a strain on married life. Rachel was always picking fights, often for no reason at all. Modena, in turn, 'would grow angry and shout and act foolishly'. His 'blood would boil', his 'heart would flutter', and his 'insides would churn up'. Sometimes, it seemed as if they did nothing but quarrel. Modena couldn't help feeling bitter. He blamed Rachel for holding him back. After one particularly turbulent summer, he claimed that her 'strange' moods had been 'the destruction, ruin, and desolation of my money, body, honour, and soul'.[76] Yet they loved each other deeply, after their own fashion. Modena described Rachel as his 'other half' – and was forever asking God to bless her name.[77] Shortly after the first anniversary of their wedding, she gave birth to a son, Mordechai, and over the next twelve years, they went on to have another six children.

Modena had long been destined for the religious life. Almost all his forebears – apart from his father – had been noted rabbis. It had simply been assumed that he would follow in their footsteps.[78] The day after his wedding, Rabbi Solomon Sforno granted him the title of *haver* (companion), signifying that he was competent to receive ordination;[79] and, two years later – after a brief, misguided attempt at running a business in Montagnana – he returned to Venice, intent on pursuing a rabbinical career.[80] At first, he was confident of finding a position. In 1593, he preached his first sermon in the Scuola Grande Tedesca to some acclaim. As he noted, '[m]any great and venerable sages were present, and the crowd was so large that the synagogue could not hold them'.[81] But his timing could hardly have been worse. Just months later, the Jewish laity, having grown tired of the rabbis' overweening influence, raised the minimum age for rabbinical ordination to thirty-five.[82] Since Modena was still only in his early twenties, this stymied his ambitions – at least for the time being.

Modena fell into a deep depression. He despaired of ever moving to Venice. 'My heart calls out for the past, is startled by the present, and is terrified of the future', he wailed.[83] But with a wife and two children to support, he could not afford to mope for long. He soon found other ways of scraping a living. He took in pupils, proofread books, and continued to preach in the synagogues.[84] He also composed poetry for various occasions – including one poem in both Hebrew and Italian celebrating the birth of the future King Louis XIII of France.

It was a meagre existence. His pupils were few and fickle, and he often complained of poverty.[85] To make ends meet, he began looking for employment elsewhere. In 1604, he accepted a job as a tutor in Ferrara, but disliked the place so much that he soon came back to Venice.[86] In desperation, he took up gambling.[87] He knew it was wrong, of course. Although Jews were not *forbidden* to gamble, the Talmud condemns it[88] – and as a boy, he had actually written a dialogue against it.[89] But once he'd started, he couldn't stop. 'Satan' kept urging him on. Inevitably, he lost more often than he won. His debts quickly mounted, until eventually, in 1608, his behaviour became 'so wild' that he had to go to live in Florence for a while.[90]

While in Tuscany, Modena finally received his rabbinical ordination. He was now able to issue halakhic judgements on his own authority; and on his return to Venice, in 1610, was chosen by the leaders of the Scuola Italiana to serve as their *hazzan* (cantor).[91] This was a prestigious, if demanding, role. Modena was required to lead prayers in the synagogue three times each day, preach every Saturday morning, and sing *kaddish* for the dead – as well as a host of other tasks. It wasn't a permanent post, either: technically, Modena had to be reconfirmed every August. But he was so highly respected by his congregation that he was shortly appointed to the synagogue's governing body – which had responsibility for electing its officials.

Modena's star was rising fast. His sermons 'blaze[d] a truly new path', while his *responsa*, once halting and uncertain, now became assured, confident, even compelling.[92] His style was, by common consent, unimpeachable. Where he excelled, however, was at interpreting the Talmud in light of social realities – both within and beyond the Ghetto walls. In the first years of his rabbinate, he defended a Jew's right to go bareheaded in public (on the grounds that, in Italy, no one thought it amiss); attacked those who played ball games; and banned Jews from taking boats on the Sabbath.[93] Such was his authority that, before long, his opinion was being sought by Jewish leaders from as far away as Hamburg and Amsterdam.[94] His fame even grew among Christians. He often boasted of preaching before Venetian nobles. On one occasion, his sermon in the 'synagogue of the Sephardim' was attended by none other than 'the brother of the king of France'. His learning was especially appreciated. He was on friendly terms with the English ambassador, Sir Henry Wotton; corresponded with the Marrano physician David Farar in Amsterdam; and was most likely the learned rabbi with whom Coryat debated the divinity of Christ in 1608.[95] In 1611, his former student Jean Plantavit de la Pause even offered him the chair of oriental languages at the University of Paris.[96]

Modena's life was still precarious, though. His salary as cantor was only 20 ducats per year – a fraction of what he needed to support his family – and teaching was as unreliable as ever.[97] Frequently short of money, he tried his hand at no fewer than twenty-six different professions[98] – from matchmaking, translating, and 'drawing up contracts' to 'selling books of arcane remedies' and trading in amulets. None of them brought him much success, however.

His family was a constant source of worry, too. Though his daughters each married into good families, they were painfully unhappy. Esther's husband had to flee the city after getting mixed up in a bribery scandal,[99] while Diana's second husband mistreated her.[100] Modena's sons, meanwhile, were haunted by tragedy. Mordechai, the eldest, died after inhaling arsenic vapours during one of his alchemical experiments; Isaac developed a gambling habit and ran away to Brazil; and Abraham died of smallpox before his first birthday.[101] Zebulun, the youngest, suffered the worst fate of all. He was a handsome young man, with an easy manner and the voice of an angel.[102] 'Wise, understanding, and cheerful', he had inherited his father's talent for writing both poetry and prose. But he could also be 'bitter' and 'impetuous' – and had caused his father no end of trouble.[103] For some years, he had been feuding with a certain Shabbetai Benincasa, against whom he had given witness in a trial.[104] One day, in the summer of 1621, their argument grew so heated that Shabbetai snatched up a butcher's knife and chased Zebulun out of the Ghetto, down to Cannaregio. Luckily, Zebulun grabbed a sword that a peasant was carrying over his shoulder and turned the tables, driving Shabbetai into the canal. At this point, Modena intervened. Before the dispute could turn *really* nasty, he called on the patrician Alvise Giustiniani to make peace between them. This should have been the end of the matter, but Shabbetai was seething. On Friday 25 March 1622 – the night before Passover – he gathered a group of roughs and attacked Zebulun in the street, only moments after passing Modena himself. Caught unawares, Zebulun didn't stand a chance. He was hit over the head, then stabbed in the throat. Blood spurted out 'like a spring'. By the time a doctor had 'bandaged his wounds', Modena wrote, 'there was no longer enough of it left to keep him alive, and his entire right side lost all feeling'.[105] Three days later, he died. He was two weeks short of his twenty-first birthday.

Life was not all sorrow, however; Modena's days were peppered with celebrations and festivals, friends and good cheer. He took an enthusiastic part in the work of Jewish societies;[106] composed songs for friends and family;[107] and was always ready to laugh at his own expense.[108] He enjoyed regaling people with his wit and took pleasure in defusing tense moments with a joke.[109] Most of all, he took joy in his writing. His output was prodigious, even by the standards of the Ghetto's unusually literary rabbis.[110] In his autobiography, he lists twenty-eight books – both published and in manuscript – and almost as many poems and prefaces in other volumes.[111] Even this represented only a small part of his literary output. He admitted to writing a great many more verses – most of which he had forgotten – and 'no end' of additional sermons and commentaries. By necessity, most of his works were devoted to Jewish religion and law; but his interests were anything but narrow. His writings included *Rachel and Jacob*, a pastoral comedy; the *Galut Yehuda* ('Exile of Judah'), a 'translation of words [from] the Bible into Italian, accompanied by some grammatical rules'; the *Ari nohem* ('Roaring Lion'), an attack on kabbalah; and the *Lev ha-aryeh* ('Heart of the Lion'), on 'place' memorization.[112] Perhaps his most remarkable work was the *Historia de' riti Hebraici*. Written at the request of Sir Henry Wotton, who intended to present it to King James I, this was a brief account of Jewish customs and beliefs. It contained nothing particularly surprising, least of all to anyone living in the Ghetto, but it was the first Jewish text aimed at an exclusively gentile audience since Josephus' *Antiquities* almost 1,500 years before.

*

No one, however, better encapsulates the assurance, excitement, and uncertainties of the Ghetto's golden age than Sara Copia Sullam. She was born in around 1592 to a wealthy family of Venetian Jews and was related, on her father's side, to Leon Modena's wife. Recognizing her evident intelligence, her parents took care to provide her with a good education. As well as Italian, Venetian, and *giudeo-veneziano* – the local dialect of Venetian Jews – she understood both Spanish and French, as well as some Hebrew and Latin.[113] She knew vernacular poetry as well as she did Jewish scripture, if not better; and her interests extended from philosophy and theology to astrology and music. One of her correspondents later recalled that, even as a child, she 'delighted in reading books of poetry and [on] various odd subjects'.[114]

As was the custom, she was married at a young age.[115] Her husband, Giacob Sullam, was a prominent banker. Like Leon Modena, his family most likely came from Provence, spending some time in Mantua before settling in Venice. He was a gentle, kindly man, whose wealth allowed him to provide his young wife with a comfortable – if not luxurious – life. He was active in community life, served as one of the Ghetto's tax assessors, and was a leading figure in the Scuola Italiana.[116] Most importantly, he seems to have placed a high value on learning and actively encouraged Sara's literary interests.

In 1618, Sara had a miscarriage. While she was recuperating, she happened to read Ansaldo Cebà's poem *La Reina Esther*.[117] It was a forgivable choice. Cebà was a Genoese nobleman who had enjoyed some fame as a love poet before taking holy orders – and *La Reina Esther* was meant to be his masterpiece. All of Italy was talking about it. Copies had been sent to the leading men of letters, and when the book finally reached Venice, it was eagerly snapped up. But sadly, Cebà had no talent for epic. Critics mocked his pompous, overwrought style and poked fun at the 'vanity' of the ageing cleric.[118] Sara, however, was so enchanted that she wrote Cebà a letter to express her admiration. She claimed that she cherished *Esther* so greatly that she kept a copy on her pillow – and even compared it to Homer's *Iliad*.[119]

Cebà was understandably flattered, and the two struck up a lively correspondence. Their letters were, at first, rather theological: Cebà trying to convert Sara to Christianity, and Sara cheerfully defending her Jewish faith. But their tone soon became more playful and intimate. They began to exchange poems: sonnets heavy with classical allusions, *canzone* 'composed out of tears', even teasing little madrigals.[120] Presents flew back and forth: books, a comb case, keepsakes – 'meagre' things, perhaps, but all the more precious for being so.[121] They even sent each other their portraits – a sure sign that affection was blurring into love. The sonnet which accompanied Sara's likeness left Cebà in no doubt about her feelings, or about the pain the distance between them was causing:

> The image is that of her who, in her heart,
>   Carries, sculpted, your image alone,
>   And who, with her hand on her breast, indicates to the world:
>   'Here I carry my idol, let everyone adore him.'
> With her left hand she supports love's weapons
>   That were your poems, her right hand signals
>   The place where she is wounded, pale and bewildered,
>   She says: 'Ansaldo, my heart is dying for you.'
> She comes before you as a prisoner
>   Asking help and she offers you that

> Chain from which my love is faithful and constant.
> Oh, accept the shadow of your faithful handmaiden,
> And may my feigned appearance enjoy, if anything,
> What an auspicious star denies these eyes.[122]

Cebà more than reciprocated. His own poems were written in a consciously Petrarchan style and overflowed with delicate, if occasionally rather strained, compliments. Hailing Sara as the 'queen of my heart', he praised her 'charms', her 'golden . . . hair', her 'reddish cheeks', her 'beautiful eyes and beautiful tresses'. He admired her pride, her compassion, her 'lynx-like' shrewdness, and especially her modesty and virtue, while teasingly chiding her for her make-up.[123] In his eyes, she was perfect – and he asked nothing more than to be her 'most ardent servant'.

The two never met. Even had it been possible, they each knew that faith and convention would keep them apart. Their love was, by choice and necessity, platonic. Sometimes, however, Cebà could still forget himself. His professions of love, though always couched in terms of propriety, came perilously close to compromising both his vows and Sara's friendship. On 18 October 1619, he cheekily noted that her name *Coppia*, with a double 'p', meant 'couple'; and hoped that this meant they might one day be 'a "couple" as a Christian and a non-Christian'.[124] Sara was appalled. Straight away, she 'removed a consonant' from her name, 'reducing it from Coppia to Copia' – and spelt it that way for the rest of her life.

Around the same time, Sara also began hosting a salon (*salotto*).[125] Meeting regularly at her home in the Ghetto, this informal and eclectic gathering of learned men – both Christian and Jewish – discussed the latest trends in literature, art, and philosophy, and was no doubt intended to help Sara establish herself as a serious writer.[126] Other than her kinsman, Leon Modena, the group included Baldassare Bonifacio, a scholar and future bishop of Capodistria; Giovanni Basadonna, a prominent senator, renowned for his skill in Latin letters; Alessandro Berardelli, an artist of modest, if uninspired, talent; and Numidio Paluzzi, a dissolute Roman poet whom Sara employed as her tutor – as well as four or five others.

Sara proved to be a glittering hostess. Poems were composed and read; Cebà's portrait was displayed; and music was performed, including by Sara herself. She sang so delightfully 'that she almost removes souls from bodies and returns them to heaven among the blest'.[127] Above all, the discussion sparkled. Later recollections show that learning, worn lightly, was leavened with delicate wit; and even the most leaden of subjects discovered its charm.

Yet every Eden has its snake, and every paradise its fall. Although Sara's guests were happy enough to accept her hospitality – not to mention her financial support – they soon turned on her. In 1621, after a brief exchange of letters, Baldassare Bonifacio published a treatise accusing Sara of denying the immortality of the soul.[128] This was a serious charge: if found to be true, Sara could have been prosecuted for heresy by both Jewish and Christian authorities. Realizing the danger, Sara hastily penned a 'Manifesto' in her defence.[129] It was a masterpiece of wry condescension. Why, she asked, had Bonifacio attacked her, a woman of modest learning? Clearly, it wasn't because she was guilty. She had always regarded the immortality of the soul as 'indisputable'.[130] Nor could she believe it was out of malice. Most likely, she reasoned, Bonifacio had simply wanted to seem learned – and had used her as his foil. But if this was his goal, he had blundered. Anyone could see that he was 'neither a Philosopher nor a Theologian'.[131] His Latin was poor, his Hebrew worse.[132] His argument was 'so replete with erroneous conceptions . . . inappropriate quotations . . . and errors of language' as to be almost laughable.[133] Far from being a brave soldier of truth, she chuckled, he was a clerical Don Quixote – marching across the field of battle, 'striking blows in the air' and shouting 'victory' to no one in particular.[134] Bonifacio was evidently hurt. He rushed a response into print.[135] It was a tawdry, confused little affair. Protesting that he had never meant to attack Sara, he claimed he had acted merely out of friendship and insinuated that Modena must have been the brains behind the 'Manifesto' all along. It cannot have convinced many, but the damage had already been done. Now that Sara's orthodoxy had been publicly questioned, Cebà took fright. While her dispute with Bonifacio had been rumbling on, he had been accused of 'obscenity', and *La Reina Esther* had been placed on the Index of Forbidden Books.[136] He could not afford to take any more risks. Forgetting all his previous protestations of love, he abruptly broke off their correspondence.

After Bonifacio withdrew from the salon, Paluzzi slunk towards centre stage. Having contracted syphilis some years earlier, he was in a bad way. Out of kindness, Sara paid for him to take the cure at a steam bath. When he returned, she then arranged for him to lodge with her laundress, Paola Furlana. Not long after he had settled in, Paola told him about a scam she had cooked up with Sara's Moorish maid, Arnolfa. Playing on Sara's love of the occult, they pilfered whatever valuables they could, then convinced her that 'aerial' spirits must have stolen them. Paluzzi needed no encouragement to join in; but since he was still too weak to stand, he recruited Berardelli to help. Together, they added another layer of absurdity to the scheme. Appealing to their patron's vanity, they told Sara that a 'great [French] prince' had heard of her spectral visitations and wanted to learn more.[137] Sara was thrilled. After reading letters purportedly written by the 'prince', she was persuaded to send him a portrait – painted, of course, by Berardelli – together with a 'jewelled ornament, which in its gold, gems, and construction, rose in value to a hundred ducats'.[138] Needless to say, the tricksters pocketed the lot.

In July 1624, Giacomo Rosa – a former acquaintance of Cebà's – stumbled on the plot and immediately went to tell Sara.[139] Understandably, she was furious. She dismissed Paluzzi as her tutor and reported Berardelli to the authorities. Neither Paluzzi nor Berardelli had any shame. Perhaps recalling Bonifacio's strategy, they published a pamphlet accusing Sara of plagiarizing Paluzzi's poems, and after Paluzzi died in the summer of 1625, Berardelli kept the fantasy going. Though patently ridiculous, it played on the contemporary prejudices against female writers and gave a glutinous credence to Bonifacio's earlier insinuations. This stung Sara where it hurt most. Fortunately, an anonymous manuscript soon appeared in her defence.[140] This rather eccentric work is cast, for the most part, as a record of Paluzzi's fictional 'trial' on Mount Parnassus, the home of the muses. Apollo, the god of truth and philosophy, presides over the proceedings; Pietro Aretino (1492–1556) acts as the chief prosecutor, while the poets Vittoria Colonna (c.1490–1547) and Veronica Gambara (1485–1550) – assisted by Sappho and Corinna – are tasked with weighing the evidence. It is all very proper. The court is presented with transcripts of Berardelli's trial before the Signori di Notte al Criminal; witnesses are called; and the accused is given a chance to present his side of the story.[141] There are even some calls for mercy.[142] But the verdict is never in any doubt. Found guilty, Paluzzi is sentenced to be pilloried, branded, and forced to wear bells around his leg for all eternity – a fitting punishment for so flagrant a fraud.

For Sara, it brought little satisfaction, though. She had been betrayed too many times. The fire which had once blazed so brightly within her had been extinguished for ever. After Paluzzi's death, she gave up writing altogether – a grievous loss for Italian and Jewish literature alike.

Sara was in every way exceptional. She was hardly a typical Jewish wife. Her salon, her poetry, and her correspondence set her apart from most women, who were largely constrained by custom to the care of their families.[143] Nor was she a typical Venetian *salonnière*. Though she sought to emulate great literary hostesses of the past, whose gatherings were almost as famous as their verse, she was barred by religion from taking her rightful place in their ranks. Simply because she was *not* a Christian, her friendship could be accepted without loyalty and her patronage abused without regret. Yet precisely for this reason, she embodies the Ghetto's fragile brilliance. Her hunger for learning, her cosmopolitanism, her restless ambition, her suffering – all spoke to the excitement and vulnerability of Jewish life. In her short, glittering career, she showed that despite everything, the Ghetto was there, not just to stay, but to shine.

PART III

Decline

8

Bodily Sickness

(1630–1663)

The future looked bright. By 1630, Venice was the best place in the world to be a Jew. With only scattered exceptions – Guyenne, Strasbourg, the Low Countries – Christian Europe was growing ever darker and more unwelcoming. In Muscovy, persecution was the norm; in France, the edict of expulsion was reaffirmed; while in England, the presence of a few court doctors did nothing to temper the long centuries of exclusion.[1] Even in Poland-Lithuania, the proverbial *Paradisus Iudaeorum*, new hostilities were stirring.[2] Almost alone, Venice stood apart. There, surrounded by the shimmering waters of the lagoon, Jews could live in relative peace and prosperity. As the rabbi Simone Luzzatto (c.1583–1663) observed, nowhere else did they enjoy such freedom, such 'exemplary justice', such abundant wealth.[3] To be sure, the Ghetto had gone through some difficult times. Then nearly fifty years old, Luzzatto had seen more than his fair share of troubles.[4] Born into a wealthy family from north-eastern Germany, he had been ordained just as the interdict was imposed, witnessed at close quarters the complex negotiations for the renewal of the *condotta*, and, as rabbi of the Scuola Grande Tedesca, had often been called upon to rule on the disputes which were so much a part of Ghetto life.[5] But had he paused to look back, all that would have seemed 'as chaff before the wind'.[6] Anyone could see that the Ghetto was indispensable to Venice's survival. Now that the Republic's days of glory were past, its fragile economy was reliant on Jewish enterprise. When the city prospered, they both shared the profits; when it did not, the Ghetto still gained. Seated comfortably in the synagogue, Luzzatto could have been forgiven for thinking that a glittering future lay ahead.

But just as the Ghetto seemed to be embarking on its most glorious years, disaster struck. In the autumn of 1630 – as a futile war over Mantua was grinding to a close – Venice was hit by plague. Since the first cases had been identified in Piedmont and western Lombardy the previous winter, it had spread across northern Italy with slow but inexorable determination. The devastation was staggering – even worse than in 1575–7. Over the next two years, the pestilence killed over 60,000 people in Milan alone; in Parma and Verona, 61 per cent of the population was wiped out.[7]

The Venetians were slow to recognize the danger. Despite a flood of reports from the mainland warning of the plague's approach, the government refused to place the city under quarantine. Professors from the University of Padua assured the Provveditori alla Sanità (Board of Health) that the epidemic was not 'really' the plague – and its officers were only too ready to believe them. One of the few doctors to disagree, Giovanni Battista Fuoli, was ordered to keep his mouth shut, so as not to disturb trade.[8] By the time the government realized its error, it was too late. In a frantic attempt to stem the tide of infection, the Arsenale was ordered to make 1,000 new beds for the plague hospitals; a fleet of barges was built to take dead bodies away for burial; and convicted criminals were offered pardons to work as *pizzigamorti* (body clearers).[9] It was to no avail. Soon, the *lazzaretti* were overflowing with the sick and dying. Shops closed; taverns shut; businesses folded. Even the churches bolted their doors. Venice became a ghost town. As one contemporary recorded,

> in a short time the city was left almost completely derelict; those who could escaped the blaze [of the disease] and the afflicted city remained diminished, emptied of courage and filled instead with unhappiness and misfortunes.[10]

The Ghetto was no exception. No sooner had the plague been reported in Venice than people in the Ghetto Vecchio started falling sick. The Ghetto authorities did their best to contain the spread. Anyone who was infected was confined to their home;[11] and, in all probability, the healthy were advised to take precautions similar to those recommended by the Paduan physician Abraham Catalano at about the same time, such as social distancing and stockpiling provisions.[12] It did no good. By March 1631, around 170 people had perished. Panic set in. Many Jews, especially Sephardim, fled to Verona, or even the Levant. Those who stayed faced a grim prospect. In Leon Modena's building, almost no one was spared. 'Above me and below me', he wrote, 'and on all sides . . . people have been taken ill and died'.[13] All he could do was pray – less in hope than in desperation.

Then, quite suddenly, the impossible happened. While the plague was 'growing in severity elsewhere in the city', the mortality in the Ghetto began to ease off. For three months, Modena claimed, not a single person 'fell ill or died'.[14] Ironically, the Ghetto's high walls and prison-like gates seem to have shielded it from infection. To Modena, it was little short of a miracle. 'Even the gentiles were astonished', he claimed. Indeed, if his complaints about the increase in 'stealing, cursing [and] lying' are any guide, it seems that some semblance of normal life may even have resumed.

Any hopes of escaping the worst were soon dashed, however. Though segregation may have reduced the contagion for a time, it could not eliminate the pestilence altogether. By the early summer, cases started to rise once again – and 'many people began to die in both ghettos'. Even if the 'death toll . . . never reached the rate of mortality in the rest of the city' and fell far short of that experienced by Jewish communities elsewhere, it was still high enough for men to curse their hubris. As one contemporary put it, 'daily one sings lamentation and moans'.[15]

*

When the plague eventually subsided, in November 1631, the city erupted in celebration. At the height of the epidemic, the Senate had commissioned Baldassare Longhena to build a new church dedicated to the Virgin Mary at the entrance of the Grand Canal.[16] Now the danger had passed, the Venetians naturally attributed their deliverance to her. On 28 November, the doge and his suite solemnly processed across the Grand Canal on a bridge of boats to do her homage with all the pomp and splendor the Serenissima could muster – and it was declared that, for ever after, the Feast of the Presentation of the Virgin would be a day of public thanksgiving.

In the Ghetto, all the old rivalries were forgotten. A fast was decreed for the first night of the month of Kislev (25 November), and the following day, the 'Nishmat Kol Chai' – a hymn of rejoicing usually reserved for the Sabbath – was added to the prayers for the new moon. A collection was taken in every synagogue to commemorate the community's salvation, and everywhere there was 'the pleasant sound of joyfulness'.[17]

Yet no rejoicing could obscure the pitiable state in which Venice had been left. In a little under a year, 46,490 people had died – almost a third of the total population.[18] When the rest of the lagoon was included, the figure rose to over 90,000. Losses were especially pronounced among children. In 1630 alone, more than half of infants died before their first birthday.[19] The elderly were not far behind. So many died that, by 1640, the average age had plummeted from a pre-plague high of 31.95 to just slightly over 20 years old.[20] Quite suddenly, Venice found itself a city of fatherless sons and childless mothers – lost souls, just setting out on life, looking at the past with regret and to the future with fear.

The Ghetto fared little better. Though the demographic blow was not so severe as elsewhere in the city, the Jewish population fell precipitously. Some 454 residents died – which, assuming a pre-plague population of around 3,000, represented about 15 per cent of the community.[21] It was impossible to bury them all properly. In the Jewish cemetery on the Lido, the monument reads simply '1631 Hebrei' – as if a whole people had perished.

The survivors faced an uncertain future. During the epidemic, Jewish merchants had been forbidden to trade; shopkeepers had seen custom dry up; and rag dealers had been forced to surrender their stock to prevent further contagion. According to Modena, '[s]even hundred and fifty bales worth much money were sent to the Lazzaretto, and almost all of them were destroyed or lost'.[22] No one seemed to be earning anything. Despite this, the Venetians had continued to make heavy financial demands. In total, the Jewish community was forced to hand over 'more than 120,000 ducats'. Worst of all, prices had risen dramatically. This caused 'many Jews . . . to become impoverished'. Even the comfortably off now struggled to put food on the table.

Yet in synagogues like Luzzatto's own, faith in providence still burned brightly. Just as God had brought Moses out of Egypt, reasoned the rabbis, so He would surely come to the Ghetto's aid now. He would not – could not – let His people perish. All that was needed was a little faith. 'In Midrash Tilim', explained one of Luzzatto's Paduan colleagues, 'you will find that God will save anyone who trusts in Him'.[23] Provided Jews remained true of heart, He would neither 'withdraw His eye from the righteous' (Job 36:7) nor forsake them in their need.

Such confidence was not misplaced. In the summer of 1630, the Levantine and Ponentine community had asked the Venetian government for permission to expand the Ghetto – partly to alleviate overcrowding and partly to make space for any additional families who might come in future. Now, this might have seemed almost redundant – if anything, there was too much housing in some areas. But so gravely had the plague damaged the Venetian economy that the government wanted to take another look. During the epidemic, what was left of the Mediterranean trade had virtually ceased; the Arsenale's workforce had been decimated; and the treasury had been starved.[24] It was vital to revive international commerce by any means necessary. Even before the epidemic had abated, the government had taken the unusual step of asking the rectors of subject cities to suggest ways of attracting more foreigners to the capital.[25] It was only logical to encourage more Jewish merchants to come, too. On 15 February 1631, the Senate therefore approved the request and ordered the Cinque Savi to find a suitable location.[26] Naturally, there was some opposition: Christian landlords objected that, if new accommodation was made available, no one would want to rent the properties already standing empty elsewhere in the Ghetto. Somewhat surprisingly, the German Jews protested, too – on similar grounds. Although they could not legally own property, they were worried that the new area would make it impossible to sublet the rickety buildings they had built on rented land. But the Senate refused to be deflected. Commerce *had* to come first. On 3 March 1633, approval was granted for the creation of a new area for Jewish merchants, across the canal from the Ghetto Nuovo. Soon to become known as the 'Ghetto Nuovissimo' (Newest Ghetto), this would consist of twenty dwellings, just behind the Ca' Zanoli, which were to be sealed off from Cannaregio and linked to the rest of the Ghetto by means of a bridge.[27] To appease the Christian landlords who had protested, the Senate decreed that, for a period of three years, only new arrivals would be allowed to rent properties there. Just to be sure, it also stipulated that the heads of the Levantine and Ponentine community would be responsible for attracting twenty new families and would be obliged to pay a fine of 3,000 ducats, or a suitable proportion thereof, if they failed.

The Senate need not have worried. Less than three years later, the Cinque Savi reported that the requisite 20 families were already living in the Ghetto Nuovissimo.[28] Indeed, had it not been for the Thirty Years War, even more Jewish merchants would have come. Some had, in fact, already sent goods to Venice for safekeeping, in the hope of being able to follow later once hostilities were over.

No one could have expected this to restore Venice's fortunes straight away. Though public finances rebounded soon enough, the damage to trade – especially in the eastern Mediterranean – was too severe to be easily repaired.[29] Shipbuilding remained stagnant; Barbary pirates continued to harass fleets returning from the Levant; and mounting tensions with the Ottoman Empire cast a pall over businesses of all kinds.[30] The Venetians were nevertheless confident that, sooner or later, Jewish merchants would turn things around. Indeed, the deeper Venice's malaise grew, the greater the hopes it placed in them – and the more concessions it was ready to make to ensure their success. In 1634, the Senate even granted the Tedeschi Jews permission to engage in Levantine trade.[31] Such a privilege was not given lightly. Every time the Tedeschi had asked for it in the past, they had been turned down flat; the Senate had also rejected similar petitions from 'English, Dutch, and Flemish merchants'.[32] But such was the government's faith in Jewish acumen that it was now willing to bend.

*

Buoyed by the foundation of the Ghetto Nuovissimo, the Jewish population quickly recovered from the plague – more quickly, indeed, than the rest of the city.[33] In 1642, the Ghetto comprised some 3,300 people, divided between 549 households. A decade later, that number had grown to 4,870 – the highest ever recorded.

The urban environment struggled to keep pace. Housing came under intense pressure, albeit in a rather uneven manner. In some parts of the Ghetto, properties were still listed as 'empty' even thirty years later; but in others, the overcrowding was worse than ever.[34] Apartments, already cramped, now became even smaller. By 1661, some had been reduced to no more than a 'room'.³⁵ This forced residents to make the most of what little space they had. Wooden platforms were set up outside properties for displaying homemade goods for sale, and within a few decades, almost a quarter of apartments were equipped with a terrace (*altana*) overlooking the canals.³⁶

Synagogues, too, scrambled to adapt to their growing congregations. Although some of the more ambitious pre-plague projects appear to have been temporarily paused, building work soon started up again.³⁷ The Scuola Canton was refurbished twice, in 1638–9 and again in 1657–8;³⁸ Baldassare Longhena – who had only recently designed Santa Maria della Salute for the Venetian government – was commissioned to redesign the interior of the Scuola Spagnola;³⁹ and a completely new synagogue – the Scuola Mesullamim – was founded before 1635.⁴⁰

There was no lack of activity among Jewish merchants. Quite apart from the trading privileges which they had been granted, they possessed a flexibility which their Christian counterparts could only envy, edging out the competition and assuming a prominent – even dominant – role in Venetian commerce. But the promise of economic recovery nevertheless failed to materialize. Jewish merchants were, after all, still part of the wider Venetian economy. No matter how hard they tried to swim against the current, they could not avoid being caught up in its tide. By the late 1630s, it was clear the Serenissima's days of glory were now numbered. Although a few domestic industries clung on, international trade was in terminal decline. The spice routes were firmly in the hands of the Dutch, and the Adriatic had become a mere backwater. There would be no recovery – only a gradual slide into irrelevance. In the years after the plague, Jewish trade through the Balkans began to tail off – and as the volume of goods declined, so too did the revenues accruing to the treasury.⁴¹ In 1637, Simone Luzzatto estimated that Venice was earning approximately 70,000 ducats each year from duties on Jewish trade.⁴² This was still a considerable sum, but a sharp drop from the high of 100,000 ducats only a decade or so before. As Venice's woes grew, the losses only mounted.

An air of weariness, even decay, began to fall over the Ghetto. Though the synagogues were filled to bursting and the squares thronged with traders, daily life was losing its former vitality. Jewish confraternities, which had once prided themselves on their generosity, now became inward-looking and cautious – almost to the point of parsimony. Aid was granted only sparingly; and even then, mainly to kith and kin.

Theatre and poetry managed to retain some of their vibrancy. Benedetto Luzzatto's *L'Amor possente* – a pastoral drama written at the height of the plague – was performed to great success before both Christians and Jews; and the poet Moses Zacuto, often feted as the 'Jewish Dante', enjoyed the pinnacle of his fame in the late 1650s while serving as a rabbi in Venice.[43] But music grew noticeably quieter. By 1639, Leon Modena's musical academy was already in decline. As Modena told a young Jewish choral director in 1639, the plague had robbed the group of its 'best members', and without them, it was difficult to carry on.[44] Over the years that followed, meetings became more spasmodic – until eventually, they stopped altogether. Some doubted whether music should even be permitted. Back in 1604, Modena's singers had faced criticism from the rabbi Moses Coimbran,[45] who believed there had been no place for music in Jewish life since the destruction of the Second Temple. Lamentation, not rejoicing, should be their lot. Modena had seen this challenge off with a typically well-crafted *responsum*, but he evidently failed to silence his critics completely. In 1645, a controversy in Senigallia, near Ancona, stirred up opposition once again.[46] At heart, this revolved around the 'problem' of whether singers should repeat God's name during prayer services, but it prompted some of the more conservative Jews to call for a complete ban on singing in synagogues. So heated did this dispute become that the aged Modena was eventually asked to step in. This time, however, he could muster no more than a half-hearted response.

*

Among the Venetians, a coolness began to creep in. Though few doubted the Jews' vital role in Levantine trade, necessity made them suspicious; and the deeper the city's malaise grew, the quicker they were to take offence.

Even before the plague had passed, there were fears that Jews were exploiting Venice's weakness to their own advantage. Back in May 1631, a dispute broke out between the heads of the Tedeschi community and an association of shopkeepers.[47] It was a trivial matter, no more important than any other; but it became so heated that the shopkeepers apparently asked the Venetian courts to intervene. This infuriated the Tedeschi. They reminded the shopkeepers that the Università had passed a statute banning Jews from appealing against its decisions in the secular courts, on pain of excommunication. There was nothing particularly surprising about this. As Daniel Malkiel has pointed out, Talmudic law had long regarded arbitration within Jewish communities as the 'normal method for the resolution of civil cases' – and up until then, the Venetian government had done little more than grumble.[48] But now things looked different. When word of the statute reached the ears of Zuane Morosini, one of the Avogadori, he was frankly alarmed. Fearing that the Università was trying to set up a 'state within a state', he called the Ghetto's leading men in for questioning, including Leon Modena.[49] They did not reassure him. Although they insisted there was nothing stopping Jews from accessing the secular magistracies, they did not deny the statute's existence – or that threats of excommunication had been made. Now more suspicious than ever, Morosini decided to investigate further. Since the community's records – known as the *Libro grande* – were in Hebrew, he commissioned two Jews, Leon Modena and Jacob Levy, to translate the relevant sections into Italian, and passed them on to one of Venice's theological jurisconsults, Gaspar Lonigo, for evaluation. Lonigo was appalled. In a vitriolic report for the Senate, he argued that the Jews were indeed trying to usurp the government's authority and set up 'a Republic separate from any other Dominion'. He therefore recommended that the *Libro grande* be burnt and that the Ghetto's leaders be punished as severely as the law allowed.

The Senate was understandably concerned, but it was wary of jumping to conclusions too quickly. It therefore decided to commission a translation of the complete *Libro grande* and asked Lonigo's colleague, Fra Fulgenzio Micanzio, for a second opinion.[50] It was a fortuitous choice. Of the two jurisconsults, Micanzio was by far the subtler mind. Originally from a village near Brescia, he had been invited to Venice by Paolo Sarpi during the interdict, and the two men had quickly become close friends and collaborators. He was pathologically incapable of taking anything at face value. Despite his advanced age, he went through the *Libro grande* with a fine-tooth comb, frequently asking rabbis for advice whenever he encountered difficulties. And he found plenty that should have troubled him. It turned out that, when Morosini had asked Modena and Levy to translate the suspect statute, they had tried to protect the Ghetto's interests by translating a similar – but less incriminating – piece of legislation, instead. Since neither Morosini nor Lonigo could read Hebrew, they had been none the wiser. But Micanzio must surely have spotted the ploy – and realized that the *real* statute was even more of a threat to the government's prerogatives than Lonigo had supposed. For whatever reason, however, he kept the truth to himself. Discreetly rubbishing Lonigo's report, he assured the Senate there was nothing to worry about and advised that no further action be taken.

The Ghetto did not escape punishment altogether. A few months later, several leading members of the Jewish community were imprisoned, presumably for colluding in the deception. And in 1633, Levantine and Ponentine merchants were expressly forbidden to interfere in any non-commercial dispute 'with duress, violence, or by means of excommunication'.[51] But given Micanzio's report, the Senate had to let the matter drop.

A lingering suspicion nevertheless remained. Many Venetians felt that, even if Jews may not have been usurping the state's authority, they were probably trying to undermine it in other, more subtle ways. Merchants, tired of their meagre cargoes, grew jealous of their Jewish neighbours; shipowners blamed them for tipping off Barbary corsairs; while shopkeepers were ready to attribute their success to theft.[52] All that was missing was the 'proof' – and it was not long in coming.

On Friday 21 March 1636, the Ghetto was celebrating Purim – usually the happiest time of the year – when a company of armed men suddenly burst through the gates. This attack was sparked by a daring, if foolhardy, robbery a few weeks earlier, in which four Christians had broken into a shop in the Merceria and stolen 70,000 ducats in goods and cash.[53] Slipping away to the Ghetto, they handed their loot over to a man named Grassin (Gershon) Scaramella for safekeeping. With the help of his cousin, Isaac Scaramella, and Menahem d'Angelo, Grassin hid everything in Jewish houses for a time, before moving it, bit by bit, to different places around the city in the hope that this would keep the crime from being detected. Inevitably, things did not turn out that way. The very next day, the Council of Ten launched a major investigation, and before long, one of the gang's associates turned informant. Most of the money was recovered, but since the culprits had still not been found, the authorities ordered a brutal raid on the Ghetto. As Leon Modena recalled, 'the [G]hetto compound was closed off' while the soldiers conducted a 'house-to-house search'. The next morning, a great outcry was raised against the Jews. Everyone – 'nobles, citizens, and commoners' – seemed to grow angry. Though only a few individuals were implicated, the whole community was held responsible. Jews were cast as a 'band of thieves' and the Ghetto itself a hotbed of criminality.

All seven of those directly involved in the crime were soon in custody. On 6 May, they were banished from the Venetian state. They were threatened with execution should they ever dare to set foot in Venice again, and their property was confiscated to reimburse the victims for any stolen property that had not yet been recovered. Unusually, the Council of Ten also asked leading rabbis to excommunicate the guilty parties for failing to inform the authorities of the crime sooner – although this understandably met with some resistance.[54]

Just as the matter seemed to be fizzling out, however, it suddenly took a turn for the worse. For the past three years or so, the Venetian authorities had been investigating a seemingly unconnected case of corruption. They were beginning to give up hope of cracking it when, out of the blue, Grassin Scaramella offered to spill the beans in exchange for a reprieve. It turned out that a wealthy Venetian merchant named Marc Antonio Marta had tried to secure a favourable ruling in a lawsuit by bribing some of the judges. Rather than risk handling the money himself, however, he had paid two Jews – Mordecai and Jacob Zorzetti – to act as his go-betweens.[55]

When word of this leaked out, it caused an immediate scandal. Under pressure to 'protect [its] honour', the Venetian government stripped the guilty judges of their nobility and banished them from the Venetian state for life.[56] But it reserved its harshest punishment for the Jews. The Zorzetti brothers were immediately placed under arrest. Jacob was condemned to the galleys, while Mordecai later died in prison after converting to Christianity.[57] Scaramella, far from getting off, was sentenced to ten years in the galleys.[58] Leon Modena's son-in-law, Jacob Motta – who had been friendly with the Zorzetti brothers – fled to Ferrara after being implicated in the crime.[59] Modena himself came under suspicion for a while. Others were dragged into the net, too. According to an anonymous Hebrew chronicle, several families were expelled – even though they had nothing to do with the 'evil affair' – simply to satisfy the public desire for vengeance.[60]

For the Jewish community, this could hardly have come at a worse time.[61] The previous year, the *condotta* of the Levantine and Ponentine merchants had expired and had still not been renewed by the time the armed raid on the Ghetto took place. Although most patricians recognized the need to keep as many Jewish merchants in Venice as possible, others were more sceptical. The Cattaveri, in particular, were convinced that Jews were set on undermining Venetian courts – and most likely saw the theft as vindicating their fears.

After much debate, pragmatism carried the day. On 10 July 1636, the *condotta* was finally reconfirmed in broadly favourable terms.[62] Provided Levantine and Ponentine merchants wore the yellow hat and respected Venice's laws, they were free to live as they wished. They were guaranteed 'complete freedom of movement and trade'. They would pay no more tax than any other merchant living in Venice. And no one, secular or religious, would be permitted to interfere with them, except in the most egregious circumstances.

Yet when Scaramella's revelations became known, many patricians regretted their decision. If any proof of the Jewish 'threat' to Venetian justice was needed, this was surely it. According to an anonymous Hebrew chronicle, 'the ministers of the Senate and especially the Council of Ten with Doge Francesco Erizzo at their head, thought of expelling all the Jews from their land'.[63]

The seriousness of this threat is unclear, but the possibility was evidently real enough for the Jewish community to be alarmed. They hastened to change the government's mind before it was too late. Rabbi Samuel Meldola – an old friend of the doge's – was summoned from Verona to plead with him on their behalf, while the eminent scholar Rabbi Israel Conegliano did his best to intercede with a sympathetic prelate.[64]

By far the most striking effort was made by Simone Luzzatto. Shortly after the scandal broke, he began writing the *Discorso circa il stato de gl'hebrei et in particolar dimoranti nell'inclita città di Venetia* ('Discourse on the State of the Jews, Particularly Those Dwelling in the Illustrious City of Venice').[65] Addressed to all 'Lovers of Truth', this set out to demonstrate that the Jews, far from harming Venice, actually brought it 'considerable profit' – and were hence vital to its future prosperity.⁶⁶

The *Discorso* is a densely written piece, littered with allusions to ancient history, classical literature, and scripture. But Luzzatto's argument is simple. Even before the plague, he began, Jews had been central to Venice's maritime trade. They imported a wide range of goods from distant lands – not just everyday necessities, but also luxury items 'meant to adorn civil life'; they kept artisans and workers supplied with raw materials, such as wool, silk, and cotton; and they sold goods manufactured in Venice abroad.⁶⁷ All of this not only generated huge tax revenues, but also boosted employment and helped guarantee peace between Venice and its neighbours.

Granted, there were some who felt that Jews had an 'unfair' share of international trade. But it would be quite wrong to claim that they had 'usurped' anything.⁶⁸ After all, the Venetians had abandoned maritime trade of their own free will, and they could quite easily have taken it up again if they had wished.⁶⁹ But they had long preferred the security of their landed estates. The only question was whether the Venetians – having renounced the sea – wanted eastern Mediterranean trade to be in the hands of foreigners or Jews. Foreigners had their attractions, of course. But once they were allowed to trade in Venice, it was difficult to stop them from taking their profits back home.⁷⁰ Jews – who had no homeland to return to – clearly did not suffer from this problem. In fact, given Venice's attractions, they wanted nothing more than to stay there as long as possible. What was more, they were uniquely well suited to trade.⁷¹ They were used to hardship; they boasted an unrivalled network of contacts; and since they couldn't own property, they were effectively tied to commerce. And there was no danger of them becoming rich – let alone rich enough to give up trade.⁷² High taxes chipped away at their assets, while their fondness for large families meant that their estates always got broken up.

The benefits were clear. According to Luzzatto's calculations, Jews brought in 222,000 ducats in taxes per year.⁷³ That was more than the gross revenue Venice received from all but one of its subject cities in 1633. But when expenses were deducted, it turned out to be about the same as 'the entire Venetian *terraferma*' and 'almost twenty times the amount yielded by . . . the *stato da mar*'.⁷⁴ This was to say nothing of the three Jewish loan banks – then known as the Red, Green, and

Black banks, after the colour of their signs. Although Luzzatto did not venture to put a figure on their contribution to the wider Venetian economy, there was no question that they kept the poor fed and the state safe from unrest.[75]

The risks, meanwhile, were negligible. There was little chance Jewish banks would abuse their position. Given that Jews were 'weak and badly thought of', the poor would not hesitate to report them if they stepped out of line. Nor were Jews likely to cause trouble. Having neither a homeland nor a protector, they were naturally 'obedient and inclined to remain subjected'.[76] This was why the Ghetto did not need 'a garrison to guard it, nor a citadel to defend or retain it'.[77] Indeed, as a people, Jews were anything but threatening. In an obvious attempt to pander to his readers' prejudices, Luzzatto insisted that they were 'fainthearted, cowardly, and half-hearted . . . incapable . . . of any political government . . . and . . . quite unobservant of the present course of things'.[78] As for their beliefs, there was even less cause for alarm. Although Jews were subject to all manner of 'slander and infamy', anyone with a modicum of 'learning or insight' could see that the accusations levelled against their rites were nonsense.[79] The Mosaic Law required 'generosity and kindness' to be 'practised towards all humankind' – while the obligations of ritual purity precluded any 'contamination' of the Ghetto's Christian neighbours.[80]

Naturally, there were always going to be a few bad apples. But the Venetians shouldn't let the crimes of a few individuals besmirch the Jewish community as a whole. All that was needed, Luzzatto argued, was to expel the guilty parties – as the government had already done – and let the law-abiding majority get on with helping Venice to prosper. 'For just as a well-cultivated terrain often produces useless and harmful herbs along with the harvest', he explained, 'a wise farmer does not abandon the intemperate and thriving soil for this single reason, but uproots the harmful plants and continues with the tiring work of tending to the good plants, and keeping the useful ones alive'.[81]

As such, Luzzatto urged the doge and his ministers to grant mercy to the Ghetto, and promised that, if the Jews were allowed to go on living in Venice, they would surely repay the kindness many times over.

Luzzatto's *Discorso* marked a watershed in Jewish apologetics. As

Benjamin Ravid has emphasized, it 'constituted the first systematic exposition of the role of the Jews in international trade' – and the earliest serious attempt to justify their presence on the grounds of commercial *raison d'état*.[82] At some level, it must have reflected thinking in government circles. As soon as the first shock of the corruption scandal had faded, any talk of expulsion was quietly dropped. Yet its reception was nevertheless rather mixed. Although the anonymous Hebrew chronicle mentions that ministers 'were impressed with [Luzzatto's] wisdom and style', there is no evidence that it played any direct role in persuading them not to take any further action.[83] In some quarters, it even aroused opposition. Three years after the *Discorso* appeared in print, the musician Melchiorre Palontrotti published a *Breve risposta a Simone Luzatto* ('Brief Response to Simone Luzatto [*sic*]').[84] This was a spectacularly antisemitic screed, which misunderstood – or misrepresented – much of Luzzatto's argument, but which nevertheless made up for a want of rigour with a surfeit of bile. It dismissed out of hand any economic justification for the Ghetto and instead focused on 'proving' that the Jewish presence posed a real threat to the spiritual life of the Christian faithful.

Outside Venice, the *Discorso* fared much better. It was greatly admired by the Portuguese rabbi Menasseh Ben Israel, whose own *Vindiciae Judaeorum* (1656) played a part in convincing Oliver Cromwell to readmit Jews to England, and influenced Isaac Cardoso's defence of the Jewish people in *Las Excelencias y Calumnias de los Hebreos* (1679). Arguably its greatest admirer, however, was the Irish philosopher John Toland. A committed freethinker, Toland recognized that Luzzatto's work chimed with his own views on religious liberty.[85] In his *Reasons for Naturalizing the Jews in Great Britain and Northern Ireland* (1714), Toland laid out a case for extending both citizenship and full legal rights to Jewish residents, based largely on arguments borrowed from the Venetian rabbi. For a time, he even toyed with the idea of translating the *Discorso* into English.

The contrast was, in many ways, a parable of the Ghetto's situation. While states elsewhere in Western Europe would soon look to Venice as a model for their own treatment of the Jews, in the Serenissima itself, an altogether more tortured relationship was taking hold. More so than ever before, the Jews' presence was dictated by economic necessity – and by that alone. In that respect, Luzzatto had been right. Yet Venice was now entering its dotage. And as its remaining wealth slowly slipped away, so did the Jews' own. The more insistent the Venetians' demands grew, the harder it became to satisfy their expectations – and the more grudging, even resentful, their tolerance became. Having once eaten the lamb, Venice's Jews would now have to taste the bitter herbs.

9

A Spiritual Crisis

(1663–1688)

In the years after the plague, Venice's Jews had found strength in their faith. It had given them hope amidst the darkness of disease and helped them look beyond the difficulties which had followed. It had also bolstered their wavering self-confidence. In prayers and rituals, in the Torah and the Midrash, they discovered a way to make sense of the Ghetto's existence – and the determination to maintain a separate, special identity of their own. Yet within a matter of decades, even this would be irretrievably shaken.

As with the plague, the crisis came unexpectedly, like a peal of thunder from a clear sky. In early October 1665, the Jewish community received word that the Messiah had finally come.[1] At any other time, they might have greeted this with scepticism, even disbelief. There had been no shortage of frauds and con men in the past. A little over a century before, the Senate had expelled an adventurer named David Reubeni, who had tried to trick the Venetians with tales of his 'kingship'.[2] But there was something about this one – Sabbatai Sevi, as he was known – that was different.

Sabbatai was not an obvious candidate. The son of a merchant from Smyrna (modern Izmir), he was said to be 'very stout and corpulent', with a bushy black beard.[3] He could claim no kinship with the ancient kings of Israel. Nor, indeed, was he much of a religious scholar. Though he had received the usual Talmudic training and may even have received the title of *hakham* (wise man) while still in his teens, he seemed little more than competent.[4] His only real distinction was his asceticism. After completing his studies, he reputedly devoted himself to the spiritual life, 'renounc[ing] all pleasures' and 'rejecting . . . frivolity'.[5] In time, this led to a profound interest in kabbalah. But even in this respect, he was far from unusual.[6]

For the Ashkenazi communities of Central and Eastern Europe, however, these were strange times. Back in 1648, the Khmelnytsky Revolt in Poland-Lithuania had led to the slaughter of as many as 100,000 Jews.[7] The suffering was so terrible that, for many survivors, it took on a millenarian significance.[8] Already, kabbalists had prophesied that the Jewish year 5408 – that is, 1648 in the Gregorian calendar – would mark the beginning of the messianic age.[9] The massacres were a sure sign that the Jews' redemption was now at hand. Soon enough, it was thought, the Messiah himself would come to lead them back to the Promised Land.

One night, shortly after the outbreak of the revolt, Sabbatai Sevi was walking in solitary meditation just outside Smyrna, when he heard the voice of God calling to him: 'Thou are the saviour of Israel, the messiah, the son of David, the anointed of the God of Jacob, and thou art destined to redeem Israel . . .'[10] Modern scholars have sometimes interpreted this as an indication of mental illness. According to Gershon Scholem – the author of the most authoritative biography – Sabbatai almost certainly 'suffered from a manic-depressive psychosis, possibly combined with some paranoid traits'.[11] But to Sabbatai, it evidently felt real enough. From that moment on, his whole demeanour changed. As a friend later recalled:

> he was clothed with the Holy Spirit and with a great illumination; he pronounced the [ineffable] name of God [traditionally forbidden to all but the High Priest in Jerusalem] and performed all sorts of strange actions as seemed fit to him . . .[12]

At first, Sabbatai kept his messianic claims to himself. He didn't even share his revelation with his family. But his behaviour was too strange, too heretical, to escape the notice of the rabbinical authorities. Their patience finally ran out when he went up a hill with some friends and commanded the sun to stand still. At some point between 1651 and 1654, they banished him from Smyrna.[13]

Leaving the city alone, most likely on foot, Sabbatai began his long years of wandering. He travelled back and forth, through Greece and the Levant, seemingly without any sense of purpose or direction. He lived in 'miserable' conditions and often scandalized rabbis with his eccentric manner.[14] On one occasion, he caused outrage in Salonika by publicly 'marrying' the Torah.[15] By 1664, he had finally had enough. Returning to Egypt after a brief sojourn in Jerusalem, he decided to put a stop to the absurd behaviour which had caused him such trouble. He longed to be nothing more than a simple rabbi – a wise man among his people.[16]

Sabbatai's story might easily have ended there, had it not been for two strange and unexpected events. The first was his marriage. This was a baffling affair.[17] Although it is sometimes difficult to separate fact from slander and legend, Sabbatai's wife, Sarah, evidently had a difficult – even shady – past. Born into a Jewish family in Galicia (modern Poland), she was reputedly orphaned during the Khmelnytsky Revolt. She was probably forced to convert to Christianity soon afterwards – and it is possible she spent some of her childhood either in a Polish convent or in the household of a Polish nobleman. By 1655, she had escaped to Amsterdam, from where she drifted to Italy and passed at least a few years in Mantua and Livorno. Her behaviour was, by all accounts, scandalous. Starting out as a maidservant, she soon gained a reputation for promiscuity. Some later claimed that she became a prostitute – possibly even a 'witch'. She was also prone to strange delusions. Exactly when these began is unclear, but by the time she arrived in Livorno, she had already become convinced that she would marry the Messiah. This caused much amusement among the townspeople, but their mockery seems only to have strengthened her belief.

According to Jacob Sasportas – who had known her in Amsterdam – news of Sarah's eccentricity eventually reached Sabbatai in Cairo. This rekindled all his old dreams. Recalling the words of the prophet Hosea ('Go, take unto thee a wife of whoredoms'), he became convinced that it was his destiny – as the Messiah – to marry her. Without wasting a moment, he summoned her to Egypt, and on 31 March 1664, the two were wed.

Some traditions hold that it was Sarah – deluded and possibly unstable – who encouraged Sabbatai to pursue his messianic pretensions. But it was a man called Nathan of Gaza who would provoke the next decisive twist in Sabbatai's tale. The son of a noted rabbi in Palestine, Nathan was 'an extremely gifted' scholar with a rare passion for kabbalistic learning.[18] Sometime in late February or early March 1665, he reputedly had a mystical vision lasting a whole day, during which it was revealed to him not only that he was a prophet, but also that a man named Sabbatai Sevi – whose name he had previously never heard – was the Messiah.[19]

Rumours of Nathan's vision reached Egypt soon afterwards.[20] Intrigued, one of Sabbatai's friends sent emissaries to Palestine to learn more. When they returned, they testified to Nathan's charismatic preaching and to the large following he had already attracted. Strangely, none of them seems to have realized that Nathan had identified Sabbatai as the Messiah. It was enough to pique Sabbatai's curiosity, however. Abandoning his work, he headed straight for Gaza. Why he did so is unclear. Later accounts suggest that, even then, he was plagued with doubts – and may have been seeking peace rather than validation. But when the two men met, all that changed. As soon as Nathan saw him, he 'fell to the ground before him' and 'hailed him as an exalted soul'. Most likely, he then explained his vision. At first, Sabbatai was wary, even amused. Little by little, however, he let himself be persuaded.

All of Sabbatai's messianic dreams now burst into the open. In late May 1665, he revealed himself at a prayer service in Jerusalem. With Nathan, his 'prophet' at his side, his 'kingship' was joyfully accepted by the congregation – and, accompanied by the blowing of shofars, his messianic age began.[21] With his message of simplicity and redemption, he reawakened long-forgotten hopes and brought unfamiliar promise to a dejected people. The liturgy was changed, fasts abandoned, and prohibitions eased. Soon enough, his followers were calling him AMIRAH, a Hebrew acronym meaning 'Our Lord and King, His Majesty be Exalted'.

Not everyone was convinced. The rabbinical authorities were appalled. Denouncing Sabbatai as a heretic, they excommunicated him and drove him from the city. Accompanied by his acolytes, Sabbatai then made for Smyrna, where his journey had begun so many years before. No longer the timid mystic, he quickly seized control of the Jewish community, pushed out the chief rabbi, and began issuing apocalyptic prophecies. Letters proclaiming the 'good news' were soon fanning out across Europe – and rumours of an imminent Jewish awakening abounded.[22]

*

The reaction in Italy was swift. Jewish communities throughout the north embraced the new creed almost en masse. As early as December 1665, children in Siena were being given Sabbatai's name.[23] In Mantua and Verona, virtually the whole population became believers; while in Casale, tidings of the Messiah's coming had reportedly 'caused such great rejoicing that many wept for excess of joy'.[24] Penitential movements sprang up; preparations for Purim were called off; and a great campaign of moral reform took flight.

In Venice, the response was more mixed. Among the working classes, enthusiasm was keenly felt. Even some rabbis came over to the cause. Moses Zacuto, widely regarded as the foremost kabbalist in Italy, was a notable, if cautious, convert. But Sabbatai's message was far from universally accepted. At the *yeshiva* – home to 'the "high" culture of Talmudism' – many rabbis and scholars struggled to reconcile the accounts they had received with traditional views of the Messiah.[25] It seemed unlikely, if not downright impossible, that Sabbatai was who he claimed to be. This put them in a difficult position, though. They could not challenge believers openly without provoking a schism. Yet nor could they let popular enthusiasm run wild. When the Venetian government had got wind that something was up, it had summoned the leaders of the Jewish community for questioning. Prudently, the leaders had feigned ignorance, but there was still a danger that, if Sabbatean passions ran too high, anti-Jewish riots might easily follow. Caution therefore seemed the wisest course of action. Without obstructing the penitential revival Sabbatai's 'kingship' had inspired, the *yeshiva* urged the Ghetto's inhabitants to show restraint. Samuel Aboab, the chief rabbi of Venice, argued that in such uncertain times, believers and 'infidels' alike should remember the words of Lamentations 3:26: 'It is good that a man should both hope and quietly wait for the salvation of the Lord'.

What troubled the *yeshiva* most was the paucity of information. The letters they had received were not only vague, but also written by the converted. If Sabbatai *was* the Messiah, why had they not heard from rabbis in the Levant? Why did travellers from the Levant not mention anything about the great events that were supposedly taking place? The silence was puzzling. Despite the recent decline in trade, Venice was still the crossroads of the Jewish world. Any news worth hearing usually passed through its quays, but at this most pivotal of moments, its network of Jewish contacts seemed to be faltering.

Without reliable information, it was impossible to contain the interest Sabbatai had aroused – let alone reach a definitive verdict on his claims.

It was vital to get some sense of what was really going on. In mid-March, letters were therefore dispatched to the rabbis of Jerusalem and Constantinople. Of these, the latter has survived. It gives a clear impression of how serious the divisions within the Ghetto were growing. 'Everywhere you can see groups of people vociferously and noisily discussing the stream of news regarding our redemption', it explained. 'Some are firm believers, whereas others have doubts and reservations . . . everybody is in great trouble and confusion, and the consequences may be grave'.[26] If the rabbis could just give some indication of 'whether it is a day of glad tidings . . . or whether the rumours have no foundation', that would be enough.

In early July, a reply arrived from the rabbis of Constantinople. Dated a little over three months earlier, it was a strange, almost mystical, letter, couched in deliberately opaque language. Its meaning was clear enough, though. The rabbis explained that they had made careful enquiries and had found the 'merchandise' to be impeccable. Any doubts that Venetian Jews might have should therefore be banished from their minds.

This was not what the *yeshiva* had been hoping for. Rather than the dispassionate account they had needed, they had got more Sabbatean propaganda. At a meeting of the Ghetto's leading rabbis in July 1666,[27] the letter provoked a violent dispute about whether it should be published or not. Some – presumably the 'doubters' – wanted it kept secret, while a vocal minority called for it to be given wide circulation. More damagingly, it also exposed a wider question of jurisdiction. Since no agreement could be reached at the meeting, the *yeshiva* took matters into its own hands. Fearing that the letter might worsen religious divisions, it issued a proclamation banning any discussion of Sabbatai's 'kingship' either with gentiles or within the Ghetto itself. This infuriated the Small Assembly. Even though it agreed that silence was the best policy, the letter was clearly a matter of public safety, rather than mere theology. The decision therefore rested not with the *yeshiva*, but with the secular authorities. As such, the Small Assembly annulled the proclamation and issued its own decree, banning anyone from being called 'our master'.

These measures calmed tensions for a time, but it was difficult to stop people talking.[28] Messages flew back and forth, spreading all manner of gossip – little of it bearing the slightest relationship to the truth. To make matters worse, another letter from the Levant arrived soon afterwards. Written by Sabbatai's private secretary, Samuel Primo, it was even more provocative than the last. It repeatedly identified Sabbatai as the 'righteous messiah', and called upon believers to 'beat to death' anyone who doubted his kingship.[29] This only intensified the possibility of a schism.

*

Sabbatai's own situation had changed dramatically by this point. At the end of 1665, he had left Smyrna for Constantinople amidst a flurry of anticipation.[30] Various 'prophets' had predicted that, if Sabbatai ever returned to the capital, he would depose the sultan and seize the Ottoman Empire for himself.[31] Whether he actually intended to do so is unclear, but the risk of civil disorder was too great for the Turkish authorities to ignore. The moment Sabbatai's ship landed, the Grand Vizier, Ahmed Köprülü, had him arrested and thrown in jail.[32] It seemed inevitable that he would be executed. Back in 1657, Köprülü had sentenced the Orthodox patriarch Parthenios III to death for similar offences, and there was no reason to suppose that he would deal any more leniently with an Anatolian Jew – 'messiah' or no.[33] Much to everyone's surprise, however, Sabbatai was spared, and was instead sent to 'quite a comfortable prison' in Constantinople. According to a Venetian diplomat, Köprülü was charmed by Sabbatai's 'eloquence and uncommon virtue'.[34] More likely, he simply wanted to avoid making a martyr out of the 'messiah'.

To Sabbatai's followers, his deliverance came as a vindication.[35] Wild rumours were spread about the 'wonders' he was working in captivity – and it was confidently expected that, sooner or later, the prophecies would be fulfilled. This was the opposite of what the Vizier had envisaged. Then preoccupied with the conquest of Venetian Crete, he could not afford to let Sabbatai destabilize the capital at such a crucial moment.[36] He therefore had the 'false messiah' transferred to a fortress in Gallipoli.

Even there, Sabbatai managed to cause trouble. Pilgrims flocked to see him; wealthy supporters donated a king's ransom in gold and jewels; and tales of his 'miracles' grew more fantastical by the day. He assured his followers that redemption was close at hand. Before long, all Europe seemed to be in the grip of a millenarian frenzy. In Poland-Lithuania, Jews fasted so relentlessly that they 'gave no food even to little children'; in Baghdad, people gathered on the roofs of their houses so angels could carry them to Jerusalem; and a man in Arta died trying to fly there himself.[37]

This was too much for the Ottoman authorities to tolerate. On 16 September 1666, Sabbatai was brought before the sultan's court in Adrianople on charges of sedition.[38] He was offered a choice: unless he either performed a miracle 'proving' he was the Messiah or converted to Islam, he would be executed on the spot. Sabbatai did the only thing he could – and converted. Now known as Mehmed Effendi – in honour of the sultan – he was rewarded with a sinecure in the palace and a handsome pension.

*

When word of Sabbatai's apostasy reached Venice some six weeks later, the shock was immense. Believers scarcely knew how to react.[39] Some – perhaps the majority – refused to believe that he could have converted. Others thought he had merely 'pretended' to convert, so as to win the sultan's confidence and undermine the Ottoman government from within. Even more bizarrely, a third group even insisted that it had been Sabbatai's ghost – rather than Sabbatai himself – that had converted.

The *yeshiva*, meanwhile, was exultant.[40] Now that Sabbatai's deceit had been exposed, the rabbis were determined to rid the Ghetto of his influence, once and for all. Over the protests of believers, the penitential practices of recent months were banned, all the traditional fasts were reinstated, and Sabbatai was never to be spoken of again. Letters were sent to Jewish communities throughout Italy, ordering them to burn any documents which mentioned him, even in passing. Any trace of him was to be obliterated. Thenceforth, the rabbis declared, his name would be anathema, his memory damned. It was to be as if he had never existed.

Sabbatai's movement was not so easily extinguished, however. Since there was no *proof* of Sabbatai's apostasy, many believers continued to practise their faith in secret. Nor were they alone. The following spring, letters arrived from Ragusa and Adrianople which made it clear that, in those cities, Sabbatai was still regarded as a Jew by a sizeable portion of the community.[41] Within months, bulletins and treatises came flooding in from the East, either justifying his apostasy as a necessary step towards redemption or explaining it away as mere fantasy. From the broken ashes, a new flame began to stir.

It was providential – or perhaps portentous – that Nathan of Gaza chose that moment to appear in Venice. Arriving shortly before Passover in 1668, he had most likely come to reassure believers and, if possible, stay the hand of their oppressors.[42] He must have known that, regardless of how many Sabbateans remained, the *yeshiva* would oppose his every move. Yet little could have prepared him for the hostility he met. As soon as he stepped off the ship, Samuel Aboab informed him that he was not welcome; the chronicler Baruch of Arezzo reports that the rabbis threatened to excommunicate anyone who offered him lodgings. Only when two Venetian magistrates who had taken pity on him ordered the Jewish community to rescind the ban did he manage to force his way into the Ghetto.

Nathan remained in Venice for two weeks, during which time he was understandably the object of much curiosity. He was visited regularly by believers and spent long hours discussing the finer points of kabbalism. But the *yeshiva* was not going to let him off the hook so easily. Before he left, the rabbis and elders of the community summoned him for questioning.[43] At this, his resolve crumbled. According to the official 'Memorial', he was unable to answer any of the rabbis' questions satisfactorily and was so ashamed that 'he could hardly speak'. At the end, he was obliged to sign a document repudiating everything. In this, he confessed that he had been 'mistaken' about his vision and wrong to recognize Sabbatai as the Messiah.

This dealt a devastating blow to the movement. After Nathan's departure, on 9 April 1688, the *yeshiva* circulated copies of his confession, together with an account of the interrogation, both within the Ghetto and further afield. Inevitably, some believers still refused to be swayed. Meir of Mestre wrote an open letter denouncing the proceedings as a 'farce', while Nathan himself later claimed that he had signed his confession under duress.[44] But Sabbatai's credibility had nevertheless been severely weakened. Most believers saw it was time to face up to their mistake. Moses Zacuto – previously one of Sabbatai's most respected supporters – now became one of the movement's bitterest critics. Writing to a friend in Vienna, he admitted that the whole thing had been a lie. Nathan's confession had proved it. Anyone who still clung to the faith after that, he believed, was a 'fool'.[45]

It had been a sorry affair – debilitating, dispiriting, and divisive. Born of a single man's fantasy, it had fed on the Ghetto's insecurities, and left inhabitants without hope or unity. The rabbis' authority had been gravely compromised. Although they may have won in the end, they had struggled to defend their faith in the face of a blatant heresy. As Samuel Aboab ruefully noted, Sabbatai had humiliated them.[46] More than that, he had challenged the very religious order they upheld. Tradition (*masoret*) had been questioned, discipline forgotten, and truth itself cast into doubt. Such damage could not be quickly – or easily – repaired.

*

It took many years for religious life to recover some of its former vigour. As the dying embers of the Sabbatean heresy fizzled out, Sephardic and Ashkenazi congregations gradually resumed their habits, and differences of belief were quietly forgotten – if not always forgiven. In the Ghetto Vecchio, synagogues once again became an object of concern. For some time past, the Scuola Levantina had been in a state of disrepair. In the early 1660s, masons had already begun restoring the rooms set aside for travellers; but in 1680, it was decided to demolish the entire building and start again from scratch.[47]

Almost everything about the new Scuola Levantina was novel. In contrast to the synagogues of the Ghetto Nuovo, it was clearly identifiable as such from the outside – and remains so today. It stands apart from the surrounding tenements, proudly, even boldly – much like the temples which had recently been constructed in Amsterdam.[48] Faced in Istrian marble, the two facades are elegant and harmonious, with fine portals and restrained detailing. The prayer hall, meanwhile, is dignified without being overbearing. The light streaming in through the enormous, two-storeyed windows lifts the heavy sobriety of the *aron ha-kodesh* (Torah ark) and *tevah* (pulpit), so that the worshipper is elevated, rather than merely awed, before the divine. Everywhere, there is an air of richness and finery.

Yet the Scuola Levantina's novelty also betrays how little

confidence the community still had. Almost every break with Jewish convention can be traced to a Christian archetype.⁴⁹ The facades are plainly modelled after Venetian *palazzi*. There are unmistakable echoes of Giuseppe Sardi's nearby Palazzo Savorgnan – just opposite the entrance to the Ghetto Vecchio on Cannaregio – not to mention Longhena's Collegio Flangini. The *aron ha-kodesh* could easily be mistaken for an altar in a Venetian church. And as the architectural historian Ennio Concina has rightly noted, the dark, Solomonic columns of the *tevah* recall nothing so much as Gian Lorenzo Bernini's *baldacchino* for St. Peter's Basilica in Rome. It is as if the community was trying to build the still-fragile Ghetto into an imitation of the Christian world beyond.

It is hard to escape feeling that the Ghetto's distinctively Jewish identity was beginning to fray. Though still bound by the obligation to wear a distinctive head-covering, Jews were already asking for – and receiving – exemptions more frequently than in the past.⁵⁰ So, too, the social boundaries between the Ghetto and the Christian city seem to have become more porous. A vivid indication of this is provided by Alexandre Toussaint Limojon de Saint Didier, who served for a time as secretary to the French ambassador in Venice. In his description of the city, published in 1680, he repeated the familiar boast that Jews were 'better treated' in Venice than anywhere else in Italy. Indeed, such was Venice's tolerance that 'every noble household' had at least one Jew among its 'beloved and trusted' friends.⁵¹ This was probably an exaggeration; but even so, it was clearly not unusual to see Jews and Christians conversing as equals in salons and squares.

Assimilation did not come easy, however. Despite the friendship Jews enjoyed with some patricians, the government's policy of tolerance was no less grudging than before. Jews were never allowed to forget that they were 'different'. Their legal rights – such as they were – remained unstable. In 1665, the Avogadori di Comun granted the German Jews permission to access the Fondaco dei Tedeschi, the warehouse set aside specifically for German merchants. Just three years later, the Senate abruptly rescinded the decision.⁵² A German was not the same thing as a German Jew – and neither was the same as a Venetian. Popular hostility also continued unabated. Indeed, the more Jews tried to integrate, the more antisemitism they encountered. The most violent attacks came from Jewish converts to Christianity. By far the worst was Giulio Morosini.

Known before his baptism as Samuel Nahmias, Morosini had been born into a wealthy family of Spanish Jews who had arrived in Venice after a period in the Levant.[53] As a young man, he studied with Leon Modena.[54] After seeing Simone Luzzatto debate with a Christian friend, he lost faith in Judaism and converted. On 22 November 1649, he was received into the Catholic Church, along with his son and one of his brothers. Some ten years later, he went to Rome, where he was eventually appointed to a research fellowship in the Vatican Library and a lectureship in Hebrew at the Collegio de Propaganda Fide. His real passion was for proselytizing, however. Filled with all the zeal of the neophyte, he longed to convert other Jews. To that end, he composed the *Via della Fede*.[55] Published in 1683, this vast, compendious work was intended – at least in part – to expose the superstitions which defiled the Jewish religion and refute all the objections which prevented Jews from embracing the Christian faith.

As a window onto Jewish practices in the Ghetto, Morosini's work is rivalled perhaps only by Modena's own *Historia de' riti Hebraici*.[56] Few details of Jews' daily life escaped Morosini's notice, yet his encyclopedism was more than matched by his vehemence. No insight was ever unaccompanied by calumny. Jews, Morosini opined, were comparable to 'prostitutes and vile animals'. They were cruel by nature and 'by inclination . . . perverse', 'obstinate', 'ignorant', and untrustworthy – not to mention 'bloodthirsty'.[57] Contrary to what Simone Luzzatto had argued, they were proud when they should have been humble.[58] Worst of all, they posed a direct threat to Christianity. According to Morosini, they enjoyed defiling images of Christ, thirsted after Christian blood, and had slaughtered Christian children many times in the past.[59] Indeed, there was scarcely a crime he did *not* accuse them of.

The violence of Morosini's views was likely not shared by many in Venice, even among the Jews' opponents. As Benjamin Ravid has pointed out, his influence in the Serenissima was negligible.[60] But the *Via della Fede* was merely a more extreme version of the prejudices still circulating in Venetian society. The 'otherness' of the Ghetto continued to arouse ire – and Jews themselves remained the objects of scorn.

Not even the dead were immune. For the last 300 years, Venice's Jews had buried their dead on a small plot of land on the Lido. Since this was on the opposite side of the city, the Jewish dead had to make the long journey by boat, passing around the back of Castello, then skirting around the Basilica di San Pietro, before venturing out into the lagoon. As they did so, boys standing on the bridge of San Pietro shouted curses and threw stones at them. Such things were not unknown in other cities. In Umbria, the sight of a strange cortège weaving its way through the streets often provoked similar displays of anger and resentment.[61] But so severe did this grow that, in 1668, the Venetian government had no choice but to order a new canal to be cut through the northern end of the Patriarch's gardens.[62]

Known as the Canale degli Ebrei (Canal of the Jews), it was only short – barely a few hundred metres end to end – but it was more than enough to allow funeral boats to avoid the San Pietro bridge. Now, a cortège could pass directly from the Rio delle Fondamente Nuove, behind the Arsenale, to the Canale dei Marani, and then out to the Lido, without ever risking trouble from bystanders. After being enlarged twenty years later, the new canal also served another unexpected purpose. Since it was deep enough to accommodate even heavy barges, it soon came to be used as a major route for traffic between the north of the lagoon and the Adriatic. The effect of this must have been galling. While Jewish funeral boats may not have suffered any more abuse from the bridge, they still had to contend with being buffeted by cargo ships on the water. Even on their 'own' canal, they were on the back foot.

It was a poignant testament to the spiritual crisis which had taken hold of Venice's Jews – and a painful foretaste of the future that lay ahead.

10

Orphans of the Storm

(1688–1714)

On the night of 5 July 1691, Simcà Todesca was returning home from buying some bread when she spotted something unusual in the entranceway of her tenement in the Corte Scala Matta, just opposite the Scuola Levantina.[1] Bending down with her candle to get a better look, she found a basket (*sporta*) covered with a piece of cloth. 'Heavens, what's this?' she cried out.[2] A moment later, the porter, Jacob Aboaf, came running downstairs, alerted by her shout. Together, they opened the basket – and there, inside, was a baby. Attached to the swaddling was a note giving the time of birth and a few lines from the Torah – but no indication of where the poor little mite had come from. Jacob was scared stiff. 'You take it out,' he said, 'I don't have the guts.'[3] Simcà was made of stronger stuff. Scooping the child up in her arms, she asked a friend to take care of him for the night, while she and Jacob went to alert the Ghetto authorities, who, in turn, placed the matter before the Cattaveri. An inquiry was immediately opened. The first priority was to find out who had left the basket in Simcà's doorway. But here, the magistrates drew a blank: the gates had been shut hours before Simcà found the baby, and the guard who had been watching the Cannaregio entrance hadn't seen anyone coming or going since then. None of Simcà's neighbours seemed to know anything, either. The baby's parents seemed to have disappeared into thin air.

This raised a painful question. If the parents couldn't be found, who should look after the baby? As far as the heads of the Ghetto were concerned, the answer was obvious: since the boy was self-evidently Jewish, he should be looked after by the community. But the situation wasn't quite that simple. Since before the Ghetto had been founded, the Venetian government had recognized that no Jewish child could be baptized before the age of fourteen without the permission of its parents.[4] This had done little to deter the more zealous Christians, of course. There were cases of Jewish children being baptized while in the care of a nurse or even carried off to live in the House of Catechumens (*Pia Casa dei Catecumeni*) until they came of age.[5] But it did at least provide a measure of legal protection. Orphans and foundlings were another matter.[6] Unless it could be *proved* that both a child's parents were Jewish, there was always a chance that at least *one* might have been a Christian – in which case, the child could be taken away and lost to Judaism forever.

To prevent this, the heads of the Ghetto hastily appealed to the Cattaveri for custody.[7] This was about more than just one baby. In a community of several thousand people, it was inevitable that children would be abandoned from time to time – especially if they were illegitimate. When this happened, parents took care to leave the children near where the heads lived, so that they could be raised at the Università's expense. This provided a vital safeguard – and it needed protecting. After all, if parents could not be sure of a decent Jewish upbringing for their unwanted children, there was no telling what might happen. A married woman who conceived a child through adultery, for example, might decide to kill herself – or the baby – rather than risk public disgrace by raising the infant in her own home. No one wanted that, surely?

Besides, there was no reason why the baby shouldn't be allowed to remain in the Ghetto. It was almost certain that *both* parents were Jewish. If the mother was Jewish, and had given birth out of wedlock, as seemed likely, she did what any reasonable Jew would have been expected to do: she left her baby where he would be taken into Jewish care, with a Hebrew prayer and his date of birth so that he could be circumcised according to the Law. The father was clearly Jewish, too; the alternative simply made no sense. If he was a Christian, he would surely have taken the boy to be raised in a foundling hospital, rather than leaving it to be raised in poverty among the Jews. As such, the heads boldly declared that the 'child belonged to the Ghetto' – and that there was 'no chance of [their] being persuaded otherwise'.[8]

Without hard evidence, however, the Cattaveri would be difficult to convince. It was vital to flush out the truth. The rabbis placed a ban of excommunication on anyone with information about the child's origins who failed to come forward and sent word to all the communities of the *terraferma*. A few days later, a Jew named Ercole Rieti appeared before the chief rabbi of Padua.[9] Tormented by his conscience, Rieti confessed that the baby had been born at his house in Castelfranco Veneto, not far from Treviso, and went on to provide 'a list of names' of people involved. Hurriedly, the rabbi dispatched a messenger to Venice. Witnesses were called, interviews held – and soon enough, the Cattaveri finally found out what had really happened.

As Rieti testified, the baby's mother was a Jewish woman by the name of Corona Levi. About eight years before, she had taken a job as a maidservant in the house of Sansone Sacerdote in Nomi, a little way outside Trent.[10] Sometime later, Sansone seduced her, and by late 1690, Corona had fallen pregnant. It was a heavy blow. If people knew that she had conceived out of wedlock, her honour would be in tatters – and Sansone's besides. She had to leave before she started showing. Since her parents would surely not let her come home, Sansone arranged for her to stay with Rieti, across the border in Venetian territory, instead. She remained there for three months. The day after she gave birth, Sansone came and took the baby away – where, she did not know. He refused to tell her anything, no matter how hard she pleaded.[11] Recounting those terrible exchanges, weeks later, she could scarcely hold back the tears.

Sansone confided to Rieti that his plan was to abandon the baby in the Ghetto. Gregorio Bellotto was recruited to help, and his wife, Anzola, agreed to feed the child on the journey.[12] Both were Christians.[13] Together, the little band made their way from Castelfranco to Mestre – where they stopped at a hostelry[14] – and from there, to Venice. It was the night of 5 July when they arrived. Huddling down in a travellers' shelter in Cannaregio, they prepared for the final act of the drama.[15] As soon as they had changed the baby, they settled him down in a basket Sacerdote had bought, with a cushion under his head and the paper tucked into his swaddling. They then scouted out the Ghetto. While Rieti and Anzola kept watch outside with the basket, Sacerdote and Bellotto went to look for a suitable spot. Soon enough, Sacerdote returned, covered the baby with Anzola's apron, and went to leave him in the Corte Scala Matta. At the last moment, Bellotto had a pang of conscience.[16] 'Watch out that the child doesn't come to any harm,' he muttered. Sansone wasn't worried, though.

Someone was bound to come along. And with that, they made their escape.

Just half an hour later, Simcà found the basket on her way home. By then, the group was already well away. After reuniting on the *fondamenta*, they took a gondola to San Casciano, where one of Bellotto's brothers lived.[17] When they were unable to find him, they then headed to the Rialto and caught a boat back to Mestre. There, Sansone paid Anzola and Gregorio for their help – and the four of them went their separate ways, no doubt hoping never to hear of the child again.

Such testimony removed any doubt. On 24 July 1691, the Cattaveri ruled that, since the baby was clearly Jewish, he could remain in the Ghetto. There was no point trying to foist him back on the parents, after all. They plainly did not want him, and, though Sansone's actions may have been heartless, his reasons were, if not forgivable, then at least understandable. He was, in any case, beyond redemption. He was not fit to be a father – and he had no intention of changing his ways. Just two years later, he got into trouble with the Jewish community of Modena for getting a servant girl pregnant again.[18] The baby was better off in the Ghetto. What became of him, however, is anyone's guess.

*

It was a sorrowful affair, which did little credit to anyone except perhaps Simcà Todesca. Yet it is indicative of the pitiable state into which the Ghetto had fallen by the end of the seventeenth century.

Shortly after Sabbatai Sevi's apostasy, Venice's long struggle for Crete had ended in defeat.[19] The island – her oldest and most cherished colony – was gone. Only three tiny fortresses remained. There had been nothing inevitable about the loss. At times, the Ottoman Empire had even been brought almost to the point of surrender. Nor could Venice reprove itself for wanting resolve. For twenty-four years, the Republic had strained its every reserve and sacrificed many of its greatest commanders to save the island. But as the banner of St. Mark was lowered over Candia for the last time, on 26 September 1669, such consolations counted for little.

The blow to trade was immense – perhaps greater even than the loss of Cyprus had been.[20] Since the thirteenth century, Crete had been a vital waypoint for Venetian ships travelling from the Levant, or on to Spain, North Africa, and Flanders.[21] Now that it was gone, Venetian cargoes would be not only more vulnerable to piracy, but also significantly less profitable. Given that Venice had already ceded much of its Mediterranean trade to English, Dutch, and French merchants, it could not fail to be alarmed by the jeopardy in which the meagre remains now stood.

Scarcely less severe was the damage to Venice itself. Having fought almost without allies for the duration of the war, it had been obliged to shoulder the costs alone. The treasury had been bled dry. In 1668, the Republic had spent more than 4 million ducats on defence – almost as much as it had spent on an entire war against the Uskoks, half a century before.[22] It was not at all clear how – or even if – the deficit might be repaired.

A cautious optimism nevertheless remained. Over the next fifteen years, strict economies and renewed taxation allowed some order to be restored to the public finances; and, before long, there was talk of a renewed campaign against the sultan. When, in 1684, Emperor Leopold, fresh from driving the Turks back from the gates of Vienna, invited Venice to join him in an anti-Ottoman league, the perfect opportunity seemed to present itself.[23] Under the command of Francesco Morosini – first as captain general, then as doge – Venetian forces swept through Greece with surprising ease. The Peloponnese was conquered and, for a time, even Athens itself was occupied. The Venetians went wild with joy. Not since Lepanto had they tasted a victory as crushing – or as sweet. At a stroke, the Stato da Màr had been renewed, the dream of empire revived. More gratifying yet, the Ottoman Empire had at last been broken. The Turks – more so even than the Venetians – had been exhausted by years of war. Though their ambitions still burned brightly, their history was, from that moment, marked only by decline.

For Venice, the fruits of conquest proved less than might have been imagined. In practical terms, the Morea (as the Peloponnese was known) contributed little to Venice's fortunes and almost nothing to its commercial standing.[24] Without control of the central Mediterranean, even the once-great ports of Coron and Modon were of limited value as staging posts to and from the Levant. Venice had survived before without them, and it gained nothing by their recovery. Though ships continued to dock at its quays, and some industries enjoyed a modest recovery, its role in international trade continued to decline, and compared to its neighbours – especially France and England – its commercial standing soon seemed paltry.[25] Within a few years of the Treaty of Karlowitz, in 1699, the last patricians still engaged in trade gradually withdrew their interests, until barely a few remained. Seeking solace on their estates, they took on the indolent, if gilded, character of the European aristocracies, and the last, sputtering flames of Venice's once great mercantile spirit were extinguished forever.

Venice's Jews could not help being affected. Now that the city's commercial standing was in decline, it was harder for the wealthiest merchants to justify staying in the Ghetto, and a good many families left for more promising harbours. By far the most popular destination was Amsterdam, which had enjoyed strong ties with Venice since the late sixteenth century; but an appreciable number also emigrated to Livorno, Hamburg, Marseilles, Bordeaux, London, and a host of other European ports.[26]

This led to a precipitous drop in the population. As the heads of the Ghetto had noted in their letter to the Cattaveri, the community numbered no more than 3,000 by the end of the century, down from nearly 5,000 only a few decades before.[27] More importantly, it was also accompanied by a dramatic shift in the distribution of wealth.

For those merchants still left in the Ghetto, the exodus of the 1680s and 1690s proved an unexpected boon. Although trade with the Levant may have dropped off, ships continued to frequent Venice's quays and, if you were willing to take the risk, there was still decent business to be done. Now that most of the competition had either left the city or retired from commerce, the remaining Jewish merchants were able to capture the lion's share – so much so that, by the turn of the century, they had come to dominate Venetian trade with the Ottoman Empire.[28] It has been estimated that, in the 1680s, around 80 per cent of Venice's 'remaining cloth output was sold in the Balkans, chiefly by Jews'.[29] Their role in shipping, too, had never been greater. In 1699, the Cinque Savi reported that, of the sixty-nine ships then in Venice, no fewer than twelve belonged to Jews, many with suitably picturesque names like *The Sacrifice of Abraham*, *The Beautiful Esther*, and *Prophet Daniel*.[30] And as a result, a handful of Jewish families soon became extremely wealthy.

For most Jews, however, the new century brought further hardship. As in other parts of Venice, a sizeable proportion of the Ghetto's inhabitants were engaged in piecework or other forms of small-scale manufacturing.[31] Since their products were intended chiefly for export, the decline in trade inevitably caused demand to fall away and their already pitiful incomes to sink even lower.[32] The poorer they grew, the graver the impact on the wider Ghetto economy. Soon enough, bakers, tailors, shopkeepers, and even teachers would all have felt the pinch – and once-prosperous households grew accustomed to want.

*

Matters were not helped by the arrival of a small but steady stream of Jews from Poland-Lithuania. A good many were refugees. Following the Khmelnytsky Revolt almost half a century before, the Ghetto had grown used to welcoming Jews who had fled persecution in Eastern Europe. A typical example was the chronicler Nathan Nata Hannover. After escaping from Zasław, in modern Ukraine, in 1648, he had travelled 'first to [the] German lands, then to Amsterdam, before finally settling in Venice, where in 1652, he published the *Yeven Metsulah* ('Abyss of Despair').[33] In all probability, the number of arrivals like Hannover had been limited at first, as most refugees generally preferred to settle in Silesia, Bohemia, and Moravia,[34] but a larger wave had since followed. The outbreak of the Russo-Swedish War in 1656, followed by the expulsion of Jews from Vienna in 1670, had forced entire communities to seek refuge elsewhere – and Venice, for all its travails, was still an attractive destination.[35]

As well as refugees, there were also former slaves. In the wake of the Khmelnytsky Revolt, thousands of Polish Jews had been taken captive by Crimean Tartars and sold on the slave markets of Istanbul.[36] There, local Jews had tried to save as many as they could, and an international fundraising network was quickly set in motion. Jewish communities throughout Europe sent whatever they could raise, and, naturally, Venice had taken a leading role. A dedicated fund (the *pidyon shevuyim*) had been set up to finance the freeing of captives, and some of the Ghetto's leading figures, including Moses Zacuto and Samuel Aboab, played an active role in soliciting donations.

Understandably, most former slaves wanted to return home as

soon as possible; but few found it easy to do so. Since families were generally split up when they were captured, once one member was freed, they almost invariably set about looking for – and trying to ransom – the rest. As a leading source of funds, Venice was a natural place to begin; and some inevitably ended up staying for longer than they anticipated. Take Ya'akov Koppel Margolis. Originally from Ukraine, he came to Venice as a former slave in 1658, hoping to raise the money to ransom his children, who remained – as he put it – 'in the clutches of cruel and evil men'.[37] He even tried publishing a book to drum up some cash.

It is impossible to know how many Polish Jews had settled in Venice by the end of the seventeenth century. It seems few stayed more than a couple of months, but even a small number would have put the Ghetto's struggling economy under additional pressure. They almost always arrived with little, if anything, to their name and were desperate to earn a living. But with work already in short supply, it is unclear how they were able to survive without being a burden on the community and widening the gap between rich and poor still further.

*

If Venice's Jews were hoping that their financial obligations to the state would be lessened, however, they were cruelly mistaken. Such was the parlous state in which the Republic found itself by the end of the century that the government needed every ducat it could lay its hands on. Between 1669 and 1700, the Università had already contributed no less than 800,000 ducats to the public purse.[38] But the difficulties which Venice faced after the Treaty of Karlowitz were so great that, on 6 January 1700, the government was obliged to ask the Ghetto for an additional 150,000 ducats, ostensibly as a proof of its loyalty.

This sum would have been difficult for the Ghetto to pay even in its heyday; but now, it must have seemed practically impossible. The departure of the richest families had robbed the community of its largest taxpayers, and there were fewer people than ever to make up the shortfall. The Venetian government was not blind to this, of course. Even before the situation had become serious, it had tried to stop the flight of taxable wealth. As early as 1630, the Senate had ruled that no Jew could leave Venice without paying their fair share of the Ghetto's tax bill. In 1695, 1696, and 1697, it granted the heads of the Università full discretion to decide how much each person should pay before being allowed to go.[39]

As the Senate must have realized, however, this was an ad hoc measure at best: good for limiting individual losses in a particular year, but not much else. What the Ghetto really needed was a way of boosting the number of taxpayers overall. In October 1706, the heads of the Tedeschi therefore asked the Senate to allow foreign Jews to reside in Venice for short periods, on the condition that they contribute to the community's tax bill.[40] It was a sensible idea. Even the Cattaveri were in favour. But it cannot have attracted many new residents – and did nothing to alleviate the Ghetto's growing financial shortfall.

*

Little by little, the Ghetto was growing steadily poorer. Despite the lingering prosperity of a few families, many – if not most – found themselves struggling as never before. Unable to support themselves, let alone feed extra mouths, parents abandoned their children with depressing regularity, as Simcà Todesca's discovery revealed. Already in a poor state of repair, some buildings now showed signs of an 'unstoppable deterioration'.[41] Especially in the Ghetto Nuovo, tenements were little more than dingy warrens of tiny, insanitary garrets. With mounting urgency, residents scrambled to make the best of what they had. Scarcely a week seems to have gone by without apartments being divided between brothers, contracts renegotiated, and rickety extensions thrown up.

The Ghetto, formerly so full of life and vigour, had become tired and shabby. Though cultural life continued, it no longer shone as it once did. After the death of Moses Zacuto in 1697, Hebrew poetry became almost listless. Now that the academies were gone, music was less often celebrated. Even funeral processions had been scaled back.[42]

The Venetians' coolness now shaded into fresh hostility, and the fear of religious 'contamination' was once again keenly felt. There were hence repeated efforts to clamp down on all forms of 'illicit' contact between Jews and Christians. In March 1703, the Esecutori contro la Bestemmia tried to discourage Christian servants from working in Jewish households by having the relevant rulings printed and posted around the Ghetto on the first Sunday of every month. The most striking of these stipulated that 'no Christian children under the age of sixteen were to enter the houses of Jews at any time' and that Christian women should not stay in the Ghetto overnight under any circumstances.[43] Two years later, the Cattaveri took similar steps to keep the Jews away from Christian homes. On the grounds that certain Jews, having fraudulently acquired exemption from wearing the yellow hat, were sneaking out of the Ghetto at night and committing all manner of 'delinquencies', the Cattaveri ordered that Jews would henceforth be banned from wearing black hats anywhere in the city, and forbidden to leave the Ghetto outside the permitted hours.[44]

If this weren't bad enough, the old myth of the 'blood libel' was resurrected as well. In April 1705, a large painting of a young boy being killed by a group of Jews was displayed on the Rialto bridge.[45] The Jewish community was appalled. A complaint was immediately lodged with the Senate. It was pointed out that, in 1475, Doge Pietro Mocenigo had prohibited anyone from making such images – and had commanded the chancellery to preserve his decree to prevent preachers from 'stir[ring] the population towards insults of this kind' in future. The Senate immediately had the painting torn down and destroyed. But the damage was already done. Word of the painting quickly spread across Italy. Just two months later, some Jewish visitors in Viterbo were accused of trying to kill a twelve-year-old Christian boy for his blood; and as the ensuing trial gripped imaginations everywhere, memories of the original outrage were further ingrained in Venetian minds.

Impoverished and victimized, the Jews of Venice seemed like orphans of a terrible storm – reeling from the blows fate had rained upon them, and frightened that worse might be to come.

11

The Age of Unreason

(1714–1789)

Even now, the Jewish community may have hoped that somehow the Ghetto might still be saved. By the early eighteenth century, Venice was, after all, tasting the first fruits of the Enlightenment. Though its commercial standing had declined, science flourished, reason was exalted, and – despite the air of decadence which had fallen upon the city – there was a growing belief that the material and spiritual conditions of life could be improved by applying the lessons of 'political economy'. In Naples, the philosopher Antonio Genovesi had outlined how even the poorest state could lift its people out of 'obscurity', while in Milan, Pietro Verri had developed a complete theory of wealth. It would not have taken much for the Venetian Senate to have put such ideas into practice, and to have rescued the Ghetto from impending disaster.

In 1714, the moment for action arrived. Still seething at its defeat a few years before, the Ottoman Empire launched a surprise attack on Venice's possessions in Greece.[1] Their advance was rapid. Venetian rule had not been popular and, as often as not, local communities, worn down by heavy taxes, welcomed the Turks as liberators. Town after town fell, until, by the end of the year, all that remained of Venice's Greek empire was the island of Corfu.

Just as the Ottomans were about to deliver the coup de grâce, however, Venice's luck changed. In August 1716, the Holy Roman Empire joined the struggle – and an army under the legendary Prince Eugene was soon on its way. Desperate to avoid fighting on two fronts, the Turkish forces threw everything they had at the city of Corfu. It was a foolish blunder. They were easily repelled, and the next day, the whole army withdrew in disarray.

Now that Corfu was saved, the Venetians went on the offensive. On land and at sea, the Ottomans were pushed back, until the sultan had no choice but to sue for peace. But it was a pyrrhic victory. Distracted by the Spanish invasion of Sardinia, the Holy Roman Empire forced the Republic to sign a hastily negotiated treaty, renouncing her claims to the Morea in exchange for nothing more than a handful of tiny islands.

The war marked a turning point in Venice's history. After more than two and a half centuries, her struggle with the Ottoman Empire was finally at an end. Thenceforth, there would be no more conquests or losses, no more fleets to equip, no more armies to supply. Now that her ties with the Levant were all but broken, her thoughts – unclouded by rivalry – would be bounded by the *terraferma*, and her aspirations by an Italic peace.

For the Ghetto, however, the war only added to its financial woes. Heavy loans were demanded by the government; interest rates were raised; and the banks had to be placed under the control of the heads of the Università.[2] Soon, the situation was so grave that, when the last remaining *condotte* of the Tedeschi Jews ran out, no one even talked about renewing them, for either merchants or moneylenders.[3] The government was alarmed. On 4 August 1722, the Cinque Savi summoned the Ghetto's leaders to give an account of their financial situation. It was worse than they might have expected. In total, the Ghetto owed around 1.2 million ducats,[4] an almost incredible sum. By the middle of the century, the annual revenue of the entire Republic was only 5.5 million ducats.[5] In apparent panic, the Cinque Savi immediately banned the Jewish community from spending or borrowing a ducat more until stringent reforms could be made.

It was too little, too late. Barely a month later, the Ghetto was effectively bankrupt. To prevent the collapse of the loan banks – on which many of Venice's poor still depended – the Senate hastily stepped in. Implicitly blaming the crisis on the Jews' 'incompetence', the government gave control over the Ghetto's finances to a committee of patricians known as the 'Inquisitori sopra l'Università degli ebrei', who were empowered to do whatever necessary to ensure 'the smooth functioning of the banks, the repayment of [its] debts ..., and the general restoration of the community to its former state'.[6]

The committee set about its work sensibly enough. The following year, it froze the debt of 14,000 ducats which the Università owed the state treasury and exempted the Jewish community from paying any further taxes for the next eight years – most likely to prioritize the repayment of private creditors.[7] It then began looking for new sources of income. One scheme was to raid dowries, which some of the wealthier families had been using to hide their assets from tax assessors.[8] Another, more ambitious plan was to attract more migrants. 'Foreign' Jews were offered the chance to live in the Ghetto for up to a decade, tax-free, in return for a payment of 500 ducats per year.[9] Controversially, the committee also made Jewish communities elsewhere in Venetian territory share responsibility for the Università's debts – a move which no doubt rankled but at least spread the liability.[10]

These were all reasonable enough ideas. But since none of them raised nearly enough money, the Inquisitori had to resort to more drastic measures. After some deliberation, they eventually hit on the idea of selling lifetime annuities.[11] This was nothing new. A few years before, the Università had tried to stave off the crisis in exactly the same way – and, by offering attractive rates, had raised a decent amount. In 1717, the duchess of Massa had bought an annuity for 13,000 ducats, in return for a guaranteed revenue of 10 per cent per year; and she was evidently so satisfied that, four years later, she had purchased another for 4,000 ducats, on the same terms.[12] But there was an important difference. Given that the Università's financial situation was now much worse, the only way of attracting new investors was to offer sky-high returns – up to 30 or even 50 per cent. This, of course, had the potential to raise a lot of money in the short term – as much as 500,000 ducats, if all the annuities had been sold. But it only stored up bigger problems for the future. If the Ghetto was struggling now, how was it ever going to pay the gigantic returns it was offering when the time came?

When the committee realized its error, it scrambled for a solution. In 1728, the Jews' major creditors were called in, assets were frozen, and the possibility of restructuring debts was raised, albeit in vain.[13] So panicky did the committee become that it even began selling privileges again, granting wealthier Jews exemptions from any rules they cared to name – a familiar solution, but one which was unlikely to raise more than a trivial amount.[14]

It did not help matters that the Ghetto's bankruptcy had also inflamed anti-Jewish feelings. All the fears of religious 'contamination' that had been simmering away over the past twenty years now came to the boil. The Cattaveri were swamped with complaints about the 'abuses' allegedly taking place in Jewish households – and the smallest incident could become a major scandal. When, in 1720, a group of masked Jews were caught enjoying the Carnevale fun, long after the Ghetto gates had been closed, there was such an outcry that they were immediately arrested and charged, even though, in happier times, such an infraction would scarcely have raised an eyebrow.[15] Before tempers could spill over, the government took steps to keep Jews and Christians apart. Decrees reiterating the ban on wearing black head-coverings were posted in public places; Christians were forbidden to purchase kosher wine; and rewards were offered to anyone who caught a Jew breaking the rules.[16] Prosecutions became common. Understandably, the majority of cases concerned Jews caught defying the clothing regulations or living in Christian neighbourhoods without permission; but even the most trivial aspect of Jewish life could attract the magistrates' ire – especially if it happened to affect the interests of Christian businesses. In 1713, a group of Jews was hauled before the Cattaveri for illegally selling turkeys, thereby depriving the Arte dei Luganegheri (sausage-makers' guild) of its business; and five years later, the chemist Benedetto Sarfatti found himself in court after arousing the envy of one of his Christian competitors.[17]

*

The Ghetto's financial position was now becoming untenable. In 1735, the Inquisitori presented the Senate with a stark assessment. As Cecil Roth aptly noted, it was 'a confession of their own failure'.[18] After thirteen years of work, the Jewish community owed almost as much as it had when the committee had been set up – and money was still flowing out at a terrifying rate. A little while before, the interest on outstanding annuities and loans was already costing the Università over 100,000 ducats per year on its own, and there were no signs of that figure coming down any time soon.[19]

With the loan banks facing near-certain collapse and confinement little more than a polite fiction, the rationale for the Ghetto's existence had all but disappeared. Elsewhere in Europe, such institutions were increasingly regarded as an anachronism. The rights of man were on everyone's lips. Although some *philosophes* – such as Voltaire and Diderot – remained hostile towards Judaism, both as an ethnicity and as a creed, a growing number were outspoken in their defence of Jewish emancipation.[20] In *Lettres persanes* (1721), Montesquieu maintained that Christians

> are beginning to rid ourselves of the spirit of intolerance which animated us . . . We have realized that zeal for the advancement of religion is different from the attachment we must have to it; and that, in order to love it and respect it, it is not necessary to hate and persecute those who do not share it.[21]

A short time later, Jean-Baptiste Boyer, Marquis d'Argens argued strongly for tolerance, even while pouring scorn on rabbinical 'superstition';[22] and Jean-Jacques Rousseau called for the establishment of schools, universities, and even a free state where Jews could 'speak and argue without danger'.[23]

There was also a growing realization that the reform of the Jewish economy was both necessary and overdue. Christian Wilhelm von Dohm's *Über die bürgerliche Verbesserung der Juden* (1781) and Abbé Grégoire's *Essai sur la régénération physique, morale et politique des Juifs* (1788) both recognized that it was folly to shackle Jews to usury. If they could be freed to pursue other commercial activities as they wished, they would enrich not only themselves, but *everyone* in the state.

Throughout Europe, legal barriers came tumbling down. In 1740, Jews were readmitted to the Kingdom of the Two Sicilies; thirteen years later, the British parliament passed a short-lived bill allowing Jews to become naturalized subjects; and in 1782, Joseph II – the epitome of the 'enlightened despot' – granted Jews unheard-of freedoms throughout the Habsburg lands.

It was pointless – even counterproductive – to keep the Ghetto in place. The loan banks were no longer capable of fulfilling their original function, and debt was crushing the remaining life out of the community. As some of the more 'enlightened' patricians soon came to realize, it would have made much more sense to have closed the banks and set up a *monte di pietà* instead. In 1735, the Quarantia al Criminal asked for advice about how a *monte* might be organized, and a short time later, petitioned for at least one of the banks to be shut down.²⁴ The Senate, seized by unreason, steadfastly refused.

The Inquisitori were now out of options. Since the Jews were clearly unable to support their debts, the only course left was to suspend repayments until a new arrangement could be negotiated. This was never going to be easy. Back in 1732, the heads of the Ghetto had pointed out that, if the Jewish community was to stand any chance of getting back on its feet, the debt needed to be drastically reduced – chiefly by buying back existing life annuities using money raised from the sale of cheaper alternatives, offering much lower returns.²⁵ Inevitably, when creditors were presented with the proposals, in early 1736, there was strong opposition.²⁶ Sixty creditors – representing claims worth a little under 300,000 ducats – voted against the restructuring. But not everyone was so blind to reality. More than twice that number – who were owed more than 600,000 ducats – were in favour, including several influential patricians. Under Venetian law, this was enough for the proposals to pass. Repayments were duly cut; the organization of the banks was streamlined; and the pressure on the Jews was eased – at least for a time.²⁷

This bought the Ghetto some breathing space. Some new means of meeting the Università's obligations now had to be found – and fast. In 1737, the Università therefore sent Jacob Saraval to negotiate a suitable loan with Jews in England and the Low Countries.²⁸ He was a shrewd choice. Though not yet thirty years old, Saraval was already recognized as a rabbi of uncommon brilliance. His sermons attracted huge crowds. Even Venetian patricians came to listen. He was a staunch defender of traditional Judaism and was a firm favourite of the *yeshiva*, but was sufficiently clear-eyed to see the need for reform – and even assimilation. He championed Italian-language education, corresponded with the English Hebraist Benjamin Kennicott, and, in later years, even translated Handel's oratorio *Esther* from English into Hebrew. Most of all, he was a compelling apologist. When a certain Giovanni Battista Benedetti published a viciously anti-Jewish screed, Saraval replied with a rejoinder so devastating – and so charming – that it is clear he could have persuaded even the most sceptical lenders.

Saraval's mission was hugely successful. Between the Jewish communities of London and Amsterdam, and the bank of Aron Uziel de La Haye, no less than 100,000 ducats was put at the Ghetto's disposal.²⁹ The terms were remarkably generous, too. The rate of interest was modest, and repayments were to be made gradually, over a period of ten years – or longer, if circumstances required.

The Venetian government was evidently reassured. In 1738, the Senate finally renewed the Jews' *condotte*, putting an end to many years of legal uncertainty.³⁰ In a break with the past, however, a single ten-year charter was issued for all Jews then living in Venice: Tedeschi, Levantines, and Ponentines alike. This was not a new idea. The idea of a unified *condotta* had first been put forward by Daniel Rodriga in the late sixteenth century. But now that the practical differences between the communities had been eroded by the financial crisis, the Senate could hardly refuse. A single charter was simpler for everyone, too. It would greatly speed up the Università's dealings with the government, reduce the scope for disputes, and – if the Ghetto was lucky – possibly even grease the wheels of commerce.

But Saraval's loan was a stopgap, rather than a solution. Although it allowed the Università to meet its immediate obligations, it did nothing at all to remedy the underlying problem. An enormous mountain of debt remained; and once the loan had been spent, no one seems to have had any idea how the Ghetto was going to get out from under it. The Università couldn't keep taking out new loans to repay the old, nor could it see a way to break the cycle. Within a few years of Saraval's return, it had already defaulted on its repayments.³¹ A new arrangement had to be negotiated so that smaller repayments could be made over a longer period. But even this proved a struggle. In 1740, the situation was so desperate that the Jewish community seriously thought about accepting an invitation from Charles III to leave Venice and settle in Naples and Sicily instead;³² and just two years later, during a slump in maritime trade, the Università even resorted to plundering the fund for freeing Jewish slaves – a previously unimaginable sacrilege.³³

*

The outlook was not always so bleak. By mid-century, many Venetian patricians had started to fall under the influence of the physiocrats. Though still in its infancy, physiocracy was a new school of economic theory then emerging in France.³⁴ It held that a state could only increase its wealth if it exploited its agricultural resources to the full – and placed as few restrictions on trade as possible. This made a good deal of sense. After all, Venice was already halfway there. Most patricians had taken up farming long ago; and anyone could see that protectionism was doing them no favours. Every year, high tariffs caused the Republic to lose more business to nearby Ancona. It did not take much to persuade the Senate to change tack – and by 1759, maritime trade was once again on the rise.[35]

At the same time, a cool realism settled over Venetian foreign policy. While most of Europe was convulsed by the Seven Years War, the Serenissima wisely stood apart.[36] It could no longer see any sense in maintaining either a large army or an expensive navy. This, naturally, only encouraged trade the more; but it also had a salutary effect on public finances. State expenditures – once so ruinous – were more modest; and, as tax revenues from the quays increased, the public debt was brought down to a manageable level for the first time in living memory.[37]

The Ghetto also benefitted. When the *condotta* was renewed in 1760, several new clauses were introduced in the hope of improving the Jews' financial situation. They would be allowed to participate in trades other than *strazzaria*, provided this didn't harm Christian businesses; they were given greater opportunities to recover debts owed to them in court; and new measures were taken to encourage 'foreign' Jews to come to Venice.[38] And for once, the effects were encouraging. Indeed, in 1761, the Senate was more positive about the Ghetto's financial outlook than it had been for decades.[39]

But these rays of sunlight were passing moments in a darkening sky. By the late 1760s, Venice was plunged into one of the most severe food crises in its history. After several years of plenty, heavy rains caused a series of catastrophic harvests. Cereals were particularly badly hit.[40] In some regions, entire crops were lost. Prices shot up. The situation wasn't limited to Venice, either. Across Europe, farmers saw their produce decimated. In England, the shortage of grain was so severe that parliament had to ban exports altogether, just so that people could eat. For Venice's Jewish merchants, this was too good an opportunity to miss. Taking advantage of the government's laissez-faire policy, they engaged in the most flagrant speculation – both at home and abroad. And the worse the shortages got, the more money they stood to make.

Olive oil was even more gravely affected. Since the sixteenth century, olive oil from Corfu and the Ionian islands had been one of Venice's most valuable cargoes.[41] Such was its importance that the Venetian government had tried to regulate the market by centralizing control of its distribution in the capital. The effect of this, of course, was to inflate the cost for consumers. As long as harvests had been abundant, this had not been too much of a problem.[42] Now that prices were rising, however, it only served to encourage black-market trade. Many Jewish merchants began buying oil 'unofficially' and selling it under the counter for less than the official rate. This allowed them to undercut the competition – and left the government increasingly out of pocket.

A political backlash was inevitable. In Venice, a group of mercantilist patricians – many in financial difficulties – were incensed by the government's slow and fumbling response to the crisis. They demanded not only urgent political reforms, but also a complete reversal of the physiocrats' laissez-faire policies. Most of all, they wanted the Jews cut down to size. They accused Jewish merchants of profiting from peasants' hardship and depriving landowners like them of a legitimate income. In November 1770, Francesco Tron and Zuan Alvise Emo set out to strangle the Jews' involvement in the food trade.[43] At their urging, it was decreed that Jews would be banned from exporting any goods purchased in Corfu or the Venetian mainland and restricted solely to importing food from abroad. They had until the end of the year to wrap up their business.

Fortunately, this measure was reversed at the last minute. The physiocrats successfully persuaded the Senate to allow Jews to go on trading freely, with only a handful of limited exceptions. But the issue was far from settled – not least because the agricultural crisis kept getting worse. As the *condotta* came up for renewal, there was intense debate about whether free Jewish trade in food helped or harmed Venice. As the French consul noted, 'the nobility is very divided on the problem of the Jews'.[44] In the end, a compromise of sorts was struck. But it was the mercantilists who got the better of it. Confirmed in 1777, the new *condotta* granted Jews the ability to trade freely, with the full protection of the Venetian state, in any goods except grain.[45]

This came as a serious blow to the Jewish community. Even though they still had the right to trade in oil, the loss of such an important commodity deprived many of a valuable source of revenue at a critical time. It also seems to have discouraged 'foreign' Jews from moving to the city – so much so that, in 1774, the heads of the Università were forced to acknowledge that the privileges designed to attract newcomers had not done the Ghetto any good at all.[46]

Any hope of escaping – or even mitigating – the Ghetto's financial problems had been definitively crushed. The community was now locked in a state of continual crisis, always scrabbling for enough money to stave off the worst, yet never quite managing to free itself from the never-ending cycle of debt and default. Shortly before the *condotta* was renewed, the capital invested in the banks was valued at a little over 215,000 ducats, but their annual income stood at just 12,324 ducats – a far cry from the bulging bags of gold shown in Giovanni Grevembroch's portrait of a typical Jewish banker.[47]

*

Already pronounced, socio-economic differences within the Jewish community now became even starker. By 1779, only 143 families earned enough to pay the *tansa* – probably significantly less than half the population of the Ghetto.[48] Of these, fourteen (10 per cent) paid more than 500 ducats. Most (79 per cent) paid as little as 1 ducat. Hundreds more paid nothing at all. Bewilderingly, the Venetian government failed to see the problem. Indeed, it almost went out of its way to worsen the situation. On 17 January 1780, it was decreed that trading licences should be limited to families in the highest tax brackets. This had a certain logic to it – better-off merchants could take bigger risks than poorer ones. But it pushed middling and small-scale traders into further difficulties, with inevitable knock-on effects for the wider community. That strict limits were also placed on Jewish manufacturing, notionally to prevent 'undue' competition with Christian craftsmen, must have depressed artisans' incomes even further.[49]

This redrew the map of Jewish life. The wealthiest families – who had profited most from the food crisis – paid for the privilege of living outside the Ghetto and put on airs of bourgeois respectability. In 1773, Salomon Treves rented a palazzo near the church of San Geremia for the princely sum of 500 ducats.[50] His father, Isaac, who had made his fortune in the Baltic fur trade, had commissioned at least two portraits from Bartolomeo Nazari, in which he and his family were portrayed in fashionable Venetian dress, in an effort to ape his Christian neighbours.[51] Now, Salomon set out to assimilate still further by procuring a seat worthy of his name. In June 1780, he and his family succeeded in 'acquiring' a magnificent palace between the Rio di San Girolamo and the Ponte degli Ormesini by means of a perpetual lease.[52]

Most Jews did not have this option. Stuck in the Ghetto, they saw their living standards fall still further.[53] Buildings – built far too high for their flimsy foundations – began to buckle and creak; lintels sagged; and chimneys broke. After years of neglect, the wall around the tiny garden in the Ghetto Vecchio was in such a tumbledown state that it was feared robbers would creep in unnoticed and steal the pledges held in the banks next door. Even the streets were in a mess. All the way from Cannaregio to the Agudi bridge, the cobbles needed replacing. Complaints were incessant.

Since few of the Ghetto's landowners were willing to spend money on renovations, the most foolish – and dangerous – structural changes were undertaken. In 1757, two adjoining buildings near the Scuola Spagnola were literally cut in half, from top to bottom, so that the apartments would be more clearly separated – and hence easier to rent.[54] Work had already begun by the time anyone realized that one half was now without a set of stairs. By then, it was too late to put in a proper staircase, so a rickety set of wooden steps, known as the 'mad stairs' (*scala matta*), was simply flung between them, without anything to hold it up beyond a bit of mortar and a few beams. How nobody died walking up them is a mystery.

We have little direct evidence of what daily life was like for the poorest in this period. Of all the Ghetto's history, these decades are by far the most sparsely studied. But the signs of growing privation are unmistakable. For most of Venice's Jews, the only question was whether death or destitution would get them first.

PART IV

Death and Afterlife

12

The Burning of the Gates

(1789–1797)

For Venice's Jews, the Fast of Tammuz was traditionally one of the saddest days of the year. Commemorating the moment the Romans breached the walls of Jerusalem in AD 70, it was a time of lamentation. Between dawn and dusk, no food would be eaten, no music would be played, and no celebrations of any kind would take place. The only sound was that of sobbing or prayer. But in 1797, things were different. Rather than being consumed with grief, the Ghetto was ablaze with joy. The *campo* was a riot of colour; music blared from impromptu bands; and in the middle of it all, a crowd of jubilant Jews were dancing in the glow of a gigantic bonfire.

Eight years before – just when times had seemed darkest – a faint light had appeared on the horizon. On 14 July 1789, the French Revolution had broken out. The *ancien régime* had been toppled, and a new, constitutional government had been set up in its place. At first, the rest of Europe had regarded the unfolding drama with more curiosity than concern. But as the revolution grew more radical, alarm quickly mounted. Threatened from abroad, the revolutionaries went on the offensive. On 20 April 1792, France declared war on Austria – and an invasion of the Austrian Netherlands was immediately launched. Almost from the first, it was a disaster. The undisciplined and poorly armed French troops were quickly pushed back, and before long, enemy troops were advancing on Paris. In the ensuing panic, the monarchy was abolished, and summary executions became the norm. Not until the Battle of Valmy did the French army begin to turn the tide. Evidently a new strategy was required. If France was to stand a chance against Austria and her allies, it would need a diversion. The decision was therefore taken to attack northern Italy. The thinking was that, if

Austria's possessions in Lombardy could be threatened, it would be forced to divert troops from the Rhineland – and thereby relieve pressure on French forces fighting on the eastern front. No one thought it would be a long campaign. Undermanned and badly equipped, the Army of Italy was in the worst condition of any of France's field armies. It was to cause as much bother as it could and then retreat. At least, that was the plan.

To lead the attack, the French government appointed the young Napoleon Bonaparte. Then just twenty-six years old, he had distinguished himself at the siege of Toulon – and was already marked out for great things. Rallying his ragtag forces, he marched into Piedmont and, in less than two months, knocked Sardinia out of the war. He then crushed the Austrians at Lodi and captured Milan. By the end of May 1796, the only significant fortress remaining in Austrian hands was Mantua.

The Venetians hardly knew what to do. Under Doge Lodovico Manin – a thin, sickly man, popularly known as *sior spavento* (Mr Frightened) – the Republic had hoped that its traditional policy of neutrality would keep it safe from the French storm.[1] But Napoleon was advancing too quickly for Venice simply to stand aside. Mantua could neither be held by the Austrians nor be taken by the French without troops crossing Venetian territory. Whether Venice liked it or not, therefore, it would have to choose a side.

The prospect of a French alliance did not appeal. The Venetian nobility was pro-Austrian, almost to a man, and instinctively hostile to revolutionaries. Nor, when Venetian officials encountered Napoleon for the first time, were the reports particularly favourable. Although no one could deny his early success, some felt that he might be running out of steam. Gian Battista Contarini, the *podestà* of Crema, was frankly unimpressed. He was 'struck by the young general's physical frailty, and by the fact that he made no effort to conceal his fatigue'.[2] Others found him too hostile to be trustworthy. On 26 May 1797, Alvise Mocenigo wrote from Brescia that, during their brief interview, even the most innocent remark was met with a torrent of angry abuse.[3] With such a man in command, Venice did not feel able to accept France's offer of an alliance – no matter how attractive it was made to seem.

But Venice was in no position to fight, either.[4] Since the Austrians – harried and hopelessly overstretched – had made it clear that Venice could expect no help from Vienna, the Republic would have to go it alone. The government seemed paralysed by indecision. It called up the fleet from Corfu, then abruptly changed its mind and appointed a *provveditore alle lagune* – an admiral of the home fleet – to draw up a report on the resources near to hand. This made for pitiful reading; but inexplicably, no effort was made either to build more ships or to raise additional troops. Already, Venice was struggling to keep control over the *terraferma*. Discontent had been stirring in the countryside, and there had been attacks on Venetian landlords in several key towns.[5] Against the French army, Venice's chances would be slim at best.

A precarious neutrality was the only alternative. Venice would stand by its friendship with Austria. But it gave Napoleon everything he asked for, too. He would have free access to Verona, control over the Adige bridges, and whatever supplies he might need. It was a clumsy compromise. The Venetians were not so foolish as to believe that it would last. As the French campaign had already shown, Napoleon would never be able to settle the affairs of northern Italy without curtailing – or even destroying – Venice's rule over the *terraferma*. But the longer they could postpone any fighting, the better. If they were lucky, Napoleon might soon come unstuck, anyway. If not, who knew? Maybe a diplomatic solution could still be found.

*

For Venice's Jews, Napoleon's advance should, in theory, have promised hope. Back in France, all the former restrictions on Jewish life had been swept away. Granted, popular prejudices remained strong. In the early days of the Revolution, there had been riots in regions like Alsace, chiefly in response to food shortages; and many revolutionaries openly despised Jewish 'superstition'.[6] But the Constituent Assembly had eventually recognized that, if the Declaration of the Rights of Man was not applied equally to *all* men, irrespective of their creed, it would have no value at all. On 27 September 1791, the Jews of France were therefore granted full citizenship – thereby becoming the first population in Europe to be emancipated.[7]

Venetian Jews could not help being suspicious at first. As their French cousins had discovered, civic liberties were not all they were cracked up to be. They had been gained at the price of severe economic disadvantages. To appease the opponents of emancipation, the Constituent Assembly had decreed that any debts owed to Jews were to be reviewed by specially appointed assessors and, where appropriate, forgiven.[8] In 1792, thousands of debts were cancelled. Even more were simply ignored – with predictably devastating results. Still more worryingly, French Jews found that citizenship was no guarantee against persecution. As Revolution gave way to Terror, a wave of anti-religious attacks swept across France. Synagogues were closed; leading Jews were hounded in the street; and several Jews suspected either of associating with the more liberal Girondins or of conspiring with counter-revolutionaries were executed.[9] In late 1793, the Convention's commissioner in Alsace even called for a campaign of *régénération guillotinière* against the Jews – and it was only by good luck that a more general bloodletting was avoided.[10]

For all the upheavals of recent years, the Jewish community therefore remained loyal to the Venetian Republic, despite its obvious weaknesses. Giuseppe (Iseppo) Treves – one of the richest men in the Ghetto, perhaps the whole city – offered the government a huge loan, and the synagogues donated an enormous quantity of gold and silver plate to the state treasury.[11]

*

For a time, the uneasy peace held.[12] On 2 February 1797, Mantua fell to the French after a long siege. The last vestiges of Austrian power in Italy were destroyed for ever. Napoleon had now far exceeded the original objectives of his campaign. But with the Austrians on the run, he saw no need to stop. Leaving behind garrisons in Bergamo, Brescia, and Verona, he led the bulk of his army north, across the Brenner Pass, into Habsburg territory.

There, matters might easily have ended – with Venice humbled, but otherwise largely unscathed. But to everyone's surprise, Bergamo and Brescia, emboldened by the presence of foreign soldiers, suddenly rose in rebellion. At first, the French stood back, wary of inflaming the situation. Soon enough, however, they were helping the rebels to take control of nearby Crema. The Venetian government was horrified. It had to stop the rebels before any more of its territory was lost. But how? Without an army to speak of, it had no choice but to raise a militia from the peasantry. The Venetians did not want to do anything to anger the French, no matter how badly Napoleon's men had behaved, so the militia was given orders to act only against the rebels. The peasants had other ideas, though. They were more interested in settling scores with the French than with their countrymen. Almost immediately, violence broke out – and soon enough, French soldiers were lying dead.

Napoleon was furious. He demanded that the Venetians hand over the guilty parties and disband the militia immediately. Before the Senate could offer its apologies, worse news arrived. On Easter Monday (17 April), anti-French riots broke out in Verona.[13] Hundreds of soldiers were taken prisoner. This was too much for Napoleon. He had had enough of Venice. It had clearly lost control. Since he could not continue his campaign in Austria while unrest threatened his rear, he made peace with the Habsburgs – and turned his attention to the lagoon.

Seizing on a minor incident, in which a French boat was attacked by overzealous Venetian officials, Napoleon now ratcheted up the pressure. As he told the Republic's terrified emissaries, he would be 'an Attila for the State of Venice' unless they gave him satisfaction. He wanted the *terraferma* evacuated, the governing oligarchy dismissed, and the constitution reformed. In short, he wanted the Venetian Republic to abolish itself.

It was impossible to refuse. Though the working classes were ready to fight, the patricians had resigned themselves to defeat. French troops had already been sighted on the banks of the lagoon, and the mood in the city was getting ugly. On 12 May, the Great Council was convened for the last time. The doge, pale and trembling, proposed a motion, accepting all of Napoleon's terms. Before the debate could open, gunshots rang out in the piazza. The patricians panicked. Unaware that some Slav mercenaries were just firing their guns in salute as they left the city, they assumed that an invasion – or a revolution – had begun. Rushing to the urns, they voted their approval and hurried away to safety. It was to an almost empty hall that the doge announced the end of the Venetian Republic.

Four days later, Napoleon's forces entered the city in triumph. A Provisional Municipality – composed of representatives from all social classes – was set up to administer the occupied city, and a few weeks later, the French commander presided over a grand celebration of Venetian 'freedom'. A tree of liberty was erected in the Piazza San

Marco; the doge's *corno* was burnt, along with the *libro d'oro*; and a new symbol – celebrating the 'Rights of Man and the Citizen' – was chosen.

*

All at once, the Jews of Venice realized their lives were about to change. The new constitution made all men, including Jews, equal before the law. Three of the Ghetto's leading figures – Mosè Luzzatto, Isaac Grego, and Vita Vivante – were chosen to serve on the Municipality.[14] Some rabbis were even seen cheering at the great celebration of Venetian liberty in the Piazza San Marco. And *libertà, egualità, fratellanza* was on everyone's lips.

But the question of what would happen to the Ghetto itself was still to be resolved. For the Provisional Municipality, the answer was far from obvious. If Jews were citizens, like everyone else, there was surely no need for the Jewish community to be kept apart, much less accorded a distinct corporate status. Back in France, many revolutionaries had vehemently opposed any such idea. At a stormy debate on 23 December 1789, Stanislas de Clermont-Tonnerre had declared that:

> everything must be refused to the Jews as a Nation in the sense of a corporate body and everything must be granted to the Jews as individuals . . . They must make up neither a political body nor an order within the State; they must individually be citizens.[15]

It was only reasonable to apply the same logic in Venice. The Ghetto – along with its system of self-government – would have to go. But there was a problem. If the Jewish community was fully integrated into the citizen body, what would happen to the banks? For almost 200 years, the banks had been reliant on the taxes paid by the community, and – less regularly – on loans raised through collective action. It was impossible to abolish Jewish self-government without also destroying the banks. That meant no more loans, and no one in the Municipality wanted that. Prior to the French invasion of Italy, Venetians had been using the banks with growing frequency. In June 1793, when agricultural prices were once again on the rise, the Black bank is estimated to have lent 60,328 ducats – more than four times what it had lent the previous summer.[16] As always, it was the poor who relied on loans the most. Granted, the economic situation had improved a little since then, but there was no way Venice could survive without the banks – especially without an alternative to fall back on.[17]

The Jews had cause to be sceptical of complete integration, too. One of the principal reasons was security. During the Republic's final days, tensions over Venice's abysmal public finances came to the boil. There were protests about the level of debt, and it seemed probable that violence would be directed against Jewish banks. So great was the threat, in fact, that troops were dispatched to surround the Ghetto and ensure 'the necessary tranquillity'.[18] A leading rabbi affixed three special *mezuzot* to the gates to guarantee God's protection.[19] However burdensome the Ghetto might be, the Jews still had cause to feel safer together than dispersed around the city. If all distinctions were abolished, a vital safeguard might be lost – or at least weakened.

The Provisional Municipality was careful not to act too rashly. On 2 July, an edict was issued, apparently in the hope of soothing jangled nerves. For the moment, at least, there would be no radical changes to Jewish self-government.[20] The current heads of the Università were to remain in office for another two weeks. During that time, a meeting of all Jewish citizens was to be held in one of the scuole, so that three replacements could be elected. Most importantly, everything possible should be done to ensure the banks kept lending. Anyone who tried to interfere with their business was to be immediately reported to the authorities.

Five days later, the Municipality passed another decree.[21] This began innocuously enough. It set out what security there would be at the meeting, who would have the right to vote, and what title the new heads should be given – all routine stuff. But then, at the very end of the decree, came the crucial clause: '[t]he gates of the Ghetto should be removed forthwith, so that there should not seem to be any separation between [Jews] and the other Citizens of this City'.[22]

No one had any illusions about this, of course. Although the decree appeared to recognize that, after almost 300 years, Jews would finally enjoy the same legal rights as everyone else, it left the Jewish community essentially intact and unchanged. Apart from the gates, everyday life would carry on much as it had before – with the same institutions, the same corporate identity, and the same financial responsibilities. The banks would remain a heavy burden; and there were still a lot of issues which needed clarifying before anyone would be fully satisfied.

But it was enough. When the Ghetto's residents met in the Scuola Spagnola on 9 July, they struggled to conceal their delight.[23] As soon as they had elected the new heads (or 'Jewish citizen deputies', as they were now known), they rushed through a measure renouncing what little judicial autonomy they had retained. For years, rabbis had used the threat of excommunication to dissuade Jews from appealing to – or even co-operating with – the civil authorities. Now, any constraint 'incompatible with the . . . new constitution' was banned. Henceforth, excommunication would be used only for religious matters, and the city magistrates, long viewed with suspicion, would be given a free hand. It was a clear show of confidence, even optimism. And with that, the meeting closed amidst tumultuous cries of 'Long live Fraternity, Democracy, and the Italian Nation'.

*

On 10 July – the Fast of Tammuz – the stage was set for the great event. Overseeing matters was Pier Gian Maria de Ferrari, a suitably aristocratic officer from the new National Guard.[24] Early that day, he sat down with the three citizen deputies – Daniel Levi Polacco, Vidal d'Angeli, and Moisè di David Sullam – to discuss how they could keep the celebrations as 'decorous and peaceful' as possible. They needed to let the Jewish population enjoy the moment, of course; but they also had to find a way of keeping order without giving the impression that the Ghetto was being 'occupied' by the Municipality. Nothing could be left to chance.

At five o'clock in the afternoon, a battalion of guardsmen, led by Ferrari, set off for the Ghetto from the Fondamenta San Girolamo, dressed in their finest uniforms, and accompanied by the gay sound of trumpets and drums. Cheering crowds lined the route; the air was alive with music; and the streets seemed to blaze with colour. On arriving in the Campo del Ghetto Nuovo, Ferrari's men formed up in a circle, alongside another detachment of National Guardsmen and 'numerous' members of the Patriotic Society. Then, as Ferrari's adjutant read out the decree ordering the destruction of the gates, the three citizen deputies stepped forward. It was the moment of truth. Everyone held their breath. Slowly, solemnly, the keys to the Ghetto were presented to Ferrari, who in turn handed them over to a group of Arsenalotti. The crowd went wild. In the excitement, the keys seem to have been snatched away and paraded around the square. 'It is impossible to describe the satisfaction and the happiness of the people who rushed up,' Ferrari recalled, 'who with joyful cries of "Liberty" couldn't get enough of dragging those Keys across the ground, blessing the time and place of [their] Regeneration'.[25] Then, the real work began. The Arsenalotti swung their axes – and in no time, the gates came crashing to the ground. Any vestiges of restraint were now forgotten. As Ferrari put it,

> people of both sexes thronged together, without any distinction, in joyful democratic Dances in the middle of the Piazza, where members of the National Guard still stood, and even rabbis dressed in the Mosaic fashion were spotted dancing, rousing the Jewish Citizens to still greater exertions.[26]

The gates were carried in triumph into the square, smashed to pieces, and thrown onto a fire. Moments later, National Guardsmen chopped down a tree in a nearby garden and set it up in the middle of the *campo* as a 'Liberty Tree', whereupon a woman immediately pulled off her cap and hoisted it on top.

Then it was time for the speeches. Raffael Vivante – the son of Vita, and himself an officer in the National Guard – jumped up onto one of the wells.[27] 'The music, the blows of the axes, the confusion, and the excitement of the people made it impossible for everyone to hear' everything he said. But for those who could, his words seemed to capture the sense of providence fulfilled and forgiveness granted. 'Brothers,' he cried,

> The happy day has finally come when prejudice and superstition have been brought low and the injuries and offenses which we have so unjustly suffered have been avenged . . . That vast abyss which separated us from other nations has been completely overcome, and here you have toppled the terrible doors which held our Nation as if locked up in a prison, and which were reinforced by thousands upon thousands of iron bars, devised by the most hateful arrogance. Yes, my

brothers, those same men who previously looked down with indifference on us, humiliated and oppressed, now give us the means to rise up, enlighten and better ourselves, inviting us to love them and invite us to consider them no longer in the revolting guise of our persecutors.[28]

Others, too, rose to speak – Isaac Grego, who was then the president of the Patriotic Society, and even a Dalmatian priest.[29] But the light was probably growing too dim and the festivities too raucous for anyone to pay much attention. At Vivante's house, an enormous party – open to all – was already in full swing. The Scuola Spagnola was lit with brilliant illuminations; shouts of happiness echoed through the streets; and – with all thought of lamentation now banished from people's minds – the dancing went on till dawn. Where once Jerusalem had fallen, the Ghetto was free at last.

13

The Price of Freedom

(1797–1835)

When everyone woke up the next day – many with sore heads and aching joints – the burning of the gates must have seemed like a dream. Yet sure enough, down in the *campo*, the ashes were still there; and as the days passed, further proofs of the Jews' new-found freedom only multiplied. On 11 July, the Ghetto's name – long a mark of segregation – was changed to the 'Contrada dell'Unione' (District of the Union); and when the French held a regatta to celebrate their triumph a little while later, Jews took part alongside their Christian neighbours in gaily decorated boats.[1]

An unfamiliar sense of optimism now swept over the Ghetto. Only a few weeks earlier, this had been elegantly foreshadowed in a speech by 'citizen' Vincenzo Dandolo. A dashing, if heavyset, young firebrand, Dandolo was the son of a Jewish convert. After a dazzling career in chemistry, he had emerged as one of the most prominent members of the new Municipality – and had immediately recognized the significance of the changes then being wrought. As he proudly declared, a 'monstrous and terrible' government had been swept away, and an age of 'regeneration' had begun.[2]

Yet however keenly Jews looked forward to the future, hope could not blind them either to the realities of daily life or to the challenges which still lay ahead. True, the gates were gone; and, in theory, Jews were citizens like any other. But little else had changed. The Jews' condition was almost exactly the same as it had been before the gates had been burnt. They were still treated separately; they were still subject to heavy financial obligations; and they were still bound by countless petty restrictions. And this was to say nothing of the banks.

A painful reminder of the Jews' unequal status was not long in coming. By late July, the Provisional Municipality was struggling with unexpected financial obligations. The French army, still in the field, needed supplying; and Napoleon had made it clear that he expected the Venetians to contribute.[3] A tax of 867,900 ducats was hence imposed on Venice's merchants and shopkeepers; and of this, the disproportionate sum of 223,100 ducats – more than 25 per cent of the total – was to be paid by Jews.[4]

Since this was a tax on products, rather than people, the burden fell most heavily on a narrow elite. Just six Jewish families contributed a massive 174,000 ducats. The Vivante and the Bonfil-Treves (who were united through marriage into a single family a few years later) each paid 68,000 ducats – by far the largest amount in the whole of Venice. A further 104 Jewish households paid the remaining 49,100 ducats, contributing anything between 20 and 10,000 ducats each. Since the Jewish community then consisted of 421 nuclear families, this meant that 311 households (74 per cent) – around 1,200 people – paid nothing at all.[5]

But the tax assessment only tells part of the story. A census (*anagrafe*) carried out by Saul Levi Mortera on 5 October 1797 indicates that economic activity, while far less vigorous than in the past, was still not confined to a minority.[6] Jews practised a range of professions; though some were certainly wealthier than others, incomes may have been more evenly distributed than products alone suggest.

According to Mortera's *anagrafe*, the Jewish community consisted of 820 men and 806 women. Of these, more than a third had been born outside Venice. Most had emigrated to the Ghetto from the *terraferma*, especially Verona; but a few had also made their way from Friuli. Out of 473 heads of household, over 200 were engaged in trade or ran businesses of one size or another. There were fifty-five merchants, seventy-five second-hand rag salesmen, twenty-four unspecified 'agents', six change-brokers, three jewellery dealers, four haberdashers, twenty-three food sellers, one furniture dealer, and one bookseller – to name just a few. Then came the artisans: eight tailors, three printers, three painters ('probably only decorators'), one chair-fixer, and one stone-cutter. A third group was made up of 'professionals': fifteen schoolteachers, twenty-one rabbis and other officiants, five doctors, three surgeons, and one midwife, as well as five porters, three letter carriers, and two custodians of the poorhouse. Lower down the social scale, there were eighty-four servants and cooks – the large number of which is probably best explained by the fact that richer families, like the Vivante and Treves, each employed at least a dozen domestic staff, generally of German or Polish origin. There were also nineteen industrial labourers, who found day work without any security, and, unusually, a lone farmer. Then, at the very bottom, there were twenty-nine beggars, who lived entirely on alms.

Yet even if the Ghetto economy was more varied than the tax suggests, its outlook wasn't exactly promising. There was no getting around the fact that most Jews pursued comparatively humble professions. Almost a quarter of the population either depended on employment with a wealthy minority or were destitute. Only merchants enjoyed a reasonable income; but thanks to the war, even their prospects were far from secure.

*

To this uncertainty was added another, even greater. Now that Napoleon had succeeded in driving the Austrians out of northern Italy, he was desperate to cement his glory by securing a peace with Holy Roman Emperor Francis II before any of his rivals could reach Vienna. Unbeknownst to the Venetians, he therefore made Francis an offer he couldn't refuse. In exchange for the Austrian Netherlands and Lombardy, the Habsburgs would receive Venice and all of its mainland possessions. When this was made public, in the Treaty of Campoformio, on 17 October 1797, the sense of betrayal was acute. The poet Ugo Foscolo, who had only recently hailed Napoleon as Venice's liberator, rose in public meetings 'to vomit forth all the imprecations possible against Bonaparte'.[7] Everything the Venetians had gained now seemed in jeopardy. 'All is lost,' wailed Foscolo in *Ultime lettere di Jacopo Ortis*; while the playwright Carlo Gozzi lamented that democracy may have been nothing more than a 'sweet, delusive dream'.[8] There was already talk of reprisals. Fearing arrest, Vincenzo Dandolo fled to Milan.[9] Many others followed.

What the Austrians would do about Venice's Jews was anyone's guess. Austria had led Europe in the emancipation of Jews a few decades earlier, but there was no telling how durable its liberalism would prove in the lagoon. Yet despite the uncertainty, the Jews were not prepared to accept just anything. Having tasted freedom, they wanted to be sure their existing status would be preserved – and, if possible, improved.

In the summer of 1798, the Università tested the waters by drawing attention to the paradoxical nature of the Jews' economic position. As part of the compromise which had led to the toppling of the gates, the Provisional Municipality had insisted that the Jewish community should continue to be treated as a separate corporation. The Università would still be responsible for acting on the Jews' behalf in any dealings with the authorities, and for administering its internal affairs. Since this was exactly how Venice's guilds worked, the Municipality had simply absorbed the Università into the guild system. As part of this, each Jewish male was required to pay two additional financial obligations: a membership fee (known as the *taglione*) and a percentage of his profits (the *tansa*).[10] Taken together, these brought the state 11,000 ducats each year.

Just because the Municipality treated the Università like any other group of artisans, this did not mean that Jews benefitted from the same rights and privileges, however. They were barred from practising any of the 'protected' trades, like shoemaking, carpentry, or gold-beating; and they were still the only people in Venice to be taxed not as individuals but collectively.

When the last *condotta* expired, the Università saw an opportunity to settle the matter. On 30 July 1798, three representatives of the Jewish community – all prominent businessmen – informed the new authorities that they would no longer accept the burdens of guild-like status unless they also enjoyed the same rights and privileges. Until this demand was granted, they would not pay either the *taglione* or the *tansa*. As Mario Berengo has noted, their 'tacit, but manifest intention' was to present the Municipality with a choice: either Jews would be treated as if they belonged to a guild like any other, in which case they would be allowed to practise 'protected' trades; or – as they would undoubtedly have preferred – they would be treated as individuals and taxed accordingly.[11]

In principle, Venice's new Austrian rulers were not unsympathetic. Everything the Jewish delegates had said was perfectly reasonable. The Università *was* an anomaly. Back in Austria, the Jews' demands had already been granted. In 1782, the Edict of Toleration had lifted 'Jewish' taxes and granted Austrian Jews the right to practise all trades, albeit not as master craftsmen; and 'assimilation' had become the linchpin of imperial policy.[12]

The sticking point was – as ever – the banks. Without the Università, there would be no banks. And without the banks, cash-strapped Venetians would have nowhere else to turn. Nowhere else, that is, unless an alternative could be found. Fortunately, just such an alternative was at hand. The previous year, shortly before the Ghetto's gates were torn down, the 'old corps of Jewish citizens' (*corpo Vecchio de' cittadini ebrei*) – most likely descendants of those who had signed the *condotta* in 1738 – had offered to liquidate the three Jewish banks and hand over their capital to the state, so that a *monte di pietà* could be set up instead. The Provisional Municipality's interest had been piqued. It had ordered plans to be drawn up; and, for a time, the scheme had seemed quite realistic.[13] It had been calculated that such a *monte* would have an annual turnover of around 8 million ducats, and would need six branches – one for each *sestiere* – to handle the business involved.[14] There had been plenty of enthusiasm for it. Vincenzo Dandolo had promoted the *monte* as 'a matter of the greatest importance for the good of the people'; and a certain Marco Piazza had published a pamphlet defending its merits.[15] According to Piazza, a *monte* would encourage the circulation of money, reduce inequalities, and even foster civic engagement. It would also reduce the abuse perpetrated by Christian moneylenders operating 'under the radar'.

In the event, nothing had come of this. The Provisional Municipality had been too short-lived – and too pressed for cash – to see the idea through to fruition. As far as the Università could see, there was no reason why it should not be resurrected now that the Austrians were in charge. It was, in many ways, the perfect solution to the Jewish community's economic problems. And this was the perfect moment to discuss it, too. The Università had already refused to pay the *taglione* and the *tansa*. It reasoned that, if it refused to renew the *condotta* as well, the Austrian authorities would *have* to agree to the dissolution of the banks. This, in turn, would allow the Università to be abolished, the 'Jewish' taxes to be set aside, and the Jews to take their place as ordinary citizens. It wasn't as if the Austrians could threaten Venice's Jews with expulsion – so how could they lose?

Unfortunately, Johann von Thugut – the de facto Austrian foreign minister – didn't see things the same way.[16] He had no principled objection to granting the Jews anything, of course. His concern was purely pragmatic – or rather, political. Although he could see the merits of a *monte di pietà*, he was also keenly aware of the danger it would pose. Since taking over, the Austrian government had increasingly relied on the co-operation of the old Venetian aristocracy, whose traditional antisemitism had only grown worse under French rule.[17] Thugut could not risk offending them with anything so favourable to Jewish interests. He therefore decided to call the Jews' bluff. Even if he couldn't threaten them with expulsion, he was reasonably sure they wouldn't leave – and he was ready to use this to preserve the status quo.

At Thugut's urging, the Imperial Council in Vienna argued that the Università, having assumed responsibility for the banks, could not just shake it off. It was part of their heritage now, as immutable and enduring as the Jewish faith. In 1801, a new *condotta* – continuing all the obligations the Università had taken on under the Venetian Republic – was issued.[18] Technically speaking, it was not a *condotta* at all. It did not lay out the usual rules and norms governing the condition of Jews in Venice, nor was it an agreement.[19] The Università was not consulted; and, given the choice, the Jewish community would never have accepted some of its terms. Rather, it was an order imposed from on high. And in contrast to how things had been under the Republic, the Jewish community simply had to accept it.

As long as the banks remained open, Thugut had no real incentive to consider the Jews' other demands. This left Jewish workers in limbo. Some Jews, impatient at being stuck in low-paying professions, had already begun practising 'protected' trades illicitly – no doubt hoping that, in the circumstances, the Austrians would turn a blind eye. But Thugut insisted on enforcing the existing labour rules to the letter. A raft of prosecutions followed. In 1801, Laudadio Fano, who had boldly (or foolhardily) given his occupation as *tapezzier* (upholsterer) in the *anagrafe*, was repeatedly denounced and found guilty of engaging in a forbidden activity.[20] In December of the same year, the Austrian authorities received a petition for six Jews to be imprisoned for having practised money-changing outside the Ghetto.[21] Even when Jews applied for an exemption, they were invariably turned down – or simply ignored. In August 1805, Samuele Emmanuel Coen Mondovì's request to 'be able to practise the profession of a chemist and to open a spice shop (*speziaria*) like every other subject of His Majesty' was not even heard.[22]

No less importantly, the Austrian courts also had an alarmingly ambivalent attitude towards Jews' property.[23] That Jews had the right to own property was not in doubt. Once they had acquired a piece of real estate, their title was – in theory – beyond question. The purchasing process was another matter, however. There was no guarantee that, when a Jew offered to buy a property, he (or she) would be allowed to complete the transaction. Local officials – drawn mostly from the old Venetian patriarchate – would decide on a case-by-case basis whether a Jew could be a property owner or not; and neither Thugut nor any of his colleagues in Vienna saw any need to interfere.

The combined effect of all this was to strengthen the judicial walls separating the Ghetto from the rest of the city. Although all Venetians were theoretically equal, the Austrians had plainly decided that some were more equal than others. Jews were not merely second-class citizens; they were even worse off than they had been under the French. What had originally been an awkward compromise was now enshrined in policy. They would go on shouldering crippling obligations without gaining any benefits in return; their rights, far from being assured, were contingent; and their economic opportunities were, if anything, even more constrained than before. Under Austrian rule, it seemed, freedom was just a different class of discrimination.

*

As it turned out, this did not last long. Far from settling the affairs of Italy, the Treaty of Campoformio merely marked a pause in hostilities. Soon enough, France and Austria were at war – and once again, it was Napoleon who took the advantage. Following his victories at Austerlitz and Jena, he forced Francis II to sign the Peace of Pressburg, returning most of the territories ceded to Austria only a few years before. Venice – together with the *terraferma*, Istria, and Dalmatia – was integrated into the new kingdom of Italy; and on 4 February 1806, the viceroy, Eugène de Beauharnais, Napoleon's stepson, entered the city in triumph.[24]

Beauharnais was a dashing, elegant figure. He was no fool, though. He knew that, however much the Venetians may have resented Austrian rule, their enthusiasm for the French was only skin-deep. He could not simply turn back the clock. He would have to work both with returning members of the Municipality and with the old patricians. Yet even if he could not 'renew the former rhetoric of liberty and fraternity', his arrival nevertheless marked a transformation in the city's fortunes – no more so than for its Jews.[25]

Soon, reforms were coming thick and fast. In keeping with the spirit of the Napoleonic Code, all distinctions between Jews and Christians were formally abolished. Henceforth, Jews would be taxed as individuals, rather than as a separate group. Their right to own property was confirmed. And every profession was opened to them.

By far the most important reform concerned the banks. On 4 August 1806, representatives of the Jewish community wrote to the Municipality offering, once again, to hand over the capital still left in the banks.[26] This amounted to about 130,000 ducats, less than two-thirds of what it had been thirty years earlier, but still a sizeable sum. Claiming to be moved only by 'affectionate patriotism', they expressed the hope that it could be used to set up 'the most charitable work of a *monte di pietà*'. They even suggested that Jewish officials could help run it.

Unlike the Austrians, the French authorities had no hesitation in accepting. On 28 October, a *monte di pietà* was finally established. It was to be floated with a combination of public funds and private donations, and loans would be capped at 15 Italian lira. Four days later, the Jewish banks were formally united, under a board composed of both Christians and Jews, and soon the first loans were made. Since it was fully owned by the state, it was not technically a *monte di pietà*, and only years later would it become a truly charitable institution. Nor did anyone seem to appreciate the irony of a *monte* – which had previously served as a prelude to the expulsion of Jewish populations from Italian towns – being founded at the Jews' own suggestion. But these were minor quibbles. What mattered was that the Jewish banks were gone. The heaviest – and longest-lasting – burden on the Jewish community had now been lifted.

For some Jews, a new dawn had broken. The Ghetto's great families found doors which had hitherto been closed to them suddenly flung open. When, in 1807, Napoleon himself visited Venice, brightly decorated boats belonging to the Treves, Vivante, and Malta families joined the procession sent to escort him.[27] Giuseppe (Iseppo) Treves – who had given the Republic money to defend itself against Napoleon only a decade earlier – now found himself feted by Venice's new ruler. By then, he was already president of the newly founded Camera di Commercio.[28] Three years later, when a statue of the emperor was erected in the *piazzetta*, he delivered the speech of dedication and, in return, was created a baron in the kingdom of Italy. It was not long before he was garlanded with even more honours.

For most Jews, the effects of the second French 'liberation' were more muted. While the legal barriers to their assimilation had been removed, few saw any improvement in the material conditions of life. The Ghetto itself was in a dreadful state. During the last decades of the eighteenth century, the fabric of the Jewish quarter had steadily declined. There had been several collapses. Many houses were left empty, and storerooms – once overflowing with produce – went unused.[29] Since then, things had only got worse. The unrest that had reigned since the fall of the old Republic had destroyed any pretence of upkeep. The Università – unsure of where its responsibilities lay – did little, if anything, to maintain the streets and bridges. Apartments were seldom, if ever, repaired. Either landlords stopped receiving rent, and so refused to spend money on improvements; or, more often, the owners were simply unknown. The fragmentation of families, the division of inheritances, and sheer administrative confusion had made it virtually impossible to determine to whom many buildings belonged.

The French were not insensible to this. Almost as soon as Beauharnais had set up a new municipal authority, the French Commissioner General of Police, Pierre Lagarde, warned that the city was in urgent need of renovation.[30] It was in such a pitiful state that the novelist and philosopher Madame de Staël noted that 'a feeling of sadness seizes the imagination as you enter Venice'.[31] There was a swift response. On 20 May 1806, a decree was issued ordering that, if any building overlooking a public thoroughfare fell into disrepair, the authorities were empowered either to compel the owner to effect repairs at his own expense or, in the most extreme cases, to tear it down. Curiously, no effort was made to apply this to the Ghetto. Whether from fear of the patricians' reaction or mere bureaucratic inertia, it was simply left to crumble.

Some of the richer families began to leave for other parts of the city. Granted, it was no exodus. Over the next decade, only a handful of Jews moved out.[32] But their departure was indicative of the immense chasm opening up within Jewish society. The Vivante are a telling example of these families.³³ Already distinguished, they had invested heavily in real estate after the Austrians' departure. In 1812, they moved to the Palazzo Bonfadini, on the Cannaregio canal, first as tenants, then, in 1815, as owners. They decorated it in magnificent style. Giovanni Carlo Bevilacqua was commissioned to adorn it with frescoes in the new Empire style; and it was soon one of the smartest *palazzi* in the area – a stark contrast with the condition into which the Ghetto was then slipping.

*

By then, however, French rule was already crumbling.³⁴ The Austrians, aware of how crucial Venice was to Napoleon's ambitions in the Adriatic, had gone back on the offensive. An early assault on Mestre achieved little; but by September 1813, Beauharnais was on the back foot. The following month, Venice was placed under siege. There was nothing Napoleon could do to help. After his defeat at the Battle of Leipzig, he was forced to retreat into France and needed every last soldier for his own defence. Beauharnais was on his own. His counsellors urged him to sue for a separate peace, just as Murat had done in Naples. By the time he made up his mind, it was already too late. On 11 April 1814, Napoleon abdicated – and within days, the Austrians returned to Venice.

For Venice's Jews, this marked a moment of jeopardy. In Austria itself, attitudes towards the Jews had, admittedly, grown no harsher. Throughout the empire, assimilation had become the cornerstone of imperial policy; and in the great cities, bourgeois Jews were welcomed into social circles which had previously taken pride in excluding them.³⁵ Indeed, at the Congress of Vienna – at which the post-Napoleonic order was to be settled – the Austrian Chancellor, Klemens von Metternich, had boasted that 'Jewish communities [had] long enjoyed a treatment which accords with the requirements of humanity' – and urged Hanseatic towns to adopt a more conciliatory manner.³⁶

Yet the upheavals of recent years had shaken Austrian confidence – and its reforming instincts now pulled against a more trenchant conservatism.³⁷ The government saw conspiracies and revolutionaries everywhere. A new campaign of political repression began. Policing was strengthened, censorship was tightened, and the number of spies was dramatically increased. Anything perceived as harmful to public order, to the institution of monarchy, or to the Catholic faith was suppressed – albeit rather less severely than historians were once inclined to believe.[38] Most suspicious of all was the taint of Bonapartism, especially in the new kingdom of Lombardy–Venetia.[39] Any legislation passed, or decree executed, by Napoleon was automatically suspect, no matter how rational or uncontroversial it might be. And, naturally, this included the emancipation of the Venetian Jews.

The question facing the Austrians was simple. Should Venice's Jews be allowed to go on living as before, in the name of economic expediency, even though their current status had been granted by Napoleon's viceroy? Or should they be treated as a potentially troublesome minority who needed to be separated from the city's Christians for everyone's sake? For Anton von Raab, the new police commissioner, the answer was obvious. He was a 'tolerant, fair-minded man', but he had serious doubts about the Jews' loyalty.[40] On 3 July 1815, he bluntly informed the Austrian prefect of Venice that 'the Jews are not in favour of the present government'.[41] This was not entirely inaccurate, but the Jews' wariness was likely motivated more by fear than by antipathy. Either way, it could not be tolerated. Von Raab therefore recommended that the Ghetto be reinstated, a strict separation between Jews and Christians maintained, and any land purchased by Jews since 1805 confiscated.

A less suspicious mind held sway in the prefecture, however. Just three days later, von Raab's suggestions were firmly rejected – and he was ordered not to molest the city's Jews in any way. This was not from any sense of humanity or justice, but economic expediency. They 'have in their hands,' the reply read, 'three quarters of the entire remaining business in this market, and they are thus almost the only capitalists that can be counted upon'.[42] Yet now that the French had freed them from their collective obligations, there was nothing, in principle, to keep them in the city. If Raab was allowed to antagonize them, they might easily leave.

The question was far from resolved, though – and as time went on, the Jewish community grew ever more concerned. None more so than Rabbi Jacob Emanuele (Yakov Menahem) Cracovia. Then a little over seventy years old, he was one of the Ghetto's leading religious authorities. He had represented the new Adriatic prefecture at the Grand Sanhedrin in Paris in 1806, and, having admirably acquitted himself before the French, was a natural choice to present the Ghetto's grievances to the Austrians.[43] The issue at stake was, if not trivial, then certainly of little moment. Following Napoleon's invasion, all charitable bodies and hospitals in Venice were closed or restructured, and consolidated under the control of a new body, known as the Congregazione di carità.[44] Since this had sole responsibility for distributing alms, it was meant to be even-handed – tending to the poor based on need, rather than religion. Just recently, however, it had not been living up to expectations. What made this failure so significant was that it exposed the double standards with which Jews were being treated.

On 22 August 1817, Cracovia wrote to the patricians who headed the Congregazione, asking that poor Jews receive the same alms as Catholics.[45] The Jewish community had always made generous donations to charitable institutions in the past, so – he argued – it was only right that the neediest should benefit. He was not asking for anything unusual, he stressed. All he wanted was for Jews to live on an equal footing with the rest of the population, just as they had under the French.

The Congregazione was less than impressed. Ruthlessly political creatures who embodied all the most reactionary tendencies of the Venetian elite, its administrators dismissed Cracovia's request out of hand.[46] It was obvious, they argued, that the Jews' charitable donations had not been made sincerely but cynically, with an eye to benefit. The 'poor' whom Cracovia had talked about weren't needy at all; they were just 'bums' (*accattoni*) who spent their days lounging around in cafes and salons. As such, they suggested that Jews stop bothering the Congregazione and look after their own.

Not until the following year was the question of the Jews' status settled. Now that new constitution – preserving many elements of the Napoleonic system – was in place, and a viceroy appointed, the Austrian authorities felt secure enough to drop their more paranoid suspicions.[47] There was to be no more talk of re-establishing a closed Ghetto. Jews were recognized as 'ordinary citizens', with the right to own property, access education at all levels, and practise any trade or profession they chose.[48]

Yet while the Austrians may have been willing to accept Jews as citizens, there was still marked reluctance – both at court and amongst local elites – to treat them as equals. Over the following years, a series of new restrictions were steadily introduced, each inspired by enduring fears of Jewish 'deceitfulness'. Between 1829 and 1837, Jews were banned from working as pharmacists, arbitrators (*probiviri*) in criminal cases, assessors in commercial disputes, and even notaries.[49] If this was freedom, it was not all it was cracked up to be.

A correspondingly qualified transformation took place in the Ghetto itself. Now that it was in a thoroughly ruinous state, the Austrian government could no longer afford to leave it to the fates. Two years earlier, a new 'Civic Commission for dilapidated housing' had been established to pick up where the French regulations had left off. In the Ghetto, an even more active strategy was required. Since the owners of many buildings could not be traced, there was no point wasting time with demands and threats. Over the following two decades, a programme of radical restructuring was set in motion.[50] Wherever possible, emergency repairs were undertaken; when these proved insufficient, whole buildings were simply pulled down. In the Ghetto Nuovo, the buildings along the San Girolamo canal were demolished. Four years later, so was another building next to the Scuola Italiana. A group of tenements near the Scuola Coanim, full of 'rich woodwork', had to be braced to prevent it collapsing. And a number of empty houses were transferred to new owners, in the hope of encouraging renovation work. Meanwhile, in the Ghetto Vecchio, the dense streets, thick with high apartment blocks, were dramatically thinned out. Particularly along the Calle Barucchi, a number of rickety buildings were razed to the ground. Behind the Scuola Levantina, foundations were strengthened, and several of the tallest structures reduced in height. Pipes were relaid, apartments replastered, facades repaired, and terraces patched up.

There was an irony in this. By 1835, the Ghetto looked better – and no doubt felt better – than it had done in decades. But there was no escaping the fact that most of the buildings that had been repaired or destroyed had been abandoned. Everyone who could had already moved out. As one site manager put it, 'the better-off households were domiciled outside the Ghetto'.[51] Most of those who remained were poor – and, as a consequence, even newly renovated buildings were worth practically nothing. For all the improvements, the Ghetto was becoming a shell.

Religious life did not escape untouched, either. Although years of

French rule appear to have imbued much of the Jewish population with the Enlightenment ideals of reason and progress, the example of Jacob Emanuele Cracovia was enough to show that rabbis still enjoyed a position of considerable importance in mediating between the community and the wider world. For the Austrians, this was naturally a matter of some concern. As long as the rabbis dominated – and fostered the use of 'sectarian' languages like Hebrew, Yiddish, and Ladino – the Jewish community would always stand apart, and the government's view of its activities would always be obscured. Since it was impossible to do away with the rabbis altogether, the only other alternative was to reform their relationship with congregations – so that it was more conformant with the idea of a unitary kingdom.

In early 1820, Emperor Francis issued an edict dealing, amongst other things, with the ordination of rabbis. Henceforth, aspiring rabbis would be subject to an examination to verify their knowledge of 'fundamental concepts in the philosophical sciences and in Hebrew religious instruction'. Once they had passed, they would be entitled to a secure living – subject, of course, to the community's approval. It was further established that Italian was to be the language not only of teaching in the *yeshivas*, but also of liturgy and prayer in the synagogues.[52]

After consultation with the communities of the Veneto, it was decided that, to accomplish this, it was necessary to establish a new seminary along the most up-to-date lines. Opened on 10 November 1829, this was given the form of a *convitto* (boarding school), so that students could enjoy a regimented and quiet life. The curriculum would, understandably enough, be broad. Students would learn both religious and human sciences; and, though it was obviously necessary to continue with the traditional Talmudic studies, the goal was to produce a truly modern institution of the highest academic standing.[53] An impressive roster of teachers was lined up. Of these, the most striking was perhaps Samuel David Luzzatto (1800–65).[54] A distant relation of the great Simone Luzzatto, Samuel – then still in his twenties – was already recognized as one of the leading Jewish scholars of his generation. While still a schoolboy, he had begun a Hebrew grammar in Italian, published a short volume of poetry, and translated a book of daily prayers from German.[55] He would go on to pioneer the critical study of the Bible, concluding that Ecclesiastes could not have been Solomon, as had previously been assumed – and defied popular consensus by attributing the whole of the Book of Isaiah to the prophet.[56]

Disappointingly, the new seminary was located in Padua, rather than Venice. It was an understandable decision. Padua boasted one of Italy's foremost universities and was already well placed to attract students from around Europe. It was also easier to get to and possessed all the usual amenities that students expected. Indeed, most rabbis – even in Venice itself – agreed that Padua was the best choice. For the Venetian Jews, however, it must still have been something of a disappointment. Having once been a capital of Jewish learning, Venice was now a mere backwater – condemned to stagnation and discontent.

The Ghetto's freedom – partial, qualified, and incomplete – had been won at a price. And by 1835, many of Venice's Jews could be forgiven for wondering if it hadn't been too high, after all.

14

Risorgimento

(1835–1866)

Over the past fifteen years, Venice had undergone a change for the better. Commerce was beginning to recover.[1] The city had been declared a free port in 1830; a railway bridge was built linking the city with the mainland; and the roads across the *terraferma* were improved. To be sure, there was no return to past glory. Venice's days as a major transit port were, by now, firmly behind it. Trieste had long been enshrined as Austria's pre-eminent trading hub, and nothing could change that. But as a local entrepôt, Venice recovered much of its vigour. Goods and agricultural produce from the Veneto were exchanged for commodities from the *terraferma*, the Adriatic littoral, and southern Italy, and the quays once again bristled with masts. This, in turn, breathed fresh life into industry. New forms of manufacturing sprang up. Workshops began using 'power-driven machinery'; a steam-driven mill was opened in an empty church; and the city boasted at least two sugar refineries. There was even a factory producing white lead.[2] For the first time in years, employment was booming.

As the population began to grow, the city itself was renewed. In 1839, gaslights were installed to illuminate narrow *calli*, and a concerted programme of repair and restoration was embarked upon.[3] Tourism suddenly grew. In 1844, no fewer than 112,644 people visited Venice. Just two years later, the city boasted eleven luxurious hotels; a magnificent complex of public baths was moored off the Punta della Dogana; theatres were sold out; and guidebooks were all the rage.[4] Everyone who was anyone came to stay.

The Jewish community was no exception to this. Jews were at the forefront of Venice's economic renewal. Isacco Pesaro Maurogonato was a key figure in the new insurance firm Assicurazioni Generali; Cesare Della Vida was the owner of a major shipping company; and Giacomo Treves de' Bonfili was among the richest men in the city. In 1835, Princess Metternich estimated that three members of the Chamber of Commerce who had been sent to Vienna to offer condolences on the emperor's death – of whom Treves was the leading member – were worth 30 million Austrian lira, '*ce qui est une jolie fortune*'.[5]

The Ghetto, too, was improving. In 1842, a full land registry was compiled; and, based on its findings, the Austrians were at last able to assess the effects of the changes that had taken place over the past two decades. That the Ghetto felt more spacious went without saying. By then, the whole of its north side had been demolished; the street leading between the Ghetto Nuovo and the Ghetto Vecchio had been remodelled to make it 'open, airy, and sunny'; and the Agudi bridge, long in a state of disrepair, was given new steps and a far more 'modern' design.[6]

Venetian relations with the Austrian government were nevertheless increasingly strained. The bourgeoisie, in whose hands commerce and industry were concentrated, bitterly resented the high taxes, the customs barriers separating the Veneto from the rest of Italy, and the unnecessary censorship. Most of all, they disliked the lack of political representation. Unlike other areas of the Austrian Empire, neither Venice nor the kingdom of Lombardy–Venetia had any diets through which grievances could be aired or policy shaped. The working classes, too, were struggling. Although there was no lack of employment, it tended to be precarious. Most had to live from hand to mouth; and many were often left wanting. An estimated 40,000 Venetians needed some form of assistance just to survive.[7]

Jews were more frustrated than most. In the atmosphere of economic growth, they chafed against the legal restrictions that had been placed on them since their 'emancipation' and found the Austrians' refusal to listen galling. In May 1840, the governor of the Veneto, Johann Baptist von Spaur, was presented with a petition asking for an improvement in Jewish civil rights, signed by Jewish leaders throughout Lombardy–Venetia. It was far from radical, but von Spaur rejected it out of hand. By way of justification, he offered them nothing more than the tired old antisemitic tropes: Jews, being cunning businessmen, would only cheat Christians; Catholics would take exception to Jews witnessing their wills; it would be inappropriate for Jews to officiate at any public function with a religious element, on account of their 'inherited guilt for the death of Jesus Christ'; and so on.[8]

*

Had the Austrians shown a little more sense, all might yet have been well. But it was not to be.[9] In 1835, Emperor Francis died and was succeeded by his son, Ferdinand. A kindly, if feeble, epileptic, he was physically incapable of ruling effectively. His unofficial regent, Archduke Ludwig, was little better. A man proud of his idleness, addicted to procrastination, and apparently indifferent to politics, he allowed government to slide into paralysis. The chancellor, Klemens von Metternich, was locked in a bitter struggle with the interior minister, Franz von Kolowrat; and without a steady hand to restrain them, their rivalry prevented serious decisions from being taken. The state finances were worst affected. Since no one could agree whether to raise taxes, the only alternative was to borrow more heavily – with the result that an ever-larger proportion of revenues went on servicing the debt. This crippled almost every other area of government. There was simply not enough money to go around. Soldiers had to put up with low pay and poor equipment, and unexpected challenges quickly spiralled into crises.

In Venice, the Austrian government's fiscal inertia proved a serious problem. In 1845, harvests around Europe failed; and over the next two years, the shortages only grew worse. Whereas Francis had dealt with a similar disaster swiftly, Ferdinand's government had its hands tied. Conspicuously, it failed to prevent the export of grain until it was too late, meaning that what little was produced on the *terraferma* flowed out for sale on the international market, rather than being consumed at home. Prices shot up; famine took hold; and, inevitably, tempers frayed.

In Daniele Manin, the Venetians – and Venice's Jews – found exactly the solution they were after. He didn't look much, to be sure. Short and squat, with a receding hairline and small, myopic eyes, he had the air of a weary village schoolmaster or a timid clerk. But that unremarkable exterior belied the spirit of a revolutionary.[10] Born into a family of Jewish origin, not far from the Campo Sant'Agostin, he had been raised in the best traditions of the Jewish Enlightenment.[11] Having read Locke, Rousseau, and Helvétius while still a young man, he enrolled in the University of Padua at the age of just fourteen, and by the time he qualified as a lawyer, he was already a committed republican. He had a deep hatred of the Austrian occupation and longed to see Venice and Italy restored to liberty and glory. It was to him that Venice's Jews now looked for their emancipation.

By 1845, there was already a growing sense that the Italian states were being held back from enjoying the fruits of modernization by their disunity, maintained and exacerbated by the Austrians. To many, it seemed obvious that the Austrians should be thrown out and a new 'Italy' created. But opinion was divided over how this should be achieved.[12] For Giuseppe Mazzini and the members of 'Young Italy', the only route to freedom and unity was force. A violent revolution, led by the young, should eject the Austrians in one fell swoop and weld the Italian states into a single republic, whether they liked it or not. For Manin, by contrast, a more moderate path seemed wiser. Despite having flirted with armed insurrection a few years earlier, he, like many Venetians, had grown wary of radical change, and instead favoured a more gradual path to Italian nationhood. He favoured expanding Venice's trade links with the rest of Italy, reducing or removing customs duties, and making taxation more equitable. In time, this would naturally lead to a united Italy; but he envisaged it as a federation, in which independent states – like Venice – would participate as equals. After the election of the reforming Pius IX in 1846, he even followed the 'neo-Guelphist' idea that it should be headed by the pope.

Venetian Jews were not, by instinct, revolutionaries, but Manin's vision of Italy nevertheless struck a chord with them. Under French domination, they had absorbed the ideals of liberty, equality, and regeneration, and yearned for full emancipation.[13] Yet recent experience had convinced many that this would never be achieved under Austrian rule – at least not as it was currently constituted. Thus, the cause of emancipation came to be united with nationalism. Some were, of course, attracted by Mazzini's easy promises; but most found Manin's approach more plausible. They had no desire to risk the gains it had taken them so long to win by acting rashly, or to antagonize the Austrians any more than necessary. Rather, it was through the progressive accretion of rights and the separation of Venice from direct imperial control that they hoped to win their emancipation. Somewhat unexpectedly, there was even strong support for neo-Guelphism. Writing to a friend in April 1848, Samuel David Luzzatto opined that, considering the pope's opposition to the Austrians, Jews should 'wear the sign of the Cross on their garments . . . with gaiety and joy'.[14]

*

Manin did not disappoint. Ambitious and energetic, he set about his task with vigour.[15] He first rose to prominence during a dispute over the route of a proposed railway from Milan to Venice. Recognizing that this was crucial to Venice's future relations with the rest of northern Italy, he successfully opposed a Viennese-backed plan to divert the track across hilly terrain to Bergamo, and guaranteed that trains would run direct. This achieved, he burnished his renown by organizing a banquet for the British free-trade campaigner Richard Cobden, and launching a legal battle aimed at securing a separate status for the kingdom of Lombardy–Venetia within the Habsburg empire.

Venice's Jews were certainly encouraged. In early January 1848, the community sent two of its most distinguished members – Cesare Della Vida and Isacco Pesaro Maurogonato – to talk with Manin.[16] Clearly expecting him to win the legal struggle, they asked him to include the demand for Jewish emancipation in any future reforms. If he agreed, they added, he would receive the support of the entire Jewish community. Manin accepted without a second thought. And he meant it. A short time later, his close collaborator, Niccolò Tommaseo – who had also been present at the meeting – published a short essay entitled *Diritti degli Israeliti alla civile eguaglianza* ('The Israelites' rights to civil equality').[17]

Before Manin could make any further progress, however, revolution broke out in Palermo on 12 January 1848. Although this was ostensibly a local affair, directed against the absolutist rule of Ferdinand II of the Two Sicilies, the shock was felt far and wide.[18] In Venice, the Austrians, fearful of public dissent, immediately clamped down on freedom of expression. Carnevale was banned, opera houses were closed, and Manin and Tommaseo were arrested.[19]

A more provocative – and foolhardy – course could hardly have been chosen. The situation in Venice was already febrile. Although the famine of previous years had abated, grain prices remained stubbornly high, and unemployment was still at record levels. Instead of calming public tensions, the arrest only caused protests to grow.

Meanwhile, the revolutionary fire, first sparked in Palermo, was spreading fast. On 11 February, a liberal constitution was promulgated in Tuscany; two weeks later, King Louis Philippe of France abdicated; and by the end of the month, unrest even reached Vienna itself. Under pressure from the Imperial Diet, Metternich resigned and fled for his life. All of a sudden, it was apparent that the Austrians – previously so sturdy, so unyielding – were on the back foot. The fire, already raging, had become a Europe-wide inferno.

When news of Metternich's fall reached Venice, on 17 March 1848, the people immediately rushed to the Palazzo Reale, demanding Manin and Tommaseo's release. The Austrian governor, Alajos Pálffy, had no choice but to agree. Amidst huge cheers, the two men were carried in triumph from the prison to the Piazza San Marco. By then, Manin was already a changed man. Now realizing that revolution was indeed possible, he renounced his former gradualism. Such an opportunity would not come again. As he told the crowd: 'sometimes there come moments when insurrection . . . is not only a right, but a duty'.[20]

The very next day, the fighting began. At around midday, a crowd of workers and students – excited by news of a revolt in Milan – gathered in the Piazza San Marco, wearing patriotic cockades and waving tricolour flags.[21] A detachment of Austrian troops was sent to contain the disturbance. Enraged, the Venetians began tearing up paving stones and hurling them at the soldiers. The Austrians responded by opening fire. Six were killed. More were wounded.

There was no turning back.[22] A civic guard was hastily raised; and on 22 March, Manin seized control of the Arsenale. The Venetians now controlled not only the fleet, but also the bulk of the Austrians' munitions. Pálffy was at a loss. Although he could still have called for reinforcements and fought on in the streets, he did not have the heart to turn Venice into a battleground. He had no choice but to surrender. At 6:30 pm, the capitulation was signed; and by nightfall, a new Venetian state – the Republic of San Marco – had been declared.

It was like nothing Venice had experienced before. Clambering onto a table to address the crowds in the Piazza San Marco, Manin promised that, while the new provisional government would not forget the city's 'ancient glory', it would be 'enhanced by modern liberty'.[23] With him as president, it would be a truly egalitarian regime, committed to improving the lot of Venetians, and to uniting all Italians into a single body.

The city exploded with excitement. Flags flew from every window; women sang patriotic songs; and – as one visitor noted – everyone seemed to be smiling. No one was happier than the Jews. Many had taken part in the revolt; and now that the old regime was gone, they could scarcely conceal their delight. 'My heart is brimming over, my mind is on fire,' exclaimed the lawyer Leone Fortis. 'At last we can breathe; there's air, by God! [...] A century divides today from yesterday. Brothers! [...] The dreadful heritage of hatred and vendetta is at an end'.[24]

Manin lost no time in rewarding their optimism. When he formed his government, he appointed his old friend, Leone Pincherle, to be his minister of commerce; and on 29 March, the government, in its first official act, decreed that all citizens, of whatever religion, would henceforth 'enjoy perfect equality of civil and political rights'.[25] At a stroke, the last, onerous constraints on Jewish life were swept away.

We should not be under any illusions about the motivations for this. Although Manin's decree rested on the recognition of a common humanity, government support for the Jews was far from just a matter of liberal egalitarianism – or even dispassionate altruism. For at least some of Manin's colleagues, the cause of emancipation was still grounded in a deeply conservative, Catholic attitude towards Judaism. Niccolò Tommaseo is a telling example. By March 1848, Tommaseo already had a long history of philosemitism. In Rome, some years before, he had befriended the great rabbi Mosè Hazan; he had intervened with the archbishop of Ferrara on the Jews' behalf; and he counted the Venetian banker Abramo Errera among his friends.[26] Like the novelist Alessandro Manzoni, he regarded Jews as the model of people yearning for freedom. He identified closely with their plight and urged his fellow Catholics to support civic equality as a matter of religious obligation.[27] Yet his enthusiasm for emancipation was not without condescension – even a certain contempt. On 11 September 1844, he wrote in his diary:

'I love the Jews, but they . . . do not know how to love. They enjoy the misfortune of others, too mindful of having been so ferociously oppressed themselves'.[28] His arguments in favour of emancipation, while well motivated, were tired rather than daring, reactionary rather than modern. In *Diritti degli Israeliti alla civile eguaglianza*, he raked over all the ideas that Venetians had been using to justify the Jews' presence for years, if not centuries. The Christian bourgeoisie had a pressing need for credit, he argued, which Jews – and Jews alone – could satisfy. Since the foundation of the *monte di pietà*, many had opened private banks, and they deserved to be compensated as fully as Christians would be for the same services. So too, Tommaseo suggested that emancipation might pave the way to conversion. Although he was adamant that Jews should never be coerced, he nevertheless hoped that, once the last legal barriers were removed, they would be more easily persuaded to accept Christ's teachings.[29]

Not all Jews were convinced of the government's sincerity, either. It was all very well to celebrate the revolution by singing Samuel Salomone Olper's ditty:

> Jews and Christians – we are all Italians
> Christians and Jews – we are all brothers.[30]

But no one was under any illusions about the strength of popular antisemitism. They had all seen countless decrees in the past, ostensibly defending their rights. And how many attacks had those stopped? Fearing that the unrest might unleash a fresh wave of violence, the Jewish community therefore appropriated many of the muskets left behind by the Austrians – just in case they needed to defend themselves.[31] Most were never recovered.

There was no denying the fact of emancipation, though. However serious the concerns, however qualified the government's support, it was impossible for Jews to ignore the fact that they were finally free; and for a blissful, fleeting moment, it might have seemed that the Ghetto really had been reborn – not as a downtrodden quarter of a marginal group, but as a truly equal part of a city in triumph.

*

How long that triumph would last was another matter. Within days, it became painfully apparent to everyone that Manin had underestimated not only Austria's resilience, but also the safety afforded by the sea. Already, the Austrian army was regrouping, determined to bring the revolutionaries to heel. An urgent effort to prepare Venice for the worst swung into action. The civic guard was enlarged; great monuments, including the Palazzo Ducale itself, were mortgaged; and all manner of fundraising schemes were put forward.[32]

The Ghetto threw its weight behind the city's defence. On 27 March, Giacomo and Isacco Treves de' Bonfili donated 5,250 lire to purchase supplies for the civic guard; and a few days later, Rabbi Abraham Lattes reassured his co-religionists they could carry out military duties on the Sabbath without incurring any sin. Indeed, they would actually be honouring the Jewish faith by 'employing one's work for the Fatherland in the best way possible'.[33] It was a clear indication, not merely of the strength of patriotic feeling in the Ghetto, but also of the extent to which it was possible for Jewish identity to be subsumed into a broader Venetian (and even Italian) identity.[34]

From the first, Manin's strategy was founded on the idea of organic collaboration. His hope was that, as revolution spread across northern Italy, more republics would be founded, which would then co-operate as equals to drive Austria out of the peninsula for good. If foreign aid was required, Manin anticipated that it would come from France – the alma mater of revolution. But in this he was disappointed. The Milanese insurrection failed to lead to the declaration of a republic; and when Mazzini returned to the city on 7 April, he had come to believe that King Carlo Alberto of Piedmont – rather than France – should play the decisive role in the struggle ahead.[35] That Piedmont was a monarchy and had never been under Austrian rule did not seem to trouble him.

Unexpectedly, Venice looked like the exception, rather than the rule. Manin was afraid that, by declaring the Republic of San Marco so quickly, he might inadvertently have jeopardized the formation of an anti-Austrian coalition. He therefore performed an abrupt volte-face. Setting aside all questions of domestic politics, he devoted himself entirely to the Italian cause and – despite lingering concerns about Carlo Alberto's motives – accepted the necessity of Piedmontese help. Among Venetian Jews, there was even a measure of optimism. Writing to a friend from nearby Padua, Samuel David Luzzatto was positively buoyant:

> Already the armies of Piedmont are arriving to help us, and we hope that in a day or so they will enter Verona and chase the Germans [*sic*] from there. I am sending you a poem in Italian which they printed here yesterday, from which you will be able to see that all Italy is fraternal like a single man, that the spirit of the Lord is pushing it to liberate itself from the yoke of the foreigners.[36]

By mid-April, it was obvious that such optimism had been misguided.[37] Carlo Alberto refused to help Venice unless Manin agreed to merge Lombardy–Venetia with Piedmont to form a new 'Italian' kingdom, with him at its head. This presented Manin with an unenviable choice. Either he could stand by Venice's independence, in the hope that Piedmont would *have* to intervene at some point, or he could give up on the republican dream. Of the two, Manin preferred the former; but as the Austrians advanced across the *terraferma*, he increasingly found himself in the minority. On 3 June, an assembly was therefore convened to decide what Venice's course should be. Two hundred representatives were elected by parishes. Of these, three were Jews: Isacco Pesaro Maurogonato, now the minister of finance; Giacomo Treves de' Bonfili, the minister of the post, and Rabbi Samuel Salomone Olper.[38] At least some of these may have spoken in Manin's defence. Maurogonato had previously declared that 'the only government appropriate to free and civil men is the republic' – and he had little cause to change his mind.[39] The assembly's decision was, however, never in doubt. To Manin's dismay, it voted overwhelmingly for annexation by Piedmont.[40]

It was a fateful decision. After suffering a catastrophic defeat at the Battle of Custoza just three weeks later, Carlo Alberto began having doubts about the campaign. Facing desertions in the field and growing unrest in Turin, he withdrew his forces and opened negotiations with the Austrians. He had to try to save as much of his army as possible – even at the expense of those he had pledged to defend. In early August, he therefore concluded an armistice. Carlo Alberto agreed to surrender Milan; and in return, the Austrians would allow his troops to retreat to Piedmont unmolested. Militarily, perhaps, it was the only option. But to the Venetians, it was a betrayal of the most ignominious kind.

Venice now stood alone. There was no one it could call on for aid; and, despite Mazzini's untiring efforts to stir up fresh revolts in Lombardy, no possibility of reviving the idea of a federal Italy. A negotiated peace was Venice's best chance of saving its freedom. Britain and France agreed to mediate; and – for a few tense months – everyone held their breath.

While discussions went on, Manin returned to his dream of making Venice truly democratic. In December 1848, new elections were called for a reduced assembly along more satisfactory, egalitarian lines – conceived, in part, by Maurogonato.[41] This time, even more Jewish candidates were returned than before. All three of the previous deputies were re-elected. They were joined by Rabbi Abraham Lattes, Cesare Della Vida, the bankers Angelo Levi and Abramo Errera, and Manin's old collaborator, Leone Pincherle.[42] This was exceptional, by any standards. Although there were only a little over 2,000 Jews living in Venice in 1847, out of a total population of 127,925 (c.1.56 per cent), they nevertheless accounted for 6.25 per cent of deputies.[43]

Such influence was useful in consolidating their civil rights. When the government showed an interest in regulating how Jews should take oaths in court, in early 1849, a delegation was invited to present its advice.[44] This was composed of the deputies Abraham Lattes, Samuel Salomone Olper, Isacco Pesaro Maurogonato, and Giacomo Treves de' Bonfili, as well as Samuele Della Vida, Leone Fortis, and Giacinto Namias. Thanks to their intervention, the resulting decree ensured that Jews would have the right to swear on the Torah – with their heads covered, but otherwise in exactly the same way as Christians.

No one could ignore the wider danger, though. However much Manin was hoping for the best from the Anglo-French mediation, Venice had to prepare for the worst. Its defences desperately needed strengthening. To help pay for this, another huge loan was arranged. Jewish merchants contributed to this even more lavishly than before.[45] Angelo Levi gave 100,000 lire, while Cesare Della Vida contributed so much that he virtually bankrupted himself. A host of younger men also chipped in. But when the time came to *use* this money, Manin seemed oddly paralysed. No serious preparations were made; and Venice – lost in dreams of liberty – began sleepwalking towards disaster.

*

In February 1849, Anglo-French negotiations collapsed. Now that Austria had recaptured Lombardy, it saw no sense in yielding the advantage. In Piedmont, the alarm was acute. Fearing Austrian retribution, even Carlo Alberto's critics agreed that the war should be resumed. The Venetians should, by rights, have been delighted. But before Manin's government could react, it was already over. Following a crushing defeat at Novara, Carlo Alberto was forced to abdicate – and with the rest of the peninsula in disarray, 'the Austrian reconquest of Italy seemed inevitable'.[46]

The Venetians were defiant. On 2 April, a tumultuous assembly decreed: 'Venice will resist the Austrians at any cost'.[47] Manin was granted unlimited powers. As he rose to accept, seemingly overcome by the awesomeness of his responsibility, the deputies leapt to their feet, crying 'resist at any cost'. A huge red flag was flown from the pole outside the palazzo, and the people – determined to fight to the last – wore red ribbons in their buttonholes.[48]

By then, the Austrian army, led by Lieutenant-Marshal Julius von Haynau – the 'butcher of Brescia' – had already reached the lagoon and immediately began laying siege to the city. At first, fighting was concentrated around Mestre. It did not take long for Jewish lives to be lost. On 1 May, twenty-six-year-old Isacco Finzi was fatally wounded by a mortar – as Tommaseo put it, 'one of the first to die worthily for Venice'.[49]

As the pressure mounted, the Venetians decided to make a stand at the fortress of Marghera, right by the new railway bridge.[50] Alessandro Levi was in the thick of the battle.[51] A sensitive, kindly soul, he evidently felt the tug of family keenly. He arranged to send news to his mother Enrichetta by concealing a note in the collar of his dog and having it run back to the family palazzo in San Felice. A short while later, the dog would return with a reply. Back and forth it went, until the Austrians got wise to the dog's movements, caught it, and killed it.

After three days of intense bombardment, the government ordered the evacuation of the fortress. The focus of the fighting then shifted to the railway bridge itself. Alessandro Levi was among those posted there. His mother was beside herself with worry. After not hearing anything from him for days, she feared the worst. Somehow, she learned that he was in the Ospedale di Santa Chiara, and was directed to a bed where a wounded man was lying with his head covered in bandages. At first, she did not recognize him. Only when she saw the prayer shawl that she had stitched into his jacket did she realize that he was her son.

It was a fruitless sacrifice. On 29 July, von Haynau – now completely in control of the mainland – unleashed the full might of the Austrian army on Venice itself. A furious bombardment rained down on the city. Nowhere was spared. Houses were destroyed. Fires raged, day and night. Given its proximity to the railway, the Ghetto was especially vulnerable. On 17 August, a bomb even fell on the Scuola Spagnola during prayers. It broke the marble steps leading to the Ark but, miraculously, failed to explode.[52] Few other buildings were so lucky. Terrified, those Jews who could sought refuge elsewhere in the city. Among them was Enrichetta Levi. After her kitchen was destroyed by a bomb, she scooped up her grandchildren and fled to her parents' home, not far from the Ponte dell'Angelo in San Marco.[53]

Daily life became all but impossible. With no food coming in, famine took hold – and tempers quickly began to fray. As one priest reported, women who tried to buy bread in the Campo SS. Giovanni e Paolo were 'swearing . . . and tearing the earrings from their ears and the . . . rings from their fingers'.[54] Elsewhere, there were riots, and cholera was soon tearing through the poorer quarters. Rabbi Abraham Lattes did his best to help. A member of the Health Board, he refused to leave his home, devoting himself day and night to the care of the sick and dying.[55] But nothing could stop the epidemic. By 23 August, no fewer than 2,788 people had died from the disease – significantly more than the entire population of the Ghetto.[56] And it showed no sign of abating.

Venice didn't stand a chance. Though Manin fought the inevitable as long as he could, he had no choice but to surrender. On 27 August 1849, Austrian troops marched into the city – and later that afternoon, Manin was carried away into exile, never to return.

*

He was not alone. As part of the surrender terms, the Austrians had demanded that forty leading members of the provisional government also leave the city – including several prominent Jews. They scattered to the winds.[57] Most emigrated to cities with a strong anti-Austrian presence, or with which they already had commercial ties. Manin's old friend Leone Pincherle settled first in Turin, then Paris; Isacco Pesaro Maurogonato fled to Corfu; and Leone Serena went to London. Some followed more wandering paths; and a few – like Samuel Salomone Olper – were kept under police surveillance wherever they went. But for none of them did exile mark the end of their political journey. Quite the reverse. Most remained committed to the cause of Italian liberty. They kept in contact with other Venetians abroad; formed patriotic societies; and followed events in the lagoon with keen interest. Most importantly, they also seized the opportunity to establish closer relations with revolutionaries elsewhere – a fact which was later to prove important. Alessandro Levi is a case in point. After recovering from his wounds, he escaped to Turin. There, he joined the Venetian Central Political Committee, led by Alberto Cavalletto, and quickly became one of its most vocal members. He even bankrolled its activities.

For the Jews left in Venice, the hopes stirred by the revolution were swiftly crushed. The Austrians had no intention of forgiving – or forgetting – their involvement. All the old restrictions were reinstated. Indeed, they were enforced even more strictly than before. Services in the synagogues were now attended by Austrian guards; and those leading figures who had gone into exile were subject to arbitrary impositions.[58] Alberto Errera, a professor of law and industrial economics, was convicted of high treason and imprisoned in Padua. The banker Angelo Levi was fined 30,000 florins for his republican views (a sum which was later reduced) and barred from serving on the Communal Council. And Abramo Errera was only allowed to take up his seat on the new Camera di Commercio thanks to what appears to have been a clerical error.

While the Austrians did not actively encourage popular antisemitism, they did little to discourage it, either. The reassertion of authority in Lombardy-Venetia brought with it the return of officials, either of foreign extraction, or – more often – drawn from established patrician families. Like most other segments of Catholic society, they were far from homogeneous; but for every liberal, there were many more whose prejudices still ran strong. Even if Jews notionally enjoyed equal legal rights to Christians, there was no guarantee they would be respected to quite the same degree – if at all.

This was illustrated by a criminal case brought in Badia Polesine, not far from Rovigo.[59] On 25 June 1855, a young peasant girl named Giuditta Castilliero returned home after being missing for eight days. When she was asked where she had been, she claimed that she had narrowly escaped a ritual murder. According to her, she had been kidnapped by a group of Jews and carried off to Verona. There, they planned to sacrifice her and a little girl. Before doing so, they tortured her by repeatedly draining blood from her arm and collecting it in a pot. She would surely have died, she related, had it not been for a Catholic servant, who helped her to slip away. She then made her way, via Legnano, back to Badia Polesine – with wounds on her arm as testament to her suffering.

Giuditta publicly identified one of her kidnappers as Caliman Ravenna. Then a little under forty years old, Caliman was a respected member of the Jewish community. He was a merchant, a money-lender, and a tax collector – and his wealth had bought him entry into local bourgeois society. He was a regular guest at salons and had even bought a share in the town theatre. The accusation hit him hard. Though it was patently ridiculous, enough Catholics believed it for his standing to be severely damaged.

When Caliman responded by lodging a complaint with the district police commissioner, things took a turn for the worse. Although the commissioner didn't believe a word of Giuditta's accusation, he felt obliged to pass the complaint on to a magistrate. The magistrate made no attempt to conceal his dislike of Jews. Ignoring Caliman's complaint, he instead opened an investigation into Giuditta's allegation, evidently impressed by the cuts on her arm. On 28 June, Caliman was charged with 'public violence' and imprisoned, pending trial.

A furore erupted across Lombardy–Venetia. A report in the *Annotatore friulano*, playing on similarities with the story of Simon of Trent, stoked antisemitic feeling. In Padua, Jewish cafegoers were abused; and in Venice, Jews were threatened with death if they dared to show their faces in public.

Not everyone believed Caliman was guilty. On 12 July, the *Corriere Italiano*, the leading government newspaper, denounced the *Annotatore friulano* for stirring up unrest. A more forceful Jewish response came from the indefatigable rabbi Abraham Lattes. In a lengthy, front-page article in the *Gazzetta Uffiziale*, Lattes lamented the re-emergence of the myth of blood libel. He challenged the credibility of Giuditta's testimony and attacked her for the 'repulsive wickedness' (*ributtante nefandezza*) of her accusation. Lattes was careful to stress the Jewish community's confidence in the justice system. He nevertheless concluded by urging 'good' people to help 'eradicate from the ignorant masses the shameful prejudice, with which some wicked people try to imbue them'.[60]

The case soon fell apart. On 9 July, Giuditta was arrested for committing a theft in Legnano at exactly the same time as she claimed she was being tortured in Verona. It was impossible for her accusation to be true. She quickly confessed to her deceit; and five days later, Caliman was released.

Giuditta's trial was still something of a worry, however. Although the main charge against her was slander, the Jewish community had been so shocked by the popular reaction that they felt even a guilty verdict would not be sufficient to counteract her lies. On 23 October, representatives from each of the kingdom's five major communities therefore met at Graziadio Vivante's house in Venice to discuss how best to respond. Among those in attendance were Abramo Errera, by then the president of the rabbinical college in Padua, and Abraham Lattes. After much discussion, it was decided to prepare a thorough refutation of the blood libel myth. Two preliminary briefs were first written by Abram Mainster, the scholarly rabbi of Rovigo, and Samuele Romanin, a Venetian historian of considerable repute. These were then used as the basis for a report published in the *Eco dei Tribunali* the following year. It was a masterpiece of historical reasoning. It conclusively demonstrated that accusations of ritual murder, such as the 'martyrdom' of Simon of Trent, were based not on fact but on an antisemitic frenzy generated by Franciscan preachers and perpetuated by a perversion of Christian belief.

Giuditta was sentenced to six years of 'hard' imprisonment (*carcere duro*) in the Giudecca prison in Venice. Her conviction no doubt offered some consolation, most of all to Caliman, but the case had illustrated with painful clarity what Manin had known all along: that, under Austrian rule, Jews would never be fully integrated in Venice – or in Italy.

*

Over the next decade, the Ghetto underwent a change of heart. Many Jews, tired of the obstacles to their equality, saw little point in remaining. Little by little, they began to leave. In 1857, 2,023 Jews were living in Venice, down from around 2,500 in 1821 – a decline of almost 20 per cent.[61] Others refused to be so easily discouraged. A spirit of discreet resistance and Italian patriotism gradually began to show itself again.

The outbreak of war between Piedmont and Austria in April 1859 provided the spur. Far from giving up on the idea of unifying Italy by force under the House of Savoy, Carlo Alberto's successor, Vittorio Emanuele II, had realized that it could only be achieved with foreign support. He therefore concluded an alliance with France and marched into Lombardy. It was a short campaign – barely two months in all – but the gains were out of all proportion to the blood spilt. Thoroughly bested, Austria ceded Tuscany to Piedmont; and, all at once, the path towards unification seemed to open.

In Venice, the reaction was, at first, muted. However joyful the news of Tuscany's liberation may have been, many people could not help feeling disappointed that the Veneto had not been freed as well. And not without reason. Vittorio Emmanuele's own prime minister, Count Cavour, had resigned over the same issue. But in time, a more determined realism took hold. All that was required was patience and effort. In the Ghetto, Jews prepared themselves for the task ahead. Families began sending their children to be educated at Jewish schools in Tuscany, where they could receive instruction not only in religious studies, but in 'Italian' subjects, too.[62] When, the following year, Giuseppe Garibaldi set out to conquer the Kingdom of the Two Sicilies, several Jews gladly answered his call.

The most noteworthy was Alessandro Levi.[63] As soon as he heard about Garibaldi's expedition, he rushed to Genoa to join up. Just missing Garibaldi's boat, he made his way to Sicily with the adventurer Giacomo Medici. He immediately threw himself into the fray (this time without a dog) and once again distinguished himself by his bravery. His finest moment came after the capture of Messina. Intending to cross the straits and march into Calabria, Garibaldi desperately needed intelligence about the disposition of forces on the mainland. This would not be easy to get. The straits were patrolled by Neapolitan and English warships; and the locals were notoriously wary of outsiders. Levi volunteered like a shot. He quickly found a little boat and took to the water. Almost immediately, he was spotted. Shots were fired, and he found himself pitched into the water. After a while, he was rescued by Neapolitan fishermen, who agreed to hide him in a house just outside Naples. Disguising himself in his hosts' clothes, he then tried to sneak into the city – but once again, his luck was out. He was quickly caught, arrested, and condemned to death for espionage. Had it not been for Garibaldi's lightning advance northwards, he would surely have been executed. As it was, he was freed, promoted, and given a command in the artillery. Nothing could have suited him better.

It did not take long for Garibaldi to complete the conquest of the Kingdom of the Two Sicilies. The path to unification was clear. On 17 March 1861, the first 'Italian' Parliament declared Vittorio Emmanuele II King of Italy. Only the Papal States and Venice remained – and of the two, Venice seemed the more likely to fall next. Excitement ran high, especially among Venice's Jews. Alessandro Levi's mother, Enrichetta, even made tricolour cockades in secret and hid them in her bedroom in readiness.[64] Eventually, in 1866, the time came. After concluding an alliance with Prussia – which had its own reasons for wanting to cut Austria down to size – Vittorio Emmanuele II's forces invaded the Veneto. It was a short, unsatisfactory, almost anticlimactic campaign. There were no great victories, no heroic escapes, only grim, fruitless exchanges. But it was enough to convince Austria that further fighting would be futile. Venice was surrendered – and after a plebiscite, the city formally became a part of the new kingdom of Italy. The only question was: what would become of its Jews?

15

The Emptying of the Ghetto

(1866–1945)

On 7 November 1866, King Vittorio Emanuele II entered Venice in triumph. Regally installed aboard a red and white barge, he was rowed up the Grand Canal to the Palazzo Ducale, where a gigantic tricolour was already flying.[1] Crowds lined the square; gondolas the route. Shouts of 'Viva Italia!' filled the air. As a British journalist later recalled, the city was 'in a state of . . . joyous delirium all night long'.[2] At La Fenice, the orchestra struck up a *canto popolare* dedicated to the new king.[3] Waiters at Florian's handed out drinks for free, and the celebrations went on till dawn.

Few were as exuberant as Venice's Jews. One of the largest parties that night was thrown by Angelo Levi at his *palazzo* on the Grand Canal, and – as in cities up and down the peninsula – it would have been difficult to find a single Jew who was not full of praise for the new monarch.[4] And who could blame them? As a rabbi in nearby Ferrara exclaimed, unification seemed at last to have raised them 'from the miserable condition' in which they had previously lived 'to the level of our beloved fellow citizens'.[5]

This wasn't hyperbole, either. Although unification may have been hard won, it nevertheless marked the culmination of the long process of Jewish emancipation which had begun back in 1797. According to the Albertine Statute, which became the basis of the new Italian Constitution, religious freedom was firmly established. While Roman Catholicism remained the state religion, other creeds were tolerated, and Jews' civil rights were formally confirmed.[6]

Anti-Jewish sentiment had not been abolished, of course, and attacks on Jews remained common. Some years later, a number of candidates in Padua's municipal elections insisted that Jews should

19. Images from Giovanni Grevembroch's richly illustrated volume of Venetian dress. Grevembroch was an artist of Dutch origin who had been commissioned to paint the costumes, habits, and occupations of Venetians from all walks of life. *Clockwise from top left*: a Levantine Jew, a banker, 'Jewish refinement', a Jew wearing the yellow circle.

20. Cross-section of buildings in the Ghetto Nuovo,
by Giorgio Fossati and Pietro Checcia, February 1778.

21. The 'tree of liberty' erected in the Piazza San Marco after Napoleon's troops
entered the city, as depicted by Giuseppe Borsato in 1797.

22. An 1865 engraving of Samuel David Luzzatto, one of the leading Jewish scholars of his generation.

23. Marble sculpture of Margherita Grassini Sarfatti, while she was Mussolini's mistress, by Adolfo Wildt, 1929.

24. Portrait of Letizia Pesaro Maurogonato, daughter of minister of finance Isacco Pesaro Maurogonato, by the painter Giacomo Balla, 1901.

25. Antisemitic cartoons from *Il Travaso delle idee*, a satirical magazine, in August 1938: 'Business is business' (right) and 'At the beauty salon' (below).

26. Arbit Blatas's *Monument to the Victims of the Holocaust* in the Campo del Ghetto Nuovo, which was installed in 1980.

27. Arbit Blatas's *The Last Train*, erected in 1993 to commemorate the fiftieth anniversary of the deportation of Venetian Jews from the Ghetto.

28. The Calle di Ghetto Nuovissimo.

29. Aerial view of the Ghetto Nuovo.

not have the vote.⁷ Yet antisemitism was still much less pronounced than in other European countries. There was no equivalent in Venice, or anywhere else in Italy, of Édouard Drumont's violently antisemitic newspaper *La Libre Parole*, or the French Antisemitic League. Nor indeed were there any public scandals akin to the Dreyfus affair, in which a Jewish officer had been wrongfully found guilty of passing French military secrets to the Germans and imprisoned for five years on Devil's Island before being pardoned. It was only natural to compare Italy favourably. In 1905, *Il Corriere Israelitico* declared that: '[o]ne cannot deny that Italian Jewry is great and fortunate. Our foreign brothers from the Alps look south with envy'.⁸

*

Over the next thirty years, Venice's Jewish elite, now scattered throughout the city, played an ever-greater part in urban and national life. Many of those who had been exiled after the revolution of 1848–9 returned to the lagoon and took up public office once again. One of the most striking was Isacco Pesaro Maurogonato. First elected in 1866, he sat in the Camera dei Deputati continuously until 1890, when he was nominated for the Senate. He was widely regarded as an economic savant; and had it not been for the opposition of reactionary elements, he would certainly have been appointed minister of finance in 1873.⁹ Even more impressive was Luigi Luzzatti. After being elected to the Camera dei Deputati in 1871, he went on to serve in a variety of ministerial roles, before finally becoming prime minister on 31 March 1910.¹⁰

Growing in confidence and stature, wealthy Jewish families led the field not only in commerce, but in medicine, law, education – and any number of other professions. Baron Alberto Treves de' Bonfili was the chairman of the Italian Company of Grand Hotels, the bedrock of the Lido's emergence as a holiday destination.¹¹ Adele Della Vida founded and ran the first Froebelian kindergarten in Italy, with the express intention of teaching children 'about God, about the *patria*, about liberty'; while Luigi Luzzatti, her son-in-law, was for many years a professor at the University of Padua before going into politics.¹²

In matters of culture, this Jewish elite admitted few equals. They were artists, poets, and musicians; adherents of decadentism and *verismo*; frequenters of cafes and salons; raconteurs, philosophers, and mystics.[13] Isacco Pesaro Maurogonato's daughter, Letizia, had her portrait painted by the Futurist painter, Giacomo Balla;[14] Enrico Castelnuovo – an admirer of Garibaldi – penned a stream of novels exploring the world of politics and business;[15] and the composer Samuele Levi, though somewhat past his prime by the time of Vittorio Emanuele II's visit, continued to write popular *canzonette*.[16]

Especially towards the end of the nineteenth century, mixed marriages – between Jews and non-Jews – began to become more common; Jewish children were given more 'Italian-sounding' names (e.g. Dante, Umberto); even worship came to be regarded as more of a patriotic ritual than a religious practice.[17] As Maurogonato's son-in-law, Marco Besso, later recalled:

> The religious solemnity which was once and still is most scrupulously observed is that of Kippur . . . an absolute and total fast, from one sunset to the next, accompanied by prayers, by meditation, and reconciliation . . . If there is a religious practice which deserves respect . . . it is precisely that which is . . . a civil and national precept, prescribed to all citizens, so that once a year they had a day of full and complete concentration, with their thoughts turned solely towards the fulfilment of their moral duties, to righting their own faults.[18]

Indeed, in spirit, these well-to-do Jews were as Venetian – or rather, as Italian – as anyone else.

Yet the same could not be said for *all* Jews – at least not to the same extent. Unification exposed a 'clear and persistent stratification' in Jewish society, between a narrow elite on the one hand, and the middle and working classes on the other.[19] This latter group consisted both of families who had lived in Venice for generations and of a growing number of immigrants arriving from mainland communities in decline. They practised a wide range of professions. Many struggled to make ends meet. On several occasions, in fact, the Jewish community was obliged to distribute household items to avoid any further decline in health. In 1886, for example, it handed out no fewer than twenty-three beds, sixty-two straw palliasses, ninety-four bedsheets, and 3,500kg of straw.[20] As a result, their integration into Venetian society was necessarily more limited. Though the surviving sources leave no doubt that most considered themselves to be Italians, they were precluded by wealth and social standing from participating in urban society to the same degree – and they preserved traditional habits to a far greater extent.

This social stratification was reflected in the Ghetto itself. Thanks, in part, to immigration, the Jewish population remained broadly steady in the years after unification – and, initially at least, the greater part still resided in or near the Ghetto. In 1869, some 579 Jews – out of a total of 2,415 – lived in the parish of San Geremia, where the Ghetto was located.[21] But for 'emancipated' Jews, whose wealth allowed them to look elsewhere, the Ghetto represented a past they preferred to forget. Despite the extensive remodelling undertaken by the Austrians, it was often characterized by contemporaries as a 'degraded quarter' – crumbling and, in places, almost derelict.[22] Those who remained there tended to be from lower socio-economic groups. The 1911 census shows that the Ghetto's residents included retailers and shopkeepers, agents, artisans, manual labourers, and office workers, as well as many second-hand dealers (*rigattieri*) and tailors, not to mention a good many 'economically inactive' persons, such as housewives, students, and pensioners.[23] As we have already noted, these tended to be the least 'integrated' sections of the Jewish community, in the sense of being welcomed into, and adopting the ways of, wider Venetian society. But at the same time, Jews living in the Ghetto found themselves living alongside Christians more closely than in any period in their history. Precisely because lodgings in the Ghetto were cheap, a growing number of apartments were rented by non-Jews, and a wider range of social experiences were shared. This had the effect both of binding at least part of the Jewish population to the lowest segments of Christian society, and of pushing the Ghetto further to the peripheries of Venetian life. As Donatella Calabi has noted, 'what characterized [the Ghetto] as "peripheral" was no longer its isolation and ethnic segregation, but the fact of being poor, degraded, provided with uncomfortable and scarcely hygienic housing'.[24]

*

These social transformations raised a new and troubling question: what did it *mean* to be a Jew? In the past, Jewishness had been defined in purely religious terms and given concrete expression through exclusion and legal restrictions. But now that piety was giving way to secularism, the old laws had been swept away, and the boundaries of Jewish society were fraying, this no longer seemed to hold water. How, then, should Jewishness be understood?

By far the most influential argument was put forward by Theodor Herzl. An Austro-Hungarian Jew, he was working in Paris as a journalist for the *Neue Freie Presse* when he first became dissatisfied with existing attitudes towards Jewish identity.[25] During a conversation with the writer Max Nordau on 6 July 1895, he agreed that Jewishness had 'nothing to do with religion'.[26] If Jews had anything in common, he thought, it was their 'race'. They all belonged to the same 'nation', with its own distinct culture and personality. Of course, Herzl – like most educated Jews of the time – had previously regarded himself as fully integrated into Austro-Hungarian culture. But he and Nordau agreed that antisemitism had 'made Jews out of us'. Hatred had not only made them conscious of their own difference, but also enforced it. This brought Herzl to an important conclusion. In *Der Judenstaat* (1896), he argued that, given the alarming growth of antisemitism in Austria-Hungary and France, it was impossible for a Jew *ever* to be fully assimilated into a hostile culture. Rather than waste time trying, the Jewish 'nation' should therefore emancipate itself by creating a Jewish state in Palestine.

Der Judenstaat caused an instant sensation. Soon, Jews everywhere were discussing Herzl's ideas – and Venice was no exception. In June 1903, the first Zionist group was set up. Two years later, it had more than 100 members.[27] Then, on 22 February 1908, the sixth Italian Zionist conference was held in the city. In the wake of the Dreyfus affair – which had ended only eighteen months before – the Venetian delegates were extremely attracted by the idea of Jewish auto-emancipation. Some were tempted to emigrate to Palestine, but most understood auto-emancipation in a broader sense. As Alessandro Levi explained, it should aim not just at 'Jewish colonization of Palestine', but also at 'raising the dignity of all Jews . . . in the face of non-Jews'.[28] In other words, one should be a Jew *before* one was an Italian – or a Venetian.

Not everyone was sympathetic to Zionism.[29] Given that Venice had little experience of the antisemitism seen in France, they couldn't see the point of it. In fact, at the time of the Italian Zionist conference, several found it difficult even to understand the concept of a

Jewish 'nationality'. They did not dispute that they *were* Jews, of course – even if they were thoroughly secular. Nor did they doubt that this entailed a certain 'separateness', which deserved respect. But they could not see any conflict between their Jewish and Italian identities, either. They were not just Jewish, or purely Italian: they were *both*. They might have been hard-pressed to say exactly what *either* of them meant, but it was futile trying to pretend they could ever distinguish between the two.

*

The outbreak of the First World War put this to the test. As a member of the Triple Alliance, Italy should, in theory, have entered the conflict immediately, on the side of Germany and Austria-Hungary. But when the time came, it hesitated. Domestic opinion was bitterly divided – not just over which side to join, but over whether to fight at all. The Left was against any intervention whatsoever. Just weeks before the outbreak of hostilities, Romagna and Le Marche had been convulsed by unrest, as workers rioted in protest at the deaths of three anti-militarists in Ancona. Meanwhile, the right-wing middle classes – furious with the government for failing to keep the socialists in check – demanded that the state prove its strength by joining the war and conquering new territory at Austria-Hungary's expense. As they saw it, only through war would the Risorgimento be completed. As Luigi Federzoni argued, Italy had been waiting for a 'truly national war, in order to feel unified at last, renewed by the unanimous action and identical sacrifices of all her sons'.[30]

In Venice, the atmosphere was febrile. Even before Franz Ferdinand's assassination, there was a public brawl in the Piazza San Marco between pro-and anti-war partisans; and a week later, no fewer than 10,000 people gathered in the square calling for military action.[31] The Jewish community was split. Although there were plenty of Jews, like Cesare Sarfatti, who supported the socialists, most of the Jewish bourgeoisie were staunchly in favour of war. Having long identified civil emancipation with unification, they found it all too easy to sympathize with a war of collective action against the hated Austrians.

When Italy eventually entered the war – against the Central

Powers – many young Venetian Jews went to fight.[32] Although some were conscripted, a good many volunteered. Several, like Alberto Levi Moreno, gave up lucrative careers to do so; and Roberto Sarfatti even tried to join up before he was old enough. No doubt in part due to the exceptionally high literacy rates among Jews, a plurality were officers.[33] At least half of those named on the monument to the Jewish war dead held the rank of *sottotenente* (sub-lieutenant) or above. At least fifteen silver medals of military valour were awarded.[34] Aurelio Ancona, an infantry officer, Mario Levi Bonaiuti, an artillery captain, and Alberto Musatti, a captain in the *milizia territoriale*, each won it twice. Some years later, Roberto Sarfatti – who died on 28 January 1918 after taking thirty Austrian soldiers prisoner at the First Battle of Three Mountains – was posthumously awarded the gold medal of military valour as well.[35]

As Shira Klein has pointed out, '[f]ighting for Italy was a family affair'.[36] The Soave family sent two brothers – Amadeo and Attilio – into battle. Amadeo worked at the Banca Commerciale Italiana before the war and had seemed destined for a glittering career in finance before he joined up at the age of twenty-nine.[37] He was commissioned as a sub-lieutenant in the *alpini* – Italy's elite mountain troops – and fought high in the Alps. Attilio, meanwhile, became a captain in the *bersaglieri* (sharpshooters).[38] He served in Libya for a time before being transferred to the Isonzo front. They died within three months of each other.

Not everyone involved in the war fought on the front line, though.[39] Those men who were too old to fight but had useful skills could serve in other roles – as doctors, administrators, or reservists. Jewish women, whose identification with the Italian war effort was especially strong, often volunteered as nurses, or else made clothing for the troops at home.[40] They contributed to organizations like *Pro esercito*, which sent comforting gifts to the front. After the defeat at Caporetto, many sent money or jewellery to *Oro alla Patria* (Gold for the Homeland), a campaign to 'collect gold and silver in order to lower the exchange rates and "give proof of female sacrifice"'.[41] They usually kept up a regular correspondence with male relatives in uniform, and some even went to the front to see conditions for themselves.[42]

*

When Jewish soldiers returned to Venice after the war's end, they found the city much changed. Having once again been a 'front city', Venice had suffered its own fair share of damage. Hospitals had been bombed, and a famous ceiling painted by Giambattista Tiepolo for the church of Santa Maria di Nazareth had been 'reduced to dust by enemy perfidy'.[43] Barbed wire and trenches still stretched across beaches on the Lido. The people had changed, too. The old social divisions had fractured. Food prices were high and rising. Dockers were out of work. Strikes were common. Even looting was not unknown.[44]

The effect on Jews' relations with non-Jews was profound. Two parallel – and opposing – shifts began to take place. On the one hand, the war greatly accelerated Jewish integration. The Jews' already robust sense of patriotism was cemented further. With remarkable speed, the community harnessed memories of the war to tighten the bond between Jewish and Italian identity. Erected in 1920, the memorial erected on the wall of the Scuola Levantina proudly declared that twenty-four 'Venetian Jews fell in war for the *patria*', adding that 'the community remembers [them] with love and with pride'. Testimonials, while no doubt grounded in hard truths, were often embellished to emphasize the patriotic fervour of the deceased. According to one post-war publication, Alberto Levi Moreno, who fell while leading an attack on Monte San Gabriele, pulled a tricolour *banderuola* from his tunic after being hit, and with his dying breath cried: 'Forward first company – long live Italy'.[45]

Jews also began playing a bigger part in Venetian society. Within the Jewish community, socio-economic mobility became more apparent. In 1922, the economic roles performed by Jewish residents were noticeably more varied – and, in many cases, better remunerated – than in the past. There were 112 'professionals' (lawyers, teachers, engineers, architects, doctors, pharmacists, accountants), 152 office workers, 194 shopkeepers, 52 manual workers, and 36 day-labourers and pedlars.[46] Mixed marriages became far more common. In 1921, there were no fewer than 101 mixed marriages – accounting for around 20 per cent of those in non-nuclear Jewish families in Venice. Between 1930 and 1935, 47 per cent of marriages involving at least one Jew were 'mixed'.[47] More Jews became visible cultural consumers, too. In 1936, for example, 17 out of 51 donations made to La Fenice by the Società dei palchettisti were in Jewish names.[48]

Perhaps most significantly, the levelling effects of war also ensured that there was a high degree of exchange between Jewish and Christian communities – and, in many ways, a burgeoning respect. A good illustration is provided by an incident which took place at Lazzaro Fano's restaurant in the Sotoportego de le Acque,[49] a traditional little place known for its excellent *baccalà mantecato* (a type of creamed cod) and the friendliness of the owner. Plenty of *goyim* were regular customers, but Fano was strict about keeping *kashrut*. He closed on the Sabbath and High Holy Days, refused to serve any meat that was not kosher, and was careful never to mix meat and dairy. One day – so the story goes – an out-of-towner (*signore forestiero*) came in and ordered a *minestra in brodo* (a meat broth with pasta). When it arrived, he called the waiter back to ask for some cheese. Naturally, since cheese with broth would break *kashrut*, the waiter politely told him there wasn't any. The man was bewildered.

'How's that, there isn't any?' he asked.

'No, sir,' stammered the waiter, embarrassed.

'Well,' the out-of-towner barked, grabbing his wallet, 'send out to buy a bit, then. I'll pay, but I can't eat *minestra* without cheese. What sort of place is this!'

'Excuse me sir,' interposed Lazzaro Fano, coming out from behind the bar, 'just try the *minestra*. If you don't like it without cheese, go away, and break my glasses, and dirty my tablecloth too, if you want, to vent your anger; but you won't get any cheese to eat from me.'

The implication of the story was not that the out-of-towner was eating in a Jewish restaurant, but that any Venetian would have known that *minestra* couldn't be eaten with cheese – and wouldn't even have asked.

On the other hand, the war also greatly increased Italy's political polarization. Many were horrified that Venice did not gain more from the Paris Peace Conference. On 25 April 1919, the flamboyant writer Gabriele D'Annunzio, who had spent most of the war in Venice, gave a speech in the Piazza San Marco, railing about how Italy had been 'cheated' of its legitimate territorial claims, and demanding what amounted to a resumption of war.[50] While the bourgeoisie wanted a swift return to economic order and the protection of property rights, workers, angry at rising prices and high unemployment, demanded sweeping political reforms. Socialist parties experienced a dramatic surge in participation; and there were dark rumours of an imminent revolution. In the summer of 1920, a group of left-wingers 'invaded' the Piazza San Marco, shouting 'down with the bourgeoisie' – and throwing the normally sedate cafes into chaos.[51]

Out of this febrile atmosphere, Benito Mussolini's Fascist Party emerged. Initially founded as a loose political movement in Milan on 23 March 1919, it quickly spread across Italy. A *fascio di combattimento* – reputedly the second in the nation – was set up in Venice just a few weeks later.[52] Soon enough, its members were breaking up strikes, beating workers, and arguing with their fists whenever they could. Mussolini, however, yearned for greater respectability. Two years later, he established the Partito Nazionale Fascista in its stead. Intensely nationalistic, it was, in many senses, a party of contradictions. It emphasized the importance of history and tradition, just as it embraced aggressive modernization; it was vehemently pro-business, but favoured collaboration between employers and employees, state and corporations. Its rise was meteoric, however. When the socialists called a national strike in 1922, Mussolini staged a dramatic 'March on Rome' with 30,000 supporters and was immediately swept to power.

Among Venetian Jews, there were many prominent anti-fascists. During the 1920s and 1930s, several fought vigorously against Mussolini's influence, both in Venice and throughout the country. And more than a few suffered as a result. Gino Luzzatto, for example, was a highly respected professor of economic history; yet, as a result of his anti-fascist stance, he was eased out of the Scuola Superiore di Commercio, before being arrested and tried in 1928.[53] One of Luzzatto's acquaintances, Angelo Fano, had his office trashed by a squad of fascists in 1926. Five years later, he was arrested on charges of subversion, then released, only to be sent into confinement in Salerno a short time afterwards.[54] And so it went on.

But a surprising number of Venetian Jews actively supported the Fascists. True, the Party's rhetoric did have a markedly antisemitic undertone from the very beginning.[55] In 1919, Mussolini himself had inveighed against 'big Jewish bankers in London and New York'.[56] And the Party's rank and file were certainly not above tormenting

Jews when the will took them. However, in its early days, the Fascist Party did not conceive of Italian nationhood along racial lines and avoided adopting any explicitly antisemitic policies.[57] Indeed, Mussolini even distanced himself from the anti-Jewish prejudice then rampant in Germany. Shortly after the assassination of Germany's Jewish foreign minister, Walther Rathenau, in June 1922, he wrote an article denouncing German antisemitism, pointing out that Italian Jews not only had served their country well in the war, but were completely assimilated.[58] On 14 May 1929, when Mussolini addressed the Camera dei Deputati on the Lateran Accords, he reassured the assembled deputies that:

> Jews have been in Rome since the time of the Kings; perhaps they provided the clothes after the rape of the Sabine women; there were 50,000 of them at the time of Augustus; and they asked to weep over the body of Julius Caesar. They will remain undisturbed, as will those who believe in another religion.[59]

As late as 16 February 1938, Mussolini declared that 'the Fascist government has never thought of taking political, economic, [or] moral measures against the Jews'.[60]

Some noteworthy figures joined the Fascists. Foremost among them were the lawyer and war hero Alberto Musatti and the banker Max Ravà. Perhaps the most intriguing, however, was Margherita Grassini Sarfatti.[61] Born into an illustrious Jewish family, she had lived in the Ghetto before moving to the Palazzo Bembo, on the Grand Canal. Her family were well connected, and thoroughly integrated. Her father even counted the Patriarch of Venice, the future Pope Pius X, as a close friend. At the age of eighteen, she had married the socialist Cesare Sarfatti, and together they had a son, Roberto. While Roberto was still a toddler, they moved to Milan, where she began writing for the socialist newspaper *Avanti! della domenica* and became active in the struggle for women's emancipation. A few years later, she met Mussolini. Then an ardent socialist, he would shortly become the editor of *Avanti!*. Margherita and Mussolini quickly became lovers. For the next twenty years, she remained his mistress. After Cesare's death, in 1924, she published one of the earliest biographies of Mussolini and was regularly seen sneaking into the Palazzo Venezia in Rome for discreet assignations with him. She had considerable influence over *Il Duce* and she wasn't afraid to use it. In 1929, when Mussolini published an article distinguishing between three different types of Jews (assimilated, less assimilated, and international Zionists, who could 'not be trusted'), she wrote to the psychologist Carlo Foà, inviting him to respond. It would be helpful, she told him, if he could emphasize that the idea of 'racial purity' was a ridiculous fantasy, which, if anyone were foolish enough to try enforcing it would cause all kinds of trouble. He might also like to point out the true strength of the Italian people was their ability to assimilate 'outsiders' – especially the Jews.[62] It was perhaps also at her urging that her son, Roberto, was posthumously awarded the gold medal of military valour and commemorated with a huge monument at the spot on Col d'Echele where he fell. Eventually, though, even Margherita had had enough. In 1930, tired of Mussolini's infidelities, she converted to Catholicism – and left Italy.

*

Following the Italian conquest of Ethiopia, in May 1936, 'unofficial' antisemitism began to increase.[63] More articles critical of Jews appeared in the press; cartoons rehearsed the basest stereotypes; and in daily life, Jewish families encountered steadily more hostility. In shops, in streets, even in school playgrounds, Jews had cheap myths and prejudices casually thrown at them. In Venice, Amelia Salvadori was so upset by 'allegations of Jewish uncleanliness' that she scrubbed her children until they were red raw, just so that 'nobody would say Jews were dirty'.[64] Even Jewish Fascists came under attack. In June 1936, an informer told the police that the secretary of the local Party was planning to block 'the well-known Jew Max Ravà' from being confirmed as the head of the Istituto di Credito Fondiario adding darkly: 'We shall succeed in eliminating even this really powerful Jew from the position . . . he still enjoys in Venice'.[65]

Some Jews could see the writing on the wall. One woman recalled walking along the streets of Rome in tears. 'I felt that only something bad could come of it for everyone,' she said.[66] When the Fascist regime suddenly adopted a much harsher policy towards the Jewish population in 1938, the shock was nevertheless profound.[67]

Promulgated on 14 July 1938, the *Manifesto della razza* ('Manifesto of Race') repudiated the Fascists' formerly vague attitude towards

'Italianness' and instead embraced a purely 'racial' understanding of the nation. Italians, it declared, were members of the Aryan race. Those who belonged to other races – including Jews – were, by definition, *not* Italians. As such, if Italy was to be 'racially pure', a clear separation between Jews and Italians needed to be maintained.

At first, many Jews refused to believe that the Manifesto was true – or, if they did, they hoped that somehow it would not be put into force.[68] The link between Jewish emancipation and Italian unification was too strong to be easily forgotten; their integration too profound to be easily dissolved. Guido Weiller, holidaying in Venice a few weeks later, simply dismissed the idea that they could be serious. 'The racist issue is purely a formal concession to Hitler to keep him politically happy,' he reassured his family. 'Italy simply cannot implement racial German theories, which are foreign to the country's civilization and culture.'[69]

The *Manifesto* was no idle pronouncement, though. To draw such a distinction in practice, it was necessary to have some idea of how many Jews there actually were in Italy. On 11 August, the ministry of the interior therefore dispatched a telegram to all prefects ordering them to conduct a census of Jews, where Jewishness was taken to mean 'belonging to the Hebrew race', regardless of what religion a person professed.[70]

The results were revealing.[71] In Venice, there were 2,136 who belonged to the 'Jewish race'. Of these, some 1,471 practised the Jewish faith, 616 were Catholics, and 49 were agnostics. And the population was growing, too – albeit perhaps a little slower than before. Compared to earlier in the century, they were also more spread out. Now, only 305 (barely 14 per cent of the total) lived in San Geremia – that is, in or around the Ghetto. No fewer than 129 lived in San Marziale, 114 in San Marcuola, and 105 in San Marco. It was also clear that, by profession, there had been some changes. Over half of the community was registered 'inactive', including 424 housewives and 207 students (91 women, 116 men). The next largest group (just over 11 per cent of the population) were labourers, office workers, or other dependent workers.

The census immediately threw up a problem, however. What did it mean for someone to 'belong ... to the Hebrew race'? As Venice's Jews had already discovered for themselves several decades earlier, it was a thorny issue. Having traditionally understood Judaism in purely religious terms, the Italian government was at something of a loss – and it struggled adequately to separate the two definitions, even at this stage.[72] Some cases seemed clear enough. Anyone who had two Jewish parents and four Jewish grandparents was obviously of pure Jewish blood. So too, anyone with three Jewish grandparents was an *ebreo puro*. But what about the children of mixed marriages? Or Jews who had converted to Christianity?[73]

After much scrambling around, the government passed the first of the so-called *leggi razziali* (racial laws) in the autumn of 1938, setting out an intricate set of rules. The child of a Jewish mother and an unknown father was regarded as Jewish. So was anyone born to a Jew and a foreigner – even if the foreigner belonged to another religion. Someone who, although born to two 'Italian' parents – one Jewish, one non-Jewish – professed the Jewish faith, was registered with a Jewish community, or had otherwise demonstrated his Judaism would also be considered Jewish. Somewhat peculiarly, anyone of mixed parentage who was baptized as a child *after* 1 October 1938 was Jewish too.[74]

To say that this left room for ambiguity would be an understatement. Over the months which followed, no end of people who had been classified as Jewish in the census challenged their status on one ground or another – with varying degrees of success.[75] There were plenty of exceptions to the rules, too. Any Jews who had served in the army or rendered some other noteworthy service to the state could apply for a *'discriminazione'*, granting them the privileged status of 'honorary' Italians.[76] All this was a recipe for confusion, but the Fascists – unlike the Nazis – saw that fuzziness could be an advantage. If nothing else, it gave the regime the latitude to adapt policy to pragmatism – retaining 'useful' Jews in key posts, extorting money from the wealthy, or removing the awkward without difficulty. As such, Mussolini and his ministers were only too happy to let any 'uncertainties' be resolved by special commissions on a case-by-case basis.[77]

Now that a framework – of sorts – was in place, Mussolini's government proceeded to active discrimination. Between 5 September and 15 November, a barrage of new laws and decrees was issued, expelling foreign Jews from Italy and banning Jewish children and teachers from schools and universities.[78] As was to be expected, there were some exceptions. Whereas 'pure-blooded' Jewish children were excluded from public education, those who were merely of the Jewish race – that is to say, children of mixed marriages, baptized Jews, etc. – were allowed to continue with their studies, albeit with a stigma attached. Fifteen-year-old Ugo Finzi, for example, received good marks in his high-school entrance exams in 1939–40, but had 'Razza ebraica' written against his name in the margin.[79] After the schoolroom came the home. Mixed marriages between Jews and Aryans were prohibited; Jews were forbidden to employ Aryans as domestic servants; and the citizenship of any Jew who had taken Italian nationality after the end of the First World War was revoked – a clear attempt to exclude those who had sought refuge in Italy in the chaos which had followed the armistice.[80]

Even at this stage, Venice's Jews had some hope. 'My father had been in the army and won medals,' Lia Sacerdote recalled in an interview with the historian Shira Klein; 'we thought the laws would pass'.[81] But they didn't. In fact, they got worse. The following year, Jewish economic activity was strictly controlled. Jews had to declare all their business interests; limits were placed on the amount of property they could own; and anything above those limits had to be voluntarily surrendered to Aryans, or it would be confiscated.[82] To speed this process along, a list of Jewish-owned businesses was published in the *Gazzetta Ufficiale* in November.[83] Then it was the turn of Jewish jobs. In June 1939, tight restrictions were placed on doctors, lawyers, pharmacists, engineers, accountants, and a dozen other professions. They could go on working, of course – but only for Jewish clients. Nor could Jews belong to trades unions; and they were completely banned from some lines of work, such as journalism.[84]

Understandably, this caused considerable hardship – and not a little bewilderment. A few days before the restrictions on professional activities were imposed, an anonymous Jewish woman from Venice wrote to Alessandro Pavolini, the president of the Fascist Confederation of Professionals and Artists, pleading for help.

> My husband is one of those professionals who because of the racial measures announced is heading for starvation with his partner and his sons.
>
> A man of noble soul, honest to the point of scrupulousness, the father of an exemplary family, the most Italian of Italians, just like his ancestors for more than ten generations, he fought in the war, like his father

fought for the Risorgimento and never presented a bill for the debt incurred. [...]

Having committed no fault, we are heading for hard times: for us old people, it doesn't matter, but it breaks our hearts for the kids. How many Jews [are there] like him, honourable people, who are heading for starvation. But what does it matter to you . . . if they are of the Jewish religion? [...]

I do not wish you ill, nor do I wish that [your] children (if you have any) should one day, without having done anything wrong, be deprived of an honest crust: I wish only that the moment should come when you feel shame for the wretched act committed against some honest men, some of whom, until yesterday, you would have shaken hands with and, perhaps, called your friends. My name doesn't matter, I'm a poor woman.[85]

Few areas of life were spared. Kosher butchering was banned. Jewish newspapers were closed.[86] La Fenice, like every other opera house in Italy, was sent a list of Jewish composers whose work could not be played; and a year and a half later, Jews were forbidden to take part in theatrical performances of any kind. Venetian libraries removed Jewish books from their shelves. Jewish scholars and scientists – like the mathematician Guido Castelnuovo – were ejected from the prestigious Istituto Veneto.[87] In time, Jews would even be driven out of hotels and beaches on the Lido, too.[88]

*

As Renata Segre has pointed out, the Jewish community was driven back into a 'ghetto' – if not *the* Ghetto.[89] Though based on racial rather than merely religious prejudice, the *leggi razziali* were eerily similar to the rules which had governed the lives of Venetian Jews centuries earlier. There was the same fear of Jewish 'contamination'; the same horror of social contact, however slight; the same morbid preoccupation with sexual 'corruption'. Indeed, in some respects, the restrictions were even harsher than in the past. While they may not have confined Venice's Jews to a specific area, they limited their freedom of action – especially in the commercial sphere – to an extent that would have baffled the old doges. Never before had Jews' contribution to Venice's prosperity been so slightly valued – or so readily destroyed.

Jews worked hard to preserve a semblance of their former lives. Dedicated Jewish schools were set up so that children could go on receiving an education. There was an elementary school on the first floor of a building in Cannaregio, and a middle school, first in a refurbished apartment on the Calle del Rimedio in Castello, then at the Ponte Storto at Santi Filippo e Giacomo.[90] Beginning in February 1939, there were courses for adults, too – language classes in English and French, classes in agronomy, even classes in home economics for 'young girls'.[91] Social and therapeutic activities continued to be run. In the summer, sickly children went on brine cures and day trips organized by the community.[92] The Association for Jewish Women offered its own classes on Jewish culture and the Hebrew language, as well as parties and meals at holiday time. From August 1939 onwards, there was even a Jewish agricultural settlement at Airuno, near Lecco, where young Jews could learn the agricultural skills they would need if they ever managed to emigrate.[93]

No one worked harder than Giuseppe Jona.[94] Tall, balding, and dignified, with round glasses and an air of quiet authority, he was elected as president of the Jewish community on 16 June 1940. He was, in many ways, the perfect choice. Born in 1866, just a week after Venice voted to become part of Italy, he had enjoyed a distinguished career as a doctor. During his forty years of service at Venice's Ospedale Civile, he became well known not only for his skill, but also for his intense humanity. Nicknamed the 'doctor of the poor', he went to extraordinary lengths to treat the needy – often putting himself at great risk in the process. He was too old to fight in the Great War, but still became a senior figure in the Red Cross, serving as a consultant in military hospitals. He acquitted himself so well, in fact, that he was praised by the minister of the interior for his 'enthusiastic patriotism and unshakeable loyalty'.[95] As such, Jona was unusually – even uniquely – well placed to guide the Jewish community through its troubles. Naturally, he already enjoyed the trust and respect of the Jewish population. At one time or another, he had treated most of them – often for free. But thanks to his war record, he had the confidence of the Fascist authorities, too.[96]

The task facing Jona was immense. Just six days before his election, on 10 June 1940, Italy had belatedly declared war on France. Almost

The Emptying of the Ghetto

immediately, Jewish life became significantly worse. The previous month, Mussolini had given orders for concentration camps to be built; and soon enough, the first Italian Jews were being interned there.[97] The following year, Jewish names were removed from Venetian telephone directories, and radio sets were confiscated.[98] And in 1942, a campaign of forced labour was introduced.[99] All the while, Jewish refugees came flooding into the lagoon, shortages mounted, and poverty rose.[100]

If this wasn't bad enough, ordinary Venetians – swept up in the early excitement of the war – became complicit in state-sponsored antisemitism, too. At the San Marco cinema, the propaganda film *Süss l'ebreo* ('Süss the Jew') was greeted with rapturous applause.[101] Newspaper articles stoked suspicions that Jews were hoarding food. In the streets and squares, people hurled abuse: 'Jewish spies, Jewish traitors . . . Death to the Jews'.[102] Violent assaults became more common, too. In April 1942, the chief rabbi, Adolfo Ottolenghi, old and blind, was beaten up by a group of Fascist agitators.[103]

Jona did his best to hold the Jewish community together. He arranged help for refugees, kept the schools running, and managed the financial contributions offered by the better off. Most importantly of all, he had to deal with the threat to Jewish safety. Officially, the Fascist regime maintained that the abuse and attacks were provoked by Jews themselves. But this, Jona could not accept. On 29 May 1941, he wrote to Marcello Vaccari, the prefect of Venice, demanding that the offences stop. 'It is not human,' he wrote, 'that . . . the Jews are obliged to surrender all dignity and honour . . . The state should protect the Jews'.[104] A few months later, he protested to the Fascist Giunta about a journalist who had described the Jewish community as 'the equivalent of a criminal association' and compared synagogues with 'robbers' dens'.[105] When the danger of Allied air raids became too severe, he also arranged for valuables from the Scuola Spagnola and the Scuola Levantina to be moved to the Palazzo delle Prigioni for safekeeping, along with the city's other artistic treasures.[106]

*

The collapse of Mussolini's government on 25 July 1943 brought little improvement. Over the forty-five days which followed, there were, admittedly, some signs that a lightening of restrictions *might* be possible. The telephone company asked about putting Jewish names back in the telephone book; while the Jewish community was permitted to print service schedules for the synagogues and arrange for school prize days.[107] But no sooner had hope been kindled than it was snuffed out. When it became known that Marshal Badoglio's new government had signed an armistice with the Allies, on 8 September, the Nazis immediately swooped in. German troops poured into northern Italy, freed Mussolini from captivity, and established a new puppet regime – the Italian Social Republic – at Salò. On 9 September, Mestre was occupied. Three days later, Venice itself was in German hands.

It was not immediately clear who, exactly, was calling the shots. Although the city was under German military control, a Fascist administration was still in place and continued to administer most of its affairs. For the Jews, there was no doubt whose opinions carried the most weight. All at once, the complicated, ambiguous system introduced by Mussolini in 1938 gave way to the unyielding rigour of the Nuremberg Laws – and the 'final solution' was brought to the lagoon. For the process of extermination to begin, however, the authorities needed to know how many Jews there currently were in Venice, who they were, and where they lived. And for this, they needed Jona's help.

On 17 September 1943, a visitor appeared at Jona's door.[108] Nothing is known about his identity, or even exactly what he said. At the very least, he must have asked for the names of everyone linked with the Jewish community. Jona surely guessed what was afoot. He would have known what was happening to Jews in Germany and Poland from talking to refugees. It would have been clear to him that, if he gave this visitor the list, everyone on it was likely to be killed. Since he could hardly say no, he probably decided to play for time.

Perhaps Jona claimed he didn't have the information to hand. Or maybe he said he would have to check with his colleagues whether the list was up to date. Either way, he convinced the unsuspecting visitor to come back again later. As soon as he was alone, Jona swung into action. He collected every scrap of paper he could find and burned them. The only complete information about the community was now in his head. If others were to be saved, that too would have to be put out of harm's way. He could have fled. Or even hidden. Instead, he took down a syringe and a phial of morphine, rolled up his sleeve, and committed suicide.

Jona's courage was equalled only by the magnitude of his sacrifice. And the Germans knew it. His suicide was not just an act of defiance, it was tantamount to rebellion. They could not allow him to become a martyr. Orders were given for his funeral cortège to be kept to an absolute minimum: ten Jews – enough for the kaddish – no more. No one paid any attention, though. When the obsequies were held, on Sunday 19 September, more than fifty people turned up – Jews and Christians, fellow doctors, and friends – all united in grief, and heedless of the risk.[109]

*

Even Jona's death could not stop the Final Solution, though. At the end of November, Venice's chief of police, Filippo Cordova, warned Jews not to leave the city. It was obvious something was up. According to Girolamo Segré, some even speculated that the Fascists were 'waiting for trucks to come and pick us up'.[110] Like many others, he wasn't unduly worried. Too often already, the Fascists had tried to frighten Jews, for no other reason than to keep them on edge. It was a fatal miscalculation. Next day, the orders arrived from Guido Buffarini Guidi, the minister of the interior. All Jews, without exception – Italian or foreign, exempt or not – were to be sent to concentration camps; their property was to be confiscated; and the goods seized would be redistributed to 'destitute victims of enemy air raids'.[111]

At 2.00 p.m. on 5 December 1943, Cordova gave orders for the 'immediate arrest' of Venice's 'pure' Jews. The operation was to take place after dark – partly to avoid the risk of public protests, but mostly to catch Jewish families by surprise while they slept. Members of the police, the *carabinieri*, the militia, and the local Fascist Party were to meet at the police station, where they would be given their instructions. Officers had been given lists of names and addresses, culled from the 1938 census, and knew exactly where to go. Even if hazy on the details, none of the men involved were in any doubt about where the Jews were going to be sent. They weren't troubled, either. As far as they were concerned, the Jews deserved it. 'They're foreigners and enemies. They can't be trusted.'[112]

Once darkness had fallen, the operation began. Girolamo Segré's experience – brilliantly reconstructed by the historian Simon Levis Sullam – was typical.[113] At 2.45 a.m., the Segré family were woken by a ring at the door. At first, they didn't suspect anything. Perhaps it was just kids playing a joke, they thought. But when the bell rang again, they knew it was more serious. They got up and opened the door. Standing there were the local police chief, four plainclothes policemen, and two *carabinieri* – all familiar faces. There was no brutality. After checking Girolamo's identity, and asking about the neighbours, the police chief told him that the family were going to be taken to the police station. They were allowed to pack and take some money. Everything was very courteous. It never occurred to Girolamo or his family to put up any resistance. Nor did anyone else in Venice.

The Segrés were escorted to the San Marco police station. They walked, calmly, and without fuss. The plainclothes policemen even helped carry their bags. When they arrived, they found a group of other Jews already there: eight men and five women, all quite elderly. There was no unpleasantness. In fact, they were even allowed to go to a nearby bar for a coffee while they waited.

The next morning, transit orders arrived. The men were to be taken to the prison of Santa Maria Maggiore, women to Giudecca, and the children to reform schools. A few hours later, a boat came to collect them. It was then that the reality of their fate hit home. Before they left the station, or perhaps even at the quay, a policeman took Girolamo's daughter, Nedda, away. He was gentle, even soothing. But the scream she let out was heart-rending. 'I will always feel that scream in my heart,' Girolamo later told his son, 'and not knowing where they had taken her weighed so heavily on me.'

At Santa Maria Maggiore, Girolamo was thrown in a cell with nine others. He was thoroughly questioned – about his family, his co-religionists, his property, everything. The conditions were terrible. It was enough to make even a secular man become religious. Then, a little over a week later, Girolamo and the other men were transferred again – this time to the Casa di Ricovero Israelitico (Jewish nursing home) in the Ghetto Nuovo. Once again, it happened at night, calmly and without fuss.

In the Ghetto, Girolamo was reunited with his family. The nursing home was not what you could call comfortable. There were far too many people and not enough space. No one had any idea how long they'd be there – or what lay ahead. But for the moment, life almost seemed to go back to normal. They received visitors ('too many at times'); they held prayer services; they even celebrated the Sabbath together.

Spirits were further lifted by an act of apparent clemency. After the transfer back to the Ghetto, the Fascists released the sick, the aged, and members of mixed families. Nobody knew the real reason, of course. As the minister of the interior explained in a telegram to Cordova, the round-up of Jews across Italy had been so efficient that it would not be possible to send everyone to the camps at once. Everything had to be slowed down.[114]

At 12.20 p.m. on 31 December 1943, ninety-three Jews – including the Segrés – left Venice by train for Fossoli di Carpi, an Italian concentration camp just outside Modena.[115] Just over two weeks later, they were joined by a group of children: Mario Levi, the son of Beniamino, aged four; Lino Levi, the son of Beniamino, aged six; Sergio Todesco, the son of Eugenio, aged four; Mara Nacamulli, the daughter of Eugenio, aged three. Still, they had no idea what was happening to them. Among the other Italian Jews at the camp was Primo Levi. In his memoir, *Se questo è un uomo*, Levi recalled that there were constant arrivals – and not just Jews, either: Yugoslavian soldiers, politically suspect foreigners. It was still possible that they would just be interned there for the rest of the war. But 'the arrival of a small unit of German SS would have made even the optimists doubt'.[116]

On 21 February 1944, the 650 Jews were told that they would be leaving. 'Everyone: no exceptions. Even the children, even the old, even the sick,' recalled Levi. 'Only a minority of naive and deluded people still persisted in hope.'[117] The next morning, they were loaded onto a train, bound for Poland. Four freezing days later, they arrived at Auschwitz. Most were killed immediately. Girolamo Segré, his wife, Lea Rita Calimani, and their daughter, Nedda, were among them.[118]

*

In Venice, the remaining Jews were alert to the danger. Over the coming months, the greater part fled. At least half went to Switzerland.[119] It was a dangerous journey. The countryside was still pullulating with Fascist police and German troops. To make things worse, the Swiss authorities, while willing enough to accept Jewish refugees, would only grant entry to those who could present valid – but incriminating – legal documents proving they belonged to the 'Jewish race'. Anyone caught with these on the Italian side risked arrest or death. Others, encouraged by the Anglo-American advance in the spring, headed south, travelling under false documents. A smaller number, generally Jewish youths, headed for the hills and joined the resistance.

Several children who had been separated from their parents were hidden by churches or monasteries. In December 1944, three siblings – Franco, Pina, and Tina – wrote to their mother with touching frankness.

> Dearest Mama,
>
> Imagine how sad we are to be far from you right now, you who are so dear to us . . . O how we hope and long from the depths of our hearts that this horrible situation will end and that we will be able to be together again very soon and enjoy that peace we all love and desire so much once more. We aren't making you any promises, but you can rest sure and easy that we will do our very best. We hope we will see each other again soon with Papa.
>
> Our most affectionate and fondest wishes, hugs and kisses from your children.[120]

Still the Fascists' campaign went on. Even before the trains had left for Auschwitz, orders were given for all remaining Jewish property to be impounded.[121] Empty houses and apartments were requisitioned and, in some cases, handed over to the Party faithful. The Villa Fano, abandoned by its owners in 1943, was a good example. Although a family friend had agreed to move in to keep an eye on the belongings, the house was taken over by two families who worked for Mussolini's Italian Social Republic.[122]

Soon enough, the arrests started again – this time with the Nazis' help.[123] There would be no more exceptions, no more mercy. Perhaps the most noteworthy round-up took place in the summer of 1944. An SS detachment under Captain Franz Stangl, the fearsome, bull-necked ex-commandant of Treblinka, was sent to Venice to track down as many Jews as possible. Assisted by Mauro Grini – a Jewish collaborator from Trieste who went by the name 'Dr. Manzoni' – Stangl arrested about ninety Jews.[124] They were immediately transported to Risiera di San Sabba, a grim former rice-husking factory, just outside Trieste. Some were already dead on arrival. Those who were still alive were then herded onto trains bound for concentration camps in Germany and Poland. Among them were twenty-one elderly people taken from the nursing home in the Ghetto Nuovo – including the chief rabbi, Adolfo Ottolenghi – and twenty-two patients from the hospital (ten, too sick to travel, remained behind). They did not come back.

Others followed. All together, no fewer than 246 Venetian Jews died in, or en route to, concentration camps. More than 400 years since the Ghetto's foundation, the terrible, hateful logic of antisemitism had reached its appalling culmination.

16

Epilogue

(1945–present)

The day after Allied troops entered Venice – on 29 April 1945 – a group of Jews gathered for a photograph in the *campiello* of the Ghetto Vecchio. There were about eighty of them, all told: some old, some young – or youngish – and a handful of children. The spring air was still cool enough for some to be wearing coats; but the sun was shining brightly. In the middle of the group stood an Allied army rabbi holding the Torah scroll. A few minutes after the picture was taken, he would solemnly return it to the Scuola Spagnola, just behind where the photographer must have been standing. It was a potent symbol. Despite everything, the Jewish community had survived. The Jewish faith lived on. And now, the moment had come to give thanks.

There was little joy about it, though. In the photograph, only a few people are smiling: a girl, maybe ten or twelve years old, in the right foreground; a couple of teenagers, squeezed between the rabbi and another soldier; perhaps, faintly, a young mother holding her child, just to the left of the Torah scroll. Most have an air of defiance, almost hardness. They gaze steadily at the camera, lips pursed, jaws set. Some, in the background, don't even have the time to stop.

Who could blame them? A little over three months before Venice's liberation, Marshal Badoglio's government in Brindisi had passed two decrees revoking the Fascist *leggi razziali* and restoring full civic rights to all those belonging to the 'Jewish race'.[1] Now that the Germans were gone, it did not take long for this to take effect in Venice. On 31 May, *Corriere Veneto* published an order from the new provincial prefect confirming that the city's Jews once again enjoyed the right to own 'commercial property, real estate, and goods'.[2] All confiscations were annulled. Bank accounts belonging to Jews were unblocked. In time, provision would be made for the restitution of all goods and property confiscated by the Fascists.

No one could just turn the clock back, though. The antisemitism of recent years ran too deep for that. However laudable their intention, Badoglio's decrees still used the same racist language as the laws they were meant to replace.[3] The text consistently – even obstinately – talked about the 'Jewish *race*'. The provincial prefect's announcement, it is true, was a little better; but in Venice itself, the signs of popular antisemitism were still everywhere to be seen. The following November, there were traces of anti-Jewish graffiti on almost every street.[4] At the entrance to the park, on the via Garibaldi, you could read, in block letters, 'Jewish spies', as clear as day.

The Ghetto itself was in a dreadful state, too. True, it had been spared the worst of the bombing. In the photograph, there are no obvious signs of serious damage. But the community was struggling. In late May, it comprised around 1,100 'Italian' Jews – Venetian and other – plus about 600 displaced foreigners, mostly Poles, Hungarians, and Yugoslavs, waiting to be repatriated or transported to Palestine.[5] These all needed providing for, even though, at the time of the liberation, there was a chronic shortage of necessities. Food, wood, and coal were almost impossible to find.

The community also had to brace itself for the return of deportees and refugees. The first arrived in Venice in mid-May 1945, aboard the boat *Velebit*.[6] Those foreigners who wanted to be repatriated were dispatched by train or sea. While they were waiting, however, they had to be lodged somewhere. By November 1945, there were around 150 at a special 'welcome centre' at Chirignago, near Mestre; 72 at another in Mogliano, on the road to Treviso; and another 140 in the city centre. Most of these were placed in two hotels, requisitioned for the purpose; but a sizeable number were also put up in the Ghetto. By necessity, much of the bureaucratic work was handled by the Allied authorities; but the Jewish community still had to bear a heavy burden. Returnees were in a pitiful state. Those in the Ghetto urgently needed food, clothing, and medical care. But there just wasn't enough to go around. That summer, the community announced that it was unable to provide for the Italian Jews – or even just the Venetians – from its own, extremely limited, resources.

Help, when it came, brought its own problems. The American

Joint Distribution Committee, known as the 'Joint', was an American Jewish organization which had been set up in New York thirty years earlier to assist Jews in need around the world – and, naturally, it was responsive to the Ghetto's plight.[7] The first of its agents arrived shortly after the liberation; and soon enough, a steady stream of supplies was on its way. On 10 October 1945, two lorries left Rome, carrying five trunks of clothes and two of blankets.[8] More would soon follow. The Joint's staff weren't easy to work with, though. They were notorious for badgering Jewish leaders for information – and, on occasions, meddling in the distribution of goods.[9] As one Milanese leader pointed out, this left Jews feeling like *schnorers* (beggars).[10] It didn't help that the Joint also had a nasty habit of bossing around elderly community leaders, often in English. In 1945, two Joint workers, Reuben Resnik and Benjamin Brook, both in their thirties, unleashed an avalanche of terse instructions upon sixty-year-old Vittorio Fano and his deputy, sixty-seven-year-old Gino Luzzatto.[11]

Gradually, some semblance of life returned to the Ghetto. A new Provisional Committee of the Jewish community was established, led by Vittorio Fano.[12] The synagogues resumed regular prayer services. Although the communal oven had been destroyed by Fascist blackshirts in the spring of 1944, the Jews of Rome generously sent a supply of *matzah*. Many of the precious ritual items which had been presumed lost were recovered from under the ark of the Scuola Canton, where they had been hidden by Moisé Calimani the night before his deportation.[13] And when it became clear that Adolfo Ottolenghi had perished, a new chief rabbi, Elio Toaff, was appointed.[14]

The Jewish schools reopened.[15] In the Casa di Ricovero Israelitica medical operations began again; and warm meals – all kosher – were provided for 100–150 refugees and 50–60 children each day.[16] Clubs and associations either restarted or were founded for the first time. Particularly notable was the Association of Jewish Women of Italy, which had ceased its operations during the war.[17] At its weekly sessions, it held needlework classes, offered moral support to those in need, and distributed all manner of essential goods for newborns, infants, teenagers, and adults. In July and August 1946, it also revived the summer camp on the Lido. Surviving photos show groups of delighted children dancing on the beach and splashing around gaily in the lagoon.

Jews began participating in Venetian life again, too. Gino Luzzatto is a good example:[18] as well as serving as vice-president of the Provisional Committee of the Jewish community, he was elected to the city council in 1946 and served as the financial assessor in the administration of Mayor Giovanni Battista Gianquinto. He was also reappointed to his old academic post as an economic historian at the University and was even elected as its rector.

*

The Ghetto never fully recovered, though. It couldn't. Unlike Germany, Italy never seriously confronted its Fascist past. Just a few weeks before the summer camp reopened in Venice, Palmiro Togliatti, the new minister of justice, attempted to put an end to divisions in the country by declaring an amnesty.[19] All cases concerning criminal acts committed before 18 June 1946 were now closed. As the historian Mimmo Franzinelli has put it, '[d]enouncing a Jew, and thus condemning him to deportation and, presumably, to death, was no longer considered in any sense a crime *per se*'.[20] Indeed, in the wake of the Togliatti amnesty, leading literary figures even tried to rewrite Italy's role in the deportations.[21] Responsibility was now shifted to the Nazis. Hitler had forced Mussolini to adopt the *leggi razziali*, the argument went. There was no attempt to deny that Italians *did* take part in the deportations, of course; but a contrast was increasingly drawn between the behaviour of 'good' Italians and 'brutal' Germans. That wasn't all. Many leading antisemites were allowed to keep their government positions and their social status.[22] Some, like Gaetano Azzariti, the former president of the Tribunale della Razza (Tribunal of Race), were even loaded with further honours.

In such circumstances, what chance was there of ever adequately acknowledging the suffering of Italy's Jews, or of rooting out the legacy of antisemitism? It wasn't that Italians were unaware of the problem. There was simply no desire to take responsibility for a solution. Take Cesare Merzagora. A prominent member of the resistance, he would be appointed minister of foreign trade in June 1947.[23] In December 1945, Merzagora wrote an article recognizing that, of all the 'tragic and sorrowful remains of Nazism', antisemitism would be the hardest to eradicate. Yet he couldn't help feeling that this was partly the Jews' *own* fault. 'The Jews,' he wrote, 'have their own atavistic defects. If they did not have them, how could we explain the persecution to which they have been victim for two thousand years?'[24] It was therefore *their* responsibility to overcome this. Merzagora even set out a ten-point plan for them. It makes for staggering reading. Jews returning from Switzerland, he argued, shouldn't complain about their exile too much, because they had had it easy compared to those who had stayed and fought for the resistance. Those who went back to work in banking, finance, or insurance shouldn't grumble about being deprived of their jobs, because there had been plenty of Jews who had been Fascists, too. The Jewish community should punish those who had acquired false baptismal certificates, because they had repudiated their heritage to defend their property. And so on.

No surprise, then, that in Venice, as elsewhere in Italy, Zionism regained some of its former appeal, and many Jews, wary of the future, left for a new life in Eretz Israel.[25] Some, naturally, went as individuals. Although the soldiers of the Palestinian Brigade, stationed in Mestre, did not always have the best reputation, it was not unknown for girls to fall in love with them, marry, and move to Palestine.[26] There were more coordinated departures, too. On 5 November 1947, the Jewish community helped arrange for 794 Jews from around Europe – including, presumably, at least some from Venice itself – to leave for Palestine on board the ship *Kadima*.[27]

*

There was little change. Over the years that followed, newspapers continued to print antisemitic slurs with casual insouciance. Despite the publication of memoirs like Primo Levi's *Se questo è un uomo* (1958), questioning Italian responsibility for the Shoah, Italians continued to neglect the problem.[28] National and local governments dragged their feet over providing financial aid to recovering Jewish communities. And following the establishment of the state of Israel in 1948, the intensity of popular antisemitism rose and fell with the tides of foreign affairs.[29]

Slowly but surely, the Jewish population of Venice shrank. By 1965, the community counted just 844 members; and, as their numbers dwindled, so too did their capacity to maintain Jewish life. Though religious life remained active – despite a marked drift towards secularization – there was neither the need nor the money to keep so many synagogues open for worship. Jewish schools, already small by the liberation, became difficult to sustain; and as the opportunities for continuing Jewish education dwindled, ever more families looked to other cities for their children's future. The Ghetto became a mere husk.

*

Since then, much has been done to breathe life back into it. Today, some 500 people are estimated to live there. Housing has been dramatically modernized, chiefly in the wake of the intense building projects which took place in Cannaregio in the 1970s and 1980s.[30] There is an old people's home, a kosher guest house, several excellent kosher restaurants, and a dedicated bookshop that attracts thousands of customers each year.

A strenuous effort has also been made to transform the Ghetto into a site of memory.[31] In 1980, Arbit Blatas's Holocaust monument was unveiled in the *campo*; the following year, an archive was opened to preserve and make available the community's records; and in 1986, a superlative museum was opened 'as a sign of hope for the future of Judaism and human dignity'. Thanks to the support of the World Monuments Fund,[32] many of the monuments have been restored to their former glory. Work continues apace, even now. In 2020, a project to create a new 'Polo Museale ebraico' was announced, with €9 million of international funding;[33] and as of early 2025, no fewer than 197 Stolpersteine, commemorating the victims of the Shoah, have been placed around the city.[34]

The importance of this 'museumification' hardly needs stating. But one of its peculiar effects is that it makes the past seem more remote. It rests on the assumption that the Ghetto's history is somehow 'behind' it, that a 'forgotten' past needs rescuing. It implies that today is not just diachronically distinct from yesterday, but devoid of any necessary association with what has gone before.

This is perhaps not unreasonable. The Ghetto is clearly no longer the place it was twenty years ago – let alone five hundred. New businesses are opening, and new people are moving in. In a recent interview, one member of the local community highlighted the obvious differences between those 'who were born in the Ghetto' and recently arrived Lubavitchers, who are more strictly (and visibly) observant.[35] Even the forms of hatred have changed. As has sometimes been argued, there are differences between the early-modern anti-Judaism which underpinned the Ghetto's creation, the antisemitism of the Holocaust, and the anti-Zionism of our own day.[36] If 'museumification' helps us to learn the lessons of the past, therefore, this sense of distance – of unfamiliarity – arguably gives the Ghetto more flexibility to confront the challenges of the future.

Yet there are deeper continuities, too. In retracing the Ghetto's history down the centuries, it is striking how few decisive turning points there have been. Even those moments which seem, at first glance, to mark a clear break between 'before' and 'after' dissolve on closer examination.[37] The foundation of the Ghetto, far from being the result of a sudden crisis, was just one step in a much longer process of experimentation and debate; its expansion retained Jewish merchants who were already present; and its dissolution, while dramatic, changed little in the daily lives of its inhabitants. Even the shift from 'religious' anti-Judaism to 'racial' antisemitism is less abrupt than it might seem.[38] There are no breaks, no periods, no departures, no possibility of *truly* forgetting – no matter how hard we might try.

The Ghetto's past is *always* present – simply because it has never gone away. It has even become something of a literary trope. In Carlo Fruttero and Franco Lucentini's *L'amante senza fissa dimora* (1986), protagonist David Silvera travels to the Ghetto, where many of his ancestors had lived, in the hope of gaining a clearer sense of his identity. He discovers that it resembles not so much a neatly archived document as a living palimpsest – still covered by the past, and still being written upon even now. So too, in Jean d'Ormesson's *Histoire du Juif errant* (1991), it is no accident that Simon, the 'wandering Jew', chooses to tell his tale in Venice: for it is only there that the Jewish past and the Jewish present blur together as seamlessly as in his person.

The scars of the Ghetto's past are still plainly visible. Everywhere, there are reminders of the segregation it has embodied – from the narrow *sotoportego*, where the gates of the Ghetto once stood, to the wells, still bearing the da Brolo family arms, and the nursing home where the Segré family stayed before being taken away to the camps.

There are chilling indications of the persistence of antisemitism, too. In the *campo* of the Ghetto Nuovo, there is a guard post, manned at all hours of the day by heavily armed police. In January 2024, Dario Calimani, the president of the Jewish community and a professor of English at Ca' Foscari, warned that there is still 'hatred everywhere'.[39] And in May 2024, graffiti appeared not far from the Jewish cemetery on the Lido, which read: 'Damned Jews, we will come looking for you house by house . . . to slaughter you and your children'.[40]

Despite this, the Ghetto is a testament of hope. For every prayer that is said, every meal that is shared, every day that is spent in this most woe-begotten corner of Venice is an affirmation of survival, against all odds, and a silent, deafening cry of defiance, echoing down the centuries – for centuries to come.

Acknowledgements

It is a pleasure finally to be able to thank those whose kindness and support has made possible the writing of this book.

The Centre for the Study of the Renaissance at the University of Warwick has, as always, been an immense support. The resources it has made available have greatly enriched my thinking and opened many exciting avenues of research.

I am particularly indebted to Stephen Bowd and Brian Maxson, who were kind enough to read drafts of the manuscript ahead of submission. Their incisive comments and suggestions have been invaluable. I would also like to express my gratitude to Julien Le Mauff and Réjane Sénac for inviting me to contribute a paper on the Ghetto's foundation to their volume *Politique de l'exclusion* (Paris: PUF, 2024), which allowed me a valuable opportunity to try out some ideas at an early stage in my research; to Ester Capuzzo, for so generously sharing her work on Daniele Manin with me; and to the editors of *History Today*, Rhys Griffiths and Kate Wiles, for allowing me to reproduce parts of my article on Sabbatai Sevi in these pages.

In preparing *The First Ghetto* for publication, I have been fortunate to work with some remarkable people. At Picador, I would like to thank Alpana Sajip, Georgina Morley, Jon Mitchell, Nicholas Blake, and Kieran Sangha, as well as Vicky Cowan and Jack Alexander. Their warmth, care, and insight have made our collaboration both a pleasure and a privilege. My agent, Georgina Capel, has been similarly brilliant. I really don't know what I'd have done without her encouragement and good sense.

My friends have been a pillar of kindness and good cheer. Their companionship has sustained through even the most difficult patches.

In particular, I would like to thank James O'Connor, Luke Houghton, Christina Reuterskiöld, Dilyana Valcheva, Alexander Millar, Tim Stanley, and Paul McIntosh.

My family have been wonderful. My mother Ingrid, my brother Piers, my brother- and sister-in-law, Michaël and Julie, and their children Yoni, Ezra, and Mila, have been a never-ending reservoir of strength and goodness – not to mention patience and understanding.

As ever, my greatest debt of gratitude is to my wife, Marie, and my children, Hannah and David. They are the sunshine of my life, the source of all my joy. I cannot even begin to say how very much I love them.

Last but certainly not least, I would like to thank my parents-in-law, Henri and Catherine Sebban. No words could adequately express what amazing people they are – or how very much they mean to me. This volume is dedicated to them with love.

Notes

Abbreviations

ASV   Archivio di Stato, Venice
DBI   *Dizionario Biografico degli Italiani*
VDH   D. Chambers and B. Pullan (eds.), *Venice: A Documentary History 1450–1630* (Oxford: Blackwell, 1992).

Introduction

1. B. Ravid, 'Ghetto: Etymology, Original Definition, Reality, and Diffusion', in W. Z. Goldman and J. W. Trotter, Jr. (eds.), *The Ghetto in Global History: 1500 to the Present* (New York: Routledge, 2017), pp. 23–39.
2. B. Ravid, 'All Ghettos were Jewish Quarters but not all Jewish Quarters were Ghettos', *Jewish Culture and History* 10/2–3 (2008), pp. 5–24.
3. B. Cheyette, *The Ghetto: A Very Short Introduction* (Oxford: Oxford University Press, 2020), p. 3.
4. William Shakespeare, *The Merchant of Venice*, 1.3.102–4, 106–9:

    > JEW: Signor Antonio, many a time and oft
    > In the Rialto you have rated me
    > About my moneys and my usances.
    > ...
    > You call me misbeliever, cut-throat dog,
    > And spit upon my Jewish gabardine,
    > And all for use of that which is mine own.

5 James Baldwin, 'My Dungeon Shook: Letter to My Nephew on the One Hundredth Anniversary of Emancipation', in *The Fire Next Time* (London: Michael Joseph, 1963), pp. 13–21.

1. An Uncertain Refuge (to c.1440)

1 See esp. S. K. Cohn, Jr., 'The Black Death and the Burning of the Jews', *Past & Present* 196 (2007), pp. 3–36.
2 On Anselmo's background, see M. Lattes, 'Gli ebrei di Norimberga e la Republica di Venezia', *Archivio Veneto* 4 (1872), pp. 149–54. For discussion of his later travails, see below.
3 Pietro Casola, *Viaggio a Gerusalemme di Pietro Casola*, ed. A. Paoletti (Alessandria: Edizioni dell'Orso, 2001), p. 84: 'A mi pare non li sii una citade a chi si possa comparare Venezia, citade fondata supra el mare . . .'. For discussion, see S. Toffolo, *Describing the City, Describing the State: Representations of Venice and the Venetian Terraferma in the Renaissance* (Leiden and Boston: Brill, 2020), pp. 81–2.
4 D. S. Chambers, *The Imperial Age of Venice, 1380–1580* (London: Thames & Hudson, 1970).
5 Florence, Biblioteca Nazionale Centrale, MS II.IV.101, fol. 1v; Toffolo, *Describing the City*, pp. 89–92; K. B. Moore, 'Seeing through text: the visualization of Holy Land architecture in Niccolò da Poggibonsi's "Libro d'Oltramare", 14th–15th centuries', *Word and Image* 25/4 (2009), pp. 402–15.
6 Q. at J. J. Norwich, *A History of Venice* (London: Penguin, 1983), p. 275.
7 See B. Ravid, 'Venice and its Minorities', in E. R. Dursteler (ed.), *A Companion to Venetian History, 1400–1797* (Leiden: Brill, 2013), pp. 449–86. Statues of Moors are to be found on the facade of the Palazzo Mastelli del Cammello.
8 In 960, the Senate forbade Venetian ships to transport Jews. As Ashtor has pointed out, this is almost certainly evidence merely of transit rather than of established presence in Venice itself. It seems likely that a similar prohibition had been issued in 945. E. Ashtor, 'Gli inizi della comunità ebraica a Venezia', *La Rassegna Mensile di Israel*, 3rd ser., 44/11–12 (1978), pp. 683–703, here p. 686.
9 E. Ashtor, 'Ebrei cittadini di Venezia?', *Studi Veneziani*, 17–18 (1975–6), pp. 145–56; D. Jacoby, 'Venice and the Venetian Jews in the Eastern Mediterranean', in G. Cozzi (ed.), *Gli Ebrei e Venezia, secoli XIV–XVIII* (Milan: Edizioni di Comunità, 1987), pp. 29–58, here

pp. 34–6; D. Jacoby, 'Venetian Citizenship and Venetian Identity in the Eastern Mediterranean, Twelfth to Fifteenth Centuries', in G. Christ and F.-J. Morche (eds.), *Culture of Empire: Rethinking Venetian Rule, 1400–1700: Essays in Honour of Benjamin Arbel* (Leiden: Brill, 2020), pp. 125–52.

10   Jacoby, 'Venice and the Venetian Jews', p. 37. On Venice's treatment of Jews in Crete, see D. Jacoby, 'Jews and Christians in Venetian Crete: Segregation, Interaction, and Conflict', in U. Israel, R. Jutte, and R. C. Mueller (eds.), *'Interstizi': Culture ebraico-cristiane a Venezia e nei suoi domini da Medioevo all'Età moderna* (Rome: Edizioni di Storia e Letteratura, 2010), pp. 243–79; R. N. Lauer, *Colonial Justice and the Jews of Venetian Crete* (Philadelphia: University of Pennsylvania Press, 2019); M. Georgopolou, 'Mapping Religious and Ethnic Identities in the Venetian Colonial Empire', *Journal of Medieval and Early Modern Studies* 26/3 (1996), pp. 467–96; M. Georgopolou, *Venice's Mediterranean Colonies: Architecture and Urbanism* (Cambridge: Cambridge University Press, 2001), pp. 192–210.

11   Jacoby, 'Venice and the Venetian Jews', p. 40.

12   Jacoby, 'Venice and the Venetian Jews', p. 37.

13   For discussion, see esp. B. Arbel, *Trading Nations: Jews and Venetians in the Early Modern Eastern Mediterranean* (Leiden: Brill, 1995); E. Ashtor, 'The Jews in the Mediterranean Trade in the Later Middle Ages', *Hebrew Union College Annual* 55 (1984), pp. 159–78.

14   Jacoby, 'Venice and the Venetian Jews', pp. 38, 48.

15   Jerusalem, National Library of Israel, MS Heb. 24°5702; Ashtor, 'Gli inizi', pp. 686–7.

16   Ashtor, 'Gli inizi', p. 687; R. Calimani, *Storia del Ghetto di Venezia* (Milan: Mondadori Electa, 2001), pp. 8–9. It has sometimes been suggested that Isaiah di Trani lived in Venice and acted as the rabbi for a Jewish community there. For a refutation of this view, see B. Ravid, 'The Jewish mercantile settlement of twelfth and thirteenth century Venice: reality or conjecture?', *AJS Review* 2 (1977), pp. 201–25, here p. 218 n. 38; B. Ravid, 'The legal status of Jews in Venice to 1509', *Proceedings of the American Academy for Jewish Research* 54 (1987), pp. 169–202, here p. 171 n. 2.

17   D. Jacoby, 'Les juifs de Venise du XIVème au milieu du XVIème siècle', in *Venezia centro di mediazione tra Oriente e Occidente (secoli XV–XVI). Atti del II Congresso internazionale di storia della civiltà veneziana, Venezia 1974* (Florence: Leo S. Olschki Editore, 1977), vol. 1, pp. 163–216, here p. 165; Ravid, 'The legal status', p. 170.

18 R. Segre, 'Les Juifs à Venise aux XIIIe et XIVe siècles: médecins, neophytes et banquiers', *Revue des études juives* 170/1–2 (2011), pp. 73–116, here pp. 86, 92.
19 Ravid, 'The Jewish mercantile settlement'; B. Ravid, 'The Venetian Government and the Jews', in R. C. Davis and B. Ravid (eds.), *The Jews of Early Modern Venice* (Baltimore and London: John Hopkins University Press, 2001), pp. 3–30, here p. 3.
20 Herman Gigas, *Flores Temporum seu Chronicon Universale ab Orbe condito ad annum Christi MCCCXLIX*, ed. J. G. Meuschen (Leiden: Philip Bonk, 1750), p. 138, trans. R. Horrox, *The Black Death* (Manchester: Manchester University Press, 1994), p. 207. On the wider context of these accusations, see T. Barzilay, *Poisoned Wells: Accusations, Persecution, and Minorities in Medieval Europe, 1321–1422* (Philadelphia: University of Pennsylvania Press, 2022).
21 Heinrich von Herford, *Liber de rebus memorabilioribus sive Chronicon Henrici de Hervordia*, ed. A. Potthast (Göttingen: Dieterich, 1859), p. 280: 'Item hoc anno Judei per Theutoniam pluresque provincias alias universi cum mulieribus et parvulis ferro vel igne crudeliter et inhumaniter absumuntur . . .'.
22 Cohn, 'The Black Death', p. 17; Iohannes Latomus, *Acta aliquot vetustiora in civitate Francofortensi . . .*, in J. F. Böhmer (ed.), *Fontes rerum Germanicarum*, 4 vols. (Stuttgart: Cotta, 1843–68), vol. 4, pp. 415–16.
23 Cohn, 'The Black Death', pp. 20–1; A. Haverkamp, '"Conflitti interni" e collegamenti sovralocali nelle città tedesche durante la prima metà del XIV secolo', in R. Elze and G. Fasoli (eds.), *Aristocrazia cittadina e ceti popolari nel tardo Medioevo in Italia e in Germania* (Bologna: il Mulino, 1984), p. 162.
24 Heinrich von Diessenhofen in Böhmer (ed.), *Fontes rerum Germanicarum*, vol. 4, pp. 16–125, here p. 70.
25 Traces of the 'German' Jews' progress across Friuli are few; but the details we do have leave no doubt of their presence. 'German' Jews are, for example, recorded in Venzone in 1333; and three Jews from Rothenburg – Simelino, Lep, and Lamelino – are recorded on 30 November 1363. P. C. Ioly Zorattini, 'Gli insediamenti ebraici nel Friuli veneto', in Cozzi (ed.), *Gli Ebrei e Venezia*, pp. 261–80, here p. 265; A. Veronese, 'Migrazioni e presenza di ebrei "tedeschi" in Italia settentrionale nel tardo Medioevo (con particolare referimento ai casi di Trieste e Treviso)', in G. M. Varanini and R. C. Mueller (eds.), *Ebrei nella Terraferma veneta del Quattrocento. Atti del Convegno di studi, Verona, 14 novembre 2003* (Florence: Firenze University Press, 2005), pp. 59–70.

26 B. Pullan, 'Charity and Usury: Jewish and Christian Lending in Renaissance and Early Modern Italy', *Proceedings of the British Academy* 125 (2004), pp. 19–40, here p. 30.
27 B. Pullan, *Rich and Poor in Renaissance Venice: The Social Institutions of a Catholic State, to 1620* (Oxford: Wiley-Blackwell, 1971), p. 434; Giovanni Domenico Mansi (ed.), *Sacrorum Conciliorum Nova et Amplissima Collectio . . .*, 31 vols. (Venice and Florence: Antonio Zatta, 1759–98), vol. 21, pp. 529–30; vol. 22, p. 231.
28 *Exod.* 22:35; *Lev.* 25:35–7; *Deut.* 23:19; *Ps.* 15:5; *Ezek.* 18:8; *Luke* 6:35.
29 *Ezek.* 22:12.
30 The following reasons represent only a small number of those put forward by medieval theologians. For a discussion of other attempts to defend the Church's prohibition on usury, see J. T. Noonan, *The Scholastic Analysis of Usury* (Cambridge MA: Harvard University Press, 1957). For a recent critique of Noonan's characterization of St Thomas Aquinas' argument (the so-called 'theologians' argument'), see J. Bell, 'Thomas Aquinas, John Noonan, and the Usury Prohibition', *Nova et vetera* 19/2 (2021), pp. 469–530.
31 Dante, *Inf.*, 11.110–11; Noonan, *The Scholastic Analysis of Usury*, pp. 21–9.
32 This was known as the 'jurists' argument'; Noonan, *The Scholastic Analysis of Usury*, p. 65.
33 F. C. Lane, *Venice: A Maritime Republic* (Baltimore and London: Johns Hopkins University Press, 1973), p. 52.
34 Lane, *Venice*, p. 52.
35 Pullan, *Rich and Poor*, p. 436.
36 Mansi (ed.), *Sacrorum Conciliorum*, vol. 22, pp. 1053–6; A. Kirschenbaum, 'Jewish and Christian Theories of Usury in the Middle Ages', *Jewish Quarterly Review*, new ser. 75/3 (1985), pp. 270–89; R. P. Maloney, 'Usury in Greek, Roman and Rabbinic Thought', *Traditio* 27 (1971), pp. 79–109, here pp. 96–109; note esp. *Deut.* 23:20: 'You may charge a foreigner interest, but not a brother Israelite, so that the Lord your God may bless you in everything you put your hand to in the land you are entering to possess'.
37 Pullan, *Rich and Poor*, pp. 436–7. K. R. Stow, 'Papal and Royal Attitudes toward Jewish Lending in the Thirteenth Century', *AJS Review* 6 (1981), pp. 161–84, here pp. 162–3.
38 D. Owen Hughes, 'Distinguishing Signs: Ear-Rings, Jews and Franciscan Rhetoric in the Italian Renaissance City', *Past & Present* 112 (1986), pp. 3–59, here p. 14.
39 Lane, *Venice*, pp. 184–5.

40 R. C. Mueller, 'Les prêteurs juifs de Venise au Moyen Age', *Annales. Histoire, Sciences Sociales* 30/6 (1975), pp. 1277–1302, here pp. 1279–80; Ravid, 'The legal status', pp. 172–3. The proposals can be found at R. Cessi (ed.), *Problemi monetari veneziani fino al tutto il sec. XIV* (Padua: Milani, 1937), docs. 122, 124.

41 Mueller, 'Les prêteurs juifs', p. 1280; Ravid, 'The legal status', pp. 172–3; cit. ASV Maggior Consiglio, Novella f. 102v.

42 On variations in the treatment of Jews in early Renaissance Italy, see, for example, S. Simonsohn, 'La condizione giuridica degli ebrei nell'Italia centrale e settentrionale (secoli XII–XVI)', in *Storia d'Italia. Annali 11: Gli ebrei in Italia*, 2 vols. (Turin: Einaudi, 1996), vol. 1, pp. 95–120.

43 Giordano da Rivalto, *Prediche del beato fra Giordano da Rivalto dell'Ordine dei Predicatori recitate in Firenze dal 1303 al 1306 . . .* , ed. D. Moreni, 2 vols. (Florence: il Magheri, 1831), vol. 2, p. 225, trans. [slightly amended] from J. Cohen, *The Friars and the Jews: The Evolution of Medieval Anti-Judaism* (Ithaca: Cornell University Press, 1982), p. 239.

44 Bernardo Gui, *Manuel de l'inquisiteur*, ed. and trans. G. Mollat, with D. Drioux, 2 vols. (Paris: Librairie Honoré Champion, 1926–7), vol. 2, pp. 6–7; q. in Cohen, *The Friars*, p. 91.

45 On the origins and course of the Fourth Venetian-Genoese War – known as the War of Chioggia – see, for example, Lane, *Venice*, pp. 189–96; Norwich, *A History of Venice*, pp. 243–56; D. M. Nicol, *The Last Centuries of Byzantium 1261–1453*, 2nd ed. (Cambridge: Cambridge University Press, 1993), p. 278–80; S. A. Epstein, *Genoa and the Genoese, 958–1528* (Chapel Hill and London: The University of North Carolina Press, 1996), pp. 237–41; B. G. Kohl, *Padua under the Carrara, 1318–1405* (Baltimore and London: Johns Hopkins University Press, 1998), pp. 205–22.

46 This paragraph follows Lane, *Venice*, pp. 196–7.

47 Correr proposed that the maximum rates should be 15 per cent on pledges and 18 per cent on notes. Mueller, 'Les prêteurs juifs', pp. 1281–2; Ravid, 'The legal status', pp. 173–4.

48 Mueller, 'Les prêteurs juifs', pp. 1282–3.

49 On the Piovego, see, for example, E. Crouzet-Pavan, *Venice Triumphant: The Horizons of a Myth*, trans. L. G. Cochrane (Baltimore and London: Johns Hopkins University Press, 2002), pp. 21, 205, 335.

50 Mueller, 'Les prêteurs juifs', p. 1283.

51 Cohn, 'The Black Death', p. 28; Lattes, 'Gli ebrei di Norimberga', pp. 149–50.
52 Mueller, 'Les prêteurs juifs', p. 1283.
53 Mueller, 'Les prêteurs juifs', p. 1290.
54 Mueller, 'Les prêteurs juifs', p. 1290; A. Teja, *Aspetti della vita economica di Zara dal 1289 al 1409*, 3 vols. (Zara: Tipografia Editrice Sp. Artale, 1936–42), 1: docs. 8, 13, 15.
55 Lattes, 'Gli ebrei di Norimberga'; Mueller, 'Les prêteurs juifs', p. 1290; R. C. Mueller, *The Procuratori di San Marco and the Venetian Credit Market* (New York: Arno Press, 1977), p. 351; D. Jacoby, 'Les Juifs à Venise du XIVe au milieu du XVIe siècle', in H.-G. Beck, M. Manoussacas, and A. Pertusi (eds.), *Venezia centro di mediazione tra Oriente e Occidente (secoli XV–XVI), Atti del II Congresso internazionale di storia della civiltà veneziana, Venezia 1974* (Florence: Leo S. Olschki Editore, 1977), vol. 1, pp. 163–216, here pp. 195–6; N. Pavoncello, *Gli Ebrei in Verona (dalle origini al secolo XX)* (Verona: Vita Veronese, 1960), p. 10.
56 Mueller, 'Les prêteurs juifs', pp. 1294–5; Lane, *Venice*, p. 151.
57 On Catarino Zane's property on Torcello, see E. Crouzet-Pavan, *La Mort Lente de Torcello: Histoire d'une Cité Disparu*, new ed. (Paris: Albin Michel, 2017).
58 Ravid, 'The legal status', p. 179; Mueller, 'Les prêteurs juifs', p. 1301 n. 80.
59 Mueller, 'Les prêteurs juifs', p. 1284; Ravid, 'The legal status', p. 174.
60 Mueller, 'Les prêteurs juifs', p. 1284.
61 Giambattista Gallicciolli, *Delle memorie venete antiche profane ed ecclesiastiche, libri tre* . . . , 8 vols. (Venice: Domenico Fracasso, 1795), vol. 2, pp. 284–5 [no. 891]; R. C. Mueller, 'The Jewish Moneylenders of Late Trecento Venice: A Revisitation', *Mediterranean Historical Review* 10/1–2 (1995), pp. 202–17, here p. 204; Mueller, 'Les prêteurs juifs', pp. 1284–5; Ravid, 'The legal status', pp. 175–6.
62 This point is made particularly well at Ravid, 'The legal status', p. 176.
63 E. Concina, U. Camerino, and D. Calabi, *La Città degli Ebrei. Il Ghetto di Venezia: Architettura e Urbanistica* (Venice: Marsilio, 1991), p. 227; Ravid, 'The legal status', p. 177.
64 Mueller, 'The Jewish Moneylenders', pp. 204–5.
65 Mueller, 'The Jewish Moneylenders', p. 205; Mueller, 'Les prêteurs juifs', pp. 1285–6; Ravid, 'The legal status', pp. 177–8.
66 Mueller, 'The Jewish Moneylenders', p. 205; Mueller, 'Les prêteurs juifs', p. 1291; Ravid, 'The legal status', p. 178.

67 Mueller, 'The Jewish Moneylenders', pp. 205-6; Mueller, 'Les prêteurs juifs', p. 1291; Ravid, 'The legal status', pp. 178–9.
68 Ravid, 'The legal status', p. 180; Mueller, 'Les prêteurs juifs', p. 1286; cit. ASV Senato, Misti, r. 40, f. 143v.
69 Concina, Camerino, and Calabi, *La Città degli Ebrei*, p. 227; Ravid, 'The legal status', p. 179; Mueller, 'Les prêteurs juifs', p. 1301 n. 82.
70 Mueller, 'The Jewish Moneylenders', pp. 207, 216.
71 The banks in question belonged to Antonio Contarini and Cristoforo Zancani. They collapsed in the second half of the year. Mueller, 'Les prêteurs juifs', p. 1286.
72 The following is based on Mueller, 'The Jewish Moneylenders', pp. 207–9, 216.
73 Ashtor, 'Gli inizi', p. 698.
74 Mueller, 'The Jewish Moneylenders', pp. 212–13.
75 Ashtor, 'Gli inizi', p. 698.
76 Lattes, 'Gli ebrei di Norimberga', pp. 149, 151 (doc. I).
77 Lattes, 'Gli ebrei di Norimberga', pp. 150, 151–2 (doc. II).
78 Lane, *Venice*, p. 197.
79 See Norwich, *A History of Venice*, pp. 264–5.
80 Ravid, 'The legal status', pp. 180–1; cit. ASV Senato, Misti, r. 43, f. 24r; Compilazione delle leggi, Ebrei, 27 August 1394.
81 Ravid, 'The legal status', pp. 180–1; B. Ravid, 'From Yellow to Red: On the Distinguishing Head-Coverings of the Jews of Venice', *Jewish History* 6/1–2 (1992), pp. 179–210, here p. 182.
82 Mueller, 'Les prêteurs juifs', p. 1292. On the identity of 'Ber', see R. C. Mueller, 'Banchi ebraici tra Mestre e Venezia nel tardo medioevo', in R. C. Mueller, *Venezia nel tardo Medioevo: economia e società = Late Medieval Venice: economy and society*, ed. L. Molà, M. Knapton, and L. Pezzolo (Rome: Viella, 2021), pp. 367–95, here p. 377 n. 28.
83 Lattes, 'Gli ebrei di Norimberga', pp. 151–4 (docs. IIa-b).
84 Jacoby, 'Les Juifs à Venise', p. 170 n. 29; Ravid, 'The legal status', pp. 181–2; cit. ASV Senato, Misti, r. 46, f. 55v; Gallicciolli, *Delle memorie*, 2:290 [no. 902].
85 Ravid, 'The legal status', p. 181; cit. ASV Maggior Consiglio, Leona, r. 21, f. 78v; Compilazione delle leggi, Ebrei, 3 April 1395; Gallicciolli, *Delle memorie*, p. 2:289 [no. 900].
86 This paragraph follows Ravid, 'The legal status', pp. 182–3.
87 Jacoby, 'Les Juifs à Venise', p. 170 n. 29; Ravid, 'The legal status', pp. 181–2; cit. ASV Senato, Misti, r. 46, f. 55v; Gallicciolli, *Delle memorie*, vol. 2, p. 290 [no. 902].
88 Pullan, *Rich and Poor*, p. 446.

89 Ravid, 'From Yellow to Red', p. 182; cit. ASV Compilazione delle leggi, 5 March 1408.
90 Ravid, 'From Yellow to Red', pp. 182–3; 'The legal status', pp. 183–4; cit. ASV Maggior Consiglio, Ursa, r. 21, ff. 187v–188r.
91 Ravid, 'From Yellow to Red', p. 183; 'The legal status', p. 181 n. 23. According to Jacoby, this apparently reconfirmed a requirement already imposed on the Stato da Màr. Jacoby, 'Les Juifs à Venise', pp. 174–5 n. 49.
92 Ravid, 'The legal status', p. 185; cit. ASV Compilazione delle leggi, 5 March 1408.
93 Ashtor, 'Gli inizi', p. 700; cit. ASV Maggior Consiglio, ursa, r. 22, f. 67v.
94 For an overview of attitudes towards Jewish–Christian sexual interactions in Renaissance Italy, see R. Bonfil, *Jewish Life in Renaissance Italy*, trans. A. Oldcorn (Berkeley, Los Angeles, and London: University of California Press, 1994), pp. 111–16; R. Bonfil, 'Jews, Christians, and sex in Renaissance Italy: a historiographical problem', *Jewish History* 26/1–2 (2012), pp. 101–11.
95 Although it has sometimes been suggested that Bernardino da Siena may have visited Venice as early as 1405, there seems to be no strong evidence for his presence before 1422. He made at least two further trips, most likely in 1429 and 1442. F. Mormando, *The Preacher's Demons: Bernardino of Siena and the Social Underworld of Early Renaissance Italy* (Chicago: University of Chicago Press, 1999), p. 160; F. Sorelli, 'Predicatori a Venezia (fine secolo XIV–metà secolo XV)', *Le Venezie francescane (Predicazione francescana e società veneta nel Quattrocento: committenza, ascolto, ricezione. Atti del II Convegno internazionale di studi francescani. Padova, 26–27–28 marzo 1987)*, n.s. 6 (1989), pp. 142–8.
96 Ravid, 'The legal status', p. 186; cit. ASV Compilazione delle leggi, 19 July 1424; Gallicciolli, *Delle memorie*, vol. 2, pp. 291–2, s. 907; *Leggi e memorie venete sulla prostituzione fino alla caduta della repubblica*, 2 vols. in one (Venice: Tipografia del commercio di Marco Visentini, a spese del Conte di Orford, 1870–2), pp. 34, 40–1.
97 Jacoby, 'Les Juifs à Venise', p. 175; Ravid, 'From Yellow to Red', p. 203 n. 32; Ravid, 'The legal status', p. 186 n. 33.
98 See n. 96, above.
99 On Venetian attitudes towards sodomy, see esp. G. Ruggiero, *The Boundaries of Eros: Sex Crime and Sexuality in Renaissance Venice*, rev. ed. (Oxford: Oxford University Press, 1989), pp. 109–45.
100 Curiously, sodomy – like usury – was often tied to female pride, with the result that Jews, prostitutes, moneylending, and 'perversion'

formed a loose – but seductive – constellation in the Renaissance imagination. See Owen Hughes, 'Distinguishing signs', p. 37; Mormando, *The Preacher's Demons*, pp. 130–1.

101   Ashtor, 'Gli inizi', pp. 694–5; cit. ASV Consiglio dei Dieci, Misti X, ff. 42 a, 42 b.

102   For a recent overview of humanistic Hebraism, see D. Stein Kokin, 'The Hebrew Question in the Italian Renaissance: Linguistic, Cultural, and Mystical Perspectives' (unpublished PhD dissertation, Harvard University, 2006). On Manetti's Hebrew learning, see, for example, C. Dröge, *Giannozzo Manetti als Denker und Hebraist* (Frankfurt: Peter Lang, 1987); Stein Kokin, 'The Hebrew Question', pp. 171–225.

103   S. Bowd, 'Civic Piety and Patriotism: Patrician Humanists and Jews in Venice and Its Empire', *Renaissance Quarterly* 69/4 (2016), pp. 1257–95, here p. 1265; G. Busi and S. Campanini, 'Marco Lippomano and Crescas Meir: A Humanistic Dispute in Hebrew', in M. Perani (ed.), *Una manna buona per Mantova: Man Tov le-Man Tovah; Studi in onore di Vittorio Colorni per il suo 92° compleanno* (Florence: Olschki Editore, 2004), pp. 169–202; M. L. King, *Venetian Humanism in an Age of Patrician Dominance* (Princeton: Princeton University Press, 1986), pp. 389–90.

104   Bowd, 'Civic Piety', p. 1263; G. Fioravanti, 'Polemiche antigiudaiche nell'Italia del Quattrocento: Un tentativo di interpretazione globale', *Quaderni storici*, n.s. 64 (1987), pp. 19–37; E. Garin, 'L'umanesimo italiano e la cultura ebraica', in *Storia d'Italia*, pp. 1:359–83.

105   Busi and Campanini, 'Marco Lippomano', p. 175; Bowd, 'Civic Piety', p. 1265.

106   Niccolò Machiavelli, *Istorie fiorentine*, 6.18; trans. from Niccolò Machiavelli, *The Chief Works and Others*, trans. A. Gilbert, 3 vols. (Durham and London: Duke University Press, 1989), vol. 3, p. 1305.

2. Borrowed Time (c.1440–1492)

1   In 1420, for example, Pope Martin V rebuked Franciscan preachers in Rome for the violence of their anti-Jewish sermons. K. R. Stow, *The Jews in Rome: 1536–1551* (Leiden: Brill, 1995), p. xxix.

2   *Bullarum, diplomatum et privilegiorum sanctorum Romanorum Pontificum . . .* , 25 vols. (Turin: Seb. Franco et Henrico Dalmazzo / A. Vecco et socii, 1857–72), vol. 5, pp. 68–70; B. Pullan, *Rich and Poor in Renaissance Venice: The Social Institutions of a Catholic State, to 1620* (Oxford: Wiley-Blackwell, 1971), p. 449. This paragraph is indebted to Pullan's overview.

3. On Paolo di Castro, see N. L. Barile, 'Renaissance Monti di Pietà in Modern Scholarship: Themes, Studies, and Historiographic Trends', *Renaissance and Reformation* 35/3 (2012), pp. 85–114, here p. 93.
4. On debates about whether it was legitimate for *monti di pietà* to charge interest, see, for example, G. Barbieri, 'Il beato Bernardino da Feltre nella storia sociale del Rinascimento', in G. Barbieri, *Il pensiero economico dall'antichità al Rinascimento* (Bari: Istituto di Storia Economica, Università di Bari, 1963), pp. 376–445, here pp. 432–9; M. G. Muzzarelli, 'Il Gaetano e il Bariani: Per una revision della tematica sui monti di pietà', *Rivista di storia e letteratura religosa* 16 (1980), pp. 3–19.
5. See, for example, S. Marjarelli and U. Nicolini, *Il Monte dei Poveri di Perugia, periodo delle origini (1462–1474)* (Perugia: Banca del Monte di credito, 1962); A. Toaff, 'Jews, Franciscans, and the First Monti di Pietà in Italy (1462–1500)', in S. J. McMichael (ed.), *Friars and Jews in the Middle Ages and Renaissance* (Leiden: Brill, 2004), pp. 239–53.
6. Marjarelli and Nicolini, *Il Monte dei Poveri*, p. 489; Toaff, 'Jews, Franciscans', p. 239.
7. In Perugia, for example, the local Jews were forced to make the monte an interest-free loan of 3,000 *fl.* Marjarelli and Nicolini, *Il Monte dei Poveri*, p. 107; Toaff, 'Jews, Franciscans', p. 241.
8. Toaff, 'Jews, Franciscans', pp. 244–5, 248; A. Toaff, *Love, Work and Death: Jewish Life in Medieval Umbria* (London: The Littman Library of Jewish Civilization, 1996), pp. 242–3. As Léon Poliakov has pointed out, one of the main reasons why Christians invested in Jewish banks, aside from the opportunity for profit, was tax evasion. Although several towns, such as Siena, took steps to prevent Christians from concealing their investment in Jewish *banchi*, the *capitoli* of the Jews of Florence, reissued in 1457, specifically stated that Jews were not required either to produce their accounts or to name their investors – with the result that any money Christians had put into their businesses would be shielded from the tax-collector's gaze. L. Poliakov, *Jewish Bankers and the Holy See: From the Thirteenth to the Seventeenth Century*, trans. M. Kochan (Abingdon: Routledge, 2012), pp. 63–4.
9. Toaff, 'Jews, Franciscans', p. 245.
10. Toaff, 'Jews, Franciscans', pp. 245–6.
11. A. Pezzana, *Storia della città di Parma*, 5 vols. (Parma: Dalla Ducale tipografia, 1837–59), vol. 3, Appendix VII, pp. 15–18; E. Ashtor, 'Gli inizi della comunità ebraica a Venezia', *La Rassegna Mensile di Israel*, 3rd ser., 44/11–12 (1978), pp. 683–703, here p. 701. The pope heard

representations from Moise Museto, quondam Bonaventure di Bologna, Simone alias Samuele quondam Museti di Mantova, Dataro quondam Vitalis di Modena, Angelo quondam Danielis di Modena, Manuele Bonaventure di Urbino, Isacco di Abramo di Mantova, Giacobbe Consiglii di Toscanella, and delegates of the Jewish communities in Siena and Ferrara. It is important to note that this bull was issued during the Council of Mantua, at a time when Pius II was relying on the Jews to help finance his planned crusade against the Turks. A few months later, he announced a new tax of one-twentieth on the Jews (to apply to capital, rather than incomes). See G. B. Picotti, *La dieta di Mantova e la politica de' Veneziani* (Venice: a spese della Società, 1912), pp. 195, 205; G. B. Picotti, 'D'una questione tra Pio II e Francesco Sforza per la ventesima sui beni degli Ebrei', *Archivio storico lombardo*, 4th ser., 20 (1913), pp. 184–213; Poliakov, *Jewish Bankers*, pp. 64–5.

12 See esp. J. E. Law, 'The Venetian Mainland State in the Fifteenth Century', *Transactions of the Royal Historical Society*, 6th ser., 2 (1992), pp. 153–74.

13 J. J. Norwich, *A History of Venice* (London: Penguin, 1983), p. 301. On the arts in this period, see, for example, T. Nichols, *Renaissance Art in Venice: From Tradition to Individualism* (London: Laurence King Publishing, 2016), pp. 22–50; D. Howard, *The Architectural History of Venice*, rev. ed. (New Haven and London: Yale University Press, 2002), pp. 106–9.

14 A. Möschter, 'Gli ebrei a Treviso durante la dominazione veneziana (1388–1509)', in G. M. Varanini and R. C. Mueller (eds.), *Ebrei nella Terraferma veneta del Quattrocento: Atti del Convegno di studi, Verona, 14 novembre 2003* (Florence: Firenze University Press, 2005), pp. 71–84, here pp. 74–8; R. C. Mueller, 'Lo status degli ebrei nella Terraferma veneta del Quattrovento: tra politica, religione, cultura ed economia. Saggio introduttivo', in Varanini and Mueller (eds.), *Ebrei nella Terraferma veneta*, pp. 9–30, here p. 16. Treviso's decision followed many years of debate. Three years earlier, in 1439, it had already determined not to renew the Jews' *condotta*.

15 R. Scuro, 'La presenza ebraica a Vicenza e nel suo territorio nel Quattrocento', in Varanini and Mueller (eds.), *Ebrei nella Terraferma veneta*, pp. 103–122, esp. pp. 109–10; Mueller, 'Lo status degli ebrei', p. 16.

16 G. M. Varanini, 'Società Cristiana e minoranza ebraica a Verona nella seconda metà del Quattrocento. Tra ideologia osservante e vita

quotidiana', in Varanini and Mueller (eds.), *Ebrei nella Terraferma veneta*, pp. 141–62, here pp. 142–4.

17 Pullan, *Rich and Poor*, p. 456; D. Carpi, *L'individuo e la collettività. Saggi di storia degli ebrei a Padova e nel Veneto nell'età del Rinascimento* (Padua: Olschki Editore, 1990), pp. ix ff.; A. Ciscato, *Ebrei in Padova (1300–1800): Monografia storica documentata* (Bologna: Forni, 1967), pp. 52–5.

18 B. Ravid, 'The Legal Status of the Jews in Venice to 1509', *Proceedings of the American Academy for Jewish Research* 54 (1987), pp. 169–202, here p. 187; B. Ravid, 'From Yellow to Red: On the Distinguishing Head-Covering of the Jews of Venice', *Jewish History*, 6/1–2 (1992), pp. 179–210, here p. 183; cit. ASV Senato, Terra, r. 1, f. 93r.

19 G. Ruggiero, *The Boundaries of Eros: Sex Crime and Sexuality in Renaissance Venice* (Oxford: Oxford University Press, 1987), p. 87.

20 Ravid, 'The Legal Status', p. 187; 'From Yellow to Red', p. 183; Ruggiero, *Boundaries*, pp. 87–8; cit. ASV Senato, Terra, r. 1, f. 95v.

21 Pullan, *Rich and Poor*, p. 454.

22 E. Muir, *Civic Ritual in Renaissance Venice* (Princeton: Princeton University Press, 1981), p. 20. For further discussion of the Council of Ten, see Marin Sanudo's comments in *VDH*, pp. 54–6 (doc. II.7[a]).

23 It is perhaps worth noting in passing that Bessarion also enjoyed a unique respect among the Venetians. During his last visit to the city in 1461, he had even been named a member of the Great Council. L. Labowsky, 'Bessarione', *DBI* 9 (Rome, 1967), s.v.

24 For a recent overview of cardinals' attitudes towards the Jews in the early modern period, see M. Pattenden, 'Cardinals and the Non-Christian World', in M. Hollingsworth, M. Pattenden, and A. Witte (eds.), *A Companion to the Early Modern Cardinal* (Leiden and Boston: Brill, 2019), pp. 375–93, here pp. 385ff.

25 See, for example, K. M. Setton, *The Papacy and the Levant (1204–1571)*, 4 vols. (Philadelphia: The American Philosophical Society, 1976–84), vol. 2, pp. 138–230; N. Housley, *Crusading and the Ottoman Threat, 1453–1505* (Oxford: Oxford University Press, 2013), pp. 10–12. On Pius II's engagement with crusading, see also N. Nisaha, 'Pope Pius II and the Crusade', in N. Housley (ed.), *Crusading in the Fifteenth Century: Message and Impact* (Houndmills: Palgrave Macmillan, 2004), pp. 39–52.

26 Setton, *The Papacy and the Levant*, vol. 2, p. 265; Poliakov, *Jewish Bankers*, p. 65.

27 Pullan, *Rich and Poor*, pp. 454–5; P. Kourniakos, 'Die Kreuzzugslegation Kardinal Bessarions in Venedig (1463–1464)'

(unpublished PhD dissertation, University of Cologne, 2009), pp. 200–8. The text of Bessarion's letter can be found in L. Mohler, *Kardinal Bessarion als Theologe, Humanist und Staatsmann*, 3 vols. (Paderborn: F. Schöningh, 1923–42), vol. 3, pp. 529–30, and U. Israel, R. Jütte, and R. C. Mueller, 'Edizione commentata della lettera del Bessarione al doge, 1463, sullo *status* degli ebrei', in U. Israel, R. Jütte, and R. C. Mueller (eds.), *Interstizi. Culture ebraico-cristiane a Venezia e nei suoi domini dal medioevo all'età moderna* (Rome: Edizioni di storia e letteratura, 2010), pp. 17–27.

28 Ashtor, 'Gli inizi', p. 700; Ravid, 'The Legal Status', p. 189; Pullan, *Rich and Poor*, pp. 450–5. On the struggle in the Peloponnese, see Setton, *The Papacy and the Levant*, vol. 2, pp. 267–8.

29 For the following, see Setton, *The Papacy and the Levant*, pp. 268–70; F. C. Lane, *Venice: A Maritime Republic* (Baltimore and London: Johns Hopkins University Press, 1973), pp. 235–6; and (with caution) Norwich, *History*, pp. 345–6.

30 After Pius II's death, all but one of the cardinals signed an election capitulation guaranteeing that the Church would continue to support the war against the Ottoman Empire as fully as possible. This left existing funding arrangements in place and set aside further monies from the alum mines at Tolfa. Setton, *The Papacy and the Levant*, vol. 2, p. 271. On the plague, see *VDH*, p. 114 (doc. III.5[a][i]).

31 Ashtor, 'Gli inizi', pp. 700–1; Ravid, 'The Legal Status', pp. 185, 187–8. On the meaning of *officii* and *sacrificii*, see esp. Ravid, 'The Legal Status', p. 188 n. 36.

32 This paragraph follows S. Bowd, 'Civic Piety and Patriotism: Patrician Humanists and Jews in Venice and Its Empire', *Renaissance Quarterly* 69/4 (2016), pp. 1257–95, here pp. 1278–9.

33 On the course of the war between 1464 and 1469, see Setton, *The Papacy and the Levant*, vol. 2, pp. 272–97.

34 Among the leading supporters of Judeo-Christian commerce were Angelo da Castro and Giovanni Francesco Pavini. On Angelo da Castro, see G. D'Amelio, 'Castro, Angelo da', *DBI* 22 (Rome: Istituto della Enciclopedia Italiana, 1979), s.v. For his wider views on Christian interactions with Jews, see, for example, K. Stow, *Jewish Dogs: An Image and Its Interpreters* (Stanford: Stanford University Press, 2006), pp. 153–4. On Pavini, see D. Quaglioni, 'Propaganda antiebraica e polemiche di curia', in M. Miglio, F. Niutta, D. Quaglioni, and C. Ranieri (eds.), *Un pontificato ed una città: Sisto IV (1471–1484). Atti del convegno: Roma, 3–7 dicembre 1984* (Vatican City: Scuola vaticana di paleografia, diplomatica e archivistica, 1986),

pp. 243–66; D. Quaglioni, 'I giuristi medioevali e gli ebrei: Due "consultationes" di G. F. Pavini (1478)', *Quaderni storici* 64 (1987), pp. 7–18; M. Melchiorre, *A un cenno del suo dito. Fra Bernardino da Feltre (1439–1494) e gli ebrei* (Milan: Unicopli, 2012), pp. 71, 89–90, 92–4, 174, 178; M. Melchiorre, 'Pavini, Giovanni Francesco', *DBI* 81 (Rome: Istituto della Enciclopedia Italiana, 2014), s.v. On Nievo, see F. Bianchi, 'Nievo, Alessandro', *DBI* 78 (Rome: Istituto della Enciclopedia Italiana, 2013), s.v.; Quaglioni, 'Propaganda antiebraica', pp. 262–4; D. Quaglioni, 'Fra tolleranza e persecuzione. Gli ebrei nella letteratura giuridica del tardo Medioevo', *Storia d'Italia. Annali 11: Gli ebrei in Italia*, 2 vols. (Turin: Einaudi, 1996), vol. 1, pp. 645–75, here pp. 661–5. See also H. Angiolini, 'Polemica antiusuraria e propaganda antiebraica nel Quattrocento (Prime notizie per l'edizione dei "*Consilia contra iudaeos fenerantes*" di Alessandro Nievo e dei "*Consilia de usuris*" di Angelo di Castro)', *Il pensiero politico* 19 (1986), pp. 311–18.

35 Alessandro Nievo, *Consilia contra iudeos foenerantes* (Venice: Franz Renner with Nicholaus of Frankfurt, 1476).

36 Pullan, *Rich and Poor*, p. 455; R. M. Dessì, 'Usura, Caritas e Monti di Pietà. Le prediche antiusurarie e antiebraiche di Marco da Bologna e di Michele Carcano', in *I frati osservanti e la società in Italia nel secolo XV. Atti del XL Convegno internazionale in occasione del 550° anniversario della Fondazione del Monte di pietà di Perugia, 1462. Assisi-Perugia, 11–13 ottobre 2012* (Spoleto: Centro Italiano di Studi sull'Alto Medioevo Spoleto, 2013), pp. 169–226.

37 Setton, *The Papacy and the Levant*, vol. 2, pp. 299–313; Norwich, *History*, pp. 348–54.

38 On Simon of Trent's murder and the trial of the town's Jews, see, for example, A. Esposito and D. Quaglioni, *Processi contro gli ebrei di Trento (1475–1478)*, 2 vols. (Padua: Cedam, 1990–2008); R. Po-chia Hsia, *Trent 1475: Stories of a Ritual Murder Trial* (New Haven: Yale University Press, 1992); G. Gentilini, *Pasqua 1475: Antigiudaismo e lotta alle eresie: Il caso di Simonino* (Milan: Medusa, 2007); M. Teter, *Blood Libel: On the Trail of an Antisemitic Myth* (Cambridge MA: Harvard University Press, 2020), pp. 43–88. On the dissemination of Simon's 'story' and its later literary echoes, see, amongst others, Teter, *Blood Libel*, pp. 89–151; P. O. Kristeller, 'The Alleged Ritual Murder of Simon of Trent (1475) and Its Literary Representations: A Bibliographical Study', *Proceedings of the American Academy for Jewish Research* 59 (1993), pp. 103–35; W. Treue, *Der Trienter Judenprozess: Voraussetzungen, Abläufer, Auswirkungen (1475–1588)* (Hannover: Hahn, 1996); S. Bowd and J. D. Cullington, *'On Everyone's Lips': Humanists, Jews, and the Tale of Simon of Trent*

(Tempe AZ: Arizona Center for Medieval and Renaissance Studies, 2012); S. Bowd, 'Tales from Trent: The Construction of "Saint" Simon in Manuscript and Print', in A. K. Frazier (ed.), *The Saint between Manuscript and Print: Italy 1400–1600* (Toronto: Centre for Reformation and Renaissance Studies, 2015), pp. 183–218.

39 The text of Tiberino's account, together with an English translation, can be found in Bowd and Cullington, *'On Everyone's Lips'*, pp. 40–57. For discussion, see Teter, *Blood Libel*, pp. 47–9.

40 *Li horribili tormenti del beato Simone di Trento* (Treviso: Gerardo da Fiandra, 1475); Teter, *Blood Libel*, p. 110; Treue, *Der Trienter Judenprozess*, pp. 306–8.

41 *Hystorie von Simon zu Trient* (Trent: Albert Kunne, 1475); Teter, *Blood Libel*, pp. 128–31.

42 Pullan, *Rich and Poor*, p. 458.

43 In April 1475, Doge Pietro Mocenigo ordered the rector of Brescia to protect local Jews from violence. S. Bowd, *Venice's Most Loyal City: Civic Identity in Renaissance Brescia* (Cambridge MA and London: Harvard University Press, 2010), p. 169.

44 Teter, *Blood Libel*, pp. 132–3; F. Veraja, *La beatificazione: storia, problem, prospettive* (Rome: S. Congregazione per le Cause dei Santi, 1983), pp. 17–19.

45 Q. at Teter, *Blood Libel*, pp. 133, 135; cit. D. S. Areford, *The Viewer and the Printed Image in Late Medieval Europe* (Abingdon: Routledge, 2017), p. 167 [emphasis added].

46 Bowd, *Venice's Most Loyal City*, pp. 168–9.

47 Teter, *Blood Libel*, p. 135; A. Esposito, 'Il culto del "beato" Simonino e la sua prima diffusione in Italia', in I. Rogger and M. Bellabarba (eds.), *Il principe vescovo Johannes Hinderbach (1465–1486) fra tardo Medioevo e Umanesimo. Atti del Convegno dalla Biblioteca Comunale di Trento, 2–6 ottobre 1989* (1992), pp. 429–443, here p. 433.

48 Notable examples can still be seen in Malegno, Cerveno, Esino, Pisogne, and Pian Camuna, on which see D. E. Katz, *The Jew in the Art of the Renaissance* (Philadelphia: University of Pennsylvania Press, 2008), pp. 142–6.

49 For what follows, see esp. M. G. Muzzarelli, 'The Effect of Bernardino da Feltre's Preaching on the Jews', in J. Adams and J. Hanska (eds.), *The Jewish-Christian Encounter in Medieval Preaching* (New York: Routledge, 2014), pp. 170–94; C. R. Puglisi and W. L. Barcham, 'Bernardino da Feltre, the Monte di Pietà and the Man of Sorrows: Activist, Microcredit and Logo', *Artibus et Historiae* 29/58 (2008), pp. 35–63; V. Meneghin, 'Bernardino da Feltre, i monti di pietà e i banchi ebraici', *Archivium Franciscanum*

Historicum 73 (1980), pp. 688–703; V. Meneghin, *Bernardino da Feltre e i monti di pietà* (Vicenza: L.I.E.F. Edizioni, 1974); R. Segre, 'Bernardino da Feltre, i monti di pietà e i banchi ebraici', *Rivista storica italiana* 90 (1978), pp. 818–33.

50 Setton, *The Papacy and the Levant*, vol. 2, pp. 327–8; Lane, *Venice*, p. 236; Norwich, *History*, pp. 356–7.

51 Ravid, 'From Yellow to Red', p. 183.

52 Setton, *The Papacy and the Levant*, vol. 2, pp. 344–5.

53 Norwich, *History*, pp. 360–1; E. Crouzet-Pavan, *Venice Triumphant: The Horizons of a Myth*, trans. L. G. Cochrane (Baltimore and London: Johns Hopkins University Press, 2002), p. 131.

54 On food shortages, see *VDH* 106 (doc. III.4[a]).

55 See *VDH* 158–60 (doc. IV.11).

56 Ashtor, 'Gli inizi', p. 702; Ravid, 'The legal status', p. 198.

57 Ravid, 'The legal status', p. 198.

58 Ravid, 'The legal status', p. 198; Ashtor, 'Gli inizi', p. 702.

59 Ravid, 'The legal status', pp. 189–90.

60 H. Angiolini, 'Marco da Montegallo', *DBI* 69 (Rome, 2007), s.v.; F. Lomastro, *Legge di Dio e Monti di Pietà. Marco da Montegallo 1425–1496* (Vicenza: Fondazione Monte di Pietà, 1996).

61 L. Ongaro, *Il Monte di Pietà di Vicenza* (Vicenza: Arti Grafiche Vicentine, 1909); F. Lomastro, 'Sul Monte di Pietà di Vicenza dalla fondazione (1486) alla fine del Cinquecento', in *Il Monte di Pietà di Vicenza 1486–1986* (Vicenza: G. Rumor Editore, 1986), pp. 21–67.

62 Bowd, *Venice's Most Loyal City*, p. 171.

63 D. Zampese, *Il Monte di Pietà di Verona* (Udine: s.n., 1941); A. Ghinato, 'Il beato Michele d'Acqui e il suo apostolato in Verona', in A. Ghinato, *Studi e documenti intorno ai primitivi Monti di Pietà*, 5 vols. (Rome: Edizioni Francescane, 1956–63), vol. 4, pp. 61–117; C. Ferlito, *Il Monte di Pietà di Verona e il contesto economico-sociale della città nel secondo settecento* (Venice: Ist. Veneto di Scienze, 2009).

64 R. Calimani, *Storia del Ghetto di Venezia* (Milan: Mondadori Electa, 2001), p. 31.

65 V. Meneghin, *Bernardino da Feltre e i Monti di pietà* (Vicenza: L.I.E.F. Edizioni, 1974), pp. 263–340; J. Moro, *Il Monte di Pietà di Padova, 1469–1923* (Padua: Soc. Co-operative Tip., 1923), p. 12; Pullan, *Rich and Poor*, p. 461.

66 Mario Maragi, 'La fondazione del Monte di Pietà di Ravenna e la situazione economico-sociale ravennate alla fine del secolo XV', *Studi Romagnoli* 16 (1966), pp. 235–52.

67 For an overview, see Pullan, *Rich and Poor*, pp. 463, 466–7.

68 Ashtor, 'Gli inizi', p. 697.

69 Marin Sanudo, *Itinerario per la Terraferma veneziana*, ed. G. M. Varanini (Rome, 2014), p. 384: 'Qui sta molti zudei, et à una bella sinagoga; et quivi se impegna, perchè Venitiani non vol hebrei stagi a Veniexia.'
70 Bowd, *Venice's Most Loyal City*, p. 171.
71 Ashtor, 'Gli inizi', p. 703; Ravid, 'The legal status', p. 191; ref. to ASV Collegio, Notario 14, f. 62° (not seen).

3. Confinement (1492–1516)

1 U. B. Marvin, 'The Meteorite of Ensisheim: 1492 to 1992', *Meteoritics* 27 (1992), pp. 28–72, here pp. 29–34; O. Kammerer, 'Un prodige en Alsace à la fin du XVe siècle: la météorite d'Ensisheim', *Actes des congrès de la Société des historiens médiévistes de l'enseignement supérieur public* 25 (1994), pp. 293–315.
2 Zaccaria Contarini, 'Relazione di Francia', in E. Albèri (ed.), *Le Relazioni degli Ambasciatori veneti al Senato*, 15 vols. (Florence: Clio, 1839–63), vol. 4, pp. 1–26, here pp. 15–16: 'La maestà del re di Francia è di età 22 anni, piccolo e mal composto della persona, brutto di volto, che ha gli occhi grossi e bianchi e molto più atti a veder poco che assai, il naso aquilino . . . i labbri *etiam* grossi, i quali continuamente tiene aperti, e ha alcuni movimenti di mano spasmosi che paiono molto brutti a vederli, *et est tardus in locutione*. Secondo la opinon mia, la qual potria esser molto ben falsa, io tengo per fermo *quod de corpore et de ingenio parum valeat; tamen* è laudato da tutti in Parigi per gagliardissimo a giocar alla palla, in caccia e alla giostra, nei quali esercizi *vel bene vel male* mette e distribuisce tempo assai.'
3 D. S. Chambers, *The Imperial Age of Venice, 1380–1580* (London: Thames and Hudson, 1970), p. 61.
4 What follows is based on M. Mallett and C. Shaw, *The Italian Wars, 1494–1559: War, State and Society in Early Modern Europe* (Abingdon: Routledge, 2014), pp. 7–15.
5 Francesco Guicciardini, *Storia d'Italia*, 1.6, 1.7; ed. C. Panigada, 5 vols. (Bari: Laterza, 1929), vol. 1, pp. 45, 52, 53–4.
6 Guicciardini, 1.6; ed. Panigada, vol. 1, pp. 50–1.
7 Marin Sanudo, *La Spedizione di Carlo VIII in Italia*, ed. R. Fulin (Venice: Tipografia del Commercio di Marco Visentini, 1873), pp. 236, 262; Mallett and Shaw, *The Italian Wars*, pp. 26–7.
8 For what follows, see Mallett and Shaw, *The Italian Wars*, pp. 28–35.
9 See T. Nichols, *Renaissance Art in Venice: From Tradition to*

Individualism (London: Laurence King Publishing, 2016), p. 72; P. Fortini Brown, *Venetian Narrative Painting in the Age of Carpaccio* (New Haven and London: Yale University Press, 1988), p. 9. More generally, see W. J. Bouwsma, *Venice and the Defense of Republican Liberty: Renaissance Values in the Age of the Counter Reformation* (Berkeley and Los Angeles: University of California Press, 1968); R. Finlay, 'The immortal Republic: the myth of Venice during the Italian wars (1494–1530)', *The Sixteenth Century Journal* 30/4 (1999), pp. 931–44; repr. in R. Finlay, *Venice Besieged: Politics and Diplomacy in the Italian Wars, 1494–1534* (Aldershot: Routledge, 2008), ch. I; D. Rosand, *Myths of Venice: The Figuration of a State* (Chapel Hill: University of North Carolina Press, 2001).

10 R. C. Mueller, *The Venetian Money Market: Banks, Panics, and the Public Debt, 1200–1500* (Baltimore: Johns Hopkins University Press, 1997), p. 237.

11 M. Lowry, *The World of Aldus Manutius: Business and Scholarship in Renaissance Venice* (Oxford: Basil Blackwell, 1979), p. 128.

12 B. Ravid, 'From Yellow to Red: On the Distinguishing Head-Covering of the Jews of Venice', *Jewish History* 6/1–2 (1992), pp. 179–201, here p. 183.

13 B. Ravid, 'The Legal Status of the Jews in Venice to 1509', *Proceedings of the American Academy for Jewish Research* 54 (1987), pp. 169–202, here p. 192. The remainder of this paragraph closely follows Ravid's account.

14 Giambattista Gallicciolli, *Delle memorie venete antiche profane ed ecclesiastiche, libri tre . . .* , 8 vols. (Venice: Domenico Fracasso, 1795), vol. 2, p. 299 [no. 924].

15 Ravid, 'The Legal Status', pp. 194–5.

16 Ravid, 'The Legal Status', pp. 194–5; a slightly different version is given at Gallicciolli, *Delle memorie*, vol. 2, pp. 300–1 [no. 928].

17 The remainder of this paragraph follows Mallett and Shaw, *The Italian Wars*, pp. 43–5.

18 For the following, see Mallett and Shaw, *The Italian Wars*, pp. 47–53.

19 Mallett and Shaw, *The Italian Wars*, pp. 58–61.

20 Girolamo Priuli, *Diarii*, ed. A. Segre and R. Cessi, 3 vols. [numbered 1, 2, and 4], *RIS*, 2nd ser., 24.3 (Città di Castello and Bologna: Tipi della casa editrice, 1912–41), vol. 2, p. 162: 'A Venetia non fu facto festa alchuna di questa victoria, ma fu bem scripto in Franza al Re in bona forma in congratulatione per il Senato Veneto'.

21 For the following, see K. M. Setton, *The Papacy and the Levant*

(1204–1571), 4 vols. (Philadelphia: American Philosophical Society, 1976–84), vol. 2, pp. 508–23.
22 F. C. Lane, *Venice: A Maritime Republic* (Baltimore and London: Johns Hopkins University Press, 1973), p. 290.
23 J. J. Norwich, *A History of Venice* (London: Penguin, 1983), p. 386.
24 Priuli, *Diarii*, vol. 2, p. 225 n. 1.
25 Priuli, *Diarii*, vol. 2, p. 227.
26 On the banking crisis of 1499, see Mueller, *The Venetian Money Market*, ch. 6.ii.
27 Ravid, 'The Legal Status', pp. 198–9; Priuli, *Diarii*, vol. 2, pp. 88–9; Marin Sanudo, *Diarii*, ed. R. Fulin, F. Stefani, G. Berchet, N. Barozzi, and M. Allegri, 58 vols. (Venice: A Spesi Degli Editori, 1879–1903), vol. 3, col. 1246; Gallicciolli, *Delle memorie*, vol. 2, pp. 301–2 [no. 929]; ASV Senato Terra, r. 13, ff. 169r–71r (not seen).
28 Ravid, 'The Legal Status', p. 199.
29 B. Pullan, *Rich and Poor in Renaissance Venice: The Social Institutions of a Catholic State, to 1620* (Oxford: Basil Blackwell, 1971), p. 508; cf. Lane, *Venice*, p. 237.
30 Pullan, *Rich and Poor*, p. 508.
31 On the Arsenale's average wage bill, see R. C. Davis, *Shipbuilders of the Venetian Arsenal: Workers and Workplace in the Preindustrial City* (Baltimore: Johns Hopkins University Press, 1991), pp. 28ff.
32 B. Netanyahu, *Don Isaac Abravanel, Statesman and Philosopher*, 5th ed. (Ithaca and London: Cornell University Press, 1998), pp. 82–5; R. Calimani, *Storia del Ghetto di Venezia* (Milan: Mondadori Electa, 2001), pp. 34–7.
33 The following is based on Ravid, 'The Legal Status', p. 195. On Anselmo, see Pullan, *Rich and Poor*, pp. 481–2.
34 On Anselmo del Banco, see Pullan, *Rich and Poor*, pp. 479–83; R. Scuro, 'Banchi ebraici a Mestre e nella Terraferma alla fine del Medioevo', in D. Calabi (ed.), *Venezia, gli Ebrei e l'Europa, 1516–2016* (Venice: Marsilio, 2016), pp. 90–3. Anselmo was buried in the Jewish cemetery in Padua, where his tombstone can still be found. D. Malkiel, *Stones Speak: Hebrew Tombstones from Padua, 1529–1862* (Leiden: Brill, 2013), pp. 152–3.
35 Sanudo, *Diarii*, vol. 46, cols. 501–2: 'Anselmo *dal Banco* primo zudio di richeza di più di 100 milia ducati'.
36 On the peace, see Setton, *The Papacy*, vol. 3, p. 2.
37 Mallett and Shaw, *The Italian Wars*, pp. 61–2.
38 Priuli, *Diarii*, vol. 2, pp. 269–70; Sanudo, *Diarii*, vol. 5, cols. 30–1,

32–4; Guicciardini, *Storia d'Italia*, 5.15; ed. Panigada, vol. 2, pp. 78–81; Mallett and Shaw, *The Italian Wars*, pp. 64–6.
39 Priuli, *Diarii*, vol. 2, p. 271.
40 Malaria was reportedly rife in Rome just then. Antonio Giustinian, *Dispacci di Antonio Giustinian, Ambasciatore Veneto in Roma dal 1502 al 1505*, ed. P. Villari, 3 vols. (Florence: Successori Le Monnier, 1876), vol. 2, p. 99 (no. 472); cf. Johannes Burchard, *Liber Notarum ab anno MCCCCLXXXIII ad annum MDVI*, ed. E. Celani, *RIS* 2nd ser., 32.1, 2 vols. (Città di Castello: S. Lapi, 1907–42), vol. 2, p. 351. On suspicions of poison, see, for example, Sanudo, *Diarii*, vol. 5, col. 65. This theory was later supported by Guicciardini, *Storia d'Italia*, 6.4; ed. Panigada, vol. 2, pp. 96–8.
41 Priuli, *Diarii*, vol. 2, p. 285: 'ali 18 di questo, venere, a hora una di nocte, passò di questa vita a l'inferno'.
42 Priuli attributes this more to 'li giovani et il populo et vulgo precipitossi', who longed only for gain, than to the 'Padri Veneti', who were wary of provoking a war with the Church, to which the Romagna properly belonged. Priuli, *Diarii*, vol. 2, p. 312; cf. Sanudo, *Diarii*, vol. 5, cols. 198–9.
43 Sanudo, *Diarii*, vol. 5, cols. 201, 206; Priuli, *Diarii*, vol. 2, pp. 312–13, 314.
44 Sigismondo de' Conti, *Le Storie de' suoi tempi dal 1475 al 1510*, 2 vols. (Rome: G. Barbera, 1883), vol. 2, pp. 339–40; Setton, *The Papacy*, vol. 3, p. 39; cf. Priuli, *Diarii*, vol. 2, pp. 369–70.
45 For the following, see Mallett and Shaw, *The Italian Wars*, pp. 86–7; Guicciardini, *Storia d'Italia*, 7.12; ed. Panigada, vol. 2, pp. 233–4.
46 Pullan, *Rich and Poor*, p. 476.
47 For example, Sanudo, *Diarii*, vol. 7, col. 316: 'Fu posto, che li zudei pagino ducati 20 milia, *videlicet* la mità a dì 15 marzo, l'atra mità per tuto marzo, da esser scontadi in le decime e tanse lhoro. Et fu presa'.
48 Pullan, *Rich and Poor*, p. 476; cf. Sanudo, *Diarii*, vol. 7, col. 604.
49 Setton, *The Papacy and the Levant*, vol. 3, pp. 54–5; Mallett and Shaw, *The Italian Wars*, pp. 87–8; J. Dumont, *Corps universel diplomatique du droit des gens*, 8 vols. (Amsterdam: Chez P. Brunel, R. et G. Wetstein, les Janssons Waesberge, et L'Honoré et Chatelain, 1726–31), vol. 4.1, pp. 109–16 (nos. 51–2).
50 Machiavelli, *Il principe*, 12.26: 'in una giornata perderono quello che in ottocento anni . . . avevano acquistato'.
51 Mallett and Shaw, *The Italian Wars*, pp. 90–1.
52 Priuli, *Diarii*, vol. 4, p. 29: 'il magno et grande Idio habia permesso et ordinato questa tanta ruina delo Imperio Veneto'; R. Finlay, 'The Foundation of the Ghetto: Venice, the Jews, and the War of the

League of Cambrai', *Proceedings of the American Philosophical Society* 126.2 (1982), pp. 140–54, here pp. 143–4. For recriminations against Venetian commanders etc., see, for example, Sanudo, *Diarii*, vol. 8, cols. 256–7.
53   Sanudo, *Diarii*, vol. 8, col. 300: 'Fu divulgato una nova, la qual fu vera, brexani haver sachizato li zudei, aperto le presom e posto a sacho le monition di le arme dil palazo dil capitano'. See also Sanudo, *Diarii*, vol. 8, col. 302.
54   Sanudo, *Diarii*, vol. 8, col. 305.
55   Sanudo, *Diarii*, vol. 8, cols. 335–6: 'veronesi haveano messo a sacho le monitiom in palazo dil capitano, l'oficio dil sal et li zudei'.
56   Sanudo, *Diarii*, vol. 8, col. 340.
57   Sanudo, *Diarii*, vol. 8, col. 340: 'Come Treviso erano in moto; et questa note alcuni citadini armati sono a le caxe di zudei, et quelle meseno a sacho tutte, ma non trovono molta roba di haver, perchè il bon e mior haveano fato portar in questa terra *etc*'.
58   Pullan, *Rich and Poor*, p. 468; Finlay, 'The Foundation', p. 140.
59   Priuli, *Diarii*, vol. 4, p. 96; Finlay, 'The Foundation', p. 140.
60   Sanudo, *Diarii*, vol. 8, cols. 355–6.
61   Sanudo, *Diarii*, vol. 8, col. 406.
62   Sanudo, *Diarii*, vol. 8, col. 373.
63   Luigi da Porto, *Lettere storiche . . . dall'anno 1509 al 1528*, ed. B. Bressan (Florence: F. Le Monnier, 1857), p. 63: 'Alcuni altri, di maggior ordine ancora, si veggono con fronte priva di ogni baldanza andare per la mesta città con passo non continuato, ma ora frettoloso, ora lento; ed abbracciando ora questo ora quello, far certe accoglienze sproporzionate, ed alcune blandizie alle genti, che non amore, ma timore smisurato dimostrano palesemente. In fine, tutta Vinegia in dieci giorni è cambiata di aspetto, e di lieta è divenuta mestissima; chè oltre che molte donne hanno dimesso il loro superbo modo di vestire, non s'ode più per le piazze e per i rii nella notte alcuna sorte di strumenti, de' quali, con sommo diletto degli abitanti, questa città a tale stagione suol essere abbondevolissima. E si poco son usi a tali percosse i Viniziani, che temono, non ch'altro, di perder anche Vinegia . . . Tanto smisurato timore è entrato ne'cuori loro'. See Bouwsma, *Venice*, p. 99.
64   This paragraph is indebted to Mallett and Shaw, *The Italian Wars*, pp. 93–4.
65   Bouwsma, *Venice*, p. 100.
66   Q. at R. Finlay, 'Venice, the Po expedition, and the end of the League of Cambrai, 1509–1510', *Studies in Modern European History and Culture* 2 (1976), pp. 37–72, here p. 45.

67 For Venetian suspicions of Jewish collusion with imperial troops, see Priuli, *Diarii*, vol. 4, pp. 196–7, 253.
68 Finlay, 'The Foundation', p. 140; Priuli, *Diarii*, vol. 4, p. 253.
69 Sanudo, *Diarii*, vol. 8, col. 527: 'Da matina in colegio sonno li zudei stanno qui, *maxime* Anselmo dil banco, dolendossi di la crudeltà fata im Padoa contra li zudei, e posto a sacho li pegni, cossa insolita farssi, e pregava fosse provisto, e più voleano dar taja a le persone; *adeo* fo comandà a li capitanij dil consejo di X andaseno a Liza Fusina, et robe di valuta veniva in questa terra retenesse e tolesse per nota, e di chi era li butini; et cussì fu fato, ma valse pocho'.
70 Sanudo, *Diarii*, vol. 8, col. 548: 'sier Zuan Marin . . . [s]crive, come è stà a la expedition di Castel Franco e Axolo con zente, e intrò lì provedador, et sedò tumulti tra soldati e la terra, per causa di sachizar li zudei, e pose hordine tutto fusse restituito'.
71 On Polsella, see Finlay, 'Venice, the Po expedition'.
72 The remainder of this paragraph follows Ravid, 'The Legal Status', p. 200; Pullan, *Rich and Poor*, p. 481.
73 According to Priuli, Venice's expenses were running at around 40,000 ducats a month. Priuli, *Diarii*, vol. 4, pp. 74, 143, 171; Finlay, 'Venice, the Po expedition', p. 65 n. 41.
74 Finlay, 'Venice, the Po expedition', p. 56.
75 Mallett and Shaw, *The Italian Wars*, p. 95; Norwich, *History*, pp. 408–9.
76 Mallett and Shaw, *The Italian Wars*, pp. 96–7. In Vicenza, the brutality was particularly extreme. According to the chronicler Antonio Grumello, Gascon soldiers discovered a crowd of people hiding in a cave outside the city. When they refused to surrender, the Gascons promptly burnt them all to death. Antonio Grumello, 'Cronaca di Antonio Grumello Pavese dal MCCCCLXVII al MDXXIX', in G. Müller (ed.), *Raccolta di cronisti e documenti storici Lombardi inediti*, 2 vols. (Milan: Colombo, 1856), vol. 1, pp. 126–7; S. D. Bowd, *Renaissance Mass Murder: Civilians and Soldiers during the Italian Wars* (Oxford: Oxford University Press, 2018), pp. 86–7.
77 Mallett and Shaw, *The Italian Wars*, pp. 97–101.
78 *VDH*, pp. 189–90 (doc. V.2).
79 Sanudo, *Diarii*, vol. 12, cols. 110–11.
80 Sanudo, *Diarii*, vol. 12, col. 110; Pullan, *Rich and Poor*, p. 479.
81 For the following, see Mallett and Shaw, *The Italian Wars*, pp. 101–3.
82 Pullan, *Rich and Poor*, p. 479; Sanudo, *Diarii*, vol. 13, cols. 105–6.
83 Sanudo, *Diarii*, vol. 13, col. 517; A. Desjardins and G. Canestrini, *Négociations diplomatiques de la France avec la Toscane*, 6 vols. (Paris: Imprimerie Impériale, 1859–86), vol. 1, pp. 544, 546–7; Mallett and

Shaw, *The Italian Wars*, pp. 104–6; S. D. Bowd, *Venice's Most Loyal City: Civic Identity in Renaissance Brescia* (Cambridge MA: Harvard University Press, 2010), pp. 204–7; Bowd, *Renaissance Mass Murder*, p. 6.

84 See, for example, Mallett and Shaw, *The Italian Wars*, pp. 106–9; D. Bolognesi (ed.), *1512: La battaglia di Ravenna, l'Italia, l'Europa* (Ravenna: Longo Angelo, 2014), esp. pp. 13–138; Guicciardini, *Storia d'Italia*, 10.13; ed. Panigada, vol. 3, pp. 187–93.

85 N. Murphy, 'Henry VIII's First Invasion of France: The Gascon Expedition of 1512', *English Historical Review* 130/542 (2015), pp. 25–56; H. Wiesflecker, *Kaiser Maximilian I: Das Reich, Österreich und Europa an der Wende zur Neuzeit*, 5 vols. (Munich: Oldenbourg, 1971–86), vol. 4, p. 102; Mallett and Shaw, *The Italian Wars*, pp. 109–10.

86 C. Shaw, *Julius II: The Warrior Pope* (Oxford: Blackwell, 1993), pp. 294–6.

87 For what follows, see Mallett and Shaw, *The Italian Wars*, pp. 116–20.

88 Guicciardini, *Storia d'Italia*, 11.9; ed. Panigada, vol. 3, pp. 264–5; Norwich, *History*, p. 425.

89 For the following, see esp. Guicciardini, *Storia d'Italia*, 11.11; ed. Panigada, vol. 3, pp. 270–3; Mallett and Shaw, *The Italian Wars*, pp. 120–1.

90 Guicciardini, *Storia d'Italia*, 11.12; ed. Panigada, vol. 3, pp. 273–81; Mallett and Shaw, *The Italian Wars*, pp. 121–2; M. Troso, *L'ultima battaglia del Medioevo: La battaglia dell'Ariotta Novara 6 giugno 1513* (Mariano del Friuli: Edizioni della Laguna, 2002).

91 Pullan, *Rich and Poor*, p. 482; cit. ASV Consiglio dei Dieci, Miste, fil. 31, fasc. 182 (15 July 1513).

92 For the following, see Guicciardini, *Storia d'Italia*, 11.14–15; ed. Panigada, vol. 3, pp. 290–2; Sanudo, *Diarii*, vol. 17, col. 119; Mallett and Shaw, *The Italian Wars*, p. 123.

93 Sanudo, *Diarii*, vol. 17, col. 147.

94 Sanudo, *Diarii*, vol. 17, col. 145: 'Come i nimici non pol fuzir che non siano roti e promete vitoria certa'.

95 On the Battle of La Motta, see Mallett and Shaw, *The Italian Wars*, pp. 123–4; Guicciardini, *Storia d'Italia*, 11.15; ed. Panigada, vol. 3, pp. 294–6.

96 Sanudo, *Diarii*, vol. 17, col. 172: 'E in men di mezz'ora fu rotta cussì bela gente.'

97 Sanudo, *Diarii*, vol. 17, col. 152: 'Tutti li corse driedo, e quando lo vidi non diceva nulla, ni era Zuan Gobo corier, qual è in campo a questo effecto per portar la nontiaura batando di la vittoria, dissi fra

me: "le cose non va ben". E leto la dita letera in Pregadi . . . tutti quelli erano in Pregadi rimaseno come morti . . .'.
98 Sanudo, *Diarii*, vol. 17, col. 172: '. . . de che la colpa di cieli e la fortuna credo ne abino gran parte, perchè la vittoria era ne le man nostre'; Finlay, 'The Foundation', p. 145.
99 For what follows, see Mallett and Shaw, *The Italian Wars*, pp. 124–5; Guicciardini, *Storia d'Italia*, 11.16; ed. Panigada, vol. 3, pp. 296–8.
100 Sanudo, *Diarii*, vol. 19, cols. 369, 371–2.
101 Sanudo, *Diarii*, vol. 19, col. 397. The real cause of death is more likely to have been 'dysentery, complicated by gout, fever, and his usual weak constitution'. R. S. Love, 'Contemporary and Near-Contemporary Opinion of Louis XII, "Père du Peuple"', *Renaissance and Reformation*, n.s. 8/4 (1984), pp. 235–65, here p. 256.
102 Sanudo, *Diarii*, vol. 19, cols. 374–5, 391, 404. On the hopes and expectations aroused by Francis' expectations, see Guicciardini, *Storia d'Italia*, 12.10; ed. Panigada, vol. 3, p. 338: 'Delle virtú, della magnanimitá, dello ingegno e spirito generoso di costui s'aveva universalmente tanta speranza che ciascuno confessava non essere, giá per moltissimi anni, pervenuto alcuno con maggiore espettazione alla corona'.
103 Sanudo, *Diarii*, vol. 20, col. 71; Finlay, 'The Foundation', p. 146.
104 Sanudo, *Diarii*, vol. 20, col. 98: 'El predicator di Frari, fra' Zuan Maria di Arezo vocifera contra di loro e contra li medici hebrei, et *maxime* maestro Lazaro, che à fato disperder christiane, usato con christiane et nulla di provision si fa, concludendo si pol tuor tutto il suo haver e meterlo a defension dil Stato, perchè sono servi nostri'; Finlay, 'The Foundation', p. 146.
105 Sanudo, *Diarii*, vol. 20, col. 98: 'Non voglio restar di scriver una prava consuetudine venuta per il continuo comercio si ha con questi zudei, quali stanno in questa terra gran numero, San Cassan, Santo Agustin, San Polo, Santa Maria *Mater Domini*, che prima de la Domenica di l'Olivo non si vedevano più fin passà Pasqua. Hora fino eri sono andati atorno, et è malissimo facto . . .'; Finlay, 'The Foundation', p. 146.
106 Sanudo, *Diarii*, vol. 20, col. 98: '. . . e niun li dice nulla, perchè mediante le guerre, hanno bisogno di loro'.
107 Sanudo, *Diarii*, vol. 20, col. 138: 'In questa matina, sier Zorzi Emo savio dil Consejo fe' lezer in Colegio una parte: che li zudei, quali sono in questa terra molti in diverse caxe et contrade et danno mal exempio a li christiani tutti, siano mandati ad habitar a la Zueca etc'.
108 It is also worth noting that the idea of segregating Venice's Jews had other precedents. Back in 1468, the Senate had decreed that, in

order to prevent the spread of infectious diseases, a new *lazzaretto* should be built on the island of Sant'Erasmo, just north of the city. Marcantonio Sabellico, *Le historie vinitiane* (Venice: Curzio Trioano Navò, 1544), p. 225r: 'La quale a chi la vede di lontano ha forma d'un castello, molto ben guernito'. J. L. Stevens Crawshaw, *Plague Hospitals: Public Health for the City in Early Modern Venice* (Farnham: Ashgate, 2012), p. 46; E. Concina, U. Camerino, and D. Calabi, *La Città degli Ebrei: Il Ghetto di Venezia: Architettura e Urbanistica* (Venice: Marsilio, 1991), p. 32. On the foundation of the Lazzaretto Nuovo, see *VDH* 115 (doc. III.5[a][ii]). Likewise, since at least the mid-fifteenth century, the Venetian patriarchate had steadily strengthened its control over the physical environment of the city and had made every effort to 'enclose and confine' marginal groups wherever it could. D. Romano, 'Gender and the Urban Geography of Renaissance Venice', *Journal of Social History* 23.2 (1989), pp. 339–53, here p. 348.

109 Sanudo, *Diarii*, vol. 20, col. 138: 'Hor inteso questa parte da' zudei et *maxime* Anselmo banchier et Vivian andono a trovar i Savj, dicendo è pericoloso non siano messi a saco, stando a la Zueca, da' fantazini, et che stariano meglio a Muran; et feno tante pratiche, che il resto dil Colegio non l'asenti, et però fo soprastato.'

110 R. J. Goy, *Chioggia and the Villages of the Venetian Lagoon: Studies in Urban History* (Cambridge: Cambridge University Press, 1985), pp. 241–3.

111 For the following, see Mallett and Shaw, *The Italian Wars*, pp. 127–30.

112 Guicciardini, *Storia d'Italia*, 12.15; ed. Panigada, vol. 3, p. 367: 'Di maniera che il Triulzio, capitano che avea vedute tante cose, affermava questa essere stata battaglia non d'uomini ma di giganti'.

113 Guicciardini, *Storia d'Italia*, 12.15; ed. Panigada, vol. 3, p. 368.

114 Finlay, 'The Foundation', pp. 147–8; Sanudo, *Diarii*, vol. 21, cols. 114, 121.

115 Sanudo, *Diarii*, vol. 21, cols. 153–4; Guicciardini, *Storia d'Italia*, 12.16; ed. Panigada, vol. 3, pp. 369–73.

116 Sanudo, *Diarii*, vol. 21, cols. 230, 231, 235, 268, 284, 290, 311; Guicciardini, *Storia d'Italia*, 12.17; ed. Panigada, vol. 3, pp. 373–7; Finlay, 'The Foundation', pp. 148–9; Mallett and Shaw, *The Italian Wars*, p. 133.

117 Guicciardini, *Storia d'Italia*, 12.18; ed. Panigada, vol. 3, pp. 377–80; Finlay, 'The Foundation', p. 148.

118 Guicciardini, *Storia d'Italia*, 12.18; ed. Panigada, vol. 3, pp. 380–1; Mallett and Shaw, *The Italian Wars*, p. 131.

119 Sanudo, *Diarii*, vol. 21, col. 439: 'in Brexa è carestia grande di ogni cosa'; Bowd, *Venice's Most Loyal City*, p. 215.
120 Guicciardini, *Storia d'Italia*, 12.20; ed. Panigada, vol. 3, pp. 385–6; Sanudo, *Diarii*, vol. 22, cols. 54–8. Maximilian's unsuccessful siege of Asola was later commemorated in a painting by Tintoretto (1544–45; private collection).
121 The remainder of this paragraph is indebted to Finlay, 'The Foundation', pp. 149–50.
122 On Bartolomeo d'Alviano's death, see Guicciardini, *Storia d'Italia*, 12.17; vol. 3, pp. 374–5; Michel de Montaigne, *Essais*, 1.3.
123 Sanudo, *Diarii*, vol. 22, col. 38: 'In questa matina, la terra comenzò a star molto di mala voglia per queste cattive nove, et che francesi, per pusilanimità, si debano retrazer; et non voler far zornada; ch'è una pessima cosa'.
124 Sanudo, *Diarii*, vol. 22, col. 63.
125 Sanudo, *Diarii*, vol. 22, col. 66.
126 Sanudo, *Diarii*, vol. 22, col. 65: 'In questa matina, sul campo di San Polo, poi la predicha fata per fra' Rufino Lovato di Padoa di l'ordine di San Francesco observante, dove vi fu grandissimo populo ... or qui a San Polo, fato uno soler, dove era il reverendo domino Domenico episcopo di Chisamo aparato con la mitra, batizoe uno hebreo chiamato ... con ... fioli'. Despite what Finlay has claimed, there is no evidence that the 'Jews ... were apparently no less indiscreet about their presence during Easter than they had been the previous year' – or that this was criticized by Fra Rufino Lovato in his sermon. Finlay, 'The Foundation', p. 151.
127 On Zaccaria Dolfin, see G. Benzoni, 'Dolfin, Zaccaria', *DBI* 40 (Rome: Treccani, 1991), s.v.
128 Sanudo, *Diarii*, vol. 22, col. 72: 'In questa matina. Havendo in questi zorni proposto sier Zacaria Dolfin savio dil Consejo in Colegio che li zudei stano mal in la terra, sicome li predicatori predicano le perversità dil Stado vien da questo, e per le sinagoge fano contra la forma di le leze, però è di opinon di mandarli tutti a star in Geto nuovo, ch'è come un castello, e far ponti levadori et serar di muro'.
129 This paragraph and the next follow E. Concina, 'Parva Jerusalem', in E. Concina, U. Camerino, and D. Calabi (eds.), *La Città degli Ebrei: Il Ghetto di Venezia: Architettura e Urbanistica* (Venice: Marsilio, 1991), pp. 9–158, here pp. 12–24; E. Concina, 'The Origins of the Venetian Ghetto: The Houses, the People, the Laws, 1390–1540', in J.-M. Cohen (ed.), *Het getto van Venetië. Ponentini, Levantini e Tedeschi 1516–1797* (Gravenhage: SDU, 1990), pp. 28–45; E. Concina, 'Owners, Houses, Functions: New Research on the Origins of the

Venetian Ghetto', *Mediterranean Historical Review* 6 (1991), pp. 180–9; B. Ravid, 'The Venetian Government and the Jews', in R. C. Davis and B. Ravid (eds.), *The Jews of Early Modern Venice* (Baltimore and London, 2001), pp. 3–30, here pp. 9–10.

130   For further connotations of the word '*geto*', see D. Calabi, *Venice and Its Jews: 500 Years Since the Founding of the Ghetto*, trans. L. Rosenberg (Milan: Officina Libraria, 2017), pp. 27–9.

131   Sanudo, *Diarii*, vol. 22, col. 73: '*Et poi fo chiamà Anselmo hebreo con do altri capi hebrei, et il Principe li disse voleano andasseno ad habitar in Geto novo, et che tenivano sinagoga qui contra la forma di le leze. El qual disse che questa era cosa injusta per più rispeti: prima, perchè non stando in mezo di zentilhomeni e altri christiani sarano messi a sacho, come è stà zà principiato di far, e stano apresso le guarde di Rialto, non che tanto lontano; poi li è stà promesso, per il Consejo di X con la zonta, non innovar altro di loro, che saria romperli la fede, e li strazaroli à pagà tanti danari per tenir le botege di Rialto, hora sariano ruinati; poi li poveri judei non vorano andar habitar li e si paririano di qui, et lui Anselmo à promesso pagar per tutti, sichè non potrà pagar non havendo da chi scuoder le taxe; suplichando non li fosse innovà questo, ma quando si havesse recuperà il Stado, l'era ben onesto andaseno li hebrei fuora in le terre dove stevano, benchè a Mestre non pono più star per non vi esser caxe. Hor andò, fuora e il Dolfin più caldo che mai, vol poner in parte in Pregadi*'. Note that, since 1455, '[o]wnership of the island' had been 'divided among several members of the da Brolo family, some of whom may have sold their holdings before the Jews were confined'. Ravid, 'The Venetian Government', p. 10.

132   Sanudo, *Diarii*, vol. 22, col. 73: '*Item, che havia inteso i nimici e nostri, over francesi, erano stati a le man: morti di una parte e l'altra da numero 3000, e che Milan era sotosopra. Questo lo intese a camino; tamen non è creduto et non fu la verità*'. The remainder of this paragraph follows Finlay, 'The Foundation', pp. 151–2.

133   Sanudo, *Diarii*, vol. 22, col. 78: '*Bergamo levoe le insegne de i nimici*'.

134   Sanudo, *Diarii*, vol. 22, cols. 78–9.

135   The decree may be found at Sanudo, *Diarii*, vol. 22, cols. 85–8, and B. Ravid, 'The Religious, Economic and Social Background and Context of the Establishment of the Ghetti of Venice', in G. Cozzi (ed.), *Gli Ebrei e Venezia, secoli XIV–XVIII. Atti del Convegno internazionale organizzato dall'Istituto di storia della società e dello stato veneziano della Fondazione Giorgio Cini. Venezia, Isola di San Giorgio Maggiore 5–10 giugno 1983* (Milan: Edizioni di Comunità,

1987), pp. 211–60, here pp. 248–50. A partial translation is given at *VDH* pp. 338–9 (doc. VIII.8); Marin Sanudo, *Venice, Città Excelentissima: Selections from the Renaissance Diaries of Marin Sanudo*, ed. P. H. Labalme and L. Sanguineti White, trans. L. L. Carroll (Baltimore: Johns Hopkins University Press, 2008), pp. 339–40. The voting was as follows: 130 in favour, 44 against, 8 abstentions. Sanudo, *Diarii*, vol. 22, col. 88.

136   Sanudo, *Diarii*, vol. 22, col. 86: 'per obviar a tanti desordeni et inconvenienti, sia provisto et deliberando in questa forma, *videlicet*: che tutti li zudei che *de praesenti* si atrovano habitar in diverse contrade de questa cità nostra, et quelli che *de caetero* venisseno . . . siano tenuti et debano andar *immediate* ad habitar unidi in la corte de case che sono in Geto, apresso San Hironimo, luoco capacissimo per sua habitatione; et aziò far possino tale effecto et non vadino tergiversando, sia provisto et preso che *immediate* tute dite case siano evacuade, et essi zudei pagar debino de fitto un terzo più di quello che *de praesenti* trazino i patroni di le case predite; nè possino tenir hostaria in alcun luoco de la terra, salvo che nel prenominado . . .'.

137   For discussion, see, most notably, D. E. Katz, *The Jewish Ghetto and the Visual Imagination of Early Modern Venice* (New York: Cambridge University Press, 2017), esp. pp. 55–6; B. Ravid, 'Curfew Time in the Ghetto of Venice', in E. Kittell and T. Madden (eds.), *Medieval and Renaissance Venice* (Urbana and Chicago: University of Illinois Press, 1999), pp. 237–75, here p. 238; Calabi, *Venice and Its Jews*, pp. 7–8.

138   Sanudo, *Diarii*, vol. 22, col. 86: 'Et per obviar che i non vadano tutta la note atorno con gravissima murmuratione et summa displicentia de missier Jesù Cristo, sia preso che de la banda verso Geto vecchio, dove è un pontesello picolo, et *similiter* da l'altra banda del ponte, siano fatte do porte, *videlicet* una per cadaun de diti do lochi; qual porte, la matina, si debino aprir a la marangona, et la sera siano serade ad ore 24 per quatro custodi christiani da esser a questo deputadi e pagadi da lor zudei a quel pretio parerà conveniente al Colegio nostro; et *insuper* sieno fatti do muri alti che serino le do altre bande che guardano sopra i rivi; siano *etiam* murade tutte le rive di le case predite. *Praeterea*, esse custodi siano tenuti habitar in dito loco zorno et note soli, senza famiglie, per ben costudirlo . . . ; et *insuper*, dito Colegio li debbi deputar do barche, qual zorno et note vadino atorno il prefato loco, da esser pagade de i danari de essi zudei'.

139   Sanudo, *Diarii*, vol. 22, col. 100: 'In questa matina, fo fato le cride, justa la parte presa in Pregadi, che tutti li zudei vadino a star in Geto,

et questo in termine de zorni 10; et fo fato a Rialto et per le contrade dove i habitavano, sopra li ponti, a notitia loro, soto gran pene'.

140 Sanudo, *Diarii*, vol. 22, col. 162.

141 Sanudo, *Diarii*, vol. 22, col. 375.

4. 'Under the Protection of the Lord' (1516–1541)

1. M. Mallet and C. Shaw, *The Italian Wars, 1494–1559: War, State and Society in Early Modern Europe* (London and New York: Routledge, 2012), p. 134; J. J. Norwich, *A History of Venice* (London: Penguin, 1983), pp. 432–3.

2. As Brian Pullan has observed, a decree passed on 29 July 1516, 'fixing the wages of Christian watch-men, implied that the narrowness of the Ghetto had . . . forced many Jews to return to their homes' within months of its establishment. B. Pullan, *Rich and Poor in Renaissance Venice: The Social Institutions of a Catholic State, to 1620* (Oxford: Basil Blackwell, 1971), p. 488; Marin Sanudo, *Diarii*, ed. R. Fulin, F. Stefani, G. Berchet, N. Barozzi, and M. Allegri, 58 vols. (Venice: A Spesi Degli Editori, 1879–1903), vol. 22, cols. 390–2.

3. In late 1516, the Venetian government agreed to allow Jewish doctors to leave the Ghetto at night, so that they could tend to Christian patients outside, push back the closing of the gates, and do away with the night-time boat patrol. B. Ravid, 'The Venetian Government and the Jews', in R. C. Davis and B. Ravid (eds.), *The Jews of Early Modern Venice* (Baltimore and London: Johns Hopkins University Press, 2001), pp. 3–30, here p. 10; Sanudo, *Diarii*, vol. 23, col. 360.

4. For the complaints against Jewish moneylenders, see, for example, Sanudo, *Diarii*, vol. 23, col. 183. On financial demands, see Sanudo, *Diarii*, vol. 23, cols. 186, 329–30, 338, 360.

5. Sanudo, *Diarii*, vol. 24, cols. 50–1, 59, 298–9; Pullan, *Rich and Poor*, p. 488; B. Ravid, 'From Yellow to Red: On the Distinguishing Head-Covering of the Jews of Venice', *Jewish History* 6/1–2 (1992), pp. 179–210, here pp. 184–5.

6. Sanudo, *Diarii*, vol. 27, col. 193; Pullan, *Rich and Poor*, p. 489.

7. On 10 November 1519, Antonio Grimani, a procurator of San Marco and a Savio del Consiglio, supported renewing the *condotta*, and had Bessarion's letters read by way of justification. Sanudo, *Diarii*, vol. 28, cols. 62–3.

8. Sanudo, *Diarii*, vol. 28, col. 63: 'ni il Papa pol concieder i dagino usura'.

9 Sanudo, *Diarii*, vol. 28, col. 63: 'Spagna li cazò di soi reame, capitò a Napoli, e quel re Alfonxo perse il regno. Il ducha di Milan per aver favorido zudei e tenirli, fo cazado dil Stado, e cussi volemo far nui, conzitarsi l'ira di Dio contra'; trans. R. Bonfil, *Jewish Life in Renaissance Italy*, trans. A. Oldcorn (Berkeley, Los Angeles, and London: University of California Press, 1994), p. 40.
10 Sanudo, *Diarii*, vol. 27, col. 359: 'Dio prosperarave a questa Republica, come fe' al re di Portogalo, che, cazadi, trovono el navegar di l'India et l'ha fato Re di l'oro'.
11 Sanudo, *Diarii*, vol. 27, col. 467; Pullan, *Rich and Poor*, p. 489.
12 See, for example, R. C. Mueller, 'The Status and Economic Activity of Jews in the Venetian Dominions during the Fifteenth Century', in M. Toch (ed.), *Wirtschaftsgeschichte der mittelalterlichen Juden: Fragen und Einschätzungen* (Munich: Oldenbourg, 2008), pp. 63–92, here p. 82; B. Pullan, 'Jewish Banks and Monti di Pietà', in Davis and Ravid (eds.), *The Jews of Early Modern Venice*, pp. 53–72, here p. 65.
13 Sanudo, *Diarii*, vol. 27, col. 467.
14 For what follows, see Sanudo, *Diarii*, vol. 28, cols. 61–4. An English translation is given at Bonfil, *Jewish Life in Renaissance Italy*, pp. 39–41.
15 Sanudo, *Diarii*, vol. 28, col. 250.
16 On Tron's career prior to this point, see, in addition to Sanudo, *Diarii*, s.v., Pullan, *Rich and Poor*, pp. 491–2; F. Gilbert, *The Pope, His Banker, and Venice* (Cambridge MA and London: Harvard University Press, 1980), pp. 43, 46–7, 61–2; Pietro Bembo, *History of Venice*, ed. and trans. R. W. Ulery, Jr., 3 vols. (Cambridge MA and London: Harvard University Press, 2007–9), vol. 1, pp. 69–71, vol. 3, pp. 75, 273.
17 Sanudo, *Diarii*, vol. 28, cols. 250–1; Pullan, *Rich and Poor*, p. 492.
18 Twenty-three others abstained. Sanudo, *Diarii*, vol. 28, col. 251.
19 Sanudo, *Diarii*, vol. 28, col. 251: 'Et li rispose sier Andrea Trivixan el cavalier savio dil Consejo. Parlò con colora, ne è da far Monte di Pietà, saria servido per broio e marioli, e non chi havesse bisogno'.
20 G. Parker, *Emperor: A New Life of Charles V* (New Haven: Yale University Press, 2019), ch. 5; Mallett and Shaw, *The Italian Wars*, p. 136.
21 K. M. Setton, *The Papacy and the Levant (1204–1571)*, 4 vols. (Philadelphia: American Philosophical Society, 1976–84), vol. 3, pp. 172–97; A. Mikhail, *God's Shadow: The Ottoman Sultan Who Shaped the Modern World* (London: Faber & Faber, 2020), ch. 23.

22 Sanudo, *Diarii*, vol. 28, cols. 321–2.
23 On 3 March, a proposal to renew the *condotta* for five years was tabled by Antonio Grimaini, Andrea Trevisan, Piero Capello, and Pandolfo Moresini. Three votes were held. Although it never gained a majority, it still emerged as the favoured option of those present. The results were as follows (abstentions were not recorded; Sanudo, *Diarii*, vol. 28, cols. 321–2):

Ballot	For	Against
1	41	41
2	65	84
3	61	82

24 For the following, see Sanudo, *Diarii*, vol. 28, cols. 355–6; Pullan, *Rich and Poor*, pp. 496–8.
25 Sanudo, *Diarii*, vol. 28, col. 363.
26 Sanudo, *Diarii*, vol. 28, col. 481; Pullan, *Rich and Poor*, p. 498.
27 Sanudo, *Diarii*, vol. 28, col. 460.
28 Sanudo, *Diarii*, vol. 31, col. 495.
29 Sanudo, *Diarii*, vol. 31, col. 291.
30 Sanudo, *Diarii*, vol. 33, cols. 176 (Portugal), 315 (concerning attacks in Egypt).
31 Setton, *The Papacy and the Levant*, vol. 3, pp. 198–228.
32 Sanudo, *Diarii*, vol. 33, col. 600; Francesco Guicciardini, *Storia d'Italia*, 15.1; ed. C. Panigada, 5 vols. (Bari, 1929), vol. 4, pp. 172–4; Norwich, *History*, pp. 440–1.
33 Mallett and Shaw, *The Italian Wars*, pp. 140–5.
34 Guicciardini, *Storia d'Italia*, 15.2; ed. Panigada, vol. 4, pp. 175–6; Norwich, *History*, p. 437. On Venice's response to Pope Adrian VI's election, see B. J. Maxson, 'The Failed Regime of Pope Adrian VI', in A. Lee and B. J. Maxson (eds.), *The Culture and Politics of Regime Change in Italy, c.1494–c.1559* (Abingdon: Routledge, 2022), pp. 115–33.
35 Sanudo, *Diarii*, vol. 34, col. 392: 158 for, 15 against, 2 abstentions.
36 Sanudo, *Diarii*, vol. 35, col. 45.
37 This paragraph and the next two closely follow Pullan, *Rich and Poor*, pp. 499–500; Pullan, 'Jewish Banks and Monti di Pietà', p. 61.
38 Pullan, *Rich and Poor*, pp. 235–8; A. Bianconi, *L'Opera delle Compagnie del 'Divino Amore' nella Riforma Cattolica* (Città di Castello: S. Lapi, 1914); P. Paschini, 'Le compagnie del Divino Amore e la beneficenza pubblica nei primi decenni del cinquecento',

in *Tre Ricerche sulla Storia della Chiesa nel Cinquecento* (Rome: Liturgiche, 1945), pp. 11–32; R. Palmer, 'L'assistenza medica nella Venezia cinquecentesca', in B. Aikema and D. Meijers (eds.), *Nel regno dei poveri: Arte e storia dei grandi ospedali veneziani in età moderna, 1474–1797* (Venice: Arsenale, 1989), pp. 35–42; B. Aikema and D. Meijers, 'Gli Incurabili', in Aikema and Meijers (eds.), *Nel regno nei poveri*, pp. 131–48.

39 Pullan, *Rich and Poor*, p. 499; cit. ASV Senato, Terra, r. 1523/24, ff. 7r–v (27 March 1523).

40 Translations from Pullan, *Rich and Poor*, p. 501; ASV Consiglio dei Dieci, Miste, r. 1524, ff. 20v–21 (not seen).

41 Sanudo, *Diarii*, vol. 34, col. 299. In Sanudo's entries about this case, he sometimes refers to the Voivode of Cracow, Krzysztof Szydłowiecki, as the 'Count Palatine of Poland' (*conte Palatin di Polona*). Only later does he use the more accurate form *conte palatin di Cracovia capitanio et gran canzellier dil Regno* (here Sanudo, *Diarii*, vol. 36, col. 571).

42 Sanudo, *Diarii*, vol. 34, col. 339. Later, Sanudo clarifies that Jacob claimed to have purchased the diamond from a certain 'Francesco di Venetia': Sanudo, *Diarii*, vol. 36, col. 598.

43 In c.1518, for example, King Sigismund of Poland had sent Eliezer of Brandenburg to Venice to purchase precious stones for the Queen herself. I. M. Rodov, *The Torah Ark in Renaissance Poland: A Jewish Revival of Classical Antiquity* (Leiden: Brill, 2013), p. 35.

44 q.v. Sanudo, *Diarii*, vol. 36, col. 571.

45 Sanudo, *Diarii*, vol. 21, cols. 114–15; vol. 26, cols. 339–41; Pullan, *Rich and Poor*, p. 483.

46 On Bona Sforza and Bari, see Sanudo, *Diarii*, vol. 35, col. 443; vol. 36, cols. 187, 228, 242, 245, 277, 404; H. Barycz, 'Bona Sforza, regina di Polonia', *DBI* 11 (Rome, 1969), s.v.

47 The delays were in part due to the fact that the ambassador was obliged to leave for Bari to take possession of the town on the Queen's behalf, on 11 February 1524. He did not return until June. In his absence, two further Polish *oratores* stood in for him but seem to have lacked the authority to act on their own initiative. Sanudo, *Diarii*, vol. 35, col. 443; vol. 36, cols. 187, 245, 277, 404.

48 Sanudo, *Diarii*, vol. 36, cols. 599–600.

49 Sanudo, *Diarii*, vol. 36, col. 611; Pullan, *Rich and Poor*, p. 483.

50 Guicciardini, *Storia d'Italia*, 15.10; ed. Panigada, vol. 4, pp. 232–7.

51 Mallett and Shaw, *The Italian Wars*, pp. 150–2.

52 Mallett and Shaw, *The Italian Wars*, p. 153.

53 Setton, *The Papacy and the Levant*, vol. 3, pp. 229–38; R. Finlay,

'Al servizio del Sultano: Venezia, i Turchi e. 1523–1538', in M. Tafuri (ed.), *Renovatio Urbis: Venezia nell'età di Andrea Gritti (1523–1538)* (Rome: Officina edizioni, 1984), pp. 78–118, here p. 105 [rev. English version published as '"I am the servant of the Turkish sultan": Venice, the Ottoman Empire, and Christendom, 1523–1534', in R. Finlay, *Venice Besieged: Politics and Diplomacy in the Italian Wars, 1494–1534* (Aldershot: Routledge, 2008), paper IX, pp. 1–45, here p. 7].

54 Mallett and Shaw, *The Italian Wars*, p. 155.
55 Sanudo, *Diarii*, vol. 41, col. 57.
56 Sanudo, *Diarii*, vol. 41, col. 83.
57 For the following, see Mallett and Shaw, *The Italian Wars*, pp. 156–9.
58 Sanudo, *Diarii*, vol. 44, cols. 285, 299, 303–5.
59 Ravid, 'From Yellow to Red', p. 185.
60 Pullan, *Rich and Poor*, pp. 504–5. This paragraph closely follows Pullan's overview.
61 Mallett and Shaw, *The Italian Wars*, p. 159.
62 For the following, see Guicciardini, *Storia d'Italia*, 18.6; ed. Panigada, vol. 5, pp. 127–8; Mallett and Shaw, *The Italian Wars*, pp. 159–60.
63 Niccolò Machiavelli, *Legazioni e commissarie*, S. Bertelli (ed.), 3 vols. (Milan: Feltrinelli, 1964), vol. 3, p. 1653.
64 Mallett and Shaw, *The Italian Wars*, p. 160; Guicciardini, *Storia d'Italia*, 18.8; ed. Panigada, vol. 5, pp. 135–42. For depictions of the sack in contemporary literature, see K. Gouwens, *Remembering the Renaissance: Humanist Narratives of the Sack of Rome* (Leiden: Brill, 1998).
65 J. Maier, *The Eternal City: A History of Rome in Maps* (Chicago and London: University of Chicago Press, 2020), p. 73.
66 Sanudo, *Diarii*, vol. 45, col. 219: 'Tutta questa città è in tanta tribulatione che veramente vostra magnificentia pò considerar, che per universal dicto, l'inferno è più bella cosa da veder.'
67 Mallett and Shaw, *The Italian Wars*, pp. 162–4.
68 Sanudo, *Diarii*, vol. 45, col. 438: 'presto el stendardo de l'Imperator sarà sopra la piaza di San Marco'.
69 Sanudo, *Diarii*, vol. 45, col. 141: 'La farina è cara . . . Non c'è carne in Becaria etc. Li mestieri non fa nulla, non si fa la fiera, et si èin la guerra'.
70 Sanudo, *Diarii*, vol. 45, col. 352.
71 Sanudo, *Diarii*, vol. 46, cols. 177–8.
72 Sanudo, *Diarii*, vol. 46, col. 153; Pullan, *Rich and Poor*, p. 505.
73 Sanudo, *Diarii*, vol. 46, col. 326: 'per el gran freddo stato sti zorni,

morite alcuni furfanti et galiori sotto el portego de San Marco et de Rialto'.
74 Sanudo, *Diarii*, vol. 46, col. 380: 'ogni sera su la piaza di San Marco et per le strade et in Rialto sta puti cridando: "Pan, et muoro da fame et da fredo"'.
75 Sanudo, *Diarii*, vol. 46, col. 413.
76 Sanudo, *Diarii*, vol. 46, col. 612: 'di visentina et brexana ne veneno assai, ch'è una cosa stupenda'; trans. from Marin Sanudo, *Venice, Città Excelentissima. Selections from the Renaissance Diaries of Marin Sanudo*, ed. L. Sanguineti White and P. H. Labalme, trans. L. L. Carroll (Baltimore: Johns Hopkins University Press, 2008), p. 327.
77 Sanudo, *Diarii*, vol. 47, col. 148; trans. F. C. Lane, *Venice: A Maritime Republic* (Baltimore and London: Johns Hopkins University Press, 1973), p. 332.
78 Sanudo, *Diarii*, vol. 47, cols. 83–4; Lane, *Venice*, p. 332; P. Fortini Brown, *The Venetian Bride: Bloodlines and Blood Feuds in Venice and Its Empire* (Oxford: Oxford University Press, 2021), p. 62.
79 Pullan, *Rich and Poor*, p. 505.
80 Sanudo, *Diarii*, vol. 48, cols. 443, 450; Pullan, *Rich and Poor*, p. 506; cit. ASV Consiglio dei Dieci. Reg. comm. 1528, 86v–87v (not seen).
81 Mallett and Shaw, *The Italian Wars*, pp. 170–3; Guicciardini, *Storia d'Italia*, 19.4–20.1; ed. Panigada, vol. 5, pp. 221–93.
82 Lane, *Venice*, p. 332.
83 This paragraph and the next follow Norwich, *History*, pp. 450–4; Setton, *The Papacy and the Levant*, vol. 3, pp. 394–449.
84 D. S. Chambers, *The Imperial Age of Venice, 1380–1580* (London: Thames and Hudson, 1970), p. 50.
85 Pullan, *Rich and Poor*, p. 508.
86 Sanudo, *Diarii*, vol. 56, cols. 383, 396, 397; vol. 58, p. 521; Pullan, *Rich and Poor*, p. 506; ref. to ASV Reg. Comune 1535/36, ff. 197v–198r; 1537/38, ff. 2v–3r.
87 Sanudo, *Diarii*, vol. 50, col. 67; Ravid, 'From Yellow to Red', p. 185; N. E. Vanzan Marchini, 'Medici ebrei a Venezia nel Cinquecento', in U. Fortis (ed.), *Venezia Ebraica: Atti delle prime giornate di studio sull'ebraismo veneziano (Venezia, 1976–1980)* (Rome: Carucci, 1982), pp. 55–84, here pp. 62–3.
88 See, for example, Sanudo, *Diarii*, vol. 51, cols. 416, 427, 479; vol. 52, cols. 145, 398; vol. 55, cols. 556, 656.
89 Sanudo, *Diarii*, vol. 56, col. 511.
90 Sanudo, *Diarii*, vol. 51, cols. 416, 427; vol. 56, col. 277; Pullan, *Rich and Poor*, p. 507.

91 Sanudo, *Diarii*, vol. 58, col. 521.
92 Sanudo, *Diarii*, vol. 56, col. 33.
93 Sanudo, *Diarii*, vol. 58, cols. 563–9; Pullan, *Rich and Poor*, p. 507.
94 D. Calabi, *Venice and Its Jews: 500 Years Since the Founding of the Ghetto*, trans. L. Rosenberg (Milan: Officina Libraria, 2017), p. 29.
95 E. Concina, 'Parva Jerusalem', in E. Concina, U. Camerino, and D. Calabi, *La Città degli Ebrei. Il Ghetto di Venezia: Architettura e Urbanistica* (Venice: Marsilio, 1991), pp. 9–158, here pp. 42, 43–4; Calabi, *Venice and Its Jews*, pp. 29, 31.
96 Concina, 'Parva Jerusalem', p. 43; Calabi, *Venice and Its Jews*, pp. 29–30.
97 Concina, 'Parva Jerusalem', pp. 44–5; Calabi, *Venice and Its Jews*, p. 30.
98 Concina, 'Parva Jerusalem', p. 43; Calabi, *Venice and Its Jews*, p. 31.
99 The earliest reference we have appears, ironically enough, in a speech given by Gabriele Moro on 18 March 1527 (Sanudo, *Diarii*, vol. 44, col. 305: 'acciò se obvii ad molti inconvenienti de sinagoghe et altri disordini'). Most likely, what he had in mind on this occasion were ad hoc prayer meetings, rather than established sites of worship.
100 Concina, 'Parva Jerusalem', p. 93; Calabi, *Venice and Its Jews*, pp. 70–1; A. Ottolenghi, *Per il IV centenario della Scuola Canton. Notizie storiche sui templi veneziani di rito tedesco e su alcuni templi privati con cenni della vita ebraica nei secoli XVI–XIX* (Venice: Tipografia del Gazzettino Illustrato, 1932); D. Cassuto, 'The Scuola Grande Tedesca in the Venice Ghetto', *Journal of Jewish Art* 3/4 (1977), pp. 40–57; R. Curiel and B. D. Cooperman, *The Ghetto of Venice* (New York: Tauris Parke, 1990), pp. 61, 68. More generally, see D. Cassuto, *Ricerche sulle cinque sinagoghe (scuole) di Venezia: suggerimenti per il loro ripristino* (Jerusalem: Jerusalem publishing house, 1978).
101 O. Margolis, *Aldus Manutius: The Invention of the Publisher* (London: Reaktion Books, 2024), pp. 93–4; M. Davies, *Aldus Manutius: Printer and Publisher of Renaissance Venice* (London: The British Library, 1995), pp. 50–55; M. Lowry, *The World of Aldus Manutius: Business and Scholarship in Renaissance Venice* (Oxford: Basil Blackwell, 1979), pp. 62–3, 142; A. Marx, 'Aldus and the first use of Hebrew type in Venice', *Papers of the Bibliographical Society of America* 13/1 (1919), pp. 64–7.
102 A. Cioni, 'Bomberg, Daniel', *DBI* 11 (1969), s.v.; more generally, see J. Bloch, 'Venetian Printers of Hebrew Books', *Bulletin of the New York Public Library* 36/2 (1932), pp. 71–92; G. Tamani, 'L'attività

tipografica a Venezia fra il 1516 e il 1627', in Fortis (ed.), *Venezia ebraica*, pp. 85–98.
103   R. Zangari, 'Felice da Prato', *DBI* 46 (1996), s.v.
104   M. Marx, 'Gershom (Hieronymus) Soncino's Wanderyears in Italy, 1498–1527: Exemplar Judicae Vitae', *Hebrew Union College Annual* 11 (1936), pp. 427–501, here pp. 441–2, 445–56.
105   D. Stern, 'The Rabbinic Bible in Its Sixteenth-Century Context', in J. R. Hacker and A. Shear (eds.), *The Hebrew Book in Early Modern Italy* (Philadelphia: University of Pennsylvania Press, 2011), pp. 76–108, here p. 81.
106   Bloch, 'Venetian Printers', p. 77.
107   See E. Samuel, 'The Provenance of the Westminster Talmud', *Transactions and Miscellanies (Jewish Historical Society of England)* 27 (1978–80), pp. 148–50.
108   M. J. Heller, *The Sixteenth Century Hebrew Book: An Abridged Thesaurus*, 2 vols. (Leiden: Brill, 2004), vol. 1, p. xvii.
109   For a discussion of Bomberg's decision to prepare a new edition of the Rabbinical Bible, see also Stern, 'The Rabbinic Bible', pp. 86ff.
110   Sanudo, *Diarii*, vol. 40, col. 75; vol. 41, cols. 55, 188.
111   Cioni, 'Bomberg, Daniel'; Bloch, 'Venetian Printers', pp. 78, 79.
112   Heller, *The Sixteenth Century Hebrew Book*, vol. 1, p. xvii.
113   For what follows, see Heller, *The Sixteenth Century Hebrew Book*, vol. 1, pp. xix–xx.
114   An inscription in the Scuola Grande Tedesca, dating from its foundation in 1528, reads that the synagogue was built 'con la protezione del Signore'. Concina, 'Parva Jerusalem', p. 93.

5. Expansion (1541–1553)

1   On the term 'Marrano', see, for example, N. Roth, *Conversos, Inquisition, and the Expulsion of the Jews from Spain*, new ed. (Madison: University of Wisconsin Press, 2002), pp. 3–14. On forced conversion in Portugal, see A. J. Saraiva, *The Marrano Factory: The Portuguese Inquisition and Its New Christians 1536–1765*, trans. and rev. H. P. Salomon and I. S. D. Sassoon (Leiden, Boston, and Cologne: Brill, 2001), pp. 1–18. More generally, see C. Roth, *A History of the Marranos*, 3rd ed. (New York: Meridian Books, 1959).
2   The prevalence of 'crypto-Judaism' among 'New Christians' – that is, Jewish converts to Christianity – has been much debated. For diverse views, see, for example, Saraiva, *The Marrano Factory*; I. S. Révah, 'Les marranes et l'Inquisition portugaise au XVIème siècle',

in *Etudes Portugaises* (Paris: Fundação Calouste Gulbenkian, Centro Cultural Português, 1975), pp. 185–230.

3   Saraiva, *The Marrano Factory*, pp. 19–42. By the early sixteenth century, a belief had emerged in Portugal (and Spain) that 'New Christians' were *inherently* Jewish by blood. For this, see esp. F. Soyer, 'The Anti-Semitic Conspiracy Theory in Sixteenth-Century Spain and Portugal and the Origins of the *Carta de los Judíos de Constantinopla*: New Evidence', *Sefarad* 74 (2014), pp. 369–88. On the Portuguese Inquisition generally, see G. Marcocci and J. P. Paiva, *História da Inquisição portuguesa 1536–1821* (Lisbon: Esfera dos livros, 2013).

4   B. Ravid, 'The Legal Status of the Jews in Venice to 1509', *Proceedings of the American Academy for Jewish Research* 54 (1987), pp. 169–202, here pp. 193–4; cit. ASV Senato, terra, r. 13, ff. 24r–27v (not seen). The text is also published at D. Kaufmann, 'Die Vertreibung der Marranen aus Venedig im Jahre 1550', *Jewish Quarterly Review*, o.s., 13 (1900–1), pp. 520–32, here pp. 525–6. On the possibility that the Marranos' sharp business practices may have informed this decision, see B. Pullan, *Rich and Poor in Renaissance Venice: The Social Institutions of a Catholic State, to 1620* (Oxford: Basil Blackwell, 1971), pp. 513–14.

5   H. Kellenbenz, 'I Mendes, i Rodriguez d'Evora e i Ximenes nei loro rapporti commerciali con Venezia', in G. Cozzi (ed.), *Gli Ebrei e Venezia, secoli XIV–XVIII. Atti del Convegno internazionale organizzato dall'Istituto di storia della società e dello stato veneziano della Fondazione Giorgio Cini. Venezia, Isola di San Giorgio Maggiore 5–10 giugno 1983* (Milan: Edizioni Comunità, 1987), pp. 143–62; B. Pullan, *The Jews of Europe and the Inquisition of Venice, 1550–1670* (Oxford: Basil Blackwell, 1983), p. 171.

6   B. D. Cooperman, 'Venetian Policy Towards Levantine Jews and Its Broader Italian Context', in Cozzi (ed.), *Gli Ebrei e Venezia*, pp. 65–84, here p. 70.

7   R. Gluzman, *Venetian Shipping from the Days of Glory to Decline, 1453–1571* (Leiden: Brill, 2021), p. 329; C. Judde de Larivière, *Naviguer, commercer, gouverner: économie maritime et pouvoirs à Venise (XVe–XVIe siècles)* (Leiden: Brill, 2008), p. 66.

8   B. Arbel, 'Jews in International Trade: The Emergence of the Levantines and Ponentines', in R. C. Davis and B. Ravid (eds.), *The Jews of Early Modern Venice* (Baltimore and London: Johns Hopkins University Press, 2001), pp. 73–96, here p. 81.

9   B. Ravid, 'The Religious, Economic, and Social Background and Context of the Establishment of the Ghetti of Venice', in Cozzi

(ed.), *Gli Ebrei e Venezia*, pp. 211–60, here pp. 222–3, pp. 250–1; cit. ASV Senato Mar, r. 26, ff. 45v–46r [2 June 1541].

10 Pullan, *Rich and Poor*, p. 511; S. Simonsohn, 'Marranos in Ancona under Papal Protection', *Michael* 9 (1985), pp. 234–67, here p. 235; S. Simonsohn, *The Apostolic See and the Jews*, 8 vols. (Toronto: Pontifical Institute of Mediaeval Studies, 1988–91), vol. 3, p. 1924 (doc. 1690); B. Ravid, 'A Tale of Three Cities and their *Raison d'Etat*: Ancona, Venice, Livorno, and the Competition for Jewish Merchants in the Sixteenth Century', *Mediterranean Historical Review* 6/2 (1991), pp. 138–62, here p. 141; B. Ravid, 'Venice, Rome, and the Reversion of New Christians to Judaism: A Study in *Ragione di Stato*', in P. C. Ioly Zorattini (ed.), *L'identità dissimulata: giudaizzanti iberici nell'Europa cristiana dell'età moderna* (Florence: Olschki, 2000), pp. 151–93, here pp. 154–5 [repr. in B. Ravid, *Studies on the Jews of Venice, 1382–1797* (London and New York: Routledge, 2003), ch. V]; B. Ravid, '*Cum Nimis Absurdum* and the Ancona Auto-da-Fé revisited: their impact on Venice and some wider reflections', *Jewish History*, 26/1–2 (2012), pp. 85–100, here p. 94; L. Poliakov, *Jewish Bankers and the Holy See: From the Thirteenth to the Seventeenth Century*, trans. M. Kochan (Abingdon: Routledge, 2012), pp. 176–7; M. Radin, 'A Charter of Privileges of the Jews in Ancona of the Year 1535', *Jewish Quarterly Review* 4/2 (1913), pp. 225–48.

11 Ravid, 'A Tale of Three Cities', pp. 141–2; Cooperman, 'Venetian Policy', pp. 72, 76; A. di Leone Leoni, 'La nation portughesa corteggiata, privilegiata, espulsa e riammessa a Ferrara (1538–1550)', *Italia* 13–14 (2001), pp. 189–248; R. Segre, 'La formazione di una comunità marrana: i portoghesi a Ferrara', in C. Vivanti (ed.), *Storia d'Italia. Annali XI/1: Gli ebrei in Italia* (Turin: Einaudi, 1996), pp. 779–841.

12 Ravid, 'A Tale of Three Cities', p. 144; J. P. Filippini, 'La nazione ebrea di Livorno', in C. Vivanti (ed.), *Storia d'Italia. Annali XI/2: Gli ebrei in Italia* (Turin: Einaudi, 1997), pp. 1047–66.

13 Ravid, 'The Religious, Economic, and Social Background', pp. 211–60, here pp. 222–3; B. Ravid, 'The Establishment of the *Ghetto Vecchio* of Venice, 1541', *Proceedings of the Sixth World Congress of Jewish Studies*, vol. 2 (Jerusalem, 1975), pp. 153–67, here pp. 161–3; D. Calabi, 'Il Ghetto e la città', in E. Concina, U. Camerino, and D. Calabi, *La Città degli Ebrei: Il Ghetto di Venezia: Architettura e Urbanistica* (Venice: Marsilio, 1991), pp. 201–302, here p. 217; R. Calimani, *Storia del Ghetto di Venezia* (Milan: Mondadori, 2001), pp. 53–4; Pullan, *Rich and Poor*, p. 512; Arbel, 'Jews in

International Trade', p. 81. The text of the Senate's decision (ASV Senato Mar, r. 26, ff. 45v–46r [2 June 1541]) is reproduced at Ravid, 'The Religious, Economic, and Social Background', pp. 250–1 and at B. Arbel, *Trading Nations: Jews and Venetians in the Early-Modern Eastern Mediterranean* (Leiden: Brill, 1995), pp. 197–200.

14   D. E. Katz, *The Jewish Ghetto and the Visual Imagination of Early Modern Venice* (New York: Cambridge University Press, 2017), pp. 96–7; Ravid, 'The Religious, Economic, and Social Background', p. 224; Pullan, *Rich and Poor*, p. 512; Arbel, 'Jews in International Trade', p. 82.

15   Katz, *The Jewish Ghetto*, p. 56; B. Ravid, 'Curfew Time in the Ghetto', in E. Kittell and T. Madden (eds.), *Medieval and Renaissance Venice* (Urbana and Chicago: University of Illinois Press, 1999), pp. 237–75, here p. 257 [repr. in Ravid, *Studies*, ch. I]; B. Ravid, 'New Light on the Ghetti of Venice', in D. Carpi et al. (eds.), *Shlomo Simonsohn Jubilee Volume: Studies on the History of the Jews in the Middle Ages and Renaissance Period* (Tel Aviv: Tel Aviv University, 1993), esp. pp. 155–8.

16   Arbel, 'Jews in International Trade', p. 83; Ravid, 'New Light', pp. 152–3.

17   *VDH*, 288 (doc. VI.11).

18   G. H. Williams, *The Radical Reformation*, 3rd ed. (Philadelphia: University of Pennsylvania Press, 1995) pp. 840–1; J. J. Martin, *Venice's Hidden Enemies: Italian Heretics in a Renaissance City* (Berkeley and Los Angeles: University of California Press, 1993), esp. pp. 99–112, 141–6, 173–7.

19   Williams, *The Radical Reformation*, p. 830; cf. Martin, *Venice's Hidden Enemies*, pp. 224, 230.

20   Martin, *Venice's Hidden Enemies*, p. 25.

21   E. Concina, 'Parva Jerusalem', in Concina, Camerino, and Calabi, *La Città degli Ebrei*, pp. 9–158, here p. 65.

22   Pullan, *Rich and Poor*, pp. 514–15; Kellenbenz, 'I Mendes'; Roth, *A History of the Marranos*, pp. 202–3; C. Roth, *The House of Nasi: Doña Gracia* (Philadelphia: Jewish Publication Society of America, 1948), p. 50; M. D. Birnbaum, *The Long Journey of Gracia Mendes* (Budapest: Central European University Press, 2003), p. 40.

23   C. Mutini, 'Della Casa, Giovanni', *DBI* 36 (1988), s.v.; A. Santosuosso, *Vita di Giovanni Della Casa* (Rome: Bulzoni Editore, 1979); A. Santosuosso, 'The Moderate Inquisitor: Giovanni della Casa's Venetian Nunciature, 1544–1549', *Studi veneziani*, n.s. 2 (1978), pp. 119–210; A. Santosuosso, 'Religious

Orthodoxy, Dissent and Suppression in Venice in the 1540s', *Church History* 42/4 (1973), pp. 476–85.

24 E. Michelson, *Catholic Spectacle and Rome's Jews: Early Modern Conversion and Resistance* (Princeton: Princeton University Press, 2022), p. 46.

25 See, for example, C. Black, *The Italian Inquisition* (New Haven: Yale University Press, 2009), pp. 19–26; K. Aron-Beller and C. Black, 'Introduction' in K. Aron-Beller and C. Black (eds.), *The Roman Inquisition: Centre versus Peripheries* (Leiden and Boston: Brill, 2018), pp. 1–29, here p. 2.

26 Martin, *Venice's Hidden Enemies*, p. 53.

27 M. Mallett and C. Shaw, *The Italian Wars, 1494–1559: War, State and Society in Early Modern Europe* (London and New York: Routledge, 2012), pp. 243–6.

28 Martin, *Venice's Hidden Enemies*, p. 53; Pullan, *The Jews of Europe*, p. 79.

29 *VDH*, 229 (doc. V.19.i).

30 Pullan, *The Jews of Europe*, pp. 113, 133–4; Martin, *Venice's Hidden Enemies*, pp. 68–70.

31 Pullan, *The Jews of Europe*, p. 6; Martin, *Venice's Hidden Enemies*, p. 55. A few years later, the Patriarch of Venice also became a regular member.

32 G. Sforza, 'Riflessi della Controriforma nella Repubblica di Venezia', *Archivio Storico Italiano* 93/354 (1935), pp. 189–216, here p. 212: 'Dio mi habbia fatto grandissima gratia, havendomi conceduto d'introdurre in questo Dominio la Inquisitione tacitamente et senza alcun strepito', trans. adapted from Pullan, *The Jews of Europe*, p. 5.

33 P. C. Ioly Zorattini, 'Jews, Crypto-Jews, and the Inquisition', in Davis and Ravid (eds.), *The Jews of Early Modern Venice*, pp. 97–116, here pp. 98–9. The figures given here are for the period 1541–1600. The remainder of this paragraph follows Ioly Zorattini's superb overview. See also Pullan, *The Jews of Europe*, pp. 122–3.

34 Ioly Zorattini, 'Jews, Crypto-Jews, and the Inquisition', p. 100; cit. P. F. Grendler, *The Roman Inquisition and the Venetian Press, 1540–1605* (Princeton: Princeton University Press, 1977), p. 56. What follows is derived from Ioly Zorattini and Grendler.

35 Pullan, *The Jews of Europe*, p. 64; Ioly Zorattini, 'Jews, Crypto-Jews and the Inquisition', p. 101; Calimani, *Storia*, p. 71.

36 Pullan, *The Jews of Europe*, p. 71; Calimani, *Storia*, pp. 72–4.

37 For what follows, see Birnbaum, *The Long Journey*, pp. 36–53; Roth,

       The House of Nasi, pp. 50–114; Kellenbenz, 'I Mendes', pp. 147–8; Pullan, *Rich and Poor*, p. 515.
38 Birnbaum, *The Long Journey*, pp. 46–8.
39 The remainder of this paragraph is based on Pullan, *Rich and Poor*, pp. 518–19.
40 Pullan, *Rich and Poor*, pp. 520–1.
41 J. J. Norwich, *A History of Venice* (London: Penguin, 1983), pp. 459–60.
42 Kaufmann, 'Die Vertreibung', pp. 526–7.
43 B. Pullan, '"A Ship with Two Rudders": "Righetto Marrano" and the Inquisition in Venice', *Historical Journal* 20/1 (1977), pp. 25–58, here p. 39.
44 Pullan, *The Jews of Europe*, pp. 174–5; Arbel, 'Jews in International Trade', p. 86.
45 P. C. Ioly Zorrattini (ed.), *Processi del S. Ufficio di Venezia contro ebrei e giudaizzanti (1548–1560)* (Florence: Olschki, 1980), p. 29. This comment was made by the French ambassador, Jean de Morvillier, on whom, see G. Alonge, 'L'ambassade à Venise de Jean de Morvillier (1547–1550)', *Cahiers de recherches médiévales et humanistes* 38 (2019), pp. 201–15.
46 Pullan, *Rich and Poor*, pp. 515–16.
47 Pullan, '"A Ship with Two Rudders"', p. 42.
48 The following is based on Pullan, *Rich and Poor*, pp. 521–2.

6. The Great Fiction (1553–1589)

1 See esp. P. F. Grendler, 'The Destruction of Hebrew Books in Venice, 1568', *Proceedings of the American Academy for Jewish Research* 45 (1978), pp. 103–30, here p. 106 [repr. as 'La distruzione di libri ebraici a Venezia nel 1568', in U. Fortis (ed.), *Venezia ebraica. Atti delle prime giornate di studio sull'ebraismo veneziano (Venezia, 1976–1980)* (Rome: Carucci, 1982), pp. 99–128, here p. 102]; P. F. Grendler, *The Roman Inquisition and the Venetian Press, 1540–1605* (Princeton: University of Princeton Press, 1977), pp. 92–3.
2 F. Gaeta (ed.), *Nunziature di Venezia*, vol. 6, *2 gennaio 1552–14 luglio 1554* (Rome: Istituto storico italiano per l'età moderna e contemporanea, 1967), p. 277.
3 Grendler, 'The Destruction', p. 107; 'La Distruzione', p. 104; *The Roman Inquisition*, p. 93.
4 G. Alberico, 'Beccadelli, Ludovico', *DBI* 7 (Rome, 1970), s.v.
5 The portrait is now in the Uffizi, Florence.
6 G. Sforza, 'Riflessi della Controriforma nella Repubblica di

Venezia', *Archivio Storico Italiano* 93/354 (1935), pp. 189–216, here pp. 202–3, 209.

7   K. R. Stow, 'The Burning of the Talmud in the Light of Sixteenth Century Catholic Attitudes towards the Talmud', *Bibliothèque d'Humanisme et Renaissance* 34/3 (1972), pp. 435–59.

8   Grendler, 'The Destruction', pp. 106–7.

9   B. Pullan, *Rich and Poor in Renaissance Venice: The Social Institutions of a Catholic State, to 1620* (Oxford: Basil Blackwell, 1971), p. 528; B. Ravid, '*Cum Nimis Absurdum* and the Ancona Auto-da-Fé revisited: their impact on Venice and some wider reflections', *Jewish History* 26/1–2 (2012), pp. 85–100, here pp. 86–7; A. Milano, *Storia degli ebrei in Italia*, 2nd ed. (Turin: Einaudi, 1992), esp. pp. 244–62. The text of the bull is found at *Bullarum, diplomatum et privilegiorum sanctorum Romanorum Pontificum...*, 25 vols. (Turin: Seb. Franco et Henrico Dalmazzo / A. Vecco et sociis, 1857–72), vol. 6, pp. 498–500. An English translation is at K. Stow, *Catholic Thought and Papal Jewish Policy, 1555–1593* (New York: Jewish Theological Seminary of America, 1977), pp. 291–8.

10 A. Toaff, 'Nuova luce sui Marrani di Ancona (1556)', in E. Toaff (ed.), *Studi sull'ebraismo italiano in memoria di Cecil Roth* (Rome: Barulli, 1974), pp. 261–280; M. Saperstein, 'Martyrs, Merchants and Rabbis: Jewish Communal Conflict as Reflected in the Responsa on the Boycott of Ancona', *Jewish Social Studies* (1981), pp. 215–28; R. Segre, 'Nuovi documenti sui marrani d'Ancona (1555–1559)', *Michael* 9 (1985), pp. 130–233; S. Simonsohn, 'Marranos in Ancona under Papal Protection', *Michael* 9 (1985), pp. 234–67; P. C. Ioly Zorattini, 'Ancora sui giudaizzanti portoghesi di Ancona (1556): condanna e riconciliazione', *Zakhor* 5 (2001–2002), pp. 39–51. For a discussion of the number of those killed, see M. Mampieri, *Living under the Evil Pope: The Hebrew Chronicle of Pope Paul IV by Benjamin Nehemiah ben Elnathan from Civitanova Marche (16th cent.)* (Leiden: Brill, 2019), p. 100.

11 S. W. Baron, 'The Council of Trent and Rabbinic Literature', in S. W. Baron, *Ancient and Medieval Jewish History*, ed. L. A. Feldman (New Brunswick: Rutgers University Press, 1972), pp. 353–71, here p. 357; Stow, 'The Burning'.

12 Ravid, '*Cum nimis absurdum*'.

13 Pullan, *Rich and Poor*, p. 523.

14 Pullan, *Rich and Poor*, p. 527.

15 Pullan, *Rich and Poor*, p. 526.

16 Pullan, *Rich and Poor*, p. 527.

17 Pullan, *Rich and Poor*, p. 529.

18 This paragraph closely follows Pullan, *Rich and Poor*, pp. 530–2.
19 Pullan, *Rich and Poor*, p. 533.
20 Pullan, *Rich and Poor*, pp. 531, 533, 535.
21 For the following, see B. Arbel, 'Venice's Maritime Empire in the Early Modern Period', in E. Dursteler (ed.), *A Companion to Venetian History, 1400–1797* (Leiden: Brill, 2013), pp. 125–253, here p. 230; B. Arbel, 'The Economy of Cyprus during the Venetian Period (1473–1571)', in V. Karageorghis and D. Michaelides (eds.), *The Development of the Cypriot Economy from the Prehistoric Period to the Present Day* (Nicosia: Lithographica, 1996), pp. 185–92; J. J. Norwich, *A History of Venice* (London: Penguin, 1983), p. 466.
22 Arbel, 'Venice's Maritime Empire', p. 230.
23 K. M. Setton, *The Papacy and the Levant (1204–1571)*, 4 vols. (Philadelphia: American Philosophical Society, 1976–84), vol. 4, pp. 943–4; Norwich, *History*, p. 466.
24 B. Ravid, 'The First Charter of the Jewish Merchants of Venice, 1589', *AJS Review* 1 (1976), pp. 187–222, here pp. 191–2.
25 On Bragadin's fate, see A. Ventura, 'Bragadin, Marcantonio', *DBI* 12 (1971), s.v.
26 Norwich, *History*, p. 486; D. S. Chambers, *The Imperial Age of Venice, 1380–1580* (London: Thames and Hudson, 1970), pp. 188, 192.
27 'La victoria ... mayor que jamás vio el cielo'; q. at I. A. A. Thompson, 'La Guerra y el Soldado', in A. Feros and J. Gelabert, *España en Tiempos del Quijote* (Madrid: Taurus Historia, 2004), pp. 159–95, here p. 160.
28 Grendler, 'The Destruction', pp. 111–18.
29 B. Ravid, 'The Jews in Cyprus: New Evidence from the Venetian Period', *Jewish Social Studies* 41/1 (1979), pp. 23–40, here p. 28; P. Grunebaum-Ballin, *Joseph Naci, duc de Naxos* (Paris: Mouton, 1968), pp. 133–50; C. Roth, *The House of Nasi: The Duke of Naxos* (Philadelphia: Jewish Publishing Society of America, 1948), pp. 138ff; Pullan, *Rich and Poor*, p. 538.
30 Ravid, 'The Jews in Cyprus', p. 28.
31 B. Pullan, '"A Ship with Two Rudders": "Righetto Marrano" and the Inquisition in Venice', *Historical Journal* 20/1 (1977), pp. 25–58.
32 Pullan, '"A Ship with Two Rudders"', p. 37.
33 Pullan, '"A Ship with Two Rudders"', p. 26.
34 Ravid, 'The First Charter', pp. 191–2.
35 Pullan, *Rich and Poor*, p. 537.
36 B. Pullan, *The Jews of Europe and the Inquisition of Venice, 1550–1670* (Oxford: Basil Blackwell, 1983), pp. 180–1.

37 B. Arbel, 'Jews in International Trade: The Emergence of the Levantines and Ponentines', in R. C. Davis and B. Ravid (eds.), *The Jews of Early Modern Venice* (Baltimore and London: Johns Hopkins University Press, 2001), pp. 73–96, here p. 91; B. Ravid, 'A Tale of Three Cities and their *Raison d'Etat*: Ancona, Venice, Livorno, and the Competition for Jewish Merchants in the Sixteenth Century', *Mediterranean Historical Review* 6/2 (1991), pp. 138–62, here p. 142; A. Anselmi, 'Venezia, Ragusa, Ancona tra Cinque e Seicento', *Atti e memorie della deputazione di storia patria per Le Marche*, ser. 8, 6 (1968–70), pp. 41–87, here p. 68.

38 L. Pezzolo, 'The Venetian Economy', in Dursteler (ed.), *A Companion to Venetian History*, pp. 255–89, here pp. 264–5.

39 F. C. Lane, *Venice: A Maritime Republic* (Baltimore and London: Johns Hopkins University Press, 1973), p. 293.

40 Arbel, 'Jews in International Trade', p. 87.

41 Pullan, *The Jews of Europe*, pp. 182–3; Ravid, 'A Tale of Three Cities', pp. 144–5. More generally, see B. Cooperman, 'Venetian Policy Towards Levantine Jews and Its Broader Italian Context', in G. Cozzi (ed.), *Gli Ebrei e Venezia, secoli XIV–XVIII. Atti del Convegno internazionale organizzato dall'Istituto di storia della società e dello stato veneziano della Fondazione Giorgio Cini. Venezia, Isola di San Giorgio Maggiore 5–10 giugno 1983* (Milan: Edizioni Comunità, 1987), pp. 65–84, here pp. 70–75.

42 Pullan, *Rich and Poor*, pp. 539–40.

43 Ravid, 'A Tale of Three Cities', p. 147.

44 Pullan, *The Jews of Europe*, pp. 183–4.

45 Norwich, *History*, p. 494. For a broader study of the plague, see E. Rodenwaldt, *Pest in Venedig, 1575–1577. Ein Beitrag zur Frage der Infektkette bei den Pestepidemien West-Europas* (Heidelberg: Springer, 1953).

46 *VDH*, p. 118 [doc. III.5(c)].

47 G. Federigo, 'Descrizione della peste del 1575–1576, che desolò Venezia e parecchie città d'Italia pubblicata dallo storico Andrea Morosini, tradotta dal Latino con alcune riflessioni', *Giornale per servire ai progressi della patologia e della materia medica* 5/13 (1836), pp. 3–24, here p. 17: 'Nessuna scoperta era capace di arrestare l'impeto del furibondo morbo'.

48 E. Horowitz, 'Processions, Piety, and Jewish Confraternities', in Davis and Ravid (eds.), *The Jews of Early Modern Venice*, pp. 231–48, here p. 241.

49 *VDH*, p. 119 [doc. III.5(c)].

50 For the wider social effects of the plague, see, for example, P. Preto, *Peste e società a Venezia nel 1576* (Vicenza: N. Pozza, 1978).
51 B. Pullan, 'Wage Earners and the Venetian Economy, 1550–1630', in B. Pullan (ed.), *Crisis and Change in the Venetian Economy in the Sixteenth and Seventeenth Centuries* (London: Routledge, 2006), pp. 146–74, here p. 148 [originally published under the same title in *Economic History Review*, ser. 2, 16/3 (1964), pp. 407–26]; Pullan, *Rich and Poor*, p. 315; Preto, *Peste e società a Venezia, 1576, passim*. For slightly different estimates, see G. M. Weiner, 'The Demographic Effects of the Venetian Plagues of 1575–77 and 1630–31', *Genus* 26/1–2 (1970), pp. 41–57, here p. 42.
52 Norwich, *History*, p. 494.
53 Federigo, 'Descrizione della peste', p. 17: 'l'audacia fu seguita dal timore, la speranza dalla disperazione'.
54 Pullan, 'Wage Earners'.
55 Ravid, 'The First Charter', p. 193; Ravid, 'A Tale of Three Cities', pp. 148–9; B. Ravid, 'Daniel Rodriga and the First Decade of the Jewish Merchants of Venice', in A. Mirsky, A. Grossman, and Y. Kaplan (eds.), *Exile and Diaspora: Studies in the History of the Jewish People Presented to Professor Haim Beinart* (Jerusalem: Ben-Zvi Institute of Yad Izhak Ben-Zvi, 1991), pp. 203–23, here pp. 203–4. In the last of these, Ravid rightly points out that *scala* is 'usually rendered as a port, but [is] perhaps better understood more specifically as a wharf, quay, or area containing everything necessary for international maritime commerce'.
56 On piracy, see A. Tenenti, *Piracy and the Decline of Venice, 1580–1615*, trans. J. and B. Pullan (Berkeley: University of California Press, 1967).
57 Ravid, 'A Tale of Three Cities', p. 149.
58 Ravid, 'The First Charter', pp. 195–6.
59 Ravid, 'A Tale of Three Cities', p. 149.
60 Ravid, 'A Tale of Three Cities', pp. 149–50; Ravid, 'The First Charter', p. 194.
61 Ravid, 'A Tale of Three Cities', pp. 150–3; Ravid, 'The First Charter', pp. 194–7; B. Ravid, *Economics and Toleration in Seventeenth Century Venice: The Background and Context of the* Discorso *of Simone Luzzatto* (Jerusalem: American Academy for Jewish Research, 1978), pp. 41–3.
62 On wool and silk production, see Pezzolo, 'The Venetian Economy', p. 273; E. Demo, 'Industry and Production in the Venetian *Terraferma* (15th–18th Centuries)', in Dursteler (ed.), *A Companion to Venetian History*, pp. 291–318, here p. 304.
63 Pullan, *Rich and Poor*, p. 601; Lane, *Venice*, p. 329. For a

contemporary account of the Pisani–Tiepolo failure, see *VDH* pp. 174–5 (doc. IV.19).

64 Lane, *Venice*, p. 385.
65 Arbel, 'Venice's Maritime Empire', p. 202; G. Rothenberg, 'Venice and the Uskoks of Senj, 1537–1618', *Journal of Modern History* 33/2 (1961), pp. 148–56.
66 Pullan, 'Wage Earners', p. 173 n. 1; Pezzolo, 'The Venetian Economy', p. 279.
67 The text is given at Ravid, 'The First Charter', pp. 214–17. An English translation may be found at *VDH*, pp. 346–9 (doc. VIII.14).
68 The text is given at Ravid, 'The First Charter', pp. 217–19.
69 Trans. from Ravid 'The First Charter', pp. 200–1.
70 Ravid, 'The First Charter', pp. 219: 'Il quinto, et ultimo, è stimato da noi molto utile p indrizzo dlla scale di Spalato, la quale prenderà forma et faciliterà il suo negotio con la corrispondenza di qsta, come speriamo, et pciò le cose dimandate sono stimate da noi degne di esser loro concesse'.
71 The text of the *condotta* is given at Ravid, 'The First Charter', pp. 219–22. For further discussion, see Ravid, 'The First Charter', pp. 203–7; Ravid, 'Daniel Rodriga', pp. 204–5; Ravid, *Economics and Toleration*, pp. 30–2; Arbel, 'Jews in International Trade', p. 88; B. Ravid, 'The Legal Status of the Jewish Merchants of Venice, 1541–1638', *Journal of Economic History* 35/1 (1975), pp. 274–9, here pp. 276–7.
72 Ravid, 'The First Charter', p. 213: 'Daniel Rodriga Console et fratello nostro'.
73 Arbel, 'Jews in International Trade', p. 88; B. Ravid, 'The Venetian Government and the Jews', in Davis and Ravid (eds.), *The Jews of Early Modern Venice*, pp. 3–30, here pp. 18–19.

7. The Golden Age (1589–1630)

1 It is telling that many Italian ghettos and 'cloisters' were founded only in the early seventeenth century. This trend is especially evident in those territories which were absorbed by the Papal States. Ghettos were founded at Mirandola (1602), Padua (1603), Mantua (1612), Rovigo (1615), Ferrara (*post* 1624), Cento (1635), and Lugo (1639). As Marina Caffiero has noted, the duchy of Urbino also saw the rise of three further ghettos after being annexed by the papacy in 1631: 'at Pesaro, with the biggest population, numbering 500 individuals, at Urbino, and Senigallia'. M. Caffiero, *The History of the*

Jews in Early Modern Italy: From the Renaissance to the Restoration, trans. P. M. Rosenberg (Abingdon: Routledge, 2022), ch. 5.4.

2   S. Della Pergola, 'Aspetti e problemi della demografia degli ebrei nell'epoca preindustriale', in G. Cozzi (ed.), *Gli Ebrei e Venezia, secoli XIV–XVIII. Atti del Convegno internazionale organizzato dall'Istituto di storia della società e dello stato veneziano della Fondazione Giorgio Cini. Venezia, Isola di San Giorgio Maggiore 5–10 giugno 1983* (Milan: Edizioni Comunità, 1987), pp. 201–10, here p. 204.

3   F. C. Lane, *Venice: A Maritime Republic* (Baltimore and London: Johns Hopkins University Press, 1973), pp. 400–1; L. Pezzolo, 'The Venetian Economy', in E. Dursteler (ed.), *A Companion to Venetian History, 1400–1797* (Leiden: Brill, 2013), pp. 255–89, here p. 265.

4   W. J. Bouwsma, *Venice and the Defense of Republican Liberty: Renaissance Values in the Age of the Counter Reformation* (Berkeley: University of California Press, 1968), p. 341.

5   Lane, *Venice*, p. 401.

6   Alvise Sanudo was one of the few members of the Cinque Savi alla Mercanzia to oppose the renewal of the charter in 1598. In contrast to his more supportive colleagues, Sanudo argued not only that the alterations requested by Rodriga should be denied, but that 'even the existing privileges should be curtailed'. B. Ravid, *Economics and Toleration in Seventeenth-Century Venice: The Background and Context of the* Discorso *of Simone Luzzatto* (Jerusalem: American Academy for Jewish Research, 1978), pp. 43–4.

7   In 1591, Ferdinando I de' Medici, Grand Duke of Tuscany, issued a charter, ostensibly to merchants of any nationality, but in reality intended to encourage Jews and former Marranos to come to Livorno. This was reissued in 1593 and became known as *La Livorniana*. See, for example, B. Ravid, 'Venice, Rome, and the Reversion of New Christians to Judaism: A Study in *Ragione di Stato*', in P. C. Ioly Zorattini (ed.), *L'identità dissimulata: giudaizzanti iberici nell'europa cristiana dell'età moderna* (Florence: Olschki, 2000), pp. 151–93, here p. 173 [repr. in B. Ravid, *Studies on the Jews of Venice, 1382–1797* (Abingdon: Routledge, 2003), paper V]; S. Reuger, *The Most Tenacious of Minorities: The Jews of Italy* (Boston: Academic Studies Press, 2013), pp. 95–8.

8   B. Ravid, 'Daniel Rodriga and the First Decade of the Jewish Merchants of Venice', in A. Mirsky, A. Grossman, and Y. Kaplan (eds.), *Exile and Diaspora: Studies in the History of the Jewish People Presented to Professor Haim Beinart* (Jerusalem: Ben-Zvi Institute of Yad Izhak Ben-Zvi, 1991), pp. 203–23, here pp. 208–9.

9   Ravid, 'Venice, Rome', p. 176; Ravid, 'Daniel Rodriga', pp. 211–23;

B. Ravid, 'An Introduction to the Charters of the Jewish Merchants of Venice', in E. Horowitz and M. Orfali (eds.), *The Mediterranean and the Jews II: Society, Culture and Economy in Early Modern Times* (Ramat-Gan: Bar Ilan University Press, 2002), pp. 203–46, here p. 212 [repr. in Ravid, *Studies on the Jews of Venice*, paper IV]; B. Ravid, 'The Third Charter of the Jewish Merchants of Venice, 1611: A Case Study in Complex Multifaceted Negotiations', *Jewish Political Studies Review* 6/1–2 (1994), pp. 83–134, here p. 99; B. Pullan, *Rich and Poor in Renaissance Venice: The Social Institutions of a Catholic State, to 1620* (Oxford: Basil Blackwell, 1971), p. 567.

10 Trans. from Ravid, 'Venice, Rome', p. 176.
11 P. C. Ioly Zorattini, 'Jews, Crypto-Jews, and the Inquisition', in R. C. Davis and B. Ravid (eds.), *The Jews of Early Modern Venice* (Baltimore and London: Johns Hopkins University Press, 2001), pp. 97–116, here p. 107; cf. B. Pullan, *The Jews of Europe and the Inquisition of Venice, 1550–1670* (Cambridge: I.B. Tauris, 1983), p. 192.
12 Ravid, 'Venice, Rome', p. 176; cit. P. C. Ioly Zorattini (ed.), *Processi del S. Uffizio di Venezia contro ebrei e giudaizzanti*, 14 vols. (Florence: Olschki, 1980–99), vol. 13, p. 269.
13 See, for example, B. Tezcan, 'The Ottoman Monetary Crisis of 1585 Revisited', *Journal of the Economic and Social History of the Orient* 52/3 (2009), pp. 460–504, here pp. 499–500.
14 Bouwsma, *Venice*, p. 342; S. Pamuk, 'In the Absence of Domestic Currency: Debased European Coinage in the Seventeenth-Century Ottoman Empire', *Journal of Economic History* 57/2 (1997), pp. 345–66. The remainder of this paragraph is based on Bouwsma's masterly summary.
15 Lane, *Venice*, p. 401.
16 Bouwsma, *Venice*, p. 343.
17 On the nature and motivations for patricians' investments in land since the late sixteenth century, see esp. Pezzolo, 'The Venetian Economy', pp. 267–8; L. Pezzolo, 'Sistema di valori e attività economica a Venezia, 1530–1630', in S. Cavaciocchi (ed.), *L'impresa. Industria commercio banca secc. XIII–XVIII* (Florence: Le Monnier, 1991), pp. 981–8; G. M. Varanini, 'Proprietà fondiaria e agricoltura', in A. Tenenti and U. Tucci (eds.), *Storia di Venezia*, vol. 5, *Il Rinascimento. Società ed economia* (Rome: Istituto della Enciclopedia Italiana, 1996), pp. 807–79; R. T. Rapp, 'Real Estate and Rational Investment in Early Modern Venice', *Journal of European Economic History* 8 (1979), pp. 269–90.
18 Bouwsma, *Venice*, pp. 343–4.
19 The following is a radically simplified account of the rivalry between

the Old and the Young. It need hardly be said that their disagreements encompassed far more than Venice's relations with the papacy. Among the other issues over which they clashed were the relative authority of the Senate and the Council of Ten; Venice's stance towards Spain; and the possibility of trading partnerships with emerging rivals, such as England, France, and the Low Countries. For discussion, see, for example, Lane, *Venice*, pp. 393–4.

20 Text in E. Cornet (ed.), *Paolo V e la Repubblica Veneta: Giornale del 22. ottobre 1605–9. giugno 1607* (Vienna: Libreria Tendler, 1859), pp. 265, 268. For discussion, see Bouwsma, *Venice*, pp. 344–6.
21 Bouwsma, *Venice*, p. 347.
22 Bouwsma, *Venice*, pp. 346–7; Cornet (ed.), *Paolo V*, pp. 266–7.
23 Bouwsma, *Venice*, p. 347.
24 Lane, *Venice*, p. 396; G. Donà Dalle Rose, *L'antipapa veneziano: vita del Doge Leonardo Donà (1536–1612)* (Florence: Giunti, 2019), esp. pp. 121–5.
25 The best study of Sarpi remains D. Wootton, *Paolo Sarpi: Between Renaissance and Enlightenment* (Cambridge: Cambridge University Press, 1983).
26 Wootton, *Paolo Sarpi*, pp. 10, 78–117.
27 Lane, *Venice*, pp. 397–8; Bouwsma, *Venice*, pp. 412–15.
28 On the proposal to improve Venice's share of the Levantine trade by granting privileges to Western European merchants, see Ravid, 'The Third Charter', pp. 116–17.
29 Thomas Coryat, *Coryat's Crudities . . .* , 2 vols. (Glasgow: James MacLehose and Sons, 1905), vol. 1, p. 395; B. Pullan, 'Wage Earners and the Venetian Economy, 1550–1630', in B. Pullan (ed.), *Crisis and Change in the Venetian Economy in the Sixteenth and Seventeenth Centuries* (London: Routledge, 2006), pp. 146–74 [originally published under the same title in *Economic History Review*, ser. 2, 16/3 (1964), pp. 407–26].
30 Ravid, 'The Third Charter', pp. 119–21.
31 On the disagreement, see Ravid, 'An Introduction', pp. 213–14; Ravid, 'The Third Charter', pp. 102–21.
32 Ravid, 'The Third Charter', pp. 100–1.
33 Pullan, *Rich and Poor*, pp. 564–8.
34 D. J. Malkiel, 'The Ghetto Republic', in Davis and Ravid (eds.), *The Jews of Early Modern Venice*, pp. 117–42, here p. 121; Pullan, *Rich and Poor*, pp. 560–1; G. Cozzi, 'Società veneziana, società ebraica', in Cozzi (ed.), *Gli Ebrei e Venezia*, pp. 333–74, here pp. 344–5; D. Malkiel, *A Separate Republic: The Mechanics and Dynamics of Venetian Jewish Self-Government, 1607–1624* (Jerusalem: Magnes Press, 1991).

35 Malkiel, 'The Ghetto Republic', *passim*; Malkiel, *A Separate Republic*, *passim*.
36 Ravid, 'The Third Charter', p. 91; D. E. Katz, *The Jewish Ghetto and the Visual Imagination of Early Modern Venice* (New York: Cambridge University Press, 2017), p. 79; cit. ASV Inquisitorato alle Arti, b. 102, f. 'Casa tra li Cattaveri con li Cinqu Savii sopra le case delli Hebrei', December 1604.
37 Katz, *The Jewish Ghetto*, p. 79.
38 Ravid, 'The Third Charter', p. 107.
39 Pullan, *The Jews of Europe*, p. 23.
40 B. Cecchetti, *La republica di Venezia e la corte di Roma nei rapporti della religione*, 2 vols. (Venice: P. Naratovich, 1874), vol. 1, pp. 34–5; Ravid, 'Venice, Rome', p. 185.
41 Cecchetti, *La republica di Venezia*, vol. 1, p. 34: 'Similmente *li delitti commessi da Giudei o altra sorte d'infedeli*, di qual si voglia setta, in parole o in fatti, contra la nostra santa fede, non appartiene all'officio dell'Inquisitione, ma al magistrato secolare, perchè l'ufficio dell'Inquisitione, è contra heretici che non sono se non li battezzati . . .'.
42 Cecchetti, *La republica di Venezia*, vol. 1, p. 34: 'Li marrani non possono esser soggetti all'officio dell'inquisitione, havendo havuto salvocondotto di poter venir et habitar con le loro famiglie . . . nel Ghetto, et . . . *di esercitar li loro riti et cerimonie senza poter esser inpediti*' (emphasis in original).
43 Cecchetti, *La republica di Venezia*, vol. 1, pp. 34–5: 'Et questa facoltà gli è concessa per publico beneficio della christianità, acciò non portino in paese di turchi tante ricchezze et industrie necessarie'.
44 The following is based on Ravid, 'Venice, Rome', pp. 177–83. See also Ioly Zorattini (ed.), *Processi*, vol. 9, pp. 7–12, 37–8; vol. 13, pp. 14–15, 109–30, 355; Pullan, *The Jews of Europe*, p. 193.
45 Bouwsma, *Venice*, pp. 486, 493, 496; S. Feci, 'Gessi, Belingero', *DBI* 53 (Rome, 2000), s.v.
46 This paragraph follows Ravid, 'Venice, Rome', pp. 183–5. See also Pullan, *The Jews of Europe*, p. 53.
47 The text of Sarpi's *consulto* (ASV, Consultore in iure, f. 22, cc. 384r–v) is reproduced at Ioly Zorattini, *Processi*, vol. 13, pp. 317–19.
48 Coryat, *Coryat's Crudities*, vol. 1, p. 370.
49 Della Pergola, 'Aspetti e problemi', p. 204; cf. R. Calimani, *Storia del Ghetto di Venezia* (Milan: Mondadori, 2001), p. 169; A. C. Harris, 'La demografia del ghetto in Italia (1516–1979 circa)', *La Rassegna di Israel*, 3rd ser., 33/1 (1967), pp. 1–16, here pp. 15–16; K. J. Beloch, 'La

popolazione di Venezia di secoli XVI e XVII', *Nuovo Archivio Veneto*, 3/1 (1902), pp. 5–49; Pullan, *The Jews of Europe*, pp. 156, 158.

50   D. Calabi, 'The "City of the Jews"', in Davis and Ravid (eds.), *The Jews of Early Modern Venice*, pp. 31–52, here p. 39.

51   Calabi, 'The "City of the Jews"', p. 34; D. Calabi, 'Il Ghetto e la Città', in E. Concina, U. Camerino, and D. Calabi, *La Città degli Ebrei: Il Ghetto di Venezia: Architettura e Urbanistica* (Venice: Marsilio, 1991), pp. 201–302, here pp. 255–6.

52   Calabi, 'The "City of the Jews"', p. 39; 'Il Ghetto e la Città', pp. 238–9; D. Calabi and M.-P. Gaviano, 'Les quartiers juifs en Italie entre XVe et XVIIe siècle. Quelques hypotheses de travail', *Annales. Histoire, Sciences Sociales* 52/4 (1997), pp. 777–97, here p. 795; cit. ASV Secreta, Materia miste et notabili, b. 131: drawing of Iseppo Paolini, 1609. On some of Paolini's other projects, see, for example, S. Grillo, 'L'équilibre de la lagune de Venise au XVIIe siècle: naissance de l'approche moderne', in S. Ciriacono (ed.), *Eau et Développement dans l'Europe Moderne* (Paris: Éditions de la Maison des sciences de l'homme, 2004), pp. 169–82.

53   Calabi, 'The "City of the Jews"', p. 34.

54   This paragraph closely follows Calabi, 'The "City of the Jews"', pp. 39–40.

55   On Fidela Scaramella's grocery, see Pullan, *Rich and Poor*, p. 552.

56   On carvers and hatters, see Pullan, *Rich and Poor*, p. 552.

57   Coryat, *Coryat's Crudities*, vol. 1, p. 371.

58   E. Concina, 'Parva Jerusalem', in Concina, Camerino, and Calabi, *La Città degli Ebrei*, pp. 9–158, here pp. 113–14.

59   Concina, 'Parva Jerusalem', pp. 124–8; D. Calabi (ed.), *Venezia gli ebrei e l'Europa 1516–2016* (Venice: Marsilio, 2016), p. 78.

60   Coryat, *Coryat's Crudities*, vol. 1, p. 372.

61   Coryat, *Coryat's Crudities*, vol. 1, pp. 372–3.

62   R. Bonfil, 'A Cultural Profile', in Davis and Ravid (eds.), *The Jews of Early Modern Venice*, pp. 169–90, here p. 187.

63   Pullan, *Rich and Poor*, p. 553; D. Harrán, 'Jewish Musical Culture', in Davis and Ravid (eds.), *The Jews of Early Modern Venice*, pp. 211–30, here p. 213.

64   B. Ravid, 'Curfew Time in the Ghetto of Venice', in E. Kittell and R. Madden (eds.), *Medieval and Renaissance Venice* (Urbana and Chicago: University of Illinois Press, 1999), pp. 237–75, here p. 247; Harrán, 'Jewish Musical Culture', p. 213.

65   Malkiel, *A Separate Republic*, p. 231; Harrán, 'Jewish Musical Culture', p. 213.

66 Ioly Zorattini, 'Jews, Crypto-Jews', pp. 109–10; Ioly Zorattini (ed.), *Processi*, vol. 9, pp. 26–8, 127–80.
67 E. Horowitz, 'Processions, Piety, and Jewish Confraternities', in Davis and Ravid (eds.), *The Jews of Early Modern Venice*, pp. 231–47, here pp. 239–40; Pullan, *Rich and Poor*, pp. 562–3.
68 Calabi, 'The "City of the Jews"', p. 40.
69 Coryat, *Coryat's Crudities*, vol. 1, pp. 374–6.
70 During his stay, Coryat was struck by the level of violence he saw elsewhere in Venice, particularly the 'desperate and resolute villaines' known as *bravos*, who prowled around at night 'like hungry Lyons', and who would not hesitate to stab 'any man that is worth the rifling'. He also bitterly condemned the Venetian fondness for street fights, which he described as a 'very barbarous and unchristian' spectacle. Coryat, *Coryat's Crudities*, vol. 1, p. 413.
71 *The Autobiography of a Seventeenth-Century Venetian Rabbi: Leon Modena's Life of Judah*, trans. and ed. M. R. Cohen (Princeton: Princeton University Press, 1988). The best modern study of Modena's life remains H. E. Adelman, 'Success and Failure in the Seventeenth Century Ghetto of Venice: The Life and Thought of Leon Modena, 1571–1648' (unpublished PhD thesis, Brandeis University, 1985).
72 *Autobiography*, p. 81.
73 *Autobiography*, pp. 83, 87; Adelman, 'Success and Failure', pp. 222–4.
74 *Autobiography*, p. 91.
75 *Autobiography*, pp. 93, 96–7, 139, 140, 149, 152, 158, 160, 164, 165.
76 *Autobiography*, pp. 154–5.
77 *Autobiography*, p. 139.
78 *Autobiography*, pp. 76–80.
79 *Autobiography*, p. 92.
80 *Autobiography*, p. 95; Adelman, 'Success and Failure', pp. 251–5.
81 *Autobiography*, p. 95. On Modena's sermons more generally, see J. Weinberg, 'Preaching in the Venetian Ghetto: The Sermons of Leon Modena', in D. B. Ruderman (ed.), *Preachers of the Italian Ghetto* (Berkeley and Los Angeles: University of California Press, 1992), pp. 105–28.
82 Adelman, 'Success and Failure', pp. 265–8; H. E. Adelman, 'Modena: Autobiography and the Man', in *Autobiography*, pp. 19–49, here p. 22.
83 Q. at Adelman, 'Modena', p. 22.
84 On the importance of letter-writing in contemporary Jewish culture, see, for example, R. Bonfil, *Jewish Life in Renaissance Italy*, trans. A. Oldcorn (Berkeley and Los Angeles: University of California Press, 1994), pp. 234–7.

85 *Autobiography*, p. 99.
86 *Autobiography*, p. 103.
87 *Autobiography*, p. 97.
88 Sanhedrin 24b.
89 Adelman, 'Success and Failure', pp. 224–33; *Autobiography*, p. 136. Later, Modena would challenge the Small Council over their decision to forbid games of chance, on pain of excommunication: *Autobiography*, pp. 133–4.
90 *Autobiography*, p. 105.
91 Adelman, 'Success and Failure', pp. 419–23. See also D. Harrán, '"Dum recordaremur Sion": Music in the life and thought of the Venetian Rabbi Leon Modena (1571–1648)', *Association of Jewish Studies Review* 23 (1998), pp. 17–61.
92 Modena described his sermons thus in a letter to Rabbi Samuel Archivolti; the translation is from M. Saperstein (ed.), *Jewish Preaching, 1200–1800: An Anthology* (New Haven and London: Yale University Press, 1989), p. 411.
93 Adelman, 'Success and Failure', pp. 436–8.
94 Adelman, 'Modena', p. 29.
95 Adelman, 'Modena', pp. 25–6.
96 Adelman, 'Modena', p. 29; Adelman, 'Success and Failure', p. 449; C. Roth, 'Leone da Modena and the Christian Hebraists', in G. A. Kohut (ed.), *Jewish Studies in Memory of Israel Abrahams* (New York: Jewish Institute of Religion, 1927), pp. 338–9, 394.
97 Adelman, 'Success and Failure', p. 423.
98 *Autobiography*, pp. 161–2.
99 *Autobiography*, pp. 144–5, 159.
100 *Autobiography*, p. 158. Modena had an especially bad relationship with Diana's second husband, Moses Saltaro Fano. He wrote that Fano so 'embittered' him that their wedding became 'an agony', and later admitted to being 'irked' by Fano: *Autobiography*, pp. 153, 157.
101 *Autobiography*, pp. 75–6. 97, 108–9, 111–15, 150, 156.
102 *Autobiography*, p. 121.
103 For example, *Autobiography*, pp. 113, 115.
104 *Autobiography*, pp. 118–20.
105 *Autobiography*, p. 120.
106 Adelman, 'Success and Failure', p. 850.
107 For example, *Autobiography*, p. 117.
108 For example, *Autobiography*, p. 128.
109 Adelman, 'Success and Failure', p. 208.
110 For a survey of the literary output of Venetian rabbis, see U. Fortis, 'Rabbini e letteratura nell'età dei ghetti (1550–1750): un profilo (tra

	Leon Modena e Moshè Chayyim Luzzatto)', in U. Fortis, *La vita quotidiana nel Ghetto: Storia e società nella rappresentazione letteraria (sec. XII–XX)* (Livorno: Salomone Belforte, 2012), pp. 61–134.
111	*Autobiography*, pp. 122–8.
112	*Autobiography*, pp. 124, 153.
113	D. Harrán, 'Volume Editor's Introduction' in Sarra Copia Sulam, *Jewish Poet and Intellectual in Seventeenth-Century Venice: The Works of Sarra Copia Sulam in Verse and Prose, Along with Writings of Her Contemporaries in Her Praise, Condemnation, or Defence*, ed. and trans. D. Harrán (Chicago and London: University of Chicago Press, 2009), pp. 1–90, here p. 33. On *giudeo-veneziano*, see also U. Fortis, *La parlata degli ebrei di Venezia e le parlate giudeo-italiane* (Florence: Giuntina, 2006).
114	Letter by Angelico Aprosio, in Copia Sulam, *Jewish Poet*, p. 507.
115	For a discussion of Sara's age, see L. L. Westwater, *Sarra Copia Sulam: A Jewish Salonnière and the Press in Counter-Reformation Venice* (Toronto: University of Toronto Press, 2020), p. 191.
116	Westwater, *Sarra Copia Sulam*, pp. 192–4; Copia Sulam, *Jewish Poet*, p. 20.
117	Ansaldo Cebà, *La Reina Esther* (Genoa: Giuseppe Pavoni, 1615). On Cebà, see C. Mutini, 'Cebà, Ansaldo', *DBI* 23 (Rome, 1979), s.v.
118	E. Sarot, 'Ansaldo Cebà and Sara Copia Sullam', *Italica* 31/3 (1954), pp. 138–50, here p. 139.
119	Cebà, Letter 2 (10 June 1618); Copia Sulam, *Jewish Poet*, p. 128.
120	On 'tears', see Copia Sulam, *Jewish Poet*, p. 157.
121	Copia Sulam, *Jewish Poet*, pp. 132, 133, 134, 137, 136, 144, 145, 154, 201, 253–4.
122	Copia Sulam, *Jewish Poet*, pp. 202–3.
123	Copia Sulam, *Jewish Poet*, pp. 125, 129, 141, 143, 144, 146, 161, 166, 199, 205, 218–19, 226–7, 228, 232, 234, 244.
124	Copia Sulam, *Jewish Poet*, p. 157.
125	For a thorough treatment of Copia Sulam's salon, see Westwater, *Sarra Copia Sulam*.
126	On the wider role of salons in Venetian and Italian culture, see L. Panizza and S. Wood (ed.), *A History of Women's Writing in Italy* (Cambridge: Cambridge University Press, 2000), p. 6; M. L. Betri and E. Brambilla (eds.), *Salotti e ruolo femminile in Italia: tra fine Seicento e primo Novecento* (Venice: Marsilio, 2004). For the European dimension, see, for example, C. C. Lougee, *Le Paradis des Femmes: Women, Salons, and Social Stratification in Seventeenth-Century France* (Princeton: Princeton University Press, 1976).
127	Copia Sulam, *Jewish Poet*, p. 397. For more on Sara's musical

interests, see D. Harrán, 'A Tale as Yet Untold: Salamone Rossi in Venice: 1622', *Sixteenth Century Journal* 40/4 (2009) pp. 1091–1107.

128 Baldassare Bonifacio, *Dell'immortalità dell'anima discorso* (Venice: Antonio Pinelli, 1621). A partial translation may be found in Copia Sulam, *Jewish Poet*, pp. 279–310.

129 Sarra Copia Sulam, *Manifesto di Sarra Copia Sulam Hebrea: Nel quale è da lei riprovata, e detestata l'opinione negante l'Immortalità dell'Anima, falsamente attribuitale dal Sig. Baldassare Bonifaccio* (Venice: Antonio Pinelli, 1621). Translation in Copia Sulam, *Jewish Poet*, pp. 311–32.

130 Copia Sullam, 'Manifesto', f. B 1r; Copia Sullam, *Jewish Poet*, p. 317.

131 Copia Sullam, 'Manifesto', f. B 3v; Copia Sullam, *Jewish Poet*, p. 321.

132 Copia Sullam, 'Manifesto', f. C 1r; Copia Sullam, *Jewish Poet*, p. 323.

133 Copia Sullam, 'Manifesto', f. C 2v; Copia Sullam, *Jewish Poet*, p. 325.

134 Copia Sullam, 'Manifesto', f. C 4r; Copia Sullam, *Jewish Poet*, p. 328.

135 Baldassare Bonifacio, *Risposta al Manifesto della signora Sarra Copia* (Venice: Antonio Pinelli, 1621). Translation in Copia Sullam, *Jewish Poet*, pp. 332–43.

136 Westwater, *Sarra Copia Sulam*, pp. 105–25. His last two letters, which demonstrate the suddenness of the break with alarming clarity, can be found at Copia Sullam, *Jewish Poet*, pp. 253–6.

137 'Avisi di Parnaso', Venice, Biblioteca del Museo Correr, Cod. Cicogna 270, f. 10r; trans in Copia Sulam, *Jewish Poet*, pp. 349–498, here p. 363.

138 'Avisi di Parnaso', ff. 11r–v; Copia Sullam, *Jewish Poet*, p. 365.

139 'Avisi di Parnaso', ff. 28r–29r; Copia Sullam, *Jewish Poet*, pp. 385–6.

140 For a discussion of the authorship of this work, see Harrán, 'Volume Editor's Introduction' in Copia Sulam, *Jewish Poet*, pp. 57–61.

141 'Avisi di Parnaso', ff. 15v–16r; Copia Sullam, *Jewish Poet*, pp. 370–2.

142 'Avisi di Parnaso', ff. 69v–76v; Copia Sullam, *Jewish Poet*, pp. 443–50.

143 Westwater, *Sarra Copia Sulam*, pp. 194–5.

8. Bodily Sickness (1630–1663)

1 On the Low Countries, see T. L. Bernfeld and B. Wallet, *Jews in the Netherlands: A Short History* (Amsterdam: Amsterdam University Press, 2023), 12–28; J. Israel, *Diasporas within a Diaspora: Jews,*

Crypto-Jews and the World of Maritime Empires (1540–1740) (Leiden: Brill, 2002), pp. 185–244; M. Bodian, *Hebrews of the Portuguese Nation: Conversos and Community in Early Modern Amsterdam* (Bloomington IN: Indiana University Press, 1997). On France and its pockets of toleration, see E. Benbassa, *The Jews of France: A History from Antiquity to the Present* (Princeton: Princeton University Press, 2001), pp. 41–72. On England, see D. S. Katz, *The Jews in the History of England 1485–1850*, new ed. (Oxford: Oxford University Press, 1996), pp. 15–144.

2 A. Teller and I. Kąkolewski, 'Paradisus Iudeorum? 1569–1648', in B. Kirshenblatt-Gimblett and A. Polonsky (eds.), *Polin: 1000 Year History of Polish Jews* (Warsaw: Museum of the History of the Polish Jews, 2014), pp. 86–125; G. Hundert, 'Poland: Paradisus Judeorum', *Journal of Jewish Studies* 48/2 (1997), pp. 335–48; J. Tazbir, 'Das Judenbild der Polen im 16–18 Jahrhundert', *Acta Poloniae Historica* 50 (1984), pp. 29–56.

3 Simone Luzzatto, *Discorso circa il stato de gl'Hebrei et in particolar dimoranti nell'inclita Città di Venetia* (Venice: Giovanni Calleoni, 1638), f. 16r; crticial text and English translation at Simone Luzzatto, *Discourse on the State of the Jews*, ed. and trans. G. Veltri and A. Lissa (Berlin and Boston: De Gruyter, 2019), pp. 40–1.

4 For biographical treatments of Simone Luzzatto, see B. Ravid, 'The Venetian Context of the *Discourse*', in Luzzatto, *Discourse*, pp. 243–74, here pp. 243–7; G. Veltri, 'Individual Responsibility and Collective Punishment in the Thought of Rabbi Simone Luzzatto', in Luzzatto, *Discourse*, pp. 275–310, here pp. 278–80; G. Veltri, 'Saggio introduttivo', in G. Veltri (ed.), *Simone Luzzatto: Scritti politici e filosofici di un ebreo scettico nella Venezia del seicento* (Milan: Bompiani, 2013), pp. xii–lxxxix, here xx–xxviii.

5 Luzzatto's best-known Hebrew work is *Mish'an Mayim* (*The Support of the Waters*), printed in the volume *Mashbit milchamot* (*The End of the Wars*) (Venice, 1606). This dealt with a dispute over the purity of a ritual bath in Rovigo. See also Veltri (ed.), *Simone Luzzatto: Scritti politici*.

6 Ps. 83:14.

7 J. Henderson, *Florence Under Siege: Surviving Plague in an Early Modern City* (Yale: Yale University Press, 2019), pp. 23–4.

8 S. K. Cohn, Jr., *Cultures of Plague: Medical Thinking at the End of the Renaissance* (Oxford: Oxford University Press, 2010), p. 180; R. J. Palmer, 'The Control of Plague in Venice and Northern Italy,

1348–1600' (unpublished PhD thesis, University of Kent, 1978), pp. 278–9.
9   J. L. Stevens Crawshaw, *Plague Hospitals: Public Health for the City in Early Modern Venice* (Farnham: Ashgate, 2012), pp. 91, 113.
10 Cecilio Fuoli, Venice, Biblioteca del Museo Correr, Cod. Cicogna 1509, f. 17v; q. in Stevens Crawshaw, *Plague Hospitals*, p. 14.
11 For an example of the punishment meted out on those who failed to respect confinement, see C. Boccato, 'Testimonianze ebraiche sulla peste del 1630 a Venezia', *La Rassegna Mensile di Israel*, 3rd ser., 41/9–10 (1975), pp. 458–67, here pp. 462–4, 466–7.
12 S. L. Einbinder, *Writing Plague: Jewish Responses to the Great Italian Plague* (Philadelphia: University of Pennsylvania Press, 2023), pp. 91–2.
13 *The Autobiography of a Seventeenth-Century Venetian Rabbi: Leon Modena's Life of Judah*, trans. and ed. M. R. Cohen (Princeton: Princeton University Press, 1988), p. 135.
14 *Autobiography*, pp. 135–6. Interestingly, recent research has suggested that, in Venice, the plague did indeed have two 'peaks', with a brief pause between them. If this is true, then it would not have been unexpected for a socially isolated area like the Ghetto to have seen a sharper decline in mortality during the 'trough' than elsewhere in the city. G. Lazzari, G. Colavizza, F. Bortoluzzi et al., 'A digital reconstruction of the 1630–1631 large plague outbreak in Venice', *Scientific Reports* 10/17849 (2020).
15 Einbinder, *Writing Plague*, p. 172.
16 A. Hopkins, *Santa Maria della Salute: Architecture and Ceremony in Baroque Venice* (Cambridge: Cambridge University Press, 2000).
17 *Autobiography*, p. 137.
18 D. Beltrami, *Storia della popolazione di Venezia, dalla fine del secolo XVI alla caduta della repubblica* (Padua: Casa Editrice Dott. Antonio Milani, 1954), p. 59; C. Davis, *The Decline of the Venetian Nobility as a Ruling Class* (Baltimore: Johns Hopkins Press, 1962), p. 58; G. M. Weiner, 'The Demographic Effects of the Venetian Plagues of 1575–77 and 1630–31', *Genus* 26/1–2 (1970), pp. 41–57, here p. 42.
19 Davis, *Decline*, p. 161; Weiner, 'The Demographic Effects', p. 49.
20 Beltrami, *Storia della popolazione*, p. 97; Weiner, 'The Demographic Effects', p. 45.
21 D. Calabi, 'The "City of the Jews"', in R. C. Davis and B. Ravid (eds.), *The Jews of Early Modern Venice* (Baltimore and London: Johns Hopkins University Press, 2001), pp. 21–49, here p. 38; cit. A. Contento, 'Il censimento della popolazione sotto la Repubblica

Veneta', *Nuovo archivio veneto* 19/1 (1900), pp. 5–42, 19/2 (1900), pp. 179–240, 20/1 (1900), pp. 5–96, 20/2 (1900), pp. 171–235; G. Luzzatto, 'Sulla condizione economica degli ebrei veneziani nel secolo XVIIIo', *La Rassegna Mensile di Israel*, 3rd ser., 16/6–8 (1950), pp. 161–72; A. C. Harris, 'La demografia del Ghetto in Italia', *La Rassegna Mensile di Israel*, 3rd ser., 33/1 (1967), pp. 1–16, here pp. 15–16.
22 *Autobiography*, p. 135.
23 Einbinder, *Writing Plague*, pp. 139–40.
24 On the 'devastating' effects of the plague in the Arsenale, see R. C. Davis, *Shipbuilders of the Venetian Arsenal: Workers and Workplace in the Preindustrial City* (Baltimore: Johns Hopkins University Press, 1991), pp. 18–19. On the wider economic impact of the plague, see, for example, C. M. Cipolla, 'The Economic Decline of Italy', in B. Pullan (ed.), *Crisis and Change in the Venetian Economy in the Sixteenth and Seventeenth Centuries* (London: Routledge, 2006), pp. 127–45.
25 B. Ravid, 'The Establishment of the Ghetto Nuovissimo of Venice', in H. Beinart (ed.), *Jews in Italy: Studies Dedicated to the Memory of U. Cassuto on the 100th Anniversary of his Birth* (Jerusalem: Magnes Press, 1988), pp. 35–54, here p. 40; cit. *Venezia e la peste, 1348–1797: mostra organizzata dal Comune di Venezia, Assessorato alla cultura e belle arti a Venezia, Palazzo ducale, 1979–1980* (Venice: Marsilio, 1979), pp. 98, 147 [item 156], 370 [doc. 22].
26 The remainder of this paragraph follows Ravid, 'The Establishment', pp. 39–50.
27 D. E. Katz, *The Jewish Ghetto and the Visual Imagination of Early Modern Venice* (New York: Cambridge University Press, 2017), p. 97.
28 Ravid, 'The Establishment', pp. 50–1.
29 L. Pezzolo, 'The Venetian Economy', in E. R. Dursteler (ed.), *A Companion to Venetian History, 1400–1797* (Leiden: Brill, 2013), pp. 255–90, here pp. 277–8; R. T. Rapp, *Industry and Economic Decline in Seventeenth-Century Venice* (Cambridge, MA: Harvard University Press, 1976); D. Sella, 'Crisis and Transformation in Venetian Trade', in Pullan (ed.), *Crisis and Change*, pp. 89–105, here p. 99.
30 F. C. Lane, *Venice: A Maritime Republic* (Baltimore and London: Johns Hopkins University Press, 1973), p. 408.
31 B. Ravid, *Economics and Toleration in Seventeenth-Century Venice: The Background and Context of the* Discorso *of Simone Luzzatto* (Jerusalem: American Academy for Jewish Research, 1978), pp. 37–8; B. Arbel, 'Jews in International Trade: The Emergence of the Levantines and Ponentines', in Davis and Ravid (eds.), *The Jews of Early Modern Venice*, pp. 73–96, here p. 94.

32 Ravid, *Economics and Toleration*, p. 38.
33 For the following, see, A. C. Harris, 'La demografia del Ghetto in Italia', *La Rassegna Mensile di Israel*, 3rd ser., 33/2–3 (1967), pp. 17–32, here p. 17; C. Roth, *History of the Jews in Venice* (New York: Schocken Books, 1975), pp. 106–7 n. 12; R. Calimani, *Storia del Ghetto di Venezia* (Milan: Mondadori, 2001), p. 169; S. Della Pergola, 'Aspetti e problemi della demografia degli ebrei nell'epoca preindustriale', in G. Cozzi (ed.), *Gli Ebrei e Venezia, secoli XIV-XVIII. Atti del Convegno internazionale organizzato dall'Istituto di storia della società e dello stato veneziano della Fondazione Giorgio Cini. Venezia, Isola di San Giorgio Maggiore 5–10 giugno 1983* (Milan: Edizioni di Comunità, 1987), pp. 201–10, esp. pp. 203–4.
34 Calabi, 'The "City of the Jews"', p. 35.
35 D. Calabi, 'Il Ghetto e la città', in E. Concina, U. Camerino, and D. Calabi, *La Città degli Ebrei: Il Ghetto di Venezia: Architettura e Urbanistica* (Venice: Marsilio, 1991), pp. 201–302, here pp. 256, 259.
36 Calabi, 'Il Ghetto e la città', pp. 259–60, p. 262; D. Calabi, *Venice and Its Jews: 500 Years Since the Founding of the Ghetto*, trans. L. Rosenberg (Milan: Officina Libraria, 2017), p. 65.
37 No new work was undertaken on the Scuola Spagnola for at least a decade. E. Concina, 'Parva Jerusalem', in Concina, Camerino, and Calabi, *La Città degli Ebrei*, pp. 9–158, here p. 127.
38 Concina, 'Parva Jerusalem', pp. 105–7; Calabi, *Venice and Its Jews*, p. 74.
39 Concina, 'Parva Jerusalem', pp. 130–1; C. Herselle Krinsky, *Synagogues of Europe: Architecture, History, Meaning* (New York: MIT Press, 1985), pp. 382–3; A. Hopkins, *Baldassare Longhena, 1597–1682* (Milan: Electa, 2006), p. 257.
40 Concina, 'Parva Jerusalem', p. 117.
41 Arbel, 'Jews in International Trade', p. 94.
42 Luzzatto, *Discourse*, p. 76 [cons. 8].
43 C. Boccato, '"L'Amor possente, favola pastorale di Benedetto Luzzatto hebreo da Venetia", composta durante la peste nel 1630', *La Rassegna Mensile di Israel*, 3rd ser., 43/1–2 (1977), pp. 36–47. The best biographical treatments of Zacuto may be found in Mošèh Zacuto, *L'Inferno Allestito*, ed. M. Andreatta (Milan: Bompiani, 2016), pp. 15–25; Moses Zacuto, *Hell Arrayed (Tofteh 'arukh). A Seventeenth-Century Hebrew Poem on the Punishment of the Wicked in the Afterlife*, trans. and introd. M. Andreatta (Toronto: University of Toronto, 2023), introduction.
44 D. Harrán, 'Jewish Musical Culture: Leon Modena', in Davis and

Ravid (eds.), *The Jews of Early Modern Venice*, pp. 211–30, here pp. 228–9.
45 Harrán, 'Jewish Musical Culture', pp. 217, 221–2.
46 I. Adler, 'The Rise of Art Music in the Italian Ghetto', in A. Altmann (ed.), *Jewish Medieval and Renaissance Studies* (Cambridge MA: Harvard University Press, 1967), pp. 321–64, here pp. 349–60; I. Adler, 'Les querelles de Senigallia circa 1642–1652[?]', in *La Pratique musicale savante dans quelques communautés juives en Europe aux XVIIe–XVIIIe siècles*, 2 vols. (Paris: Mouton, 1966), vol. 1, pp. 70–9; D. Harrán, '*Nomina numina*: final thoughts of Rabbi Leon Modena on the essence of sacred music', *Italia* 17 (2006), pp. 7–63. More generally, see D. Harrán, 'Leon Modena on the Legality of Art Music in the Synagogue', in D. Harrán, *Three Early Modern Hebrew Scholars on the Mysteries of Song* (Leiden: Brill, 2014), pp. 131–50.
47 For the following, see D. Malkiel, 'The Tenuous Thread: A Venetian Lawyer's Apology for Jewish Self-Government in the Seventeenth Century', *AJS Review* 12/2 (1987), pp. 223–50; D. Malkiel, *A Separate Republic: The Mechanics and Dynamics of Venetian Jewish Self-Government, 1607–1624* (Jerusalem: Magnes Press, 1991), pp. 37–42; D. J. Malkiel, 'The Ghetto Republic', in Davis and Ravid (eds.), *The Jews of Early Modern Venice*, pp. 117–42, here pp. 117, 122, 138–9, 141–2; H. E. Adelman, 'Success and Failure in the Seventeenth Century Ghetto of Venice: The Life and Thought of Leon Modena, 1571–1648' (unpublished PhD thesis, Brandeis University, 1985), pp. 694–9.
48 Malkiel, 'The Ghetto Republic', pp. 140–1.
49 Adelman, 'Success and Failure', pp. 694–6.
50 The following is based on Malkiel, 'The Tenuous Thread'. On Micanzio, see A. Barzazi, 'Micanzio, Fulgenzio', *DBI* 74 (Rome, 2010), s.v. On the translation of the *Libro grande*, see B. Ravid, '"A Republic Separate from All Other Government": Jewish Autonomy in the Seventeenth Century and the Translation of the *Libro Grande*', in A. A. Greenbaum and A. L. Ivry, *Thought and Action: Essays in Memory of Simon Rawidowicz* (Haifa: Tcherikover, 1983), pp. 53–76 [Hebrew].
51 Malkiel, 'The Tenuous Thread', pp. 227–8.
52 On the allegation that Jews were in league with Barbary corsairs, see Luzzatto, *Discourse*, pp. 118–21 [cons. 12].
53 This paragraph follows *Autobiography*, pp. 143–4 and the excellent historical notes at pp. 249–53. Further details of this case are found in Adelman, 'Success and Failure', pp. 747–9; B. Ravid, 'The Venetian

Context of the *Discourse*', in Luzzatto, *Discourse*, pp. 243–74, here pp. 250–5; G. Miletto, P. Ferruta, and G. Veltri, with C. Boccato, 'Studi storici et documenti inediti dall'Archivio di Stato di Venezia', in G. Veltri (ed.), *Filosofo e Rabbino nella Venezia del Seicento. Studi su Simone Luzzatto con documenti inediti dall'Archivio di Stato di Venezia* (Rome: Aracne Editrice, 2015), pp. 373–479; G. Cozzi, *Giustizia 'contaminata'. Vicende giudiziarie di nobili ed ebrei nella Venezia del Seicento* (Venice: Marsilio, 1996); M. A. Shulvass, 'באיטליה סיפור הצרות שעברו' [Story of the troubles in Italy], *Hebrew Union College Annual* 22 (1949), pp. 1–21.

54 Ravid, 'The Venetian Context', p. 254; Miletto et al., 'Studi storici', pp. 441–2.
55 *Autobiography*, pp. 144, 251; Adelman, 'Success and Failure', p. 749; Ravid, 'The Venetian Context', p. 255.
56 Ravid, 'The Venetian Context', p. 255; Cozzi, *Giustizia 'contaminata'*, p. 119.
57 *Autobiography*, p. 144.
58 *Autobiography*, p. 251.
59 *Autobiography*, pp. 144–5, 251–2; Adelman, 'Success and Failure', p. 750.
60 Trans. from Ravid, 'The Venetian Context', p. 253.
61 I owe this point to Adelman, 'Success and Failure', p. 751. For further discussion of the following, see Ravid, *Economics and Toleration*, pp. 36–7.
62 For the text of the *condotta*, see Ravid, *Economics and Toleration*, pp. 100–5. See also Ravid, 'The Establishment of the Ghetto Nuovissimo', p. 51.
63 Trans. from Ravid, 'The Venetian Context', p. 253.
64 Trans. from Ravid, 'The Venetian Context', p. 253.
65 On the composition of the *Discourse*, see Ravid, *Economics and Toleration*, pp. 13–16; Ravid, 'The Venetian Context', pp. 255–6; G. Veltri, G. Miletto, and G. Bartolucci, 'The Last Will and Testament of Simone Luzzatto (1583?–1663) and the Only Known Manuscript of the *Discorso* (1638). Newly Discovered Manuscripts from the State Archive of Venice and the Marciana Library', *European Journal of Jewish Studies* 5/1 (2011), pp. 125–46.
66 Luzzatto, *Discourse*, pp. 5, 13.
67 Luzzatto, *Discourse*, p. 17 [cons. 1].
68 Luzzatto, *Discourse*, p. 18 [cons. 1, 9r–v].
69 Luzzatto, *Discourse*, pp. 22–6 [cons. 2, 10r–11v].
70 Luzzatto, *Discourse*, pp. 32–44 [cons. 3].
71 Luzzatto, *Discourse*, pp. 46–54 [cons. 4].

72 Luzzatto, *Discourse*, pp. 66–8 [cons. 7, 26r–v].
73 Luzzatto, *Discourse*, p. 80 [cons. 8, 30v]; Ravid, *Economics and Toleration*, p. 86.
74 Ravid, *Economics and Toleration*, p. 87.
75 Luzzatto, *Discourse*, pp. 84–9 [cons. 9].
76 Luzzatto, *Discourse*, p. 57 [cons. 5].
77 Luzzatto, *Discourse*, p. 81 [cons. 8].
78 Luzzatto, *Discourse*, p. 101 [cons. 11].
79 Luzzatto, *Discourse*, pp. 115, 117 [cons. 12].
80 Luzzatto, *Discourse*, pp. 123–33 [cons. 13].
81 Luzzatto, *Discourse*, p. 9 [Pref., 6r].
82 B. Ravid, 'The Venetian Government and the Jews', in Davis and Ravid (eds.), *The Jews of Early Modern Venice*, pp. 3–30, here p. 24.
83 Trans. from Ravid, 'The Venetian Context', p. 253; B. Ravid, '"Contra Judaeos" in Seventeenth-Century Italy: Two Responses to the *Discorso* of Simone Luzzatto by Melchiore Palontrotti and Giulio Morosini', *AJS Review* 7/8 (1982/3), pp. 301–51, here p. 303 [repr. in B. Ravid, *Studies on the Jews of Venice, 1382–1797* (London and New York: Routledge, 2003), no. VIII].
84 On Palontrotti's response to Luzzatto's work, see Ravid, '"Contra Judaeos"', pp. 303–28. For biographical details, see R. Wistreich, 'Palontrotti, Melchiorre', *DBI* 80 (Rome, 2014), s.v.
85 I. E. Barzilay, 'John Toland's Borrowings from Simone Luzzatto: Luzzatto's *Discourse on the Jews of Venice* (1638) the Major Source of Toland's Writing on the *Naturalization of the Jews in Great Britain and Ireland* (1714)', *Jewish Social Studies* 31/2 (1969), pp. 75–81.

9. A Spiritual Crisis (1663–1688)

1 G. Scholem, *Sabbatai Ṣevi: The Mystical Messiah, 1626–1676* (Princeton: Princeton University Press, 1973), p. 331. What follows is structurally derived from A. Lee, 'The Lost Messiah', *History Today* 74/4 (April 2024), pp. 90–3. I am indebted to the editors for permission to reproduce certain elements of this article here.
2 A. Verskin, *Diary of a Black Jewish Messiah: The Sixteenth-Century Journey of David Reubeni through Africa, the Middle East, and Europe* (Stanford: Stanford University Press, 2023), ch. 3.
3 Scholem, *Sabbatai*, p. 189.
4 Scholem, *Sabbatai*, p. 111.

5 Scholem, *Sabbatai*, pp. 112–14.
6 Scholem, *Sabbatai*, p. 123.
7 To my knowledge, there is at present no authoritative survey of the violence inflicted on the Jews of Poland-Lithuania during the Khmelnytsky Revolt. See, however, J. Raba, *Between Remembrance and Denial: The Fate of the Jews in the Wars of the Polish Commonwealth during the Mid-Seventeenth Century as Shown in Contemporary Writings and Historical Research* (Boulder: East European Monographs, 1995). The number of those killed is still debated. Shaul Stampfer of the Hebrew University in Jerusalem has apparently been working on a demographic study of Jews in Eastern Europe, suggesting a lower, but still appalling, total. G. D. Hundert, *Jews in Poland-Lithuania in the Eighteenth Century: A Genealogy of Modernity* (Berkeley and Los Angeles: University of California Press, 2004), p. 15 n. 32.
8 A. Teller, *Rescue the Surviving Souls: The Great Jewish Refugee Crisis of the Seventeenth Century* (Princeton: Princeton University Press, 2020), p. 55; Scholem, *Sabbatai*, pp. 91–2.
9 The exact role of kabbalism in the rise of Sabbateanism has been much debated. Scholem, *Sabbatai*, pp. 22–93; M. Idel, '"One from a Town, Two from a Clan": The Diffusion of the Lurianic Kabbala and Sabbatianism, a Re-Examination', *Jewish History* 7 (1993), pp. 79–104; Y. Dweck, *The Scandal of Kabbalah: Leon Modena, Jewish Mysticism, Early Modern Venice* (Princeton: Princeton University Press, 2011), p. 183.
10 Q. at Scholem, *Sabbatai*, p. 136. Sabbatean tradition records the date as 11 June 1648. D. J. Halperin, *Testimonies to a Fallen Messiah* (London: The Littman Library of Jewish Civilization, 2007), p. 4.
11 Scholem, *Sabbatai*, p. 126.
12 Scholem, *Sabbatai*, p. 136.
13 Scholem, *Sabbatai*, pp. 148–51.
14 Scholem, *Sabbatai*, p. 175.
15 Scholem, *Sabbatai*, pp. 159–60.
16 Scholem, *Sabbatai*, p. 198.
17 What follows is based on Scholem, *Sabbatai*, pp. 192–7.
18 Scholem, *Sabbatai*, p. 201.
19 Scholem, *Sabbatai*, pp. 206–7.
20 Scholem, *Sabbatai*, pp. 213–14.
21 Scholem, *Sabbatai*, p. 220.
22 Scholem, *Sabbatai*, pp. 461–77.
23 Scholem, *Sabbatai*, p. 479.
24 Scholem, *Sabbatai*, pp. 493–4, 482.

25 R. Bonfil, 'A Cultural Profile', in R. C. Davis and B. Ravid (eds.), *The Jews of Early Modern Venice* (Baltimore and London: Johns Hopkins University Press, 2001), pp. 169–90, here p. 187.
26 Scholem, *Sabbatai*, p. 501.
27 Scholem, *Sabbatai*, pp. 507–8.
28 Scholem, *Sabbatai*, pp. 508, 510.
29 Halperin, *Testimonies*, p. 55.
30 Scholem, *Sabbatai*, p. 432.
31 Scholem, *Sabbatai*, pp. 355, 367.
32 Scholem, *Sabbatai*, pp. 448–9.
33 C. A. Frazee, *Catholics and Sultans: The Church and the Ottoman Empire, 1453–1923* (Cambridge: Cambridge University Press, 2006), p. 99.
34 D. Kaufmann, 'Une pièce diplomatique vénitienne sur Sabbataï Cevi', *Revue des études juives* 34/68 (1897), pp. 305–8, here p. 308: 'Mandò pertanto a far essequir l'arresto del falso Messia, che condotto quì in catene havea già preparata la sentenza di morte ad un palo, come auttor seditioso di comotioni, e sussuri popolari, ma il sagace condoto avanti il Visir parlando linguaggio Arabo a perfettione con eloquenza, e virtù non ordinaria, della qual molto si diletta quel Ministro, seppe così ben guadagnar il suo animo, che salvò la vita, condoto in carcere assai commoda, ove tuttavia si trova sotto custodia del Casas Bassi'.
35 Scholem, *Sabbatai*, p. 450.
36 Scholem, *Sabbatai*, p. 459. On the Cretan War, see J. J. Norwich, *A History of Venice* (London: Penguin, 1983), pp. 542–60; F. C. Lane, *Venice: A Maritime Republic* (Baltimore and London: Johns Hopkins University Press, 1973), pp. 409–10.
37 Scholem, *Sabbatai*, pp. 594–5.
38 Scholem, *Sabbatai*, pp. 673–86.
39 Scholem, *Sabbatai*, p. 760.
40 Scholem, *Sabbatai*, p. 762.
41 Scholem, *Sabbatai*, p. 762.
42 Scholem, *Sabbatai*, pp. 740, 764–5.
43 Scholem, *Sabbatai*, pp. 765–7.
44 Scholem, *Sabbatai*, pp. 767, 768.
45 Scholem, *Sabbatai*, pp. 768–9.
46 Scholem, *Sabbatai*, pp. 763, 766.
47 E. Concina, 'Parva Jerusalem', in E. Concina, U. Camerino, and D. Calabi, *La Città degli Ebrei: Il Ghetto di Venezia: Architettura e Urbanistica* (Venice: Marsilio, 1991), pp. 9–158, here p. 135.
48 Concina, 'Parva Jerusalem', p. 135; D. Calabi, *Venice and Its Jews: 500*

Years Since the Founding of the Ghetto, trans. L. Rosenberg (Milan: Officina Libraria, 2017), p. 79.

49 Concina, 'Parva Jerusalem', pp. 136–9.

50 B. Ravid, 'From Yellow to Red: On the Distinguishing Head-Covering of the Jews of Venice', *Jewish History* 6/1–2 (1992), pp. 179–210, here pp. 197–8.

51 Alexandre Toussaint Limojon de Saint Didier, *La Ville et la République de Venise*, 3rd ed. (Amsterdam: Daniel Elsevier, 1680), pp. 161–2: 'In n'y a point d'endroit en Italie où les Juifs soient mieux traitez qu'à Venise . . . chaque maison de Noble en a quelqu'un d'affectionné et de confident . . .'.

52 D. Calabi, 'Il Ghetto e la città', in Concina, Camerino, and Calabi, *La Città degli Ebrei*, pp. 201–302, here p. 213; cit. ASV Senato terra, r. 176, ff. 64r–v (24 March 1668).

53 For an overview of Morosini's life, derived largely from the *Via della fede*, see B. Ravid, '"Contra Judaeos" in Seventeenth-Century Italy: Two Responses to the *Discorso* of Simone Luzzatto by Melchiore Palontrotti and Giulio Morosini', *AJS Review* 7/8 (1982/3), pp. 301–51, here pp. 328–36.

54 See D. Simonsen, 'Giulio Morosinis Mitteilungen über seinen Lehrer Leon da Modena und seine jüdischen Zeitgenossen', in A. Freimann and M. Hildesheimer (eds.), *Festschrift zum siebzigsten Geburtstage A. Berliner's* (Frankfurt: J. Kauffmann, 1903), pp. 337–44.

55 Giulio Morosini, *Via della fede mostrata a'gli Ebrei* (Rome: Sacra Congregazione de Propaganda Fide, 1683).

56 C. Roth, *History of the Jews in Venice* (New York: Schocken Books, 1975), p. 118.

57 Morosini, *Via della fede*, pp. 87, 91, 431, 1398, 1399.

58 Morosini, *Via della fede*, p. 1421.

59 Morosini, *Via della fede*, pp. 1388, 1402.

60 Ravid, '"Contra Judaeos"', p. 349.

61 A. Toaff, *Il vino e la carne. Una comunità ebraica nel Medioevo* (Bologna: Il Mulino, 1989), p. 67.

62 Calabi, 'Il Ghetto e la città', pp. 273–4; Calabi, *Venice and Its Jews*, pp. 92–3; J. Georgelin, *Venise au siècle des lumières* (Paris: École des hautes études en sciences sociales, 1978), p. 945 n. 66.

10. Orphans of the Storm (1688–1714)

1 C. Boccato, 'Il caso di un neonato esposto nel ghetto di Venezia alla fine del '600', *La Rassegna Mensile di Israel*, 3rd ser., 44/3 (1978), pp.

179–202. For discussion, see P. C. Ioly Zorattini, *Battesimi di Fanciulli Ebrei a Venezia nel Settecento* (Udine: Doretti, 1984), pp. 17–18; B. Ravid, 'The Forced Baptism of Jewish Minors in Early-Modern Venice', *Italia* 13–15 (2001), pp. 259–301, here pp. 285–6; R. Calimani, *Storia del Ghetto di Venezia* (Milan: Mondadori, 2001), pp. 244–8; F. Francesconi, 'The Venetian Jewish household as a multireligious community in early modern Italy', in N. Terpstra (ed.), *Global Reformations: Transforming Early Modern Religions, Societies, and Cultures* (Abingdon: Routledge, 2019), pp. 231–48, here p. 242.

2   Boccato, 'Il caso', p. 186: 'Seman Israel, cosa è questo'. 'Seman Israel' literally means 'Hear [or listen], O Israel' and comes from the first words of the Shema, usually recited at morning and evening prayers. Some witnesses – including Jacob Aboaf – claimed that she said 'Seman Israel, un putto' ('Heavens, a child'), but given that she had not yet opened the basket, this seems unlikely.

3   Boccato, 'Il caso', p. 186: 'Descoprite che io ho stomego.'

4   Ravid, 'The Forced Baptism', pp. 262–78.

5   On the role of the House of Catechumens more broadly, see, for example, E. N. Rothman, 'Becoming Venetian: Conversion and Transformation in the Seventeenth-Century Mediterranean', *Mediterranean Historical Review* 21/1 (2006), pp. 39–75. For a particularly striking case, in which a three-year-old boy was snatched from the Fondamenta Sant'Alvise and taken to the House of Catechumens in 1708, see Ioly Zorattini, *Battesimi*, pp. 26–32; Ravid, 'The Forced Baptism', pp. 287–91.

6   More generally, see B. Pullan, *Tolerance, Regulation and Rescue: Dishonoured Women and Abandoned Children in Italy, 1300–1800* (Manchester: Manchester University Press, 2016), pp. 125–39.

7   For the text of the appeal, see Boccato, 'Il caso', pp. 201–2.

8   Boccato, 'Il caso', p. 202: 'Questo fanciullo è di Ghetto . . . Non c'è probabilità che persuada il contrario . . .'.

9   Boccato, 'Il caso', pp. 188–9.

10   Boccato, 'Il caso', pp. 193–4.

11   Boccato, 'Il caso', p. 194.

12   Boccato, 'Il caso', p. 192.

13   Gregorio Bellotto and his wife were identified as Christians by Jacob Ferrarese. The fact that Gregorio describes the Scuola Levantina as 'una Chiesa d'essi hebrei' also strongly suggests that he was not Jewish. Boccato, 'Il caso', pp. 189, 197.

14   Boccato, 'Il caso', p. 195.

15   Boccato, 'Il caso', p. 196.

16 Boccato, 'Il caso', p. 197.
17 Boccato, 'Il caso', p. 197.
18 The servant girl was called Chella Levi. It is possible that she was the same person as Corona Levi. After an investigation by the Jewish community of Mantua, Sansone refused to accept paternità but agreed to pay a certain sum. Francesconi, 'The Venetian Jewish household', p. 242.
19 On the Cretan war, see J. J. Norwich, *A History of Venice* (London: Penguin, 1983), pp. 542–60; F. C. Lane, *Venice: A Maritime Republic* (Baltimore and London: Johns Hopkins University Press, 1973), pp. 409–10; N. D. Mason, 'The War of Candia, 1645–1669' (unpublished PhD thesis, Louisiana State University, 1972); K. M. Setton, *Venice, Austria, and the Turks in the Seventeenth Century* (Philadelphia: American Philosophical Society, 1991), pp. 104–243.
20 Setton, *Venice, Austria*, p. 363.
21 B. Arbel, 'Venice's Maritime Empire in the Early Modern Period', in E. Dursteler (ed.), *A Companion to Venetian History, 1400–1797* (Leiden: Brill, 2013), pp. 125–253, here p. 229.
22 Norwich, *History*, p. 557; M. E. Mallett and J. R. Hale, *The Military Organization of a Renaissance State: Venice, c.1400–1617* (Cambridge: Cambridge University Press, 1984), p. 484.
23 Norwich, *History*, pp. 561–74; Lane, *Venice*, pp. 410–11; Setton, *Venice, Austria*, pp. 271–425.
24 P. Topping, 'Premodern Peloponnesus: The Land and the People under Venetian Rule (1685–1715)', *Annals of the New York Academy of Sciences* 268/1 (1976), pp. 92–108.
25 Lane, *Venice*, pp. 418–20; W. Panciera, 'The Industries of Venice in the Seventeenth and Eighteenth Centuries', in P. Lanaro (ed.), *At the Centre of the Old World: Trade and Manufacturing in Venice and the Venetian Mainland, 1400–1800* (Toronto: University of Toronto Press, 2006), pp. 185–214, esp. pp. 194–6.
26 B. Arbel, 'Jews in International Trade: The Emergence of the Levantines and Ponentines', in R. C. Davis and B. Ravid (eds.), *The Jews of Early Modern Venice* (Baltimore and London: Johns Hopkins University Press, 2001), pp. 73–96, here p. 95; J. Israel, 'The Jews of Venice and their Links with Holland and Dutch Jewry (1600–1713)', in G. Cozzi (ed.), *Gli Ebrei e Venezia, secoli XIV–XVIII. Atti del Convegno internazionale organizzato dall'Istituto di storia della società e dello stato veneziano della Fondazione Giorgio Cini. Venezia, Isola di San Giorgio Maggiore 5–10 giugno 1983* (Milan: Edizioni Comunità, 1987), pp. 95–116, here pp. 99–100, 106.
27 S. Della Pergola, 'Aspetti e problemi della demografia degli ebrei

nell'epoca preindustriale', in Cozzi (ed.), *Gli Ebrei e Venezia*, pp. 201–10, esp. pp. 203–4; A. C. Harris, 'La demografia del Ghetto in Italia', *La Rassegna Mensile di Israel* 33/2–3 (1967), pp. 17–32, here p. 17; C. Roth, *History of the Jews in Venice* (New York: Schocken Books, 1975), pp. 106–7 n. 12; Boccato, 'Il caso', p. 201.

28 G. Luzzatto, 'Sulla condizione economica degli ebrei veneziani nel secolo XVIII', *La Rassenga Mensile di Israel*, 3rd ser., 16/6–8 (1950), pp. 161–72, here p. 162.

29 J. I. Israel, *European Jewry in the Age of Mercantilism, 1550–1750* (Oxford: Clarendon Press, 1985), p. 174.

30 G. Luzzatto, 'Armatori ebrei a Venezia negli ultimi 250 anni della Repubblica', *La Rassegna Mensile di Israel*, 3rd ser., 28/3–4 (1962), pp. 160–8, here p. 163.

31 Luzzatto, 'Sulla condizione', p. 167.

32 L. Pezzolo, 'The Venetian Economy', in Dursteler (ed.), *A Companion to Venetian History*, pp. 255–90, here p. 280.

33 M. Teter, 'Jews in the Polish-Lithuanian Commonwealth: An Embedded Diaspora', in H. R. Diner (ed.), *The Oxford Handbook of the Jewish Diaspora* (Oxford: Oxford University Press, 2021), pp. 230–52, here p. 238; E. Fram, 'Creating a Tale of Martyrdom in Tulczyn, 1648', in E. Carlebach, J. M. Efron, and D. N. Myers (eds.), *Jewish History and Jewish Memory: Essays in Honor of Yosef Hayim Yerushalmi* (Hanover NH: Brandeis University Press, 1998), pp. 89–112, here p. 89.

34 A. Teller, *Rescue the Surviving Souls: The Great Jewish Refugee Crisis of the Seventeenth Century* (Princeton: Princeton University Press, 2020), p. 216. See also M. A. Shulvass, *From East to West: The Westward Migration of Jews from Eastern Europe during the Seventeenth and Eighteenth Centuries* (Detroit: Wayne State University, 1971), pp. 25–51.

35 Teller, *Rescue*, p. 252; P. Rauscher, '"Auf der Schipp": Ursachen und Folgen der Ausweisung der Wiener Juden 1670', *Aschkenas: Zeitschrift für Geschichte und Kultur der Juden* 16/2 (2006), pp. 421–38.

36 For what follows, see A. Teller, *Rescue the Surviving Souls: The Great Jewish Refugee Crisis of the Seventeenth Century* (Princeton: Princeton University Press, 2020), esp. pp. 95–196.

37 Q. at Teller, *Rescue*, p. 95.

38 Calimani, *Storia*, p. 249.

39 Calimani, *Storia*, pp. 250–2.

40 Calimani, *Storia*, p. 250.

41 D. Calabi, 'Il Ghetto e la città', in E. Concina, U. Camerino, and

D. Calabi, *La Città degli Ebrei: Il Ghetto di Venezia: Architettura e Urbanistica* (Venice: Marsilio, 1991), pp. 201–302, here p. 279.
42 E. Horowitz, 'Processions, Piety, and Jewish Confraternities', in Davis and Ravid (eds.), *The Jews of Early Modern Venice*, pp. 231–47, here pp. 246–7.
43 B. Ravid, 'Curfew Time in the Ghetto of Venice', in E. Kittell and R. Madden (eds.), *Medieval and Renaissance Venice* (Urbana and Chicago: University of Illinois Press, 1999), pp. 237–75, here p. 252.
44 Ravid, 'Curfew Time', p. 250.
45 This paragraph follows M. Teter, *Blood Libel: On the Trail of an Antisemitic Myth* (Cambridge MA and London: Harvard University Press, 2020), p. 280; cit. Tranquillo Vita Corcos, *Alla Sagra Consulta Illustriss. e Reverendiss. Monsig. Ghezzi Ponente per l'università degl'hebrei di Roma. Sommario* (Rome: Stamperia della Rev. Camera Apostolica, 1706), doc. 6.

11. The Age of Unreason (1714–1789)

1 K. M. Setton, *Venice, Austria, and the Turks in the Seventeenth Century* (Philadelphia: American Philosophical Society, 1991), pp. 426–61; F. C. Lane, *Venice: A Maritime Republic* (Baltimore and London: Johns Hopkins University Press, 1973), p. 411; J. J. Norwich, *A History of Venice* (London: Penguin, 1983), pp. 575–82.
2 A. A. Viola (ed.), *Compilazione delle leggi . . . in materia d'offici, e banchi del Ghetto*, 6 vols. in 5 (Venice: Pinelli, 1786), vol. 5.2, pp. 302–3; R. Calimani, *Storia del Ghetto di Venezia* (Milan: Mondadori, 2001), pp. 252, 254; A. Milano, 'I "banchi dei poveri" a Venezia', *La Rassegna Mensile di Israel*, 3rd ser., 17/6 (1951), pp. 250–65, here p. 261.
3 B. Ravid, 'An Introduction to the Charters of the Jewish Merchants of Venice', in E. Horowitz and M. Orfali (eds.), *The Mediterranean and the Jews II: Society, Culture and Economy in Early Modern Times* (Ramat-Gan: Bar Ilan University Press, 2002), pp. 203–46, here p. 242 [repr. in Ravid, *Studies on the Jews of Venice*, paper IV].
4 M. Pompermaier, *L'économie du 'mouchoir': crédit et microcrédit à Venise au XVIIIe siècle* (Rome: École française de Rome, 2022), p. 244.
5 W. Panciera, *La Repubblica di Venezia nel Settecento* (Rome: Viella, 2014), p. 41.
6 Viola (ed.), *Compilazione delle leggi*, vol. 5.2, pp. 303–8; G. Giraudo, M. M. Ferraccioli, and A. Pavan (eds.), *Documenti veneziani riguardanti gli Ebrei (secc. XVII–XVIII). Repertori e concordanze*

(Naples: Scriptaweb, 2005), p. lxxvi; B. Ravid, 'The Venetian Government and the Jews', in R. C. Davis and B. Ravid (eds.), *The Jews of Early Modern Venice* (Baltimore and London: Johns Hopkins University Press, 2001), pp. 3–30, here p. 27.

7 Pompermaier, *L'économie*, p. 246.
8 Calimani, *Storia*, p. 256.
9 Giraudo, Ferraccioli, and Pavan (eds.), *Documenti veneziani*, p. lxxvii.
10 Pompermaier, *L'économie*, pp. 246–7; cit. ASV, Inquisitori sopra l'Università degli ebrei, b. 1, f. 12v.
11 Viola (ed.), *Compilazione delle leggi*, vol. 5.2, pp. 316–22.
12 Pompermaier, *L'économie*, p. 245.
13 Calimani, *Storia*, p. 257.
14 On 'residence privileges', see C. Boccato, 'Licenze per altane concesse ad ebrei del Ghetto di Venezia (sec. XVI–XVII–XVIII)', *La Rassegna Mensile di Israel*, 3rd ser., 46/3–4 (1980), pp. 106–16.
15 C. Boccato, 'Processi ad ebrei nell'archivio degli ufficiali al Cattaver a Venezia', *La Rassegna Mensile di Israel*, 3rd ser., 41/3 (1975), pp. 164–80, here pp. 172–3.
16 B. Ravid, 'From Yellow to Red: On the Distinguishing Head-Covering of the Jews of Venice', *Jewish History* 6/1–2 (1992), pp. 179–210, here pp. 194–5; Calimani, *Storia*, pp. 253–4.
17 Boccato, 'Processi', p. 176.
18 C. Roth, *History of the Jews in Venice* (New York: Schocken Books, 1975), p. 338.
19 Pompermaier, *L'économie*, p. 245.
20 On the ambiguities of Enlightenment attitudes towards Jews and Judaism, see esp. A. Sutcliffe, 'Judaism and the Politics of Enlightenment', *American Behavioral Scientist* 49/5 (2006), pp. 702–15; A. Sutcliffe, *Judaism and Enlightenment* (Cambridge: Cambridge University Press, 2003).
21 Montesquieu, *Lettres persanes*, 2 vols. (Amsterdam: Pierre Brunel, 1721), let. LX: 'On commence à se défaire parmi les chrétiens de cet esprit d'intolérance qui les animait . . . On s'est aperçu que le zèle pour les progrès de la religion est différent de l'attachement qu'on doit avoir pour elle; et que, pour l'aimer et l'observer, il n'est pas nécessaire de haïr et de persécuter ceux qui ne l'observent pas'. For discussion, see A. Ages, 'Montesquieu and the Jews', *Romanische Forschungen* 81/1–2 (1969), pp. 214–19, here pp. 218–19.
22 Jean-Baptiste Boyer d'Argens, *Lettres juives, ou correspondance philosophique, historique et critique, entre un Juif Voyager à Paris et ses Correspondans en divers endroits*, 7 vols. (Amsterdam: Paul Gautier, 1736–9).

23 Jean-Jacques Rousseau, *Émile, ou De l'éducation*, 4 vols. (La Haye: Jean Néaulme, 1762), bk. 4: 'Je ne croirai jamais avoir bien entendu les raisons des Juifs, qu'ils n'aient un état libre, des écoles, des universités où ils puissent parler et disputer sans risqué'.

24 Viola (ed.), *Compilazione delle leggi*, vol. 4, p. 384; vol. 5.2, pp. 346, 354–6; Calimani, *Storia*, p. 260.

25 Calimani, *Storia*, p. 259.

26 Viola (ed.), *Compilazione delle leggi*, vol. 5.2, pp. 349–50.

27 On reforms to the banks, see Viola (ed.), *Compilazione delle leggi*, vol. 5.2, pp. 350–2.

28 On Saraval and his mission, see Yaqob Rafael Saraval, *Viaggi in Olanda*, introd. P. C. Ioly Zorattini (Milan: Polifilo, 1988); G. B. De' Rossi, *Dizionario storico degli autori ebrei e delle loro opere*, 2 vols. (Parma: Reale Stamperia, 1802), vol. 2, pp. 121–2; Roth, *History*, pp. 341–4.

29 Milano, 'I "banchi dei poveri"', p. 261; Pompermaier, *L'économie*, p. 247; Roth, *History*, p. 344.

30 Ravid, 'An Introduction', pp. 242–3.

31 Roth, *History*, p. 344.

32 Pompermaier, *L'économie*, p. 247.

33 Milano, 'I "banchi dei poveri"', p. 262; Calimani, *Storia*, p. 262. On the slump in trade, see J. Georgelin, *Venise au siècle des lumières* (Paris: École des hautes études en sciences sociales, 1978), pp. 80–1.

34 See, for example, L. Vardi, *The Physiocrats and the World of the Enlightenment* (Cambridge: Cambridge University Press, 2012); E. Fox-Genovese, *Origins of Physiocracy: Economic Revolution and Social Order in Eighteenth-Century France* (Ithaca NY: Cornell University Press, 1976).

35 Georgelin, *Venise*, pp. 76–85, 1008.

36 Norwich, *History*, pp. 591, 597.

37 Lane, *Venice*, pp. 425–7.

38 Ravid, 'An Introduction', p. 243; Calimani, *Storia*, pp. 275–6.

39 Calimani, *Storia*, p. 276.

40 Georgelin, *Venise*, pp. 304–19.

41 B. Arbel, 'Venice's Maritime Empire in the Early Modern Period', in E. Dursteler (ed.), *A Companion to Venetian History, 1400–1797* (Leiden: Brill, 2013), pp. 125–253, here pp. 231–3; S. Ciriacono, *Olio ed ebrei nella Repubblica veneta del Settecento* (Venice: A spese della Deputazione, 1975), pp. 64, 91–109.

42 S. Ciriacono, 'L'olio a Venezia in età moderna. I consumi alimentari e gli altri usi', in S. Cavaciocchi (ed.), *Alimentazione e Nutrizione*,

sec. *XIII–XVIII* (Florence: Le Monnier, 1997), pp. 301–312, here pp. 308–9.
43   Calimani, *Storia*, pp. 276–7.
44   Q. at D. Calabi, *Venice and Its Jews: 500 Years Since the Founding of the Ghetto*, trans. L. Rosenberg (Milan: Officina Libraria, 2017), p. 102.
45   Ravid, 'An Introduction', p. 243; Calimani, *Storia*, pp. 277–8; G. Luzzatto, 'Sulla condizione economica degli ebrei veneziani nel secolo XVIII', *La Rassenga Mensile di Israel*, 3rd ser., 16/6–8 (1950), pp. 161–72, here pp. 163–4.
46   Calimani, *Storia*, p. 278.
47   Milano, 'I "banchi dei poveri"', p. 263.
48   Luzzatto, 'Sulla condizione', p. 165.
49   Luzzatto, 'Sulla condizione', pp. 164–5.
50   Calabi, *Venice and Its Jews*, p. 102; D. Calabi, 'Il Ghetto e la città', in E. Concina, U. Camerino, and D. Calabi, *La Città degli Ebrei: Il Ghetto di Venezia: Architettura e Urbanistica* (Venice: Marsilio, 1991), pp. 201–302, here p. 283.
51   See M. Massaro, 'I Treves dei Bonfili tra collezionismo, imprenditoria e cosmopolitismo', in D. Calabi and M. Massaro (eds.), *Gli Ebrei, Venezia e l'Europa tra Otto e Novecento* (Venice: Istituto Veneto di Scienze, Lettere ed Arti, 2018), pp. 89–104, esp. pp. 91–6.
52   Massaro, 'I Treves', p. 96. On the *ius casaca' more Hebreorum*, used to 'acquire' a property in this way, see C. Boccato, 'L'Istituzione del Ghetto veneziano. Il diritto di locazione perpetua o "Jus Gazagà" ed i banchi di pegno', *Giornale economico della Camera di commercio, industria, artigianato e agricoltura di Venezia* 26/3 (1971), pp. 336–43.
53   This paragraph follows the excellent survey at Calabi, 'Il Ghetto e la città', p. 277.
54   Calabi, 'Il Ghetto e la città', p. 279.

12. The Burning of the Gates (1789–1797)

1   D. Raines, 'Manin, Lodovico Giovanni', *DBI* 69 (Rome, 2007), s.v.
2   J. J. Norwich, *A History of Venice* (London: Penguin, 1983), p. 611.
3   Norwich, *History*, pp. 611–12.
4   Norwich, *History*, p. 615.
5   S. Woolf, *A History of Italy 1700–1860: The Social Constraints of Political Change* (London and New York: Routledge, 1979), pp. 158–9.
6   E. Benbassa, *The Jews of France: A History from Antiquity to the*

Present (Princeton: Princeton University Press, 2001), p. 81; S. Schama, *Citizens: A Chronicle of the French Revolution* (London: Penguin, 1989), pp. 266, 386.

7   Benbassa, *Jews*, p. 82; Z. Szajkowski, *Jews and the French Revolutions of 1789, 1830 and 1848* (New York: Ktav Publishing House, 1970), esp. pp. 616–17; R. Schechter, *Obstinate Hebrews: Representations of Jews in France, 1715–1815* (Berkeley: University of California Press, 2003), pp. 150–93.
8   Benbassa, *Jews*, pp. 82–3.
9   Benbassa, *Jews*, pp. 852–8.
10 Szajkowski, *Jews and the French Revolutions*, p. 409.
11 C. Musatti, 'Il Maestro Moisè Soave', *Archivio Veneto* 37/2 (1889), pp. 381–418, here p. 400n; S. Romanin, *Storia documentata di Venezia*, 10 vols. (Venice: Giusto Fuga, 1853–61), vol. 9, p. 388.
12 The following paragraphs are based on Norwich, *History*, pp. 616–33.
13 On the 'Veronese Easter', see, for example, F. M. Agnoli, *Le Pasque veronesi: quando Verona insorse contro Napoleone* (Rimini: Il cerchio, 1998).
14 A. Ottolenghi, 'Il Governo democratico di Venezia e l'abolizione del Ghetto', *La Rassegna Mensile di Israel*, 2nd ser., 5/2 (1930), pp. 88–104, here p. 88.
15 Q. at Benbassa, *The Jews of France*, p. 81.
16 J. Georgelin, *Venise au siècle des lumières* (Paris: Mouton, 1978), pp. 329–30 ; M. Pompermaier, *L'économie du 'mouchoir': crédit et microcrédit à Venise au XVIIIe siècle* (Rome: École française de Rome, 2022), p. 258.
17 Georgelin, *Venise*, pp. 330ff.
18 Ottolenghi, 'Il Governo', p. 94.
19 Ottolenghi, 'Il Governo', p. 93.
20 Ottolenghi, 'Il Governo', p. 95.
21 Ottolenghi, 'Il Governo', pp. 96–7.
22 Ottolenghi, 'Il Governo', p. 97: 'Le porte del Ghetto dovranno prontamente esser levate, onde non apparisca una separazione tra essi e li altri Cittadini di questa Città'.
23 Ottolenghi, 'Il Governo', pp. 97–9.
24 Except where stated, the following paragraphs are based on: (a) the account given in 'Feste del Ghetto per la sua Liberazione dalla Schiavitù Politica in cui lo tenne l'Aristocrazia', *Gazzetta urbana veneta* (12 July 1797), pp. 440–1; (b) Ferrari's own account, written two days after the events described and contained in *Raccolta di rapporti, decreti, processi verbali, e discorsi concernenti li cittadini ebrei di Venezia dopo la loro felice rigenerazione* (Venice: s.n., 1797), pp. 16–25. Much of

the Italian text is also reproduced in R. Calimani, *Storia del Ghetto di Venezia* (Milan: Mondadori, 2001), pp. 295–7. All translations from this source are my own; but for an accessible English rendering of Vivante's speech by Benjamin Ravid, see P.-M. Flohr and J. Reinharz (eds.), *The Jew in the Modern World: A Documentary History*, 3rd ed. (Oxford: Oxford University Press, 2011), pp. 146–7.

25 Ferrari: 'Non è esprimibile la soddisfazione, e il contento di tutto l'accorso Popolo, quale con lieti evviva di Libertà non si saziava di strascinare per terra quelle Chiavi, benedicendo l'ora, e il punto della Rigenerazione'.

26 Ferrari: 'Nel momento, che si atterravano le Porte si intrecciarono giojose Danze democratiche da Persone d'ambi i Sessi, senza alcuna distinzione nel mezzo della Piazza che restò coperta dalla Guardia Nazionale, ed è rimarcarsi che ballarono anche i Rabbini vestiti alla Mosaica, ciò che produsse una maggiore energia nei Cittadini Ebrei'.

27 On Raffael Vivante and his family background, see C. Vivante, *La memoria dei padri. Cronaca, storia e preistoria di una famiglia ebraica tra Corfù e Venezia* (Florence: Giuntina, 2009), pp. 104–6.

28 Raffael Vivante, *Discorso del Cittadino Raffael Vivante tenuto a' suoi connazionali il dì 22. Messidor Anno I. della Libertà Italiana* (Venice: Giovanni Zatta, 1797), pp. 3–4: 'Fratelli. È giunto finalmente quel giorno felice in cui atterrato il pregiudizio e la superstizione, e furono vendicate le ingiurie ed offese che abbiamo tanto ingiustamente sofferte . . . Quell'immenso intervallo che ci separava dalle altre nazioni è tolto interamente ed ecco anche qui rovesciate quelle Porte formidabili che tenevano la nostra Nazione quasi in un carcere rinchiusa e che erano rinforzate da mille e mille spranghe di ferro inventate dalla più odiosa prepotenza. Sì, miei fratelli, quegli uomini stessi che dapprima ci vedeano con indifferenza avviliti ed oppressi, ci somministrano ora i mezzi di risorgere, di illuminarci e di migliorarci, essi c'invitano ad amarli e a non considerarli più sotto il ributtante aspetto di nostri persecutori'. The text of Vivante's speech can also be found in Ottolenghi, 'Il Governo', pp. 102–3. For a recent discussion of speeches like Vivante's in the wider context of Jewish emancipation during the French campaign, see D. Mano, 'L'émancipation, l'événement et ses émotions: orateurs et patriotes juifs sous l'arbre de la liberté (Italie, 1796–1799)', *Annales historiques de la Révolution française* 415 (2024), pp. 147–70, esp. pp. 156–8.

29 Ottolenghi, 'Il Governo', p. 101.

13. The Price of Freedom (1797–1835)

1. C. Roth, *History of the Jews in Venice* (New York: Schocken Books, 1975), p. 359; R. Carnesecchi, 'Cerimonie, feste e canti: lo spettacolo della "democrazia veneziana", dal maggio del 1797 al gennaio del 1798', *Studi Veneziani* 24 (1992), pp. 213–318.
2. *Discorso che venne pronunziato nel momento che s'innalzò in Venezia l'Albero della Libertà della Città del Cittadino Dandolo . . . 2 Giugno 1797* (Venice: Giovanni Zatta, 1797); q. at M. Plant, *Venice: Fragile City, 1797–1997* (New Haven and London: Yale University Press, 2002), p. 27. On Dandolo, see P. Preto, 'Un "uomo nuovo" dell'età napoleonica: Vincenzo Dandolo politico e imprenditore agricolo', *Rivista storica italiana* 94 (1982), pp. 44–97, esp. pp. 46–8; P. Preto, 'Dandolo, Vincenzo', *DBI* 32 (Rome, 1986), s.v.
3. For discussion in context, see S. Woolf, *A History of Italy 1700–1860: The Social Constraints of Political Change* (London and New York: Routledge, 1979), pp. 175–6.
4. G. Luzzatto, 'Sulla condizione economica degli ebrei veneziani nel secolo XVIII', *La Rassegna Mensile di Israel*, 3rd ser., 16/6–8 (1950), pp. 161–72, here p. 170. I have been unable to verify Luzzatto's figures. The details given in the relevant decree – 'Tansa sopra il commercio, e navigazione, approvata della Municipalità provvisoria veneziana li 15 giugno 1797. V. S.' (21 July 1797) – apparently referenced in the only footnote in this section of his article do not correspond to what he describes: *Raccolta di tutte le carte pubbliche, stampate ed esposte ne'luoghi più frequentati della città di Venezia*, 10 vols. (Venice: Francesco Andreola, 1797), vol. 4, pp. 3–76. In this decree, Lazzaro Jacob Vita Vivante and his nephew are assessed at 35,000 ducats and Iseppo q. Emanuel Treves and the heirs of the Bonfil family at 45,000 ducats. Neither the Bonfil nor the Curiel are listed. It seems likely that Luzzatto's information comes from documents in the ASV, but it has not been possible to locate them. I therefore record Luzzatto's details in good faith, but with a note of caution.
5. M. Berengo, 'Gli ebrei veneziani alla fine del Settecento', *Italia Judaica: Gli ebrei in Italia dalla segregazione alla prima emancipazione. Atti del III Convegno Internazionale – Tel Aviv 15–20 giugno 1986* (Rome: Ministero per i Beni culturali e ambien tali Uffici o centrale per i beni archivistici, 1989), pp. 9–30, here p. 10.
6. Luzzatto, 'Sulla condizione', pp. 170–1; Berengo, 'Gli ebrei veneziani', pp. 10–12.
7. A. Alberti and R. Cessi (eds.), *Verbali delle sedute della Municipalità*

provvisoria di Venezia . . ., 14 vols. (Bologna: Zanichelli, 1928–42), vol. 3, p. 63.
8   Carlo Gozzi, *Useless Memoirs of Carlo Gozzi*, trans. J. A. Symonds (London: Oxford University Press, 1962), p. 284; q. at Plant, *Venice*, p. 39.
9   Preto, 'Dandolo, Vincenzo'.
10 H. Forbes Brown, *Venice: An Historical Sketch of the Republic* (London: Rivington, Percival, 1893), p. 254.
11 Berengo, 'Gli ebrei veneziani', pp. 14–15.
12 W. O. McCagg, *A History of Habsburg Jews, 1670–1918* (Bloomington IN: Indiana University Press, 1989), pp. 47–64; R. Judd, 'Central and Western Europe', in M. B. Hart and T. Michels (ed.), *The Cambridge History of Judaism*, vol. 8, *The Modern World, 1815–2000* (Cambridge: Cambridge University Press, 2017), pp. 11–42, here p. 16.
13 M. Pompermaier, *L'économie du 'mouchoir': crédit et microcrédit à Venise au XVIIIe siècle* (Rome: École française de Rome, 2022), p. 274; Berengo, 'Gli ebrei veneziani', pp. 18–19; *Raccolta di tutte le carte pubbliche*, vol. 1, pp. 166–7; vol. 2, pp. 136–41; vol. 5, p. 68.
14 Pompermaier, *L'économie*, p. 277.
15 *Raccolta di tutte le carte pubbliche*, vol. 2, pp. 136–9; M. Piazza, *Considerazioni del cittadino municipalista Marco Piazza intorno all'erezione d'un Monte di Pietà in Venezia* (Venice: Giustino Pasquali & Mario, 1797); Pompermaier, *L'économie*, p. 288.
16 On Thugut and his attitude towards Venice, see K. A. Roider, *Baron Thugut and Austria's Response to the French Revolution* (Princeton: Princeton University Press, 1987), pp. 231–91, esp. pp. 248, 278.
17 D. Laven, *Venice and the Venetia under the Habsburgs: 1815–1835* (Oxford: Oxford University Press, 2002), pp. 41–2.
18 *Editti regi imperiali pubblicati in Venezia dall'arrivo delle truppe di Sua Maestà I. R. A. Francesco II nel Veneto Stato, sino alla cessazione del Governo militare*, 8 vols. (Venice: Pinelli, 1798–1806), vol. 4, doc. 41.
19 Berengo, 'Gli ebrei veneziani', p. 22.
20 Berengo, 'Gli ebrei veneziani', p. 15.
21 Berengo, 'Gli ebrei veneziani', p. 15.
22 Berengo, 'Gli ebrei veneziani', p. 16.
23 This paragraph follows Berengo, 'Gli ebrei veneziani', pp. 19–21.
24 F. Boyer, 'Les débuts du régime Napoléonien à Venise, d'après les lettres inédites d'Eugène de Beauharnais (1806)', *Rassegna storica del Risorgimento* 44 (1957), pp. 636–43; A. de Fournoux, *Napoléon et Venise 1796–1814* (Paris: Éditions de Fallois, 2002), ch. 13; Plant, *Venice*, pp. 48–50.

25 Plant, *Venice*, p. 48.
26 Pompermaier, *L'économie*, p. 278; P. Bembo, *Delle istituzioni di beneficienza nella città e provincia di Venezia* (Venice: Naratovich, 1859), pp. 140–1, 169–70. This paragraph and the next closely follow Pompermaier's excellent survey.
27 Roth, *History*, p. 362; Plant, *Venice*, pp. 56–7.
28 M. Massaro, 'Napoleone: l'apertura dei cancelli e l'assimilazione', in D. Calabi (ed.), *Venezia, gli Ebrei e l'Europa, 1516–2016* (Venice: Marsilio, 2016), pp. 114–29, here p. 119.
29 G. Carletto, *Il ghetto veneziano nel Settecento attraverso i catastici* (Rome: Carucci, 1981); D. Calabi, 'Il Ghetto e la città', in E. Concina, U. Camerino, and D. Calabi, *La Città degli Ebrei: Il Ghetto di Venezia: Architettura e Urbanistica* (Venice: Marsilio, 1991), pp. 201–302, here pp. 276–84; D. Calabi, *Venice and Its Jews: 500 Years Since the Founding of the Ghetto*, trans. L. Rosenberg (Milan: Officina Libraria, 2017), pp. 104–5, 108–9; A. Ferrighi, 'The story of the Venetian Ghetto in the nineteenth century. A virtual heritage digitally revealed', in A. Gago da Câmara, C. Bottaini et al. (eds.), *Cities in the Digital Age: Exploring Past, Present and Future* (Porto: CITCEM, 2018), pp. 83–98, here p. 91.
30 Plant, *Venice*, p. 49.
31 Germaine de Staël, *Corinne ou l'Italie* (Paris: H. Nicolle, 1807), bk. 15, ch. 7: 'Un sentiment de tristesse s'empare de l'imagination en entrant dans Venise'.
32 M. Berengo, 'Gli ebrei dell'Italia absburgica nell'età della restaurazione', *Italia* 6/1–2 (1987), pp. 62–103, here p. 65; Calabi, *Venice and Its Jews*, pp. 107, 118.
33 Calabi, *Venice and Its Jews*, pp. 119–21; D. Calabi, 'Gli ebrei veneziani dopo l'apertura delle porte del ghetto: le dinamiche insediative', in G. Benzoni (ed.), *1797: Le metamorfosi di Venezia. Da capitale di Stato a città del mondo* (Florence: Olschki, 2001), pp. 147–72, here pp. 162–4.
34 R. J. Rath, *The Fall of the Napoleonic Kingdom in Italy (1814)* (New York: Columbia University Press, 1941), pp. 60ff; Woolf, *History*, p. 224; Plant, *Venice*, pp. 77–9.
35 McCagg, *A History of Habsburg Jews*, pp. 57–63.
36 E. Timms, 'The Pernicious Rift: Metternich and the Debate about Jewish Emancipation at the Congress of Vienna', *Leo Baeck Institute Year Book*, 46/1 (2001), pp. 3–18, here p. 12.
37 McCagg, *A History of Habsburg Jews*, pp. 47–8.
38 David Laven has brilliantly demonstrated that Francis I's rule after the restoration was 'far less burdensome and oppressive than that of

Napoleon' and 'much more sensitive to Venetian needs' than has generally been supposed. D. Laven, *Venice and Venetia under the Habsburgs: 1815–1835* (Oxford: Oxford University Press, 2002), *passim*, but here p. 214.

39 See, in general, R. J. Rath, *The Provisional Austrian Regime in Lombardy–Venetia, 1814–1815* (Austin TX: University of Texas Press, 1969), esp. pp. 3–53; Laven, *Venice and Venetia*, pp. 53–74; D. Laven, 'Law and Order in Habsburg Venetia 1814–1835', *Historical Journal* 39/2 (1996), pp. 383–403.

40 Rath, *The Provisional Austrian Regime*, p. 23; Laven, *Venice and Venetia*, p. 57.

41 M. Berengo, 'Gli ebrei veneti nelle inchieste austriache della restaurazione', *Michael: On the History of the Jews in the Diaspora* (1972), pp. 9–37, here p. 13.

42 Berengo, 'Gli ebrei veneti nelle inchieste', p. 14.

43 A. Ottolenghi, 'Il Governo democratico di Venezia e l'abolizione del Ghetto', *La Rassegna Mensile d'Israel*, 2nd ser., 5.2 (1930), pp. 88–104, here pp. 92–3; A. T. Desquiron, *Commentaire sur le décret impérial du 17 mars 1808, concernant les droits et les devoirs des juifs . . .* , 2nd ed. (Paris: Clament, 1810), p. 162.

44 J. Bernardi, *Antichi testamenti tratti dagli archivi della Congregazione di Carità di Venezia*, 12 vols. (Venice: Tipografia della società di M. S. Fra Comp. Tip., 1882–93); F. Masè, *Patrimoines immobiliers ecclésiastiques dans la Venise médiévale (XIe–XVe siècle): une lecture de la ville* (Rome: École française de Rome, 2006), pp. 82–4.

45 Berengo, 'Gli ebrei veneti nelle inchieste', pp. 17, 32–4.

46 Berengo, 'Gli ebrei veneti nelle inchieste', pp. 17, 34–7.

47 Laven, *Venice and Venetia*, pp. 67–73.

48 Calabi, *Venice and Its Jews*, p. 107; M. Berengo, 'Gli ebrei dell'Italia asburgica nell'età della restaurazione', *Italia* 6/1–2 (1987), pp. 62–103.

49 Berengo, 'Gli ebrei dell'Italia asburgica', pp. 72–4.

50 Calabi, *Venice and Its Jews*, pp. 109–13; Calabi, 'Il Ghetto e la città', pp. 284–9; Ferrighi, 'The Story', pp. 91–5.

51 Calabi, *Venice and Its Jews*, p. 112.

52 F. Cavarocchi, *La comunità ebraica di Mantova fra prima emancipazione e unità d'Italia* (Florence: Giuntina, 2002), pp. 43–4; M. Cotrozzi Del Bianco, *Il Collegio rabbinico di Padova. Un'istituzione religiosa dell'ebraismo sulla via dell'emancipazione* (Florence: Olschki, 1995), pp. 65–8; M. Del Bianco Cotrozzi, 'Il Collegio rabbinico di Padova: la sua istituzione ed il suo influsso sulla cultura ebraica', *La Rassegna Mensile di Israel*, 3rd ser., 57/3 (1991), pp. 359–80, here p. 360.

53   Del Bianco Cotrozzi, 'Il Collegio', pp. 372–6; N. Vielmetti, 'Die Gründungsgeschichte des Collegio Rabbinico in Padua', *Kairos* 12 (1970), pp. 1–30; 13 (1971), pp. 36–66, here 13 (1971), p. 57.
54   G. Luzzatto Voghera, 'Luzzatto, Samuel David', *DBI* 66 (Rome, 2006), s.v.; R. Bonfil, I. Gottlieb, and H. Kasher (eds.), *Samuel David Luzzatto: the Bi-Centennial of his Birth* (Jerusalem: Magnes, 2004).
55   His grammar would later grow into the *Prolegomeni ad una grammatica ragionata della lingua ebraica* (Padua: Cartallier, 1836); see Samuel David Luzzatto, *Prolegomena to a Grammar of the Hebrew Language*, trans. A. D. Rubin (Piscataway NJ: Gorgias Press, 2006).
56   S. Vargon, 'Isaiah 56:9–57:13: Time of the Prophecy and Identity of the Author. According to Samuel David Luzzatto', *Jewish Studies Quarterly* 6/3 (1999), pp. 218–33.

14. Risorgimento (1835–1866)

1   R. Greenfield, 'Commerce and new enterprise at Venice, 1830–48', *Journal of Modern History* 11 (1939), pp. 313–33, here pp. 321–2; D. Laven, *Venice and Venetia under the Habsburgs: 1815–1835* (Oxford: Oxford University Press, 2002), pp. 97–8; P. Ginsborg, *Daniele Manin and the Venetian Revolution of 1848–49* (Cambridge: Cambridge University Press, 1989), pp. 30–1.
2   Greenfield, 'Commerce and new enterprise', p. 319.
3   Ginsborg, *Daniele Manin*, p. 31.
4   M. Plant, *Venice: Fragile City, 1797–1997* (New Haven and London: Yale University Press, 2002), pp. 124–31; H. Hearder, *Italy in the Age of the Risorgimento, 1790–1870* (London: Longman, 1983), p. 279 n. 4.
5   *Mémoires, documents et écrits divers laissés par le Prince de Metternich . . .* , 8 vols. (Paris: E. Plon, Nourrit, 1880–4), vol. 6, p. 16; A. Zorzi, *Venezia austriaca, 1798–1866* (Rome and Bari: Laterza, 1985), p. 259.
6   D. Calabi, *Venice and Its Jews: 500 Years Since the Founding of the Ghetto*, trans. L. Rosenberg (Milan: Officina Libraria, 2017), p. 111.
7   For discussion, see Ginsborg, *Daniele Manin*, pp. 39–40.
8   Q. at J. Keates, *The Siege of Venice* (London: Pimlico, 2006), p. 65.
9   This and the following paragraph follow Laven, *Venice and Venetia*, pp. 221–3; Ginsborg, *Daniele Manin*, pp. 47–8; S. Woolf, *A History of Italy 1700–1860: The Social Constraints of Political Change* (London and New York: Routledge, 1979), p. 296.
10   By far the best study remains Ginsborg, *Daniele Manin*.
11   On Manin's origins, see P. Padoa, 'Daniele Manin e gli Israeliti di

Venezia nel 1848–49', *Vessillo israelitico* 52/2 (1904), pp. 281–6; A. Ottolenghi, 'Abraham Lattes nei suoi rapporti colla Repubblica di Daniele Manin', *La Rassegna Mensile di Israel*, 2nd ser., 5/1 (1930), pp. 25–35, here p. 26 n. 2. For a broader biographical survey, see M. Gottardi, 'Manin, Daniele', *DBI* 69 (Rome, 2007), s.v.

12 For a good overview, see Woolf, *History*, pp. 303–60.
13 T. Catalan, 'Italian Jews and the 1848–49 Revolutions: Patriotism and Multiple Identities', in S. Patriarca and L. Riall (eds.), *The Risorgimento Revisited: Nationalism and Culture in Nineteenth-Century Italy* (Houndmills: Palgrave Macmillan, 2012), pp. 214–31, here p. 217; cf. E. Capuzzo, 'Gli ebrei e la repubblica romana', *Rassegna storica del Risorgimento*, Special Issue: La repubblica romana nel movimento europea tra il 1848 e il 1849, atti del Convegno internazionale di studi (1999), pp. 267–86, here p. 278.
14 G. Luzzatto Voghera, '"Primavera dei popoli" ed emancipazione ebraica: due lettere dell'aprile 1848', *La Rassegna Mensile di Israel*, 3rd ser., 64/1 (1998), pp. 83–6, here p. 86; English trans. at Catalan, 'Italian Jews', p. 218. On Jewish views of emancipation under the leadership of Pius IX more generally, see G. Luzzatto Voghera, *Il prezzo dell'eguaglianza. Il dibattito sull'emancipazione degli ebrei in Italia (1781–1848)* (Milan: Franco Angeli, 1998), pp. 89–112.
15 For the following, see Ginsborg, *Daniele Manin*, pp. 51–8, 67–74.
16 E. Capuzzo, *Gli ebrei italiani dal Risorgimento alla scelta sionista* (Florence: Le Monnier, 2004), p. 52. The chapter from which this reference is taken ('A Venezia con Manin', pp. 51–78) offers an invaluable survey of Jewish involvement in the revolution of 1848–9. I am very grateful to Prof. Capuzzo for sharing a copy with me.
17 This has been published as Niccolò Tommaseo, '"Diritti degli Israeliti alla civile eguaglianza" Discorso di Niccolò Tommaseo', *La Rassegna Mensile di Israel*, 3rd ser., 41/5–6 (1975), pp. 274–8. For an important discussion of this text, see E. Bacchin, 'Per i diritti degli ebrei: percorsi dell'emancipazione a Venezia nel 1848', *Annali della Scuola Normale Superiore di Pisa. Classe di Lettere e Filosofia*, 5th ser., 5/1 (2013), pp. 91–128. See also B. di Porto, 'Niccolò Tommaseo e gli ebrei: una meditata simpatica', *La Rassegna Mensile di Israel*, 3rd ser., 35/11 (1969), pp. 505–14, here pp. 509–10; Ginsborg, *Daniele Manin*, p. 73.
18 Woolf, *History*, p. 363.
19 Plant, *Venice*, p. 139.
20 Q. at Ginsborg, *Daniele Manin*, p. 90.
21 Carlo Alberto Radaelli, *Storia dello assedio di Venezia negli anni 1848–1849* (Venice: Antonelli, 1875), p. 43; Nicolò Foramiti (ed.), *Fatti di*

    Venezia degli anni 1848–1849 . . . (Venice: Cecchini, 1850), pp. 6–7; Ginsborg, *Daniele Manin*, p. 92.

22 For the following, see Radaelli, *Storia*, pp. 43–60; Foramiti (ed.), *Fatti*, pp. 6–14; Ginsborg, *Daniele Manin*, pp. 92–104.

23 Radaelli, *Storia*, p. 57: 'essa ricorderà le nostre antiche glorie, e sarà migliorata dalle moderne libertà. Con ciò noi non intendiamo separarci dai nostri fratelli italiani; anzi, al contrario, noi formeremo uno dei centri che serviranno alla fusione graduale, successiva, della nostra amata Italia *in un solo tutto!*'

24 Q. at T. Catalan, 'Ebrei italiani del Litorale austriaco nella rivoluzione del 1848', in R. Camurri (ed.), *Memoria, rappresentazioni e protagonisti del 1848 italiano* (Verona: Cierre, 2006), pp. 221–47, here p. 227: 'Il mio cuore trabocca, la mia mente arde. Alla fine si respira; c'è dell'aria, per Dio! [. . .] Un secolo divide ieri dall'oggi. Fratelli! [. . .] Le tristissime eredità di odii e di vendette sian consumate'.

25 Foramiti (ed.), *Fatti*, p. 18: 'Tutti i cittadini delle provincie unite alla Repubblica veneta, qualunque siano le loro confessioni religiose, nessuna eccettuata, sono dichiarati godere di perfetta uguaglianza di diritti civili e politici'.

26 Di Porto, 'Niccolò Tommaseo e gli ebrei', pp. 507, 509. On Abramo Errera, see B. Nunes Vais Arbib, 'La communità israelitica di Venezia durante il Risorgimento', *La Rassegna Mensile di Israel*, 3rd ser., 27/5 (1961), pp. 219–29, here p. 223.

27 Luzzatto Voghera, *Il presso dell'eguaglianza*, p. 109.

28 Niccolò Tommaseo, *Diario intimo*, ed. R. Ciampini (Turin: Einaudi, 1938), p. 265: 'Io amo gli ebrei, ma eglino . . . non sanno amare. Godon della depressione altrui, troppo memori d'essere stati tanto ferocemente depressi'. See also di Porto, 'Niccolò Tommaseo e gli ebrei', p. 507.

29 When the patriarch of Venice, Cardinal Jacopo Monico, petitioned Tommaseo to remove some of the legal prerequisites for baptism shortly after the Republic's foundation, Tommaseo turned him down flat, on the grounds that safeguards were necessary to prevent anyone from being coerced. Luzzatto Voghera, *Il prezzo dell'eguagliana*, pp. 106–7; R. Calimani, *Storia del Ghetto di Venezia* (Milan: Mondadori, 2001), p. 304. On Tommaseo's hopes for Jewish conversions after emancipation, see Ottolenghi (ed.), *L'azione di Tommaseo*; di Porto, 'Niccolò Tommaseo e gli ebrei', p. 510; cf. Niccolò Tommaseo, *Studii filosofici di N. Tommaseo*, 2 vols. (Venice: Gondoliere, 1840), vol. 1, pp. 5, 10.

30 Nunes Vais Arbib, 'La communità israelitica', p. 224:

> 'Ebrei e Cristiani – Semo tuti Italiani
> Cristiani e Ebrei – Semo tuti fradei'.

    For discussion, see Bacchin, 'Per i diritti degli ebrei', p. 113.

31. Ginsborg, *Daniele Manin*, p. 154.
32. R. Fulin, 'Venezia e Daniele Manin: ricordi raccolti', *Archivio Veneto* 9/1 (1875), pp. v–ccxxvii, here pp. cxxi–cxxv; Plant, *Venice*, p. 141.
33. Ottolenghi, 'Abraham Lattes', pp. 27–8: 'Ciò che forse può occorrere per taluni si è di conoscere se e quanto possa ostare agli esercizi della milizia l'obbligo della santità del Sabbato e delle Feste nostre; ond'è che a tranquillare le coscienze, ed a dissipare ogni ombra di scrupolo, amplamente per me si dichiara, che non solo nulla si oppone per parte della nostra Religione a prestarsi in tali giornate puntualmente alla funzioni militari, a norma delle proprie incombenze, e degli ordini che si ricevono, ma che anzi si serve eminentemente alla Religione stessa impiegando la propria opera in prò della Patria nel miglior modo che per noi si possa'. See also Bacchin, 'Per i diritti', pp. 110–11; Ginsborg, *Daniele Manin*, p. 120.
34. See G. Luzzatto Voghera, 'La religione degli ebrei in Italia', *La Rassegna Mensile di Israel* 76/1–2 (2010), pp. 257–74, here p. 264.
35. Ginsborg, *Daniele Manin*, p. 141.
36. Q. (in Italian) at Luzzatto Voghera, *Il prezzo dell'eguaglianza*, p. 96: 'Già stanno arrivando gli eserciti del Piemonte ad aiutarci e speriamo che fra un giorno o due entrino in Verona e caccino da lì i tedeschi. Ti invio una poesia in italiano che hanno stampato qui ieri, dalla quale potrai vedere che l'Italia intera è fraterna come un sol uomo, che lo spirito del Signore la spinga a liberarsi dal giogo degli stranieri'. The original – which I have been unable to check – is in Hebrew.
37. Ginsborg, *Daniele Manin*, pp. 204–9, pp. 223–6; Woolf, *History*, pp. 380–6.
38. Calimani, *Storia*, p. 305; A. De Giorgi, 'Venezia nel 1848 e 1849: supplementi storici', *Archivio Veneto* 11 (1876), pp. 1–50, here pp. 45–7.
39. Q. at T. Catalan, 'La "primavera degli ebrei". Ebrei italiani del littorale e del Lombardo-Veneto nel 1848–1849', *Zakhor* 6 (2003), pp. 35–66, here pp. 60–1: 'l'unico reggimento appropriato ad uomini liberi e civili è la repubblica'. See also Bacchin, 'Per i diritti degli ebrei', p. 115.
40. See De Giorgi, 'Venezia nel 1848 e 1849', pp. 14–19.
41. Bacchin, 'Per i diritti degli ebrei', p. 115.

42 De Giorgi, 'Venezia nel 1848 e 1849', pp. 48–50; Capuzzo, *Gli ebrei italiani*, p. 73. On Angelo Levi and Abramo Errera, see Nunes Vais Arbib, 'La communità israelitica', pp. 223–4.
43 In 1843, there were 2,208 Jews living in Venice: G. Luzzatto Voghera, 'Gli ebrei', in M. Isnenghi and S. J. Woolf (eds.), *Storia di Venezia. L'Ottocento e il Novecento* (Rome: Istituto della Enciclopedia Italiana, 2002), pp. 619–48, here p. 622. For the total population of Venice, see Ginsborg, *Daniele Manin*, p. 41 n. 122. There were 128 deputies in the new assembly. De Giorgi, 'Venezia nel 1848 e 1849', pp. 48–50.
44 Ottolenghi, 'Abraham Lattes', pp. 33–4.
45 Calimani, *Storia*, p. 305.
46 Woolf, *History*, p. 404.
47 Fulin, 'Venezia e Daniele Manin', p. cxxxiv.
48 Ginsborg, *Daniele Manin*, p. 332.
49 B. Nunes Vais Arbib, 'Il Risorgimento italiano e la comunità israelitica di Venezia', *La Rassegna Mensile di Israel*, 3rd ser., 27/6 (1961), pp. 272–82, here p. 272.
50 Ginsborg, *Daniele Manin*, pp. 337–9.
51 For the following, see Arbib, 'Il Risorgimento italiano', pp. 272–3.
52 Arbib, 'Il Risorgimento italiano', p. 274.
53 Arbib, 'Il Risorgimento italiano', p. 273.
54 Q. at Ginsborg, *Daniele Manin*, p. 349.
55 Arbib, 'Il Risorgimento italiano', p. 274.
56 Ginsborg, *Daniele Manin*, p. 355.
57 For what follows, see Nunes Vais Arbib, 'Il Risorgimento italiano', pp. 275, 277.
58 Arbib, 'Il Risorgimento italiano', pp. 276–8.
59 The following account is closely based on E. D'Antonio, 'Jewish Self-Defence against the Blood Libel in Mid-Nineteenth Century Italy: The Badia Affair and Proceedings of the Castilliero Trial (1855–56)', *Quest. Issues in Contemporary Jewish History* 14 (2018), pp. 23–47. See also E. D'Antonio, 'Badia Polesine 1855. Storia di una calunnia del sangue nell'Italia dell'Ottocento' (unpublished PhD thesis, Università degli studi di Udine, 2015/16); E. D'Antonio, *Il sangue di Giuditta. Antisemitismo e voci ebraiche nell'Italia di metà Ottocento* (Rome: Carocci, 2020).
60 Abraham Lattes, 'Agli amici della giustizia, onesti ed illuminati', *Gazzetta Ufficiale di Venezia* (9 June 1855): 'Egli è perciò che faccio solenne appello a' buoni, i quali, scevri da sinistre prevenzioni, sanno riconoscere nell'uomo il proprio fratello . . . a sradicare dal volgo ignaro sì vergognoso pregiudizio, di cui qualche malvagio tenta

imbeverlo per riuscire ad iniquo scopo'. Q. at D'Antonio, 'Badia Polesine 1855', p. 156.
61 Luzzatto Voghera, 'Gli ebrei', p. 622; Calimani, *Storia*, p. 308.
62 Arbib, 'Il Risorgimento italiano', p. 278.
63 Arbib, 'Il Risorgimento italiano', pp. 278–9.
64 Arbib, 'Il Risorgimento italiano', p. 279.

15. The Emptying of the Ghetto (1866–1945)

1 The entry was commemorated in Girolamo Induno's *Entry of Victor Emmanuel II into Venice (7 November 1866)*. Milan, Museo del Risorgimento.
2 George Augustus Sala, *Rome and Venice, with Other Wanderings in Italy, in 1866–7* (London: Tinsley, 1869), p. 269.
3 M. Plant, *Venice: Fragile City, 1797–1997* (New Haven and London: Yale University Press, 2002), p. 159.
4 B. Nunes Vais Arbib, 'La comunità israelitica di Venezia durante il Risorgimento', *La Rassegna Mensile di Israel*, 3rd ser., 27/7–8 (1961), pp. 343–54, here p. 344.
5 Q. at S. Klein, *Italy's Jews from Emancipation to Fascism* (Cambridge: Cambridge University Press, 2018), p. 26.
6 G. Fubini, *La Condizione Giuridica dell'Ebraismo Italiano* (Turin: Rosenberg & Sellier, 1998), pp. 37–8; Klein, *Italy's Jews*, p. 24; cf. G. Luzzatto Voghera, 'Gli ebrei', in M. Isnenghi and S. J. Woolf (eds.), *Storia di Venezia. L'Ottocento e il Novecento*, 3 vols. (Rome: Istituto della Enciclopedia Italiana, 2002), vol. 1, pp. 619–48, here p. 621, which stresses the 'posizione non egualitaria' of non-Catholic faiths.
7 Klein, *Italy's Jews*, p. 37.
8 'Le Glorie dell'Ebraismo Italiano', *Il Corriere Israelitico* (1905), p. 365; q. in Klein, *Italy's Jews*, p. 38; for further context, see T. Catalan, 'Le reazioni dell'ebraismo italiano all'antisemitismo europeo (1880–1914)', in C. Brice and G. Miccoli (eds.), *Les racines chrétiennes de l'antisémitisme politique (fin XIXe–XXe siècle)* (Rome: École Française de Rome, 2003), pp. 137–62.
9 For an excellent account, see R. Calimani, *Storia del Ghetto di Venezia* (Milan: Mondadori, 2001), pp. 313–20; G. Luzzatto Voghera, 'Maurogonato Pesaro, Isacco', *DBI* 72 (Rome, 2008), s.v.; Nunes Vais Arbib, 'La comunità israelitica', p. 345.
10 P. Pecorari and P. Ballini, 'Luzzatti, Luigi', *DBI* 66 (Rome, 2006), s.v.

11 D. Calabi, *Venice and Its Jews: 500 Years Since the Founding of the Ghetto*, trans. L. Rosenberg (Milan: Officina Libraria, 2017), p. 133.
12 Nunes Vais Arbib, 'La comunità israelitica', pp. 347–8, 349.
13 On cafes and salons, see, for example, S. Levis Sullam, *Una comunità immaginata. Gli ebrei a Venezia (1900–1938)* (Milan: Unicopli, 2001), p. 65.
14 Giacomo Balla, *Letizia Pesaro Maurogonato*, 1901. Venice, Ca' Pesaro, Galleria Internazionale d'Arte Moderna.
15 B. Recchilongo, 'Castelnuovo, Enrico', *DBI* 21 (1978), s.v.
16 Nunes Vais Arbib, 'La comunità israelitica', pp. 350–1.
17 On mixed marriages, see Levis Sullam, *Una comunità immaginata*, p. 50.
18 Marco Besso, *Autobiografia* (Rome: Fondazione Marco Besso, 1925), p. 8; q. at Luzzatto Voghera, 'Gli ebrei', p. 637: 'La solennità religiosa che al tempo mio e ancor oggi è più scrupolosamente osservata è quella del Chipur, ossia dell'espiazione: un digiuno assoluto ed intero, da un tramonto all'altro, accompagnato da orazioni, da raccoglimento, e da rappacificazioni dove vi siano stati dissapori od offense. [...] Se vi è una pratica religiosa che per i suoi alti fini meriti rispetto, essa è proprio questa . . . [ch'] è precetto civile e nazionale prescritto a tutti i cittadini, perché si abbia almeno una volta all'anno un giorno di raccoglimento pieno ed intero col pensiero rivolto unicamente all'adempimento dei propri doveri morali, all'emendazione dei propri falli'.
19 Luzzatto Voghera, 'Gli ebrei', p. 624.
20 Luzzatto Voghera, 'Gli ebrei', p. 625.
21 Levis Sullam, *Una comunità immaginata*, p. 54. See also S. Levis Sullam, 'Gli ebrei a Venezia nella prima metà del Novecento', in Isnenghi and Woolf (eds.), *Storia di Venezia*, vol. 3, pp. 1663–84.
22 Luzzatto Voghera, 'Gli ebrei', p. 625.
23 Levis Sullam, *Una comunità immaginata*, p. 59.
24 D. Calabi, 'Gli ebrei veneziani dopo l'apertura delle porte del ghetto: le dinamiche insediative', in G. Benzoni (ed.), *1797: Le metamorfosi di Venezia. Da capitale di Stato a città del mondo* (Florence: Olschki, 2001), pp. 147–72, here p. 157.
25 On Herzl's period in Paris, see, for example, D. Penslar, *Theodor Herzl: The Charismatic Leader* (New Haven and London: Yale University Press, 2020), pp. 47–84.
26 Theodor Herzl, *The Complete Diaries of Theodor Herzl*, ed. R. Patai, 5 vols. (New York: Herzl Press, 1960), vol. 1, p. 196.
27 Levis Sullam, *Una comunità immaginata*, p. 36.
28 *L'Idea sionnista* (June–July 1905): '[Sono] convinto che il Sionnismo [*sic*] non dev'essere solo un movimento volto alla colonizzazione

ebraica della Palestina; ma dev'essere anche . . . un movimento diretto ad elevare la dignità di tutti gli Ebrei'. Q. at Levis Sullam, *Una comunità immaginata*, pp. 39–40. On Alessandro Levi, see A. Cavaglion, 'Levi, Alessandro', *DBI* 64 (Rome, 2005), s.v.

29 See Levis Sullam, 'Gli ebrei a Venezia', pp. 1663–5.
30 Q. at J. A. Thayer, *Italy and the Great War: Politics and Culture, 1870–1915* (Madison WI: University of Wisconsin Press, 1964), p. 253.
31 R. Bosworth, *Italian Venice: A History* (New Haven and London: Yale University Press, 2014), pp. 88, 92.
32 By far the most thorough analysis of the Jewish war effort is P. Briganti, *Il contributo militare degli ebrei italiani alla Grande Guerra 1915–1918* (Turin: Silvio Zamorani, 2009).
33 See Klein, *Italy's Jews*, p. 41.
34 F. Tedeschi, *Gli israeliti italiani nella guerra 1915–1918* (Turin: F. Servi, 1921), pp. 203, 204, 211, 228, 229, 230, 234, 244, 247, 248, 252.
35 Tedeschi, *Gli israeliti italiani nella guerra*, pp. 149–50, 295.
36 Klein, *Italy's Jews*, p. 42.
37 Tedeschi, *Gli israeliti italiani nella guerra*, pp. 37–8.
38 Tedeschi, *Gli israeliti italiani nella guerra*, pp. 38–9, 247.
39 Klein, *Italy's Jews*, p. 42.
40 R. Nattermann, 'The Female Side of War: The Experience and Memory of the Great War in Italian-Jewish Women's Ego-Documents', in E. Madigan and G. Reuvini (eds.), *The Jewish Experience of the First World War* (London: Palgrave Macmillan, 2019), pp. 233–54, here p. 247.
41 M. Miniati, *Italian Jewish Women in the Nineteenth and Twentieth Centuries* (Cham: Palgrave Macmillan, 2021), p. 250.
42 Miniati, *Italian Jewish Women*, pp. 239–43.
43 Bosworth, *Italian Venice*, pp. 77–9, 97.
44 Bosworth, *Italian Venice*, pp. 103–4.
45 *Gli israeliti italiani nella guerra*, p. 230.
46 Levis Sullam, *Una comunità immaginata*, pp. 59–60.
47 Levis Sullam, *Una comunità immaginata*, p. 51.
48 Levis Sullam, *Una comunità immaginata*, p. 67.
49 Levis Sullam, *Una comunità immaginata*, p. 69.
50 Plant, *Venice*, p. 274.
51 Bosworth, *Italian Venice*, p. 114.
52 Bosworth, *Italian Venice*, p. 118.
53 Levis Sullam, 'Gli ebrei a Venezia', p. 1672.
54 Levis Sullam, *Una comunità immaginata*, pp. 200, 202.
55 See, for example, G. Fabre, 'Mussolini and the Jews on the Eve of the March on Rome', in J. D. Zimmerman (ed.), *Jews in Italy under*

Fascist and Nazi Rule, 1922–1945 (Cambridge: Cambridge University Press, 2005), pp. 55–68.

56 Q. at Klein, *Italy's Jews*, p. 53; R. De Felice, *The Jews in Fascist Italy: A History* (New York: Enigma Books, 2001), p. 60.

57 S. Zuccotti, *The Italians and the Holocaust: Persecution, Rescue, and Survival*, new ed. (Lincoln NE, University of Nebraska Press, 1996), p. 32.

58 Q. at R. Calimani, *Storia degli ebrei italiani*, vol. 3, *Nel XIX e nel XX secolo* (Milan: Mondadori, 2015), p. 366–7.

59 Benito Mussolini, *Opera omnia*, ed. D. and E. Susmel, 44 vols. (Florence: La Fenice 1951–1961; Rome: Giovanni Volpe, 1978–1980), vol. 24, p. 82: 'Gli ebrei sono a Roma dai tempi dei Re, forse fornirono gli abiti dopo il ratto delle Sabine: erano 50,000 ai tempi di Augusto e chiesero di piangere sulla salma di Giulio Cesare. Rimarranno indisturbati, come rimarranno indisturbati coloro che credono in un'altra religione'.

60 *L'Informazione Diplomatica* 14 (16 February 1938); q. at Klein, *Italy's Jews*, p. 55; M. Sarfatti, *The Jews in Mussolini's Italy: From Equality to Persecution*, trans. J. and A. C. Tedeschi (Madison: University of Wisconsin Press, 2006), p. 122.

61 S. Urso, 'Grassini, Margherita', *DBI* 58 (Rome, 2002), s.v.

62 Calimani, *Storia degli ebrei italiani*, vol. 3, pp. 368–9.

63 Zuccotti, *The Italians and the Holocaust*, pp. 32–3.

64 Klein, *Italy's Jews*, p. 55; cit. O. Neerman, *Ebrei per caso* (Venice and Mestre: Stamperia Cetid, 2010), p. 43.

65 Q. at Sarfatti, *The Jews in Mussolini's Italy*, p. 101.

66 Q. at Sarfatti, *The Jews in Mussolini's Italy*, p. 96.

67 On this change of policy, see Sarfatti, *The Jews in Mussolini's Italy*, pp. 98–9.

68 Klein, *Italy's Jews*, p. 94.

69 G. Weiller, *La Bufera: Una Famiglia di Ebrei Milanesi con i Partigiani dell'Ossola* (Florence: La Giuntina, 2002), pp. 18–20; q. at Klein, *Italy's Jews*, p. 85.

70 R. Segre (ed.), *Gli ebrei a Venezia, 1938–1945: Una comunità tra persecuzione e rinascita* (Venice: il Cardo, 1995), p. 37.

71 Segre (ed.), *Gli ebrei a Venezia*, pp. 37–40.

72 M. A. Livingston, *The Fascists and the Jews of Italy: Mussolini's Race Laws, 1938–1943* (Cambridge: Cambridge University Press, 2014), p. 45.

73 For discussion, see Livingston, *The Fascists*, pp. 24–45.

74 Klein, *Italy's Jews*, pp. 87–8; Segre (ed.), *Gli ebrei a Venezia*, p. 41; Livingston, *The Fascists*, pp. 25–40.

75 Segre (ed.), *Gli ebrei a Venezia*, p. 41.
76 This was a status coveted particularly by Fascist Jews. See E. Asquer, 'Being a Fascist Jew in Autumn 1938: Self-portrayals from the "Discrimination" Requests Addressed to the Regime', *Quest: Issues in Contemporary Jewish History* 11 (2017), pp. 1–21; Segre (ed.), *Gli ebrei a Venezia*, pp. 48–50.
77 Livingston, *The Fascists*, p. 23.
78 Klein, *Italy's Jews*, pp. 88, 90; Sarfatti, *The Jews in Mussolini's Italy*, pp. 141–2, 155–6; Segre (ed.), *Gli ebrei a Venezia*, pp. 46–7, 51–2.
79 Segre (ed.), *Gli ebrei a Venezia*, p. 51 [no. 43].
80 Klein, *Italy's Jews*, pp. 89, 90, 91, 99, 100; Sarfatti, *The Jews in Mussolini's Italy*, pp. 109–10, 136.
81 Klein, *Italy's Jews*, p. 94.
82 Klein, *Italy's Jews*, p. 97; Livingston, *The Fascists*, pp. 53, 58–9.
83 *Gazzetta Ufficiale del Regno d'Italia*, 276 (28 November 1939), pp. 5457–8; Segre (ed.), *Gli ebrei a Venezia*, p. 60.
84 Klein, *Italy's Jews*, p. 97; Livingston, *The Fascists*, p. 49; cf. Sarfatti, *The Jews in Mussolini's Italy*, p. 137.
85 Segre (ed.), *Gli ebrei a Venezia*, p. 61 [no. 63]: 'Mio marito è uno di quei professionisti che per gli enunciati provvedimenti razziali andrà verso la fame con la sua compagna e i suoi figli. Di animo nobile, onesto sino allo scrupolo, padre di famiglia esemplare, italiano italianissimo coi suoi antenati da più di dieci generazioni, ha fatto la guerra come il padre suo combatté per il Risorgimento e non presentò mai il conto per il dovere compiuto. [...] Senza colpe andremo verso tempi duri: per noi vecchi non importa, ma ci si spacca il cuore per i figliuoli. Quanti ebrei come lui, gente di onore, che andranno alla fame. Ma che importa a voi, se sono di religione ebraica? [...] Io non vi auguro del male né che i vostri figli (se ne avete) possano un giorno senza colpe esser privati di un onesto pane: vi auguro solamente che venga il momento in cui provate tutta la vergogna per il triste atto compiuto contro dei galantuomini, a taluno dei quali, sino a ieri, avrete stretta la mano e, forse, dichiarata la vostra amicizia. Il nome non conta, sono una povera donna'.
86 Sarfatti, *The Jews in Mussolini's Italy*, p. 140; Klein, *Italy's Jews*, p. 98.
87 Segre (ed.), *Gli ebrei a Venezia*, pp. 71–8.
88 Segre (ed.), *Gli ebrei a Venezia*, p. 84.
89 R. Segre, 'Giuseppe Jona, il Presidente della Comunità Israelitica di Venezia', in G. A. Danieli (ed.), *Giuseppe Jona* (Venice: Istituto Veneto di Scienze, Lettere ed Arti, 2015), pp. 5–19, here p. 10.
90 Segre (ed.), *Gli ebrei a Venezia*, pp. 107–22.

91 Segre (ed.), *Gli ebrei a Venezia*, pp. 123–5.
92 Segre (ed.), *Gli ebrei a Venezia*, pp. 130–1.
93 Segre (ed.), *Gli ebrei a Venezia*, pp. 141–2.
94 On Jona's life and career, see Danieli (ed.), *Giuseppe Jona*; M. Battain, 'In memoria di Giuseppe Jona', *L'Ateneo Veneto* 132/1–2 (1945), pp. 51–8; N.-E. Vanzan Marchini, *Giuseppe Jona nella scienza e nella storia del Novecento* (Venice: Canova, 2014).
95 Q. at Segre, 'Giuseppe Jona', p. 8: 'patriota entusiasta e di fede incrollabile'.
96 This point is well made at Segre, 'Giuseppe Jona', p. 8.
97 Klein, *Italy's Jews*, p. 98.
98 Segre (ed.), *Gli ebrei a Venezia*, pp. 90–1.
99 Klein, *Italy's Jews*, p. 98.
100 Segre (ed.), *Gli ebrei a Venezia*, pp. 143–6.
101 Segre (ed.), *Gli ebrei a Venezia*, p. 93.
102 Segre (ed.), *Gli ebrei a Venezia*, p. 89: 'Ebrei spie, Ebrei traditori . . . Morte agli Ebrei'; from a letter addressed by Giuseppe Jona to Marcello Vaccari, the prefect of Venice, 29 May 1941.
103 Segre (ed.), *Gli ebrei a Venezia*, pp. 95–6.
104 Giuseppe Jona to Marcello Vaccari, 29 May 1941: 'Non è umano, che . . . si imponga agli ebrei di abdicare a ogni senso di dignità e di onore . . . Lo Stato doveva tutelare gli ebrei . . .'; q. at Segre (ed.), *Gli ebrei a Venezia*, p. 89; Segre, 'Giuseppe Jona', pp. 11–12.
105 Relazione (Report) of Giuseppe Jona to the Fascist Giunta, 23 October 1941: 'Il vostro giornale ha scritto ieri che 'Comunità Israelitica equivale ad associazione a delinquere' e 'che sinagoga è sinonimo di luogo di ricettazione'; q. at Segre (ed.), *Gli ebrei a Venezia*, pp. 94–5; Segre, 'Giuseppe Jona', p. 12 (in more abbreviated form).
106 Segre, 'Giuseppe Jona', p. 14.
107 Segre (ed.), *Gli ebrei a Venezia*, p. 147.
108 This paragraph and the next closely follow Zuccotti, *The Italians and the Holocaust*, pp. 139–40.
109 Segre, 'Giuseppe Jona', pp. 16–17.
110 S. Levis Sullam, *The Italian Executioners: The Genocide of Jews in Italy*, trans. O. Smyth and C. Patane (Princeton and Oxford: Princeton University Press, 2018), pp. 81–2.
111 Telegram from Guido Buffarini Guidi to provincial heads, 1 December 1943, 5:15 pm; q. at Segre (ed.), *Gli ebrei a Venezia*, pp. 151–2.
112 Levis Sullam, *The Italian Executioners*, p. 78.
113 Giuseppe Segré's account is retold at Levis Sullam, *The Italian*

Executioners, pp. 81–5. The following is heavily indebted to Levis Sullam's masterful work.
114 Segre (ed.), *Gli ebrei a Venezia*, p. 155.
115 Segre (ed.), *Gli ebrei a Venezia*, p. 155.
116 Primo Levi, *Se questo è un uomo*, ed. A. Cavaglion (Turin: Einaudi, 2012), p. 8: 'V'erano inoltre un centinaio di militari jugoslavi internati, e alcuni altri stranieri considerati politicamente sospetti. L'arrivo di un piccolo reparto di SS tedesche avrebbe dovuto far dubitare anche gli ottimisti'.
117 Levi, *Se questo*, p. 8: 'Ma il mattino del 21 si seppe che l'indomani gli ebrei sarebbero partiti. Tutti: nessuna eccezione. Anche i bambini, anche i vecchi, anche i malati . . . Soltanto una minoranza di ingenui e di illusi si ostinò nella speranza . . .'.
118 L. Picciotto Fargion, *Il libro della memoria: gli Ebrei deportati dall'Italia (1943–45)*, 2nd ed. (Milan: Mursia, 1992), ad nom.
119 Segre (ed.), *Gli ebrei a Venezia*, pp. 175–6.
120 Segre (ed.), *Gli ebrei a Venezia*, p. 175:

> Mamma adorata,
>
> Immaginati il nostro dispiacere, essere lontani da te in questa giornata, a noi sì tanto cara . . . Oh come speriamo e desideriamo nel più profondo dell'anima che questa orribile situazione termini e che noi possiamo riunirci molto presto e goderci nuovamente la nostra tranquillità a noi tanto cara e desiderata. Non ti facciamo alcuna promessa, ma puoi rimanere sicura e tranquilla che sarà nostro dovere fare il meglio possibile. Speriamo di presto rivederci con il papà.
>
> I nostri più affetuosi e cari auguri, abbracci e bacioni dai tuoi figli.

121 Segre (ed.), *Gli ebrei a Venezia*, p. 164.
122 Levis Sullam, *The Italian Executioners*, p. 90.
123 Segre (ed.), *Gli ebrei a Venezia*, pp. 158–61.
124 Segre suggests that Stangl was assisted by Carlo Grini; Levis Sullam, with stronger justification, argues that it was Carlo's brother, Mauro, who went by the pseudonym 'Dr. Manzoni'. Segre (ed.), *Gli ebrei a Venezia*, pp. 160, 223 n. 80; Levis Sullam, *The Italian Executioners*, pp. 86, 120.

16. Epilogue (1945–present)

1. R. Calimani, *Storia degli ebrei italiani*, vol. 3, *Nel XIX e nel XX secolo* (Milan: Mondadori, 2015), p. 675; G. Acerbi, *Le leggi antiebraiche e razziali italiane e il ceto dei giuristi* (Milan: Giuffrè, 2011), p. 190; R. Segre (ed.), *Gli ebrei a Venezia, 1938–1945: Una comunità tra persecuzione e rinascita* (Venice: il Cardo, 1995), p. 245.
2. Text in Segre (ed.), *Gli ebrei a Venezia*, pp. 246–7.
3. Calimani, *Storia degli ebrei italiani*, p. 675.
4. Q. at Segre (ed.), *Gli ebrei a Venezia*, p. 193: 'Mentre in alcune strade di Venezia (ad esempio in calle Pompeo Molmenti) si vedono ancora tracce di scritte contro gli Ebrei, in via Garibaldi e più precisamente all'ingresso dei giardini pubblici, si legge a caratteri cubitali la dicitura "Ebrei spie"'.
5. Segre (ed.), *Gli ebrei a Venezia*, p. 185.
6. Segre (ed.), *Gli ebrei a Venezia*, p. 202.
7. This paragraph closely follows the excellent survey at S. Klein, *Italy's Jews from Emancipation to Fascism* (Cambridge: Cambridge University Press, 2018), pp. 182–93.
8. Segre (ed.), *Gli ebrei a Venezia*, p. 204.
9. See the detailed accounts presented by the community on 21 January 1946: Segre (ed.), *Gli ebrei a Venezia*, pp. 187–9.
10. Klein, *Italy's Jews*, p. 192.
11. Klein, *Italy's Jews*, p. 193.
12. Segre (ed.), *Gli ebrei a Venezia*, p. 183.
13. Segre (ed.), *Gli ebrei a Venezia*, pp. 196–9.
14. On Toaff's tenure in Venice, see E. Toaff, *Perfidi giudei, Fratelli maggiori* (Milan: Il Mulino, 1961), pp. 131–61.
15. Segre (ed.), *Gli ebrei a Venezia*, p. 207.
16. Segre (ed.), *Gli ebrei a Venezia*, p. 201.
17. Segre (ed.), *Gli ebrei a Venezia*, pp. 211–12.
18. P. Lanaro, 'Luzzatto, Gino', *DBI* 66 (Rome, 2006), s.v.; M. Berengo, 'Profilo di Gino Luzzatto', *Rivista Storica Italiana* 76 (1964), pp. 879–925.
19. See M. Franzinelli, *L'Amnistia Togliatti. 22 giugno 1946: colpo di spugna sui crimini fascisti* (Milan: Mondadori, 2006).
20. M. Franzinelli, 'Collaborazione e delazione', in M. Flores, S. Levis Sullam, M.-A. Matard-Bonucci, and E. Traverso (eds.), *Storia della Shoah in Italia*, 2 vols. (Turin: UTET, 2010), vol. 1, p. 572.
21. Calimani, *Storia degli ebrei italiani*, pp. 687–8.
22. Calimani, *Storia degli ebrei italiani*, pp. 671–2.
23. N. De Ianni, 'Merzagora, Cesare', *DBI* 73 (Rome, 2009), s.v..

24 Q. at Calimani, *Storia degli ebrei italiani*, p. 658: 'Bisogna che gli ebrei siano consapevoli di un'amara realtà: di tutti i residuati tragici e dolorosi del nazismo quello che rimarrà più lungo in Europa e anche in Italia è l'antisemitismo . . . Gli ebrei . . . hanno evidenemente i loro atavici difetti. Se non li avessero, come si spiegherebbero le persecuzioni di cui sono vittime da duemila anni?'
25 On the rise of Zionism, see Klein, *Italy's Jews*, pp. 205–15.
26 Klein, *Italy's Jews*, p. 209.
27 M. Zanetti, 'Da Pellestina e dalla laguna di Venezia a Eretz Israel', *Mediterranea – Ricerche storiche* 48 (2020), pp. 59–80.
28 Calimani, *Storia degli ebrei italiani*, pp. 694–5.
29 Calimani, *Storia degli ebrei italiani*, pp. 689–90, 697–8.
30 M. Plant, *Venice: Fragile City, 1797–1997* (New Haven and London: Yale University Press, 2002), pp. 402–3.
31 For a good survey of this process of 'museumification', see S. Levis Sullam, 'Réinventer la Venise juive: le Ghetto entre monument et métaphore', *Laboratoire italien* 15 (2014), pp. 213–23.
32 https://www.wmf.org/project/venetian-ghetto (last accessed 24 May 2025).
33 https://www.metropolitano.it/nuovo-polo-museale-al-ghetto-di-venezia/ (last accessed 18 October 2025).
34 https://moked.it/blog/2025/01/17/venezia-con-rav-sermoneta-la-posa-di-cinque-nuove-pietre-dinciampo/ (last accessed 24 May 2025).
35 A. Di Trani, 'Histoires et pratiques dissonantes dans un ghetto en devenir. Anthropologie contemporaine du cas de Venise', *Les Cahiers de la recherche architecturale urbaine et paysagere* 15 (2022) [online]: http://journals.openedition.org/craup/10837 (last accessed 24 May 2025): 'Ce sont eux que l'on voit en premier dans les rues et sur le *campo*, mais c'est nous, les vrais juifs du ghetto, ceux de l'enclave de 1516, cela fait cinq cents ans que nous sommes là. Et certains d'entre nous sont nés dans le ghetto.'
36 For discussion, see, for example, J. Adams and C. Heß (eds.), *The Medieval Roots of Antisemitism: Continuities and Discontinuities from the Middle Ages to the Present Day* (New York and London: Routledge, 2018).
37 See J. Le Goff, *Faut-il vraiment découper l'histoire en tranches?* (Paris: Fayard, 2014).
38 For a broader discussion of this point, see, for example, Adams and Heß (eds.), *The Medieval Roots of Antisemitism*; I. G. Marcus, *How the West Became Antisemitic: Jews and the Formation of Europe, 800–1500* (Princeton: Princeton University Press, 2024).

39 https://www.ilgazzettino.it/nordest/venezia/dario_calimani_ presidente_comunita_ebraica_venezia_ebrei_odio-7884421.html (last accessed 24 May 2025).
40 https://www.repubblica.it/cronaca/2024/05/13/news/venezia_scritta_ antisemita-422942996/ (last accessed 24 May 2025): 'Ebrei maledetti vi cercheremo casa [per] casa . . . per sgozzare voi e i vostri bambini'.

Index

Aboab, Samuel 167, 171, 172, 182
Aboaf, Jacob 176
Abramo, brother of Anselmo of Nuremberg 9, 19, 23–4
Abramo, son of Fricele 48, 59, 71, 73
Abravanel, Isaac 47–8
Adelkind, Baruch 89
Adelkind, Cornelio 89, 90
Agnadello, Battle of (1509) 50–1, 58
Alexander VI, Pope 41, 42, 43, 45, 49
Ancona
   Jewish trade 24, 114, 116, 193
   papal policy towards Marranos 94–5, 98, 106, 130
Anselmo del Banco (Asher Meshullam, son of Solomon)
   brother Vivian (Chaim) 48, 55, 62, 67, 74
   complaint on antisemitic sermon 55
   death and funeral 86
   debate on second-hand trade 71, 73
   family background 48
   influence 48, 53, 61
   move to Ghetto 68
   negotiations on site of Jewish confinement 62, 67, 68
   privileges 48, 51
   son 77, 78, 86
   tax collection 54
   taxation 56
   taxation protests 73–4, 79–80, 81
   Venetian five-year *condotta* renewal (1520) 73
   Venetian five-year *condotta* renewal (1528) 83
   Venetian ten-year *condotta* (1503) 48, 51, 55, 59
   Venetian ten-year *condotta* renewal (1513) 59
Anselmo of Nuremberg, son of Samuel 9, 11–12, 19, 20, 23–4
antisemitism
   anti-Zionism 272
   attacks from Jewish converts 173
   Austrian policy 225–6, 237
   concentration camps 259, 261, 263, 265
   doge's response to 36
   Fascist policies 251–5, 256–7, 259
   fears of social contagion 128
   German 252
   Holocaust 265, 272
   illustration of **plate 25**
   Italian position 243, 246–7, 252, 269–70
   response to *Discorso* 161
   ritual murder accusations 35–6, 238–9
   Venetian 3, 16, 27
   Venetian aristocracy 214
   Venetian popular 231, 237, 267
   Venice today 273
   Zionist response to 246
Ashkenazi Jews 4, 96, 134, 164, 172
Asola 64
Asolo 53, 102
Association of Jewish Women of Italy 268
Astru, Ioste (or Joste) 26

Astruc, Samuel 26
Auser (loan banker) 19
Azzariti, Gaetano 269

Badia Polesine 104, 238
Badoglio, Pietro, Marshal 260, 266–7
banks, Jewish *see also* moneylending
   branch closures 73
   Christian investors 29–30, 108–9
   closure (1527) 81
   closure announcement 71
   contribution to Venetian economy 71, 159–60
   establishment of state *monte di pietà* 216
   liquidation proposal 213
   monte di pietà debate 75–6, *see also monti di pietà*
   monte di pietà replacement proposals 71, 213
   reopened (1520) 74
   threat of violence against 205
   union of 216
   Venetian regulation of 21, 109, 114, 118
Baruch of Arezzo 171
Basadonna, Giovanni 141
Beauharnais, Eugène de 215–16, 218
Beccadelli, Ludovico 105–6, **plate 10**
Bellini, Gentile 43
Bellotto, Gregorio and Anzola 178–9
Belluno 24
Benedetti, Giovanni Battista 191
Benedetti, Rocco 115–16
Benincasa, Shabbetai 138
Berardelli, Alessandro 141, 143
Bergamo 57, 58, 68, 107, 202
Bernardino da Feltre 36, 38–9
Bernardino da Siena 26
Bernardo Gui 16
Bessarion, Cardinal 32–3, 70
Besso, Marco 244
Bevilacqua, Giovanni Carlo 218
Black Death (1348) 9, 12, 15, 115
Blois, Treaty of (1499) 45, 46
blood libel 3, 47, 185, 239
Bologna 55, 57, 64, 83
Bomberg, Daniel 87–90

Bongi, Nicola 11
Bonifacio, Baldassare 141–3
books, Hebrew 22, 26–7, 87–90, 105–6, 158, 161
Borgia, Cesare 45, 48, 49
Boyer, Jean-Baptiste, Marquis d'Argens 190
Bragadin, Alvise 90
Bragadin, Marcantonio 110–11
Brandolino, Marcantonio 125
Brescia
   famine 81, 82
   Jewish population 40
   monte di pietà 39, 40
   ritual murder accusation 35, 36
   violence against Jews 51
   warfare 57, 58, 64, 202–3

Calimani, Dario 273
Calimani, Lea Rita 263
Calimani, Moise 268
Caliva, Johannes 26
Cambrai, League of (1508–10) 50, 52, 54–5
Cambrai, Treaty of (1529) 83–4, 85
Campoformio, Treaty of (1797) 211, 215
Cardona, Ramón de 59–60, 63
Cardoso, Isaac 161
Carlo Alberto, King 232–4, 235, 240
Carpaccio, Vittore 43
Caser (loan banker) 19
Casola, Pietro 9
Castagna, Giovanni 115, 120
Castelfranco Veneto 53, 107, 178
Castelnuovo, Enrico 244
Castilliero, Giuditta 238–9
Cavour, Count 240
Cebà, Ansaldo 140–3
Charles V, Holy Roman Emperor 72, 75, 78–81, 83–4, 96
Charles VIII, King of France 41–3, 45, 58
Chioggia 17, 52
Clement VII, Pope 79–80, 83
Cognac, League of (1526–30) 79–81
Coimbran, Moses, Rabbi 154
Compagnia del Divino Amore (Company of Divine Love) 75
concentration camps 259, 261, 263, 265

INDEX

condotte (charters), in chronological order
  Mestre moneylenders (1366) 15, 16
  Venice moneylenders (1382) 18, 19–20
  Venice – German Jewish moneylenders (1387) 20–1, 23
  Venice – Jewish loan banks from Mestre (1503) 48, 51, 55, 73
  Venice – Jewish loan banks renewal (1513) 59, 69–70
  condotta renewal debate (1518–19) 69–72
  condotta renewal (1520) 73
  condotta renewal (1523) 75, 79, 81
  condotta renewal (1528) 82–3
  condotta renewal (1533) 85
  condotta renewal (1537) 85
  Venetian territories (1547) 102
  Venice *condotta* renewal debate (1548) 102–3
  condotta renewal (1558) 108
  condotta renewal debate (1565) 108–9
  condotta renewal terms (1566) 109, 112
  condotta renewal (1573) 114
  new *condotta* (1589) 118–20
  condotta renewal (1598) 122
  condotta renewal (1636) 158
  unified *condotta* of all Jewish communities (1738) 192
  condotta renewal terms (1760) 193
  condotta renewal terms (1777) 194–5
  new *condotta* under Austrian rule (1801) 214
Conegliano 74
Conegliano, Israel, Rabbi 158
Contarini, Gian Battista 200
Contarini, Michele 21
Contarini, Troiano 47
conversions
  Christian attitudes 16, 27, 33, 98, 231
  Christian women to Judaism 85
  converts 11, 85–6, 87–8, 99, 157, 173–4, 253
  frequency 4
  Islamic 37, 170
  Levantine Jews 97–8
  Marranos *see* Marranos
  payment for baptism 100, 133
  Sabbateanism 165, 167, 170
  status under Fascism 255
Copia Sullam, Sara 6, 139–44, **plates 12, 13**
Cordova, Filippo 261, 263
Corner, Giovanni 18
Corner, Marco, Doge 17–18
Coryat, Thomas 126, 131, 132, 134, 137
Cracovia, Jacob Emanuele (Yakov Menahem), Rabbi 219–20, 222
Crema 74, 102, 107, 202
Cremona 45, 57, 105
Crescas Meir 27
Crete
  Jewish quarter in Candia 10
  Ottoman policy 169, 179
  trade 11, 179–80
  Venetian loss 179–80
  Venetian rule 10
Cyprus
  Genoese control 16–17
  Ottoman control 111–12
  Ottoman strategy 110–12
  trade 11, 110, 179
  Venetian loss 113, 179
  Venetian rule 110

da Brolo family 66–7, 87, 272
d'Alviano, Bartolomeo 60, 63, 65
Dandolo, Vincenzo 209, 211, 213
d'Angeli, Vidal 206–7
D'Annunzio, Gabriele 250
Della Casa, Giovanni 97–9, 105
Della Vida, Adele 243
Della Vida, Cesare 225, 228, 234
Della Vida, Samuele 234
Diderot, Denis 190
doctors 24, 69, 115, 147, 148, 261
Dolfin, Zaccaria 66–8
Domenico da Leonessa 28
Donà, Francesco, Doge 99
Donà, Leonardo, Doge 125, 129–30
Doria, Gian Andrea 110
d'Ormesson, Jean 272
Drumont, Édouard 243

emancipation, Jewish
  Austrian policy 190, 211, 219, 225, 227–8
  defence of 190
  Fascism 254
  French policy 201–2, 219
  Italian Constitution 242
  Jewish strategy 227–8
  opponents 202
  Venetian decree (1848) 230–1
  World War I 247
  Zionism 246
Emo, Giorgio 61–2, 66
Emo, Zuan Alvise 194
Erizzo, Francesco, Doge 158
Errera, Abramo 230, 234, 237, 239
Errera, Alberto 237
Eugenius IV, Pope 28

Fano, Angelo 251
Fano, Laudadio 214
Fano, Lazzaro 250
Fano, Menahem Azariah da, Rabbi 132
Fano, Vittorio 268
Fascist Party 251–4, 255, 258–61, 263–4, 266–70
Federzoni, Luigi 247
Felice da Prato, Fra 87–8
Feltre 24
Ferdinand I, Emperor of Austria 226
Ferdinand II, King of Aragon 41, 43, 46, 52, 56
Ferrara 38, 55, 105, 124, 242
Ferrari, Pier Gian Maria de 206–7
Finzi, Isacco 235
Finzi, Ugo 256
Foà, Carlo 253
Foscari, Francesco, Doge 31
Foscolo, Ugo 211
Fossoli di Carpi 263
Francis I, King of France 60, 62–5, 75, 79, 83–4, 98
Francis II, last Holy Roman Emperor (later Emperor of Austria) 211, 215, 222, 226
Franciscans
  anti-Jewish preaching 26, 28–9, 36–7, 54, 61–2, 239

Inquisitor 99
monte di pietà policy 35, 37, 38–9
Francoso, Giacomo 100
Fruttero, Carlo 272
Fusina 59

Garibaldi, Giuseppe 240–1, 244
Genoa
  decline 23
  Garibaldi's expedition 240
  revolt 55
  shipping 46
  trade 46
  wars with Venice 15, 16–17
German Jews (Tedeschi)
  access to Fondaco dei Tedeschi 173
  banks 18–22, 122, 127, 187
  cultural activity 22
  Ghetto residents 94, 96, 97, 131, 151, 184
  leaving Venice 22
  lending policy 20–2
  Levantine trade 152
  moneylending 14–16, 19, 20–3
  refugees in Venice 9, 11–12, 18, 22
  relationship with Levantine Jews 96, 127, 131, 192
  relationship with Ponentine Jews 127
  settlement in Mestre 14–16
  settlement in Venice (before the Ghetto) 18, 19, 25
  shopkeepers' dispute 154–5
  shops 131
  taxation 127
  Venetian *condotte* 18, 20–1, 23, 102, 152, 187, 192
  Venetian expulsion decree 23–4
  World War II experiences 260–1
Gessi, Berlinghiero 129–30
Ghetto
  balconies 95, 128, 131
  bell 68
  bridges 66–7, 68, 131, 151, 175, 217, 225
  control over finances 187–8
  demolitions and repairs 225
  destruction of gates 207–8, 209, 212
  emigration 181, 183–4, 221
  established 2, 67–8, 272

Index

existence confirmed 109
families 90
financial difficulties 107–9, 183–4, 187–92, 194–5
funeral processions 86, 175, 184, 261
gates 68, 95, 149, 176, 189, 272
government *see* Università degli Ebrei
guards 68, 75, 95, 176, 273
Holocaust memorial 271, **plate 26**
housing conditions 86–7, 95, 131, 152–3, 184, 196, 221
Jews ordered to move to 68
keys 207
kosher butchers 87, 96, 131, 257
lack of maintenance 217–18
Large Assembly 127–8
Lubavitchers 272
map xv
memorial to deportation of Jews (1943) **plate 27**
modernization 271
'museumification' 271–2
ovens 96, 268
plague (1630–1) 148–51
population (1608) 131
population (1642) 152
population (1652) 152
population (1700) 181
population (1797) 210
population (1869) 245
poverty 133–4, 184
professions and occupations of residents 4, 182, 210–11, 245
refugees and former slaves 182–3, 192
renovation 221, 224
rental of accommodation 68, 151, 217, 245
response to Napoleon's new constitution 204–6
restrictions on contact between Jews and Christians 185, 189
restrictions on Jews 3, 69, 87, 90, 221
role 3–4
Sabbatean affair 167–9, 170–2
shops 86–7, 131–2
site 2, 5, 10, 66–7
Small Assembly 128, 133, 168

socio-economic differences 195, 244–5
synagogues 4, 87, 132–3, 136, 153–4, 172–3, 202, 222, 237, 259–60, 271, *see also* synagogues
taxation *see* taxation
tensions 96, 134
visitors 93, 95–6, 134
walls 3–4, 67, 68, 87, 128, 149, 221
waste disposal 131
wells 5, 66, 87, 273
yeshiva 167–8, 170–1, 191
yeshivas 133, 222
Ghetto Nuovissimo 3, 151–2, **plate 28**
Ghetto Nuovo
balconies 131
banks 68, 122, 127
bell 68
bridge 68
Campo 87, 131, 134, 206, 273, **plate 5**
daily existence 90
demolitions and repairs 221, 225
established 3, 67–8, 94, **plate 4**
families 90
gates 68
German (Tedeschi) Jews 93, 97, 122, 127, 131
guards 68, 273
housing conditions 3, 67, 68, 95, 131, 184
Iberian Jews 93
illustrations of **plates 5, 6, 20, 29**
improvements 97
Jews ordered to move to 68
name 67
nursing home 262–3, 265
refugees 93
restrictions on residents 3, 90
segregation of Jews 67
shops 131–2
site 66–7
synagogues 132, 172
walls 68
wells 66
Ghetto Vecchio
balconies 128
demolitions and repairs 196, 221, 225
foundation 95, 104

Ghetto Vecchio (*cont.*)
  gates 95
  guards 95
  housing 3, 131
  Levantine Jews 95–6, 97
  photograph of Jewish survivors (1945) 266
  plague (1630) 148
  restrictions on residents 3
  shops 131–2
  site 95
  synagogues 132, 172–3
  visiting merchants 127
  walls 128
Giacobbe, brother of Anselmo of Nuremberg 9, 19, 23–4
Gianquinto, Giovanni Battista 269
Giordano da Rivalto 16
Giovanni da Canal 18
Giudecca 11, 61–2, 116, 239, 262
Giustinian, Michele 22
Giustiniani, Alvise 138
Giustiniani, Marco Antonio 90
Giustiniani press 90, 105
Gomez, Simon 130
Gozzi, Carlo 211
Grego, Isaac 204, 208
Grevembroch, Giovanni 195, **plate 19**
Grini, Mauro ('Dr. Manzoni') 264–5
Gritti, Andrea, Doge 60, 86
guilds 28, 97, 189, 212

Hannover, Nathan Nata 182
Hebrew publishing 4, 87–90, 105–6, 133
Heinrich von Herford 12
Herman Gigas 12
Herrera, Fernando de 111
Herzl, Theodor 246
Holy League (1511) 56–8, 59–60, 63
Hostiensis 13–14

Index of Forbidden Books (*Index Librorum Prohibitorum*) 106, 125, 142
Inquisition
  Ghetto as refuge from 4, 119
  Levantine and Ponentine Jews 119
  Marrano refugees from 93
  Mendes family 101–2
  Pisan 130
  punishments 100, 101
  Roman 98
  targets 99, 100–1, 112–13, 125, 133
  Venetian 99, 130
  Venetian independence from 122–3, 129–31
Inquisitori sopra l'Università degli ebrei (committee of patricians) 187–8, 189, 191
Isaiah di Trani 11
Italy, Kingdom of (1805–14) 215–18
Italy, Kingdom of (1866) 241, 242–3

Jews *see also* German Jews (Tedeschi), Levantine Jews, Ponentine Jews
  cemetery on Giudecca, use of 61
  cemetery on the Lido 20, 22, 150, 174–5, 273, **plates 16, 18**
  charters *see condotte* (charters)
  clothing restrictions 23, 25, 43–4, 69, 114
    exemptions 25, 37, 43, 85, 173, 185
    hats 44, 69, 80, 101, 119, 158, 173, 185, 189
    yellow signs 23, 25, 31–2, 37, 43–4, 114, **plate 19**
  decree of expulsion from Venetian territories (1571) 113–14
  deportation to death camps 263, 264–5, **plate 27**
  economic roles in Venice 182, 210–11, 224–5, 245, 249
  emancipation *see* emancipation
  expulsion from Venice (1511) 55–6
  expulsion of Jewish moneylenders from Venice 23–5
  importance to Venetian economy 4, 39–40, 61, 71, 101, 127, 153, 159–60
  kashrut 96, 250
  loan banks 18–22, 30, 48, 126–7, 159–60, 187, 189–91, **plate 15**
  merchants *see* merchants, Jewish
  moneylending *see* moneylending

Index

refugees *see* refugees
schools 30, 258, 259, 268, 271
second-hand trade (*strazzaria*) *see* second-hand trade
self-government 127–8, 133, 134, 168, 204, 205, *see also* Università degli Ebrei
survivors of German occupation 266, 267
synagogues *see* synagogues
Venetian census (1552 or 1555) 11
Venetian census (1797) 210
Venetian census (1911) 245
Venetian census (1938) 254–5, 261
Venetian elite 210, 243–4
Venetian population before Ghetto 11–12
Venetian population in Ghetto *see* Ghetto
Venetian population (1821) 240
Venetian population (1857) 240
Venetian population (1869) 245
Venetian population (1938) 254–5
Venetian population (1965) 270
Venetian restrictions on 31–2, 38, 69, 90, 103, 209, 221, 225–6, 237, 256–7
Venetian round-up of (1943) 261–3
Venetian safe conducts to Jewish settlers (1573) 114–15

Joint Distribution Committee (the 'Joint') 268
Jona, Giuseppe 6, 258–61
Julius II, Pope 49–50, 52, 58
Julius III, Pope 130

kabbalah, kabbalism 22, 132, 139, 164, 165–6, 171
Karlowitz, Treaty of (1699) 181, 183
Klein, Shira 248, 256
Köprülü, Ahmed, Grand Vizier 169

Lando, Pietro, Doge 99
Lattes, Abraham, Rabbi 232, 234, 236, 239
Lazzaretto Vecchio 115
leggi razziali (1938) 255–7, 266, 269

Legnano 238, 239
Leo X, Pope 58–9, 63, 75
Lepanto, Battle of (1571) 111–12, 113, 180
Levantine Jews
 detained during Ottoman war 113
 dress **plate 19**
 Ghetto Nuovissimo established 151–2
 Libro grande affair 156
 living in Venetian colonies 10
 occupation of Ghetto Vecchio 95–6
 origins 94
 papal policy toward 97–8, 99
 privileges 119, 122, 126–7
 relationship with German Jews 96, 127, 131, 192
 relationship with Ponentine (Iberian) Jews 119–20, 122, 126–7, 151–2
 Rodriga's proposals for status of Jewish merchants 118–19
 Rodriga's Spalato plan 116–17, 119
 suspected of being enemy agents 112–13
 synagogue 96
 value to Venetian trade 94–5, 97, 122, 154
 Venetian *condotta* (1611) 126–7
 Venetian *condotta* (1636) 158
 Venetian *condotta* (1738) 192
Levi, Alessandro 240–1, 246
Levi, Angelo 242
Levi, Corona 178
Levi, Primo 263, 270
Levi, Samuele 244
Levi Bonaiuti, Mario 248
Levi Moreno, Alberto 248, 249
Levis Sullam, Simon 262
Levy, Jacob 155
Libro grande (Jewish community's records), translation 155–6
Limojon de Saint-Didier, Alexandre Toussaint 173
Lippomano, Marco 27
Lodi, Battle of (1796) 200
Lodi, Peace of (1454) 30
Lombardy–Venetia, kingdom of 219, 225, 228, 233, 237–8, 240

Longhena, Baldassare 149, 153, 173
Lonigo, Gaspar 155–6
Loredan, Leonardo, Doge 52, 64, **plate 3**
Louis XII, King of France (Louis d'Orléans) 42, 45, 49, 52, 55–6, 58, 60
Louis XIII, King of France 136
Lovato, Fra Rufino 55, 65
Lucentini, Franco 272
Luzzatti, Luigi 243
Luzzatto, Benedetto 154
Luzzatto, Gino 251, 268–9
Luzzatto, Mosè 204
Luzzatto, Samuel David 222–3, 228, 233, **plate 22**
Luzzatto, Simone, Rabbi 147, 153, 158–61, 174, 222

Mainster, Abram, Rabbi 239
Malkiel, Daniel 155
Manifesto della razza ('Manifesto of Race' 1938) 253–4
Manin, Daniele 6, 226–30, 232–7, 239
Manin, Lodovico, Doge 200
Mantua 105, 148, 167, 200, 202
Marco da Montegallo 38–9
Marcuzo, son of Jacob 48
Marghera 59, 235
Marignano, Battle of (1515) 63–4
Marino, Rosso 21
Marranos
  burnt at the stake in Ancona 106
  enticed by Venice's rivals 114
  expulsion from Venice (1550) 103–4, 106
  Inquisition's proceedings against 98, 122–3
  origins 4, 93
  papal policy toward 94–5, 106, 122, 129–30
  refugees to Italy 93–4
  refugees to Ottoman Empire 93–4
  suspected of being enemy agents 112–13
  trade connections 94, 103–4
  Venetian policy toward 97, 103–4, 114–15, 119–20, 122–3, 128–30

marriages, mixed 244, 249, 255–6
Marta, Marc Antonio 157
Masaod, Iosef and Moise 129–30
Maurogonato, Isacco Pesaro 224–5, 228, 233–4, 237, 243–4
Maurogonato, Letizia Pesaro 244, **plate 24**
Maximilian I, Holy Roman Emperor
  anti-French league 43
  death 72
  League of Cambrai 50, 52
  Milan campaign 64–5, 67
  policy towards Jews 51
  truce with Venice 69–70
  war with Venice 49–50, 52–3, 55, 56, 58, 60, 63
Mazzini, Giuseppe 227, 232, 234
Medici, Giacomo 240
Meir of Mestre 171
Meldola, Samuel, Rabbi 158
Menasseh Ben Israel 161
Mendes, Brianda 97, 101–2
Mendes, Diogo 93, 97
Mendes, Gracia 97, 101–2, 103
The Merchant of Venice (Shakespeare) 1, 3
merchants, Jewish
  exodus (1680s and 1690s) 181
  food price speculation 193–4
  German and Italian 94
  invited to Ghetto 3
  invited to Venice 24–5
  Levantine 94–5, 113, 119, 122, 126–7, 151–2, 156, 158
  life in Ghetto 4, 122, 127, 158, 181, 210–11, 272
  life in Ghetto Nuovissimo 151–2
  life in Ghetto Nuovo 94
  life in Ghetto Vecchio 95
  life in Mestre 12
  papal policy 98
  plague epidemic effects 150
  Ponentine (Iberian) 114–15, 119, 122, 126–7, 151–2, 156, 158
  taxation 158, 195, 210
  Venetian defence loan 234
  Venetian policy 24–5, 114–15, 117–19, 122–3, 126–7, 151–3, 158

Merzagora, Cesare 269–70
Meshullam, Jacob 77–8, 86
Mestre
  German occupation 260
  Jewish migration from Venice 23, 24, 80
  Jewish migration to Venice 18, 24, 48, 51, 82–3
  Jewish moneylenders 12–15, 44, 48
  Jewish settlement 12
  Palestinian Brigade 270
  synagogue 40
  violence against Jews 47, 51
  warfare 59, 218, 235
Metternich, Klemens von 218, 226, 229
Micanzio, Fra Fulgenzio 155–6
Michele Carcano da Milano 35
Michele da Acqui 39
Milan
  Charles V's conquest 75
  duchy 42, 45, 58, 62, 64, 70, 84
  Franco-Venetian relations 45, 58, 62–4
  French campaigns 58, 79, 84
  French conquest 45, 46, 52
  Maximilian's campaign 64–5, 67–8
  Napoleon's conquest 200
  plague (1630) 148
  railway plan 228
  revolt 229, 232
  surrender (1848) 233
  Swiss attacks 55, 57
  Swiss conquest 57
  Venetian retreat 58
  Venetian victory 63
  war with Genoa 17
  wars with Venice 23, 24, 30–1
Mocenigo, Alvise 200
Mocenigo, Giovanni, Doge 37
Mocenigo, Pietro, Doge 36, 185
Modena 135, 179, 263
Modena, Leon
  autobiography 134, 138–9
  cantor 134, 137
  children 136, 138
  family background 135, 136
  finances 136, 137
  gambling 134, 136
  influence 137
  illustration **plate 11**
  Libro grande affair 155–6
  life 6, 135–7
  marriage 135–6
  musical academy 154
  plague experiences 149, 150, 154
  preaching 136, 137
  rabbi 134, 137
  relationship with Sara Copia Sullam 139, 141, 142
  teaching 136
  writings 134, 135, 136, 138–9, 174
  Zorzetti case 157
moneylending
  Christian moneylenders 14, 213
  effects of Ghetto site 62
  effects of *monti di pietà* establishment in *terraferma* 107–8
  forced loans 17, 38, 43, 59, 81
  importance of Jewish moneylenders to Venetian economy 71
  interest rates 12–15, 18, 20, 22, 33, 73, 82, 103, 109, 114, 127, 187–8
  Jewish loan banks 18–22, 30, 48, 126–7, 159–60, 187, 189–91, **plate 15**
  Jewish moneylenders in Mestre 12–13, 14–15, 24, 48
  Jewish moneylenders in Venice 2–3, 16, 18–19, 24, 48
  Jewish moneylending banned in *terraferma* 31
  loans to Venetian 'working poor' 2–3
  Mestre *condotta* (1366) 15
  monti di pietà see monti di pietà
  papal policies 28, 30, 70
  pledges 13, 18–23, 44, 48, 51, 53, 73, 102, 196
  size of loans 14–15, 19, 22, 114, 216
  taxation *see* taxation
  usury debate 13–14, 28–9, 33, 34, 70–1, 73, 85, 102, 104, 108, 190
  Venetian agreements with Jewish moneylenders 18–22, 48, 109
  Venetian *condotta* (1382) 18
  Venetian *condotta* (1566) 109
  Venetian *condotta* extension (1385) 20

moneylending (*cont.*)
   Venetian *condotta* with Jewish loan
      banks (1503) 48
   Venetian *condotta* with Jewish
      moneylenders (1387) 20–1
   Venetian expulsion of Jewish
      moneylenders (1394) 23–5
   Venetian legislation (1388) 21
   Venetian policy 2–3, 14, 16, 17–18, 48,
      62, 108–9
   Venetian restrictions on (1388) 21
Montagnana 74, 107
Monte nuovo (loan-fund) 38
Montesquieu 190
monti di pietà
   attempts to establish in Veneto 35
   calls for establishment 35, 37
   effects on Jewish moneylenders 29–30,
      39, 102, 107–8
   establishment in Italy 29–30, 35
   establishment in *terraferma* 38–40,
      104, 107
   establishment in Venice by liquidation
      of Jewish banks 216, 231
   finances 29, 76, 107, 114, 216
   monopoly in Crema 102
   papal policy 29–30
   plans for establishment in Venice
      71–3, 75–7, 78, 79, 190–1, 213–14
   role 29
Morello, Cornelio 116
Moro, Cristoforo, Doge 32, 33, 35
Moro, Gabriele 70–1, 80, 82, 86
Morosini, Andrea 116
Morosini, Francesco, Doge 180
Morosini, Giulio (Samuel Nahmias)
   173–4
Morosini, Pietro 19–20
Morosini, Zuane 155–6
Mortera, Saul Levi 210
Motta, Jacob 157
Murano 62, 66
Musatti, Alberto 248, 252
music
   call for ban on singing in
      synagogues 154
   decline in Jewish music 154, 184

Jewish celebrations 199, 206–7
Jewish musicians 4, 133, 141–2, 154, 243
Mussolini, Benito 251–3, 255, 259–60,
   264, 269

Napoleon Bonaparte 200–3, 210, 211, 215–
   16, 218–20
Nasi, Joseph 102, 112–13
Nathan of Gaza 165–6, 171–2
Niccolò da Poggibonsi 9
Nievo, Alessandro 34
Nordau, Maz 246

Ochino, Bernardino 97
Oliviero, Francisco 100–1
Olper, Samuel Salomone, Rabbi 231, 233,
   234, 237
Ospedale degli Incurabili (Hospital of
   Incurables) 75–6, 77
Ottolenghi, Adolfo, Rabbi 259, 265, 268
Ottoman Empire
   calls for crusade against 32–3
   Jewish emigrants 5
   Lepanto defeat 111–12
   Levantine Jews 93–6, 112–13, 115,
      117–18
   monetary crisis 123
   Sabbatai Sevi 169–70
   threat to Venice 30, 37–8, 42, 72,
      74–5, 110
   trade 32–3, 85, 94, 181
   war with Venice 34, 38, 46–7, 48, 84, 85,
      110–13, 179–80, 186–7

Padua
   accusations of ritual murder 35
   antisemitism 238, 242–3
   attacks on Jews 53
   banks 74, 83
   expulsion of Jews (1453) 31
   Jewish immigration 22
   Jewish refugees in Venice 51–2
   monte di pietà 35, 39
   rabbinical seminary 223, 239
   siege 59
   University 34, 88, 148, 223, 227, 243
   usury ban 102

Venetian gain 24
Venetian recapture 53
Pálffy, Alajos 229
Palladio, Andrea 116
Palontrotti, Melchiorre 161
Paluzzi, Numidio 141, 142–4
Panigo, Giacomo 19, 23–4
papal bulls 28–9, 30, 98, 106–7, 130
Parma 63, 148
Paul III, Pope 94–5, 96, 98
Paul IV, Pope 106
Paul V, Pope 125
Pavia
    Battle of (1525) 79
    Venetian siege 81
Pavolini, Alessandro 256
Philip II, King of Spain 110, 111
Pincherle, Leone 230, 234, 237
Pius II, Pope 30, 32–4
Pius V, Pope 110–11, 113
Pius X, Pope 252
plague
    Black Death (1348) 9, 12, 15, 115
    Jews blamed for 12, 18
    Venice (1575–7) 115–16, 122
    Venice (1630–1) 148–51, 152–4, 159, 163
Polacco, Daniel Levi 206–7
Polesella, Battle of (1509) 54
Ponentine Jews
    Ghetto Nuovissimo established 151–2
    name 119
    privileges 119–20, 122
    Venetian *condotta* (1611) 126–7
    Venetian *condotta* (1636) 158
    Venetian *condotta* (1738) 192
Portobuffolè 37, 74
Portogruaro 19, 74
Pressburg, Peace of (1805) 215
Primo, Samuel 169
Priuli, Antonio 104
Priuli, Girolamo 46, 51, 53

Ravà, Max 252, 253
Ravenna 39, 57, 238
Ravenna, Caliman 238–9
Ravid, Benjamin 161, 174
refugees
    from Poland-Lithuania to Venice 182
    from Spain to Venice 22, 93
    from *terraferma* to Venice 51–2, 54, 55–6, 65
    German Jews in Venice 9, 11–12, 22
    Iberian Jews in Venice 119
    Marranos in Italy 93–4
    Marranos in Ottoman Empire 93–4
    returning home 83, 267–8
    World War II 259, 260, 263–4, 267–8
Reubeni, David 163
Rieti, Camillo 133
Rieti, Ercole 178
Righetto (Enriques Nuñez, Abraham Benvenisti) 112–13
ritual murder accusations 35–7, 39, 47, 238, 239
Rodriga, Daniel 116–19, 121, 122, 127, 131, 192
Romanin, Samuel 239
Rome, Sack of (1527) 81
Rosso, Bernardino 118
Rousseau, Jean-Jacques 190, 227
Rovigo 104, 238
Ruggiero, Guido 31
Ruzini, Marco 66

Sabbatai Sevi 163–72, 179
Sacerdote, Lia 256
Sacerdote, Sansone 178–9
Sadoleto, Jacopo, Cardinal 98–9
Salamone Sansone di Vinegia 22
Salò 260
Salomon (loan banker) 19
Sanudo, Marin
    diarist 40, 52
    on famine 81–2
    on Jewish funeral cortege 86
    on Jewish moneylenders 71, 85
    on Jewish population in Venice 56, 61
    on violence against Jews 53
    on warfare 64, 65
Saraceni, Scipione 125
Saracin, Jacob 131
Saraval, Jacob 191–2
Sarfatti, Benedetto 189
Sarfatti, Cesare 247, 252

Sarfatti, Margherita Grassini 252,
    plate 23
Sarfatti, Roberto 248, 252, 253
Sarpi, Paolo 125, 126, 129, 130, 155
Sasportas, Jacob 165
Scaramella, Fidela 131
Scaramella, Grassin (Gershon) 156,
    157, 158
Scaramella, Isaac 156
Schio (La Motta), Battle of (1513) 60
Scholem, Gershon 164
second-hand trade (*strazzaria,
    strazzaruoli*)
    Ghetto establishment 68
    numbers of Jewish traders 210, 245
    permission to trade 82, 103
    restrictions on Jews 44, 70–3,
        108–9, 193
    restrictions on Levantine Jews 96
    taxation 61
Segré, Girolamo 261–3
Segré family 262–3, 272
Selim I the Grim, Sultan 72, 74
Selim II, Sultan 109–11, 112
Sephardi Jews 4, 96, 134, 137, 149, 172
sexual contact between Jews and
    Christians 26, 31–2, 101
Sforza, Massimiliano 58, 63
Simon of Trent, supposed ritual murder
    of 35–7, 238, 239, **plate 2**
Sixtus IV, Pope 30
Soave, Amadeo and Attilio 248
Soncino, Gershon 88
Spalato, port (*scala*) of 116–17, 118–19
Stangl, Captain Franz 264–5
Suleiman the Magnificent, Sultan 74, 78,
    84–5, 96, 101, 109
Sullam, Giacob 139–40
Sullam, Moisè di David 206–7
Sullam, Sara Copia *see* Copia Sullam
synagogues
    administration 127
    architecture 87, 132, 172–3
    Austrian regime 222
    donations to state treasury 202
    Fascist regime and 259–60
    forbidden in Venice 48, 68

Mestre 40
number in Ghetto 4, 87, 132, 271
prayer services resumed (1945) 268
Scuola Canton 87, 132, 153, 268, **plate 8**
Scuola Coanim 132
Scuola Grande Tedesca 87, 132, 136
Scuola Italiana 132, 137, **plate 7**
Scuola Levantina 96, 132, 172–3,
    249, 259
Scuola Luzzatto 132
Scuola Mesullamim 132, 153
Scuola Spagnola (or Ponentina) 132,
    153, 206, 208, 236, 259, 266,
    plate 9
singing 154

taxation
    Austrian regime 225
    decima 47, 61
    ecclesiastical exemption 124
    French regime 216
    German Jews 127
    Ghetto administration and collection
        127–8, 183–4, 187–8, 212–13
    Jewish moneylenders 20–1, 34
    Jews in Venice 54, 56, 59, 73, 75, 79,
        82–3, 103, 108–9, 114, 204,
        210–13
    Jews of the *terraferma* 38, 56–7, 73, 75,
        107–8
    Levantine Jews 95, 119, 158
    papal tax on Jews (1463) 33
    Ponentine Jews 119, 158
    taglione 212, 213
    tansa 195, 212, 213
    Venetian revenues from Jews 159–60
Tedeschi Jews *see* German Jews
theatre 154, 224, 257
Tiberino, Giovanni Mattia 35
Toaff, Elio, Rabbi 268
Todesca, Simcà 6, 176, 179, 184
Togliatti, Palmiro 269
Toland, John 161
Treves, Giuseppe (Iseppo) 202, 216
Treves, Isaac 195–6
Treves, Salomon 195–6
Treves de' Bonfili, Baron Alberto 243

Treves de' Bonfili, Giacomo 225, 232, 233, 234
Treves de' Bonfili, Isacco 232
Treves family 195–6, 211, 216
Treviso 22, 31, 35, 51, 56, 107
Trieste 224
Tron, Antonio 61, 71–3, 75–7
Tron, Francesco 194
Tron, Nicolò, Doge 35

Udine 107
Università degli Ebrei
   Austrian policy 212–14
   establishment 127
   leadership 184, 187, 195, 205
   legal status 155, 212
   role 127–8, 177, 187–9, 191–2, 212–14, 217
   tax administration and collection 127–8, 183–4, 212

Vaccari, Marcello 259
Venetian state institutions
   Avogadori di Comun 26, 155, 173
   Banco della Piazza 118
   Cattaveri (Ufficiali al Cattaver) 86, 126, 128, 133, 158, 176–9, 181, 184–5, 189
   Cinque Savi alla Mercanzia 94, 117–19, 126, 151–2, 181, 187
   Collegio
      complaint over treatment of Paduan Jews 53
      Ghetto site proposal 66, 67–8
      Giudecca proposal 61–2
      Jewish taxation issue 74
      Marrano safe conduct issue 129
      monte di pietà project 76
      Ottoman threat to Cyprus 110
      petition of arms manufacturer 39–40
      role 70
   Congregazione di carità 220
   Council of Ten
      book-burning policy 106
      death sentence for kidnapping 112
      investigation of attack on Ghetto 156–7
      investigation of spying 112–13
      monte di pietà policy 76–7
      policy towards Church 124–5
      policy towards Jewish bankers 33–4, 51
      policy towards Jews 32, 37, 43–4, 51–2, 82, 102, 158
      policy towards Marranos 115
      Portuguese negotiations 47–8
      response to Paduan Jews 53
      response to refugees 65
      role 32
      taxation policy 61
   Esecutori contro la Bestemmia 112, 184–5
   Great Council (*Maggior Consiglio*) 14, 15, 17, 18, 25–6, 44, 65, 203
   Piovego, Magistrato del 18, 20–2
   Quarantia 18, 21, 25–6
   Quarantia al Criminal 71, 78, 82, 85, 190–1
   Savii del Consiglio 79
   Senate
      blood libel case (1705) 185
      church building 116, 149
      condotta renewals 75, 102–3, 108, 109, 119, 192, 193, 194
      detention of Ottoman subjects (1570) 110
      ecclesiastical land legislation 124
      economic policy (1750s) 193
      expulsion of Jews (1571) 113
      Ghetto establishment 68, 69
      Ghetto Nuovissimo establishment 151–2
      Ghetto policy (18th century) 186, 187, 189, 193
      Ghetto proposal 67
      Ghetto Vecchio establishment 95–6
      Hebrew printing policy 88–9
      Jewish clothing restrictions 25, 31–2, 43–4, 80
      Jewish quarter proposals 21, 61–2
      Libro grande affair 155–6
      moneylending legislation 21, 23–5, 73, 80, 104, 109

Venetian state institutions (*cont.*)
   monte di pietà debates 75–6, 191
   Ottoman war 33
   response to Schio defeat 60
   Spalato port policy 117
   taxation of Jews 38, 47, 50, 54, 73–4, 103, 108, 109, 183–4
   treatment of Levantine Jews 95–7, 119, 122, 126–7, 151–2
   treatment of Marranos (1574) 115
   treatment of Marranos (1589) 119–20
   treatment of Ponentine (Iberian) Jews 119–20, 122, 126–7, 151–2
   treatment of Tedeschi (German) Jews 152, 173
   vote to expel Marranos (1550) 103–4
   war policies 42, 46, 64
  Sopraconsoli dei Mercanti 21, 44
Venice
  abolition of Republic by Napoleon 203–4
  anti-French league (1495) 42–3
  armies 43, 50–1, 58, 60, 63, 75, 83, 187, 193, 202–3
  Arsenale 66, 72, 73, 74, 76, 78, 110, 112, 148, 151, 229
  Austrian rule 211–15, 218–21, 239–41, *see also* Lombardy-Venetia
  Bonfadini, Palazzo 218
  Canale degli Ebrei 175, **plate 17**
  Carnevale 189, 228
  currency devaluation (1600) 123
  economic crisis (1380–2) 17–18
  economic renewal 224
  education 31, 243, 255–6, 258, 268, 271
  famine (1527) 81–2, 83
  fleet 17, 23, 38, 40, 46, 54, 73, 75, 81, 110, 111, 113, 201, 229
  food shortages (1760s) 193–4
  German military control (1943–4) 260–5, 266
  illustration of **plate 1**
  industry 121–2, 224, 225
  Interdict (1606–7) 125–6, 128, 131, 133, 147, 155
  maps xii–xiii, xiv
  maritime trade 3, 10–11, 23, 46, 123, 126, 159, 192–3
  port 46, 224
  proposal for *monte di pietà* 76–7
  proposals for a Jewish quarter 20, 21, 61–2, 122
  Provisional Municipality 203–6, 209–10, 212–13, 215
  relations with Ottoman Empire 5, 32–3, 37–8, 72, 74, 84–5, 101–2, 111–14, 180, 186–7
  relations with papacy 5, 38, 121, 124–6, 129–30
  restrictions on religious worship 25–6, 34, 222
  Rialto market 3, 10, 16, 18, 21, 46, 62
  Santa Maria della Salute 153, **plate 14**
  shipbuilding 17, 121–2, 152
  shipping 5, 10, 17, 21, 23, 54, 121–2, 181
  territories on mainland (*dominio di terraferma*)
   Austrian advance 233
   borders 30, 45, 187
   case of abandoned baby 178
   ecclesiastical lands 124
   expansion 24
   famine 226
   French threat to Venetian control (1797) 201, 203
   gains (1503) 49
   imperial threat to 79
   Jewish banks 73, 74, 75
   Jewish clothing restrictions 25
   Jewish migrants in Venice 25, 210
   Kingdom of Italy 215
   losses (1509) 50–1, 52
   maps xii–xiii
   monti di pietà 37, 38–9
   recovery of losses 53, 69, 126
   refugees from 51, 55–6, 65
   restrictions on Jews 31
   revenue from 159
   roads 224
   taxation 38, 47, 73

Index

trade 224
violence against Jews 51, 53
warfare 48
territories overseas (Stato da Màr)
10–11, 24, 25, 48, 180–1
tourism 224
'tree of liberty' in Piazza San Marco
(1797) **plate 21**
war damage (1918) 249
Verona
capture (1512) 57
emigration to Ghetto 210
German Jewish immigrants from
Venice 22
Giuditta Castilliero case 238, 239
Jewish banks 19, 74
moneylending ban 31
monte di pietà 39
Napoleonic position 201, 202, 203
occupation 63, 64
plague epidemic (1630–31) 148,
149
ritual murder accusation 35
Sabbateanism 167
usury ban 102
Venetian gain 24
violence against Jews 51

Vicenza
famine 82
German Jewish immigrants from
Venice 22–3
loan bank 19
moneylending ban 31
monte di pietà 39, 40
Spanish capture 60
Venetian gain 24
vote for expulsion of Jews 39
Vittorio Emanuele II, King 240–1,
242, 244
Vivante, Graziadio 239
Vivante, Raffael 207–8
Vivante, Vita 204, 207
Vivante family 210, 211, 216, 217–18
Voltaire 190
von Raab, Anton 219

Weiller, Guido 254
World War I 247–9
World War II 6, 258–9
Wotton, Sir Henry 134, 137, 139

Zacuto, Moses 154, 167, 171–2, 182, 184
Zionism 246–7, 270, 272
Zorzetti, Mordccai and Jacob 157